T0320123

TWO WORLDS OF COTTON

Colonialism and the Regional Economy in the French Soudan, 1800–1946

TWO WORLDS
OF COTTON

COLONIALISM AND THE

REGIONAL ECONOMY IN THE

FRENCH SOUDAN, 1800 – 1946

RICHARD L. ROBERTS

Stanford University Press
Stanford, California 1996

Stanford University Press
Stanford, California
© 1996 by the Board of Trustees of the
Leland Stanford Junior University

CIP data appear at the end of the book

Dedication

To Amy, Sam, and Sophie,
and to Al who reads it all

Preface

When I began research on this project in 1983, I would not have anticipated that the current book would be the result. Indeed, this book bears little resemblance to the original project I had in mind—namely a social history of the handicraft textile industry in the French Soudan. Elements of such a social history are present, but this book is more the result of a dialogue between research and design, theory and evidence, silences and abundances in the historical record. This give-and-take is a central characteristic of the historian's craft and it constitutes that which is distinctive about doing history. In launching a historical project, historians give life to an organism that grows, mutates, and develops, perhaps along paths we have defined, but certainly not as we originally planned. This is as it should be.

Works of history, especially those conducted over a decade or so, are also borne along by the deep intellectual currents in their fields and by prevailing winds. The past two decades have witnessed dramatic intellectual and political challenges to historical paradigms, methods, and forms of exposition. These challenges have led to significant broadening of subject matter and interpretation. But even as these winds have led to changes in the field, historians of Africa need to be mindful of the deeper currents: a commitment to providing a central space for African agency and careful attention to the range and density of our sources. The commitment to African agency provides the methodological and epistemological foundation to our historical work. But this is not an unchanging commitment: the broadening of subject matter has meant that we can no longer write of the glorious forward march of Africans without paying special attention to struggles over power, resources, and meanings, to the different experiences of women, men, elders, leaders, and subalterns, and to struggles among Africans. But we can write about these subjects only if we engage in the tedious but often pleasurable and sometimes exciting processes of collecting oral history and archival records.

I have on several occasions encountered a certain degree of incredulity on the part of various panels on the protection of human subjects when I try to explain to them the basic principles of collecting oral histories in Africa. They are concerned above all with protecting the safety and usually the anonymity of human subjects, as they should be, and find it hard to believe that historians and informants working in an oral context are engaged in a truly collaborative process. I would not say that informants and historians confront the interview process as equals, but it is true that our informants are often delighted by our interest in their histories and more or less freely provide their version of their past. This project is possible because of the genuine goodwill and enthusiasm on the part of my elderly female and male informants to share their history with me. To them, I offer a profound thanks. I have also learned an immense amount from my sustained conversations with Aliou Kone of Segu (now deceased), Soumaila Diakite of Bamako, and Mulaye Ismaila Dembele of Banamba, who helped me navigate the back roads of Segu, Banamba, and Sinsani and interpret both the past and the present.

Throughout my research in Mali, I was graciously received and assisted by Alpha Oumar Konare and Kleena Sanogo, the directors of the Institut des Sciences Humaines in Bamako, and by Ali Onoigba, the archivist of the Malian National Archives, which is a treasure trove of material, although badly deteriorating. A special note of thanks goes wholeheartedly to Saliou Mbaye, the director of the Senegalese National Archives. Not only is Saliou deeply dedicated to making the Senegalese archives the best in West Africa, he has been a model scholar-administrator. Closer to home, I wish to thank Karen Fung for building and maintaining at the Hoover Institution one of the finest Africana collections in North America, and Sonia Moss of Green Library, who scours the nation in pursuit of books hidden in distant libraries. Whether in Mali, Senegal, or France, I remain deeply grateful to the men and women who actually bring researchers the files from dark and dusty corridors lined with archival boxes. Thank you for satisfying my virtually unrelenting request for documents.

I started and finished this book at the Stanford Humanities Center. I wish I could say that I actually finished it in one year. I began writing it as a fellow in 1987–88 and finished the final version as a second-term fellow in 1993–94. During both years, the Humanities Center generated exactly the kind of interdisciplinary intellectual life I sought when I entered the academy. While my colleagues there gave generously of their time and their criticism, my more distant colleagues in my field ultimately made a deeper contribution to my thinking about cotton and colonialism. I am especially grateful to Allen Isaacman and Tom Bassett, fellow travelers in cotton, and to the participants to the University of Minnesota–Stanford University conference on the social history of cotton, held in June 1992. Until then, I felt I was alone in my pursuit of the social history of cotton and colonialism in Africa. At strategic points David Abernethy, Jean-Loup Amselle, Mary Jo Arnoldi, Jean Bazin, Judith Byfield, Fred Cooper, Marcel Fafchamps, Martin Klein, Paul Lovejoy, Paul Lubeck, Pat Manning, Claude Meillassoux, Donald Moore, David Robinson, and Michael Watts made interventions that changed this project in dramatic and subtle ways. Where their ideas end and mine begin is no longer discernible, and I am deeply grateful to them for their pushes and shoves. I also wish to acknowledge my graduate students, who, perhaps more often than they probably wished, were subjected to reading and commenting on aspects of the arguments presented here. I have benefited from all their comments.

Portions of the manuscript appeared in slightly different form in four earlier publications. Parts of the Introduction appeared in my "Reversible Social Processes, Historical Memory, and the Production of History," *History in Africa* 17 (1990). Part of Chapter 2 appeared in "Women's Work and Women's Wealth: Household Social Relations in the Maraka Textile Industry of the Nineteenth Century," *Comparative Studies in Society and History* 26, no. 2 (1984); reprinted with the permission of Cambridge University Press. Part of Chapter 4 appeared in "French Colonialism, Imported Technology and the Handicraft Textile Industry in the Western Sudan, 1898–1918," *Journal of Economic History*, 47, no. 2 (1987); reprinted with the permission of Cambridge University Press. Part of Chapter 8 appeared in "The Coercion of Free Markets: Cotton, Peasants, and the Colonial State in the French Soudan, 1924–1932," *Cotton, Colonialism, and Social History in Sub-Saharan Africa;* © 1995, reprinted by permission of the publisher, Heineman, a division of Reed Elsevier, Inc.

Research for this project was supported by a National Endowment for the Humanities Fellowship for independent research, 1983–84, a postdoctoral fellowship from the Social Science Research, summer 1987, by a fellowship from Stanford University's Humanities Center,

1987–88, and by an appointment at the Ecole des Hautes Etudes en Sciences Sociales, Paris, 1991. I also "borrowed" a little time from a second fellowship at the Stanford Humanities Center, 1993–94, to polish off the final version of this book.

Once again, I thank Norris Pope for his sustained and deep commitment to scholarly publishing and to John Feneron for his expert guidance throughout the process of bringing a manuscript to life. Although they probably don't know how much, Amy, Sam, and Sophie contributed an immense amount to this book, which, after all, was part of our lives for more than a decade.

R.L.R.

Contents

Tables, Maps, and Figures

Note on Orthography

Despite considerable efforts since independence to normalize and phoneticize Bambara and Malinke, there has been little agreement about systematization of Malinke languages. I continue in this book the practice I laid out in my previous studies. I am particularly concerned with consistency and ease of recognition. Because this project focuses on the colonial period, I have retained the colonial spelling with only minor adjustments. The long *u* sound presented in the French as *ou* (as in *Segou*) is here as *u* (thus, *Segu*). I have retained the *ou* spelling when it appears as the first vowel sound of a place name, as in the French *Bougouni*, which appears here as *Bouguni*. The retention of the French *ou* is especially important in the distinctions between the Western Sudan and the French Soudan, which I make in this study. I use the Western Sudan to refer to the precolonial space that eventually became the Soudan under French colonial rule. These distinctions help underscore the historical specificity of the colonial period.

I have translated all the French quotations used in this study and, with Aliou Kone and Soumaila Diakite, translated the Bambara. In rendering French and Bambara, I have tried to be consistent and to facilitate interpretation. For example, I translated the French *cercle* as district to retain the sense of a spatial administrative unit, rather than use the less familiar term *circle*. I have also not used French accents or phonetic marks in rendering Malian surnames and place names.

TWO WORLDS OF COTTON

Colonialism and the Regional Economy in the French Soudan, 1800–1946

CHAPTER ONE

Introduction

Two worlds of cotton intersected at the beginning of the nineteenth century in West Africa. Cotton and handicraft cotton textile production had long been part of the economies of West Africa, especially those of the savanna, and cotton textiles catered to both domestic needs and regional markets. Long-distance trade was based on comparative advantage and led to complex webs of commercial relations. The world of West African cotton in the nineteenth century was subject to profound changes, especially those associated with the decline of the transatlantic slave trade, changes in West African political economies, increased demand within West Africa for goods and services, and the rise in demand for African tropical commodities on the world market.

The other world of cotton emanated from Europe, where cotton textile production was undergoing rapid industrialization. Because cotton does not grow well in northern Europe, the cotton mills were forced to reach many thousands of kilometers away to secure a steady supply of raw materials. In the process of procuring its raw materials, the world of European cotton became linked to the Atlantic economies and other semitropical and tropical regions producing raw materials. When the French returned to the two colonial towns of Gorée and Saint Louis in 1817, they sought to build colonialism on production of agricultural commodities for export to the metropole. As they looked around them, the French saw Africans cultivating small plots of cotton everywhere. They concluded that cotton was ideally suited to the economic future of their colony. The French revived their colonization in Senegal based on metropolitan demand for cotton and other semitropical products.

Following an initially energetic start, the pace of French colonial cotton development waned until the cotton supply crisis of the 1860s. The American Civil War, commodity speculation, and hording contributed to the industrializing world's first major supply crisis

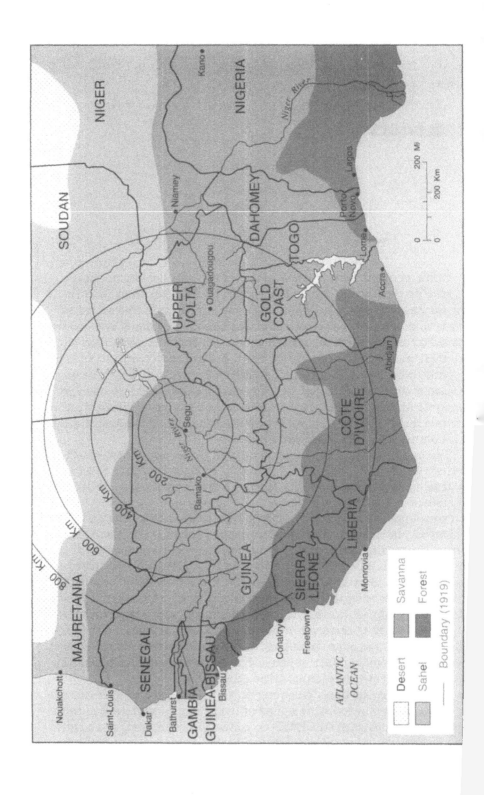

and forced a recalibration of the role of the state in the national economy. Protecting national industries and securing reliable sources of raw materials became a central component of the new political economies of European nation-states and the capitalist world economy in the last quarter of the nineteenth century. This new orientation of the economy coincided with the conquest of the West African interior. Colonial officials in the French Soudan found themselves masters of a vast new territory in search of an economic mission. The locus of cotton and colonialism shifted from Senegal to the new colony of the French Soudan. There, cotton production for export became synonymous with programs for colonial economic development from 1896 onward.

These two worlds of cotton—the world of West African cotton and handcrafted cotton textiles and the world of the European capitalist cotton textile industry—came increasingly into collision during the course of the late nineteenth century and the first half of the twentieth century. This book explores the linked history of the dynamic handicraft textile industry of the French Soudan, which was capable of absorbing the expanding cotton harvest of the colony, and French colonial efforts to capture the cotton harvest for export to the metropole. French efforts failed. Explaining that failure is this book's goal.

As I crossed the Marakala Dam astride the Niger River on my way to my research site at Sinsani on the left bank in 1976, I had no idea that this derivation dam, started in 1932 and costing tens of millions of francs and hundreds of African lives, was linked to a small invention in England 243 years earlier. In 1733 a Lancashire mechanic, John Kay, introduced a spring into each side of the shuttle of the hand loom, thus speeding up the weaving process. Although Kay's flying shuttle enabled one hand-loom weaver to do the work of two, his productivity was still dependent on the labor of spinners. Before Kay's invention, it normally took between three and eight spinsters (most spinners were women) to supply one weaver with sufficient yarn for one day's work. As Kay's flying shuttle diffused among Britain's hand-loom weavers, increased pressure on the supply of yarn induced deliberate efforts to invent labor-saving devices. In 1764 James Hargreaves invented the spinning jenny, which was little more than a spinning wheel linked to a battery of spindles instead of just one. The spinning jenny increased the productivity of spinsters significantly, and because it was not linked to mechanical power, it could be used by women in their cottages. In 1769, Richard Arkwright linked mechanical power, derived from water wheels, to spinning, thus paving the way for the concentration of spinning in factories. Samuel Compton's mule, introduced and refined between 1774 and 1779, linked Arkwright's frame to Hargreaves's jenny and provided the means to spin finer and stronger yarn. Most important, Compton's mule could be harnessed to steam power, and by 1790 coal-fired spinning factories became the model of the emerging revolution in industrial production.

Industrial yarn was still largely woven by hand-loom weavers, but the increased supply of yarn permitted a significant increase in textile production. In 1785, Edmund Cartwright solved the problem of linking mechanical power to weaving, but it was not until the late 1820s that steam-powered looms replaced hand-loom weavers throughout the English Midlands. Labor savings in spinning and weaving greatly increased productivity in the weaving industry but placed tremendous demand-side pressure on the supply of cotton.[1]

Less than 1.4 million pounds of raw cotton were imported into Britain at the beginning of the eighteenth century. Imports rose to 6.7 million pounds on the eve of the major technological developments in 1775 and rose nearly tenfold to 56 million pounds in 1800. Until the late 1790s, most of this cotton was imported from the Levant and India. Some cotton was imported from the Americas, notably the long-fiber Sea Island cotton from Georgia and the British Caribbean. Cotton production in India and the Levant did not expand sufficiently to meet rising demand. Prices for cotton in the Americas rose, especially from 1785 to 1795, inducing many planters in the antebellum South to experiment with Sea Island varieties in the upland or piedmont regions. In the interior, however, only short- or medium-staple cotton grew, yielding short, fuzzy fibers difficult to clean. Until 1793, when Eli Whitney invented the mechanical cotton gin, much of the two to three million pounds of short-staple cotton planted in the South each year was left to rot because of the difficulty of removing the seeds from the fiber.[2] Whitney's cotton gin transformed the antebellum South, making cotton king and making possible the rapid development of the European cotton textile industry. European demand for cotton eventually created a globally structured market for cotton and cotton textiles.[3]

Britain took the lead in industrializing cotton textile production, but continental Europe was not far behind. Even though the British Parliament prohibited the export of the new technologies and the

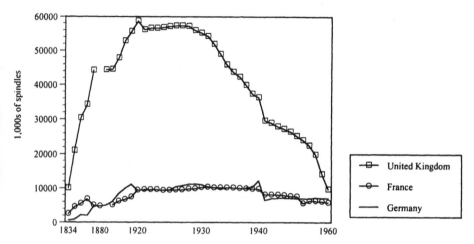

Fig. 1. Spindles in Use in Great Britain, Germany, and France, 1834–1960.
Source: Mitchell, *European Historical Statistics.*

emigration of their artisans (the most important legislation dates
from 1781–86), the industrial techniques of spinning rapidly found
their way to the Continent. The diffusion of the new technologies
was facilitated by the fairly easy movement of "experts" between
Great Britain and the Continent. Some of these experts were trained
as mechanics; others were British and foreign merchants and government officials. They were instrumental in the social reproduction of
the new factory system throughout Europe from the end of the eighteenth to the first half of the nineteenth centuries.[4]

In 1753, John Kay introduced his flying shuttle directly into
France. With royal support, British textile entrepreneurs and artisans
were encouraged to emigrate and establish textile manufactories in
Normandy. France was therefore not noticeably behind Britain in the
development of her cotton textile industry, although the French
Revolution and the Napoleonic era created political disincentives to
the expansion of the French textile industry. Nonetheless, by 1825,
textiles accounted for 20 percent of the total value of French industrial production.[5] Figure 1 shows the growth in numbers of spindles
in France, Britain, and Germany from 1834 to 1960. Britain was
clearly the industrial leader, but the pace of France's cotton textile
industrialization by 1890 made it fourth in Europe after Britain, Russia, and Germany.

There was no obvious reason for cotton textiles to become one of the leading industrial sectors in Britain and France in the nineteenth century. Manufacturers had no local supplies to draw on but had to reach thousands of kilometers away to secure steady supplies of cheap raw material to produce inexpensive commodities. By the mid-nineteenth century the vast amount of cotton circulating on the world market demonstrated the power of capitalist manufacturing to call forth the raw materials it required. But looking at the supply of cotton on the world market does not demonstrate the antagonistic and contradictory aspects of its development or how interdependent and heterogeneous were the systems of production and marketing throughout the world. French efforts to develop cotton in the West African colonies must be understood as part of worldwide engagement between globally structured markets, the expansion and periodic crises in capitalist production, and dynamic local processes.

Cotton and colonialism coincided in French West Africa because of deep imperfections in the world commodity markets of the nineteenth and twentieth centuries. The cotton supply crisis of 1861–65, which saw massive waves of industrial unemployment in the immediate aftermath of wrenching political revolutions, made crystal clear to French industrialists just how dependent they were upon one primary source of cotton for their industrial needs and encouraged the first sustained effort to promote colonial sources of cotton for French mills. These efforts waned when American cotton returned to the international markets in the late 1860s. In the 1890s, French industrialists again worried about the reliability of the American cotton supply. Their concerns coincided with the politics of neomercantilist protection and prompted yet another round of cotton development programs in the colonies.

By 1896, the lieutenant governor of the Soudan understood how to link this concern about protecting metropolitan industries through secure sources of colonial cotton to the economic development of his colony. It was also a way to justify continued metropolitan support for the colonies against a rising chorus of skeptics in France. World War I and the postwar economic reconstruction focused attention directly on colonial sources of crucial raw materials, of which cotton was one, and promoted debates about economic autarky, in which colonies would play crucial roles. Cotton colonialism in French West Africa was directly linked to real and perceived imperfections in the world supply of cotton. The Marakala derivation dam (also called the Sansanding dam), which I first crossed in 1976, was a small but central part of this story.

Cotton and Colonialism in the French Soudan

This book is about colonial efforts to shape and capture the cotton harvest of the Soudan. It is about the ideas of colonial economic development and the struggles to implement them. This book is also about the dynamism of the handicraft textile industry in the Soudan and its ability to respond to the demands of West African consumers for cloth and clothing. Indeed, the very resiliency of the handicraft textile industry, the high elasticity of demand for cloth in the Soudan and neighboring regions, and the power of African cotton producers to make decisions about how to dispose of their cotton harvest shaped the outcome of colonial efforts to develop the economy of the Soudan on cotton exports. French efforts to make the Soudan and the Soudanese economy conform to their wishes failed. This book, therefore, is about the failure of French colonial economic development.

In the elaboration of programs of colonial economic development, cotton in the French Soudan became the location of profound struggles among French administrators, agronomists, public works officials, entrepreneurs, and expatriate merchants and African peasants, traders, weavers, and consumers. Protagonists on all sides of the debates on how best to encourage cotton production for export produced not only policies but also cultural conceptions regarding colonialism more generally. The language of colonial development reflected ideological assumptions about Africans, their social and economic organization, and their capacities to work. In these assumptions, French officials drew on the cultural history of Europe's encounter with Africa but framed the issues in terms of late nineteenth- and early twentieth-century ideas about management and modernism.[6] All protagonists in the debates about colonial cotton development saw African cotton, the African economy, and African producers as amenable to change. What was needed were appropriate scientific and managerial solutions. Different solutions stemmed from different interpretations of what the problems were.

This book examines the history of two competing models of colonial cotton development: a group of senior administrators who were committed to a development plan focused on African peasants which relied on market incentives, adequate rainfall, and long-term hybridization schemes to yield large supplies of cotton at competitive prices and qualities; and a group of French entrepreneurs, agronomists, and colonial public works officials who saw cotton development as requiring massive investment in irrigation which would yield vast plantations managed by Europeans and worked by Africans. Elements of both development approaches were evident in France's efforts to promote cotton in Senegal between 1817 and 1867, when cotton was first identified as a colonial crop useful to the metropolitan economy. These two opposing camps came into open conflict in the Soudan after World War I.

This study of French colonial cotton policy provides an opportunity to examine the language of development as the protagonists in the debate about cotton struggled over the terms and practices of colonial cotton policies. The central crisis in French colonial cotton policy—and French colonialism in the Soudan more generally—was that neither of the two competing camps provided metropolitan users with sufficient cotton of the quality they wanted. One of the central paradoxes of colonial cotton development was why, in the face of such paltry results, the French did not abandon cotton for another crop or for another development strategy.

The French gravitated to cotton as the premier colonial crop of the French Soudan because everywhere they looked they saw production of cotton and handicraft textiles servicing domestic, regional, and long-distance markets. The French thought that they could easily tap into the existing supply of cotton and redirect it to metropolitan spinners and weavers. Success seemed always just around the corner. With a little more effort and a little greater commitment or resources, the anticipated results would be theirs. Moreover, colonial sources of raw materials played a central part in the politics of capitalist development in metropolitan France. In his *Empire colonial et capitalisme français: Histoire d'un divorce,* Jacques Marseille joins a long tradition of efforts to revise V. I. Lenin's arguments regarding capitalism and imperialism. Marseille proposes instead that France's twentieth-century industrial development needs to be examined in two phases, one leading up to the 1930s and the other afterward. In contrast to Lenin, Marseille argues that the period of greatest industrialization coincided with the dismantling of France's colonial empire and that by the 1930s most French capitalists had lost interest in empire. Marseille also describes the unevenness of France's industrial development, the factionalism among capitalists, and the persistence of colonies in the prevailing ideas about capitalist development. Although colonies were considered to be privileged sources of raw materials for metropolitan development, Marseille demonstrates that they were instead major markets for some sections of France's industry. Marseille develops the case of textile production and demonstrates that although France's colonies did not contribute significantly to her raw materials needs, colonies did absorb a large and increasingly important share of France's textile output. Marseille also draws attention to the lingering popular perception of the empire's importance to France, even when it no longer performed those functions for capitalists.[7]

The bulk of Marseille's study focuses on the 1930s, when the politics of autarky was in favor. By not expanding his purview to include the beginning of France's nineteenth-century colonialism and by concentrating on the metropole, he misses the ebbs and flows of France's thinking about colonialism and the periodic raw materials crises that drove both efforts to build empire and colonial development programs. Marseille's study raises important questions about Europe's industrial development, but beyond a set of fascinating statistics regarding colonial commerce, he does not examine the colonial side of the story.[8] Far from accomplishing what they understood to be the colony's role in France's industrial textile development—whether as a privileged source of raw materials or as a vast and expanding market for textiles—French colonial development in Senegal and the Soudan confronted a dynamic handicraft industry, whose persistence created significant obstacles to the success of colonial cotton development policies.

A central theme in this book is the resiliency of the regional economy of the Soudan to withstand colonial efforts to bend its production to satisfy metropolitan needs. Just as the senior colonial administrators had predicted, Soudanese cotton producers responded to market incentives and sold their cotton to the highest bidder. Unfortunately for those expecting the Soudan to export cotton, the majority of the annual cotton harvest flowed into the hands of the spinners and weavers of the domestic handicraft textile industry and into the local, regional, and long-distance circuits of the West African continental market. This outcome provides important insights into the history of local processes withstanding pressures of the world economy.

Cotton, Colonialism, and History

This story about cotton and colonialism engages in four sets of ongoing theoretical discussions that have directly or indirectly shaped the study of late precolonial and colonial African history. These discussions flow from an analysis of the same historical process: the uneven incorporation of regional economies of Africa into a modern world economy. French efforts to make their colonies in West Africa yield raw materials for metropolitan industries demonstrate the interplay of global, capitalist processes with local ones. They demonstrate most dramatically the resiliency of local processes to withstand efforts to control and shape them.

The story of the failure of French cotton colonialism in the Soudan is also linked to the weakness of the colonial state in French West Africa. Had the opposing forces within the colonial state agreed on a consistent strategy of colonial development, had it had better access to financial and ideological resources, and had the senior colonial administration been less ambivalent about the use of compulsion, perhaps the outcome would have been different. Yet the failure of the colonial state to capture the cotton harvest of the Soudan did not reside solely with its weaknesses. French colonial cotton development in West Africa was burdened by the peculiar development of the world economy for cotton and cotton textiles. French industrialists wanted a reliable supply of good quality cotton, but they were unwilling to pay more for secure sources of colonial cotton as long as cheaper supplies of good quality cotton were available on the world commodity markets. French managers of the state, however, were concerned about limiting social unrest, especially when world commodity markets failed to assure continued supplies of cotton and factories closed; they were concerned about the drain on national reserves of capital to pay for imported commodities when supplies were abundant; and they were concerned about ensuring national defense, which led them to seek raw materials from their own colonies.

In responding to the conflicting signals sent from the metropole, the managers of the colonial state in West Africa grappled with their own failure to deliver the goods to their superiors. The history of cotton colonialism in Senegal and the Soudan provides an opportunity to tease out the competing models of colonialism which undergirded the programs of colonial economic development. These programs of cotton colonialism were simultaneously expressions of state power and cultural representations of Africans, of work, and of colonial order. Exploring the history of the competing models of cotton colonialism lets us examine the cultural side of economic development and the economic and political implications of cultural constructions of colonialism.

Programs to make West Africa into France's source of cotton rested on the assumption that Europeans could control production and marketing decisions made by West Africans. The failure of cotton colonialism to make the Soudan conform to notions of colonialism and the economy established in France demonstrates the resiliency of the local processes in Africa. The story of the handicraft textile industry presented here focuses on local processes of production and consumption of cloth in the Soudan and on the regional and global factors that influenced how the female spinners and the male weavers entered into textile production. Far from being destroyed by the advance of colonialism and importation of European manufactured cloth, the handicraft textile industry persisted and provided consumers with cloth. Persistence did not mean stasis, however. Even though the production of textiles in the Soudan remained hand work, the workers of the industry engaged in ongoing but reversible struggles over the social relations of production, the factors of production, the social product of labor, and the meaning of change. The histories of French colonial cotton development and the handicraft textile industry are not so much "contrapuntal" narratives of the encounter between French imperialism and West Africa.[9] They are, instead, seamless parts of the same history.

Local Processes and the World System

Immanuel Wallerstein's *Modern World System* and *Modern World System II* have generated a great deal of debate and have profoundly shaped perceptions of European and non-Western history. "A world system," Wallerstein wrote in his first volume, "is a social system, one that has boundaries, structures, member groups, rules of legitimization and coherence. Its life is made up of the conflicting forces which hold it together by tension, and tear it apart as each group seeks eternally to remold it to its advantage."[10] The emergence of capitalism operating through worldwide systems of production and marketing in the sixteenth century drove this system. Wallerstein does not deny the preexistence of regional systems, but he is convinced that the emergence of capitalism in Europe as the single dominant mode of production structured the logic of class conflict, labor control, commodity flows, and accumulation throughout the world.

Historians and anthropologists toiling in the peripheral (and semi-peripheral) areas of Wallerstein's world system could not deny the pressures exerted upon the societies and economies they studied. Wallerstein's model, however, would have us believe that the logic of capitalist production and accumulation on a world scale orchestrated global change. But it was far from clear that these pressures were sufficient to explain the outcomes of class conflict, labor control, worker resistance, household change, gender relations, and commodity flows everywhere. In an important review of Latin American history, Steve Stern challenged Wallerstein's cavalier dismissal of the power of local processes to shape the outcome of the encounter between the world economy and regional societies. The passage quoted below concerns the emergence of African slavery in Brazil, but the implications of Stern's critique go further.

The world-system's needs and theoretically optimal labor pattern, while important, do not suffice to explain the outcome of the labor system in the sugar plantation periphery. At the heart of the labor question were conditions that made local Indian and European populations insufficiently exploitable, compared to African slave populations, for the purpose of plantation production. In the interplay between these local conditions of production and the interests and opportunities derived from the international market lies a more powerful explanation of the rise of socioeconomic structures overwhelmingly dependent upon African slavery.[11]

Viewing the interplay of the world economy and local process from the perspective of the periphery thus yields a very different conjuncture of forces. Even recognizing the power of the world economy to call forth commodities and labor systems, studies of the interplay of local forces with the larger world economy demonstrate how significant was the constellation of local processes in determining the outcome of the encounter. For example, the development of plantation slavery on Martinique in the nineteenth century seems to demonstrate the logic of the world system to dictate the form of labor in the periphery. Upon closer examination of local processes of labor formation, Dale Tomich argues that the world economy viewed from the periphery appears less to be passively responding to orders from the European core than "a heterogeneous, interdependent, antagonistic, contradictory whole—that is, the unity of the diverse." From the perspective of Africa, Frederick Cooper criticizes Wallerstein's model for failing to explain "why particular systems of production and different struggles for control of land and labor—in the context of a growing system of exchange, but not as a mere reflection of it— led to structures with different potentials for continued growth."[12] The Eurocentrism of so much of world systems analysis blinded its practitioners to the complexities of colonialism and the resiliencies of local processes. Historians and anthropologists are now much more aware of the interplay of world systemic and local processes, recognizing that the organization of labor systems was the result of long struggles and that the incorporation of peripheral regions into the world economy was drawn out, heterogenous, and messy. Many were also only partially successful.

It was, rather, the power of local social and economic processes to shape the outcome of the interplay between the world economy and the Soudanese market for the cotton harvest that determined the failure of French cotton colonialism. It would be misleading, however, to suggest that the demand for cotton by the French did not have any impact on the social and economic history of the Soudanese cotton and cotton textile markets. French cotton colonialism induced significant change in the decisions cotton producers made regarding how to cultivate and to dispose of their cotton harvest. New varieties of cotton and new methods of cultivating cotton led to profound changes in agriculture and the handicraft cotton textile industry in West Africa.

Because the handicraft textile industry of the Soudan fed a dynamic domestic and intracontinental market in West Africa, Soudanese cotton producers were able to withstand pressure from the colonial state to sell their cotton to the export sector. The outcome of cotton colonialism in Mozambique, for example, was quite different precisely because the colonial state was prepared to force Africans to produce and deliver cotton to it and because there was only a poorly developed domestic market for cotton.[13] Thus the Soudanese cotton producers' ability to resist participating in export markets lay both with the failure of the world economy to subsume the domestic handicraft textile industry in its orbit (and thus lead to the erosion of that industry) and with the colonial state's ideological commitment to the assumption that Soudanese peasants would respond positively to market incentives. This widely shared assumption led to policies that inadvertently protected the domestic cotton market. Thus the interplay of the world economy and local processes was shaped by political and economic factors as well as by the cultural assumptions of colonialism held by the colonizing power. These assumptions shaped colonial policies and directed how the state intervened in local processes.

Creating "Colonial Order" and the Culture of Economic Development

There was a certain arrogance to the idea that French colonial officials and entrepreneurs could reshape the economy and societies of the Soudan according to their notions of Africa and colonialism. That arrogance owed much of the audacity of French military leaders, who in just under two decades had conquered the immense interior of West Africa. This conquest contributed to the sense that the state could accomplish whatever it wanted.[14] It gave substance to the idea that imperialism was the natural extension of French cultural and political genius. Conquest thus built on the legacy of the power of the metropolitan state, which, over the course of the nineteenth century, had made the peasants toiling in various regions of France into Frenchmen. Making Soudanese peasants into productive commodity producers or into disciplined wage earners probably seemed simple in comparison.[15]

In *Colonising Egypt*, Timothy Mitchell links European efforts to control Egypt and North Africa to the imperial desire to create order within prevailing European cognitive categories. This desire to tame and to control also lay at the heart of how and why international and colonial exhibitions, held in European capitals in the mid- and late nineteenth century, were constructed. According to Mitchell, there was a clear relationship between these metropolitan representations of the Orient in the exhibitions and programs of control in the colonies. These colonial programs were built on new "technologies of power" elaborated in the course of constructing the modern European nation-state. Mitchell argues that the "method of building and naming" the colonial city, which was the premier representation of colonial power, "made present to the visitor the order and the institutions of colonial authority." More generally, colonization depended upon a plan. "A plan or framework"—just like the urban plan—"would create the appearance of objectiveness. . . . Egypt was to be ordered up as something object-like. In other words it was to be made picture-like and legible, rendered available to political and economic calculation. Colonial power rendered the country readable."[16] To create order and thus to control through representations, effectively making intelligible what appeared as irrational and disorderly, became the principal task of colonial rule.

The mutual empowerment of European culture and European colonialism lies at the heart of what Edward Said describes as the overlapping territorial and intellectual sides of imperialism. "The enterprise of empire," he writes, "depends upon the *idea of having an empire*. When it came to what lay beyond metropolitan Europe, the arts and the disciplines of representation—on the one hand, fiction, history, and travel writing, painting; on the other, sociology, administrative or bureaucratic writing, philology, racial theory—depended on the powers of Europe to bring the non-European world into representations, the better to be able to see it, to master it, and above all, to hold it."[17] The success of empire depended also on the simultaneous representation of the natives and the silencing of them, undermining their sense of history and the worth of their cultures.

In his introduction to a collection of essays on culture and colonialism, Nicholas Dirks cautions the reader not to think that colonialism was "monolithic" and "unchanging." Nor, Dirks argues, was colonial power fragile. He posits a "sinuous and hegemonic character of colonial power" in which "colonialism transformed domination into a variety of effects that masked conquest and rule." Colonialism accomplished this task, Dirks suggests, by linking itself with "the inexorable and universal forces of science, progress, rationality, and modernity" and displacing all else into reified categories of tradition, barbarity, and backwardness. Dirks dismisses the older tradition of resistance scholarship, which celebrated resistance to colonialism. Such resistance studies "trivialized the all-pervasive character of power, particularly in colonial regimes."[18]

Mitchell, Said, Dirks, and the host of new scholarship on culture and empire stress the hegemony of the West. They recognize that this hegemony was deeply flawed and relied on imperial adventures to contain its contradictions. All admit to local resistance and struggle but assume that colonialism induced a shift in local cultures so that these struggles occurred within structures imposed by the West. This approach stresses the European side of empire and is the cultural analogy to Wallerstein's economic and political forces emanating from the European core. This approach has a paradoxical effect of "silencing" local actors, especially those who ignored the new structures (cultural as well as economic and political) of colonialism as much as possible. When examining the colonial experience, Said, for example, is concerned largely with the impact of empire on the Western educated elite. Precisely because many came to work for the colonial state (as clerks, minor officials, or modern indigenous rulers), to work within its institutions (such as lawyers), or to think within its categories (teachers and academics), their experience of colonialism was distinct and distinctive. These groups were also most likely to leave written evidence, which could be studied as "texts."

The deep flaw of this approach to culture is that it fails to recognize sufficiently the power of local processes—or local currents of culture and practice—to withstand empire and ultimately to shape the experience of colonialism. My research on French colonial cotton development—and its failure—suggests that this view of colonialism refracts a wider and messier experience through the eyes of a segment of colonial society most susceptible to the colonial cultural program, namely a relatively small group of indigenous people who actively participated in the colonial program. The meanings of empire for peasants, local traders, and ordinary men and women were probably quite different.

My study of the failure of French colonial cotton development is indicative of the broader failure of the colonial cultural agenda to convince Africans to accomplish their assigned tasks. It points to the inherent weakness of the colonial state, its limited capacity to control the economic decisions West Africans made, and thus of the failure of the imperial cultural mission. French colonial power waxed strongest at the level of the "plan" and not at the level of the cotton fields.

I share with Dirks a sense that colonialism was sinuous, but I disagree that it was hegemonic. Colonialism affected indigenous practices unevenly. I prefer to think of colonialism as a fog, flowing over a highly variegated landscape. The fog lies deepest in the areas that open themselves most to its influence. The fog covers other zones thinly and bypasses some outcroppings altogether. The metaphor of a fog is also instructive on another level. Although the new turn to interpretation does direct our attention to fruitful inquiries regarding the cultural side of colonialism, it should not limit our view of the wider landscape of the colonial experience. Situating oneself in the deepest pools of fog may in fact narrow what we see and study. We must seek the landforms less obscured by the fog.[19] From these vantage points, the impact of colonialism may not seem so all-pervasive.

Some recent postmodern approaches to colonialism direct our attention to fruitful inquiries regarding the cultural side of colonialism. Colonial intellectual and economic development programs were both representations of European cognitive categories of society and the economy and efforts to make the colonies and natives conform to Western assumptions about economic and social behavior. It is within this context that we must examine French programs of cotton colonialism. Cotton colonialism was not merely an effort to promote commodity production; it was simultaneously an effort to see, to master, and to control the colonial territory and the lives of natives within it.

In discussing colonial India's development regime, David Ludden describes a "development discourse" that informed the debates about policy and provided a "language of legitimacy for the state." India's development regime evolved, Ludden writes, "in stages measured by the growing state power to standardize, unify, classify, count, list, compare, and compute systematically." Colonial knowledge was a "regimen of cognition, collection, and transmission of facts" and the universalization of categories. In the process, it concealed state power.[20] Ludden's depiction of colonial India's development program reflects the maturation of a highly bureaucratic colonial state. The same propensities to order, to collect, and to transmit economic observations prevailed in French West Africa, although on a smaller scale.[21] The result was what Governor-General Jules Henri Gaston Carde in 1924 called the "archive of the last twenty years of cotton debates," which he consulted before promulgating his new cotton development program.

Ludden's suggestion that the elaboration of colonial knowledge concealed state power does not translate well into the French West African case. As I develop in the section below on the *politique cotonnière*, the debate about cotton development was simultaneously about practical ways of promoting economic change and about competing models of colonialism. Far from concealing state power, agronomic and development debates fractured state power.

Ludden's emphasis on the cultural side of economic development finds a clearer resonance in the debates about colonial cotton development in French West Africa. These debates were about Africans, about their capacities as farmers and workers, and about African structures of society and economies more generally. These debates helped to narrow the field of intervention because they imposed recognizable cognitive categories on unfamiliar economic behavior. Protagonists on both sides of the debate about promoting cotton exports—those who saw African peasants as rational economic actors willing to act in their own self-interest and those who saw them as unwilling laborers toiling on vast cotton plantations managed by Europeans—represented Africans within prevailing European ideas about peasants and workers. By the 1930s, for example, these two categories of Africans had solidified into policy. Henri Labouret's studies on peasants provided empirical grounding for the pro-peasant perspective. By the end of the decade, he compiled his inquiries into *Paysans d'Afrique occidentale*.[22] Although no single text did the same for African workers, legislation on family allowances, workers' compensation, and paid vacations helped transform the amorphous, undisciplined, and potentially dangerous group of African urban laborers into modern workers.[23] Such representation lay at the base of efforts to control and to order colonial territories and natives within them.

The problem for the colonial state, however, was that its ability to actualize its programs depended upon Africans playing their assigned roles. In this, the French protagonists of cotton colonialism were woefully unsuccessful.

The Colonial State and the Colonial Economy

In its efforts to restructure physical, political, cultural, and economic space in Africa, colonialism became the site of the condensed contradictions between the world economy and local process and between culture and empire. This was most pronounced when imperialists shared a high degree of unanimity regarding the goals or outcomes of colonialism. In French West Africa—in Senegal in the first half of the nineteenth century and in the Soudan from the end of the nineteenth century until the end of colonialism itself—the rulers of empire expected this region to become *la France cotonnière*, the premier source of cotton for metropolitan mills. This goal became policy at various times and was expressed in various ways, but "the very notion of 'policy,'" as Bruce Berman suggests, "expresses the drive to extend control over social structural forces that has led to the development of a sequence of techniques to manage . . . recurrent crises and struggles" and accomplish the goals of the managers of the state.[24]

This passage suggests a certain intentionality between expectations and intervention. Berman's remark regarding policy, however, is designed instead to highlight the rather haphazard elaboration of a "diverse and ambiguous collection of parts [of the state] created at different historical junctures" to deal with specific crises. Far from being an instrument of metropolitan capitalist intervention in the colonies, the colonial state, as John Lonsdale and Berman have elaborated over the past decade, constantly grappled with its own weaknesses and its contradictions. "The colonial state," Berman and Lonsdale wrote in 1979,

indeed straddled not one but two levels of articulation: between the metropole and the colony as a whole as well as within the colony itself. It therefore had a dual character: it was at once a subordinate agent in its restructuring of local production to meet metropolitan demand, yet also the local factor of cohesion over the heterogeneous, fragmented and contradictory social forces jostling within. . . . In grappling with these dilemmas . . . the colonial state was obliged to intervene more directly in economic life than was characteristic of contemporary capitalist states.[25]

The history of the colonial state in Kenya, in particular, yields what Berman has called the "two very different and apparently contradictory forces of the colonial state." On the one hand, there was the "weak" colonial state: "the paternalistic mediator struggling to maintain a precarious sovereignty over contending interests" and hobbled by inadequate resources and little coercive force. It had only a "facade" of power. On the other hand, there was the "strong" colonial state. It continually expanded its bureaucratic apparatus, which "intervened in ever-widening areas of colonial political economy, directing change to serve the interests of metropolitan (or, in the case of Kenya, settler) capital, and containing and suppressing indigenous social forces." The colonial state, Berman concludes, was a powerful instrument of political domination and structural transformation but one that constantly faced the "dialectic of contradictory forces that drove its development."[26]

Berman and Lonsdale's theoretical and empirical writings on the colonial state have yielded important insights into the history of colonialism. They have broadened considerably the concept of the colonial state beyond the mere bureaucratic contours of its organization to place it squarely within an analysis of the uneven development of capitalism in colonial East Africa. Although their conception of the colonial state is framed as a general paradigm, it is nonetheless deeply shaped by the experience of settler colonialism and the relatively weak development of regional networks of production and exchange in Kenya. An analysis of the contradictions shaping the colonial state in French West Africa must begin with an appreciation of a different constitution of its contradictions. To be sure, the colonial state in French West Africa straddled, as the Kenyan state did, the demands of the metropolitan state and the conflicting ones emanating from the colony as a whole. At one level, the program of cotton development confronted contradictory signals from the metropole. French textile industrialists wanted a secure supply of cotton, but they set conditions that profoundly hobbled the colonial state's implementation of its objectives. Moreover, these objectives were framed in policy terms that reflected cultural assumptions about Africans. These assumptions were also subject to considerable debate. In his turn, the lieutenant governor of the Soudan straddled a level of articulation between the government-general of the French West Africa Federation (Afrique occidentale française, AOF, founded in 1895) in Dakar, which set broad policy and controlled large portions of the federation-wide fiscal resources, complex and changing African societies, and the private sector of French export-oriented commerce. But was the colonial state a factor in the cohesion of the "heterogenous, fragmented, and contradictory social forces jostling within"? The colonial state was certainly a factor in the social transformations unleashed by conquest and the subsequent shaping of a colonial economy. Instead of cohesion, the colonial state set in motion processes of change over which it ultimately had little control.[27] In the French Soudan, the colonial state paradoxically nurtured a colonial economy that remained largely independent of colonial control.

Far from being a factor of cohesion, the colonial state in the French Soudan was deeply fractured by contending programs of cotton development. In this manner, the colonial state itself became the object of competing groups seeking to control its resources as a means of implementing its view of what the colonial economy should be. In contrast to Berman's remark that policy helped to focus the combined and awesome power of the state, colonial cotton policy in the French Soudan led to considerable weakening of the colonial state, which in turn resulted in the failure to control West Africans and their economic decisions. It resulted in the failure of policy in practice: the Soudanese cotton harvest consistently slipped through its fingers.

Crawford Young has recently examined the phenomenon of the colonial state in Africa. If, as he argues, the colonial state's performance up to World War II was measured primarily by challenges to its hegemony and its ability to secure local sources of revenue, then almost all colonial states in Africa were "strong." They were so because they temporarily monopolized the means of coercion, they established few other expectations, and because Young measures challenges to hegemony in a narrowly formal manner.[28] When, Young continues, the challenges to the colonial state's hegemony both within and outside of its boundaries occurred through growing nationalist ideologies and changing assumptions about international relations, the colonial states in Africa revealed themselves to be fragile. Young's otherwise magisterial study neglects informal challenges to hegemony, as James Scott and others have explored, and he assumes that if African subjects paid their taxes, the colonial state succeeded in transforming the "natural economy" into one in which the state directed Africans to sell their labor power or the products of their labor.[29] As I will argue in this book, the reality of the colonial state's control over Africans' lives and their economic decisions was far from complete. When referring to colonial states, *weak* and *strong* are only relative terms, which must be measured against stated objectives and outcomes.

Capitalism clearly articulated the world of West African cotton in the nineteenth and twentieth centuries, but the outcome of this articulation did not neatly tie Soudanese peasants to the French metropolitan economy as colonial officials expected. On the contrary, articulation led to profound but reversible changes in the social relations of production in the handicraft textile industry. The industry remained dynamic and capable of expanding production to satisfy market demand. Moreover, the workers of the handicraft textile industry consistently outbid cotton exporters for the disposition of the Soudanese cotton harvest.

This discussion suggests a need to rethink what we mean by the term *colonial economy*. Students of colonialism have too quickly assumed that under colonial rule, the economy of a colony became in effect a colonial economy. The idea of a colonial economy was merely the projection on the colonial scene of a metropolitan category. Over the course of the late eighteenth and nineteenth centuries Europeans witnessed the simultaneous creation of modern nation-states and national economies. Armed with new technologies of state power, including the survey, the census, and the tariff, the new bureaucracies grounded their power in the production of specialized knowledge. The unit of analysis was now the nation; local or regional units were seen as smaller parts of an aggregate whole. The cognitive category of the national unit was applied unproblematically to the colonies. "In the 1920s and 1930s," A. G. Hopkins writes of the imperial idea of the colonial economy, "the colonial economy was considered as much a part of the natural order as was the House of Lords or the Third Republic."[30] Hopkins and other historians of African economic history are aware of the uneven development of "colonial economies" and of the great variations of the colonial economic experience and performance.[31] These studies make an effort to focus on regional economic experience as a way of extracting their units of analysis from the national (or colonial) category. All, however, return to the colonial entity as their smallest unit because that was how the evidence was packaged.

The idea of a colonial economy rested on the assumption that colonial officials could control the economic decisions made by those living within its boundaries. At the very least, the colonial economy meant the production of official reports and statistics reflecting a knowledge of or surveillance over the sum of economic transactions.[32] But just as colonial boundaries were for the most part administrative and international fictions, so too were the colonial units of economic accounting. "The assumption," Douglas Rimmer notes, "that economies are conterminous with national boundaries is appealing to governments that seek to manage and develop economic life, but greatly oversimplifies reality."[33]

Janet MacGaffey has argued that the "real economy" of contemporary Zaire is not the official one of government statistics but the sum of "all transactions monetized and nonmonetized, official and unofficial. Clearly, the true picture [of the economy] is not reflected in the national accounts and official economic reports: a great deal of economic activity is taking place outside the official system. It is through these unofficial activities that the economy really works; instead of looking at the official economy, we should be looking at the unofficial one. What had previously been thought of as a marginal sector of the economy is, in fact, the principal means by which it operates."[34] MacGaffey is interested in formulating new approaches to measuring the gross domestic product and therefore in generating more reliable economic data. Such data are needed for efficient government planning, international aid programs, and public and private investment. The net result of MacGaffey's efforts to devise better measurements is to perpetuate the idea of a national economy without problematizing that category.

In this book, I argue that the failure of colonial cotton development in the French Soudan is directly attributable to the persistence of the precolonial handicraft textile industry. The handicraft textile industry in the French Soudan fed demand in Senegal, Mauritania, upper Guinea, the Côte d'Ivoire, the Gold Coast, and parts of Upper Volta. It is clear that the handicraft textile industry was part of a much wider and complex regional economy that did not conform to colonial boundaries. Nor is it intellectually useful to see the movement of commodities, capital, and people across colonial borders as "imports" and "exports" or as immigration and emigration. This movement was part of a complex and changing regional economy that long predated colonialism. To be sure, the structure and performance of the handicraft textile industry changed in response to the larger colonial political economy in which it was situated. But this was exactly how it had responded in the precolonial period as well.

The underlying dynamic of the West African continental market was economic specialization shaped by the annually oscillating cycles of humid and dry air masses. These air masses created broad horizontal bands of ecologically diverse environments, which fostered specialized economic activities. With the exception of microenvironments associated with rivers, lakes, mineral deposits, and so forth, most inhabitants in each zone pursued similar economic activities. Trade was stimulated across these zones. As much as by climate, the structure and performance of the precolonial economy was shaped by dynamic regional political economies. Particularly in the nineteenth century, states throughout West Africa stimulated economic development and occupational specialization and encouraged commerce. During periods of expanded commodity production, the webs of commercial and productive relationships extended beyond regional political economies. During periods of political and climatic uncertainty, these webs weakened.[35]

Colonial conquest ushered in a sustained period of political and economic stability, which encouraged ecologically specialized producers to invest in productive and commercial activities. Many African producers increased their production of commodities for export to the metropole. Many others, particularly those in the interior of Africa, invested more in the webs of relations within well-established regional economies. Economic change in the French Soudan during the colonial period thus witnessed an acceleration of local processes of economic and social change, which responded to long-established patterns of production and exchange. Colonial economic development, by contrast, sought to integrate the Soudan into the world capitalist economy. The tensions generated by these contradictory processes are central to the story presented here. But the outcome of this encounter will make sense only if the reader remembers that the regional economy of West Africa had deep precolonial roots and remained central to servicing the needs of West African consumers throughout the colonial period. The struggles among the competing forces jostling to control the cotton harvest largely shaped the meaning of the colonial experience. Hence the failure of cotton colonialism in the Soudan is indicative of the broader failure of colonialism on economic, political, and cultural levels. The explanation for this failure lies in large part with an appreciation of African agency.

Social History and Cotton Colonialism

This book takes the perspective that Africans make their own history, but not necessarily under conditions of their own choosing. The nineteenth and twentieth centuries witnessed significant social, economic, and political change throughout the continent as Africans responded to increased demand for labor, for tropical commodities, and increasingly for African territory. Europeans attempting to direct Africans to produce cotton confronted Africans engaged in their own pursuits of economic and political change. The outcomes of cotton colonialism depended on local social processes as Africans struggled among themselves for the direction and the meaning of these changes.

Africans experienced cotton colonialism through what David William Cohen has termed the "interior architecture" of the societies in which they lived. But these societies were undergoing rapid change as women and men, wives and husbands, older men and younger sons responded to the new opportunities and new constraints associated with colonial conquest and pacification. This was a period during which "customs" were defined and redefined, yielding what Sara Berry has described as "an era of intensified contestation over custom, power, and property. The intensity of these contests and their ongoing character are keys to understanding the social dynamics of African agrarian change in the twentieth century."[36]

Students of the social history of rural change in Africa have explored the pressures affecting Africans in their daily lives, the forms of their resistance, and often their impoverishment as a result of their experiences. Some of these perspectives, inspired by underdevelopment theories, have presented Africans as victims in the face of inexorable pressures of colonialism and incorporation into capitalist world economies.[37] Simply inserting Africans into webs of forces emanating from the world economy cannot capture the complex experiences of colonialism. In a provocative assessment of European social history, Charles Tilly has argued that "the changing experiences of ordinary people" were affected by the "very large structural changes, such as the growth of nation states and the development of capitalism."[38] The development of colonial states, the establishment of colonial institutions, and the penetration of capitalism in its colonial variants undoubtedly affected ordinary Africans. These forces, however, intersected with dynamic local and regional patterns of change and conflict.

By focusing on the two worlds of cotton yet presenting them as part of a conjoined historical experience from the early nineteenth century, I have endeavored to situate small-scale local and regional processes within larger world-scale historical forces. I have identified French colonial efforts to capture the cotton harvest of the Soudan and their efforts to change the nature of work and influence cotton growers' decisions about how to dispose of their harvest as the specific fields of force affecting Soudanese cotton producers. By tracing the cultural and political struggles within the French colonial administration, within the various public and private congeries of French interests in the Soudan, and within the metropolitan state I have shown just how factious these debates were and how fractured the colonial state was as a result. No matter how fractured, however, the colonial state imposed fields of force that influenced the worlds in which Soudanese cotton and textile producers lived and worked. What Soudanese peasants did with their cotton is central to the analysis presented here.

In this book, the West African world of cotton is about the production and circulation of handcrafted textiles, for which an abundant supply of cotton was a crucial input. It was here that the two worlds of cotton collided. The supply of cotton, however, was only one—albeit central—input into the production of handcrafted textiles. West African spinners and weavers made decisions about their work and consumers made choices depending upon a complex set of factors which shaped the market for textiles in the Soudan. This book explores those decisions and examines some of the meanings they had for the patterns of change within the handicraft textile industry.

This book has been shaped by the evidence I collected and by what I could not find. Using colonial sources, I have been able to reconstruct the broad contours of the early colonial period, which hint at profound changes in the nature of the textile industry, gender relations, and household dynamics. These would, I anticipated on the basis of my previous fieldwork, be transformative social changes that would be recalled in the oral record. They ought to have become a central part of the social construction of the meaning of historical processes. But as far as I have been able to determine, this has not been the case. Details on gender relations and the productive processes appear in my informants' accounts for the period just before and after World War II, drawn from personal experience. Whereas I have been able to reconstruct the social history of the precolonial era, including the changes induced by increased use of slave labor, my informants are silent on what I would consider equally significant changes in the early colonial period. This paradox—apparently richer evidence in the oral record for an earlier era than for a chronologically closer one—has implications for both fieldwork strategies and for social history.

Yarn, as I will argue in Chapters 2, 4, 9, and 11, was central to the complementarity of gender tasks in the handicraft textile industry. Changes in the access to and availability of yarn outside the bonded limits of household complementarity, I hypothesized, would have provided men and women with new opportunities to renegotiate work, household relations, and control over marketable commodities.

The lack of vivid historical recollection of what I would have presumed to be a significant social transformation has forced me to think about historical processes and the collection of oral history in different ways. Some, if not most, historical processes involved small-scale, indirect, and reversible changes that left no clear historical markers. Historical processes that do not produce conclusive change may be harder to trace. Precisely because they are harder to trace (and to remember), they may not become part of the past over which men and women struggle.[39] This lack of an imprint in the oral record is a central methodological issue that affected the kind of social history I was able to do.

From the standpoint of a social and economic historian, there seems to be a significant difference in the oral record between processes of change that led to "conclusive" change and those I have identified as "reversible," that is, the short-term patterns of small fortunes and misfortunes composed of gradual advances and partial retreats. Reversible social processes may not have left imprints in historical memory precisely because they may not have been recognized by those who lived through them. In contrast, conclusive change may be remembered because it involved significant and identifiable social change. The dislocations and disruptions that followed became opportunities to struggle over the meaning of the past anterior to these transformative social processes. For example, if male informants could present the precolonial handicraft textile industry as one based on household reciprocity, they could blame the contemporary loosening of household complementarity on women's acquisitive tendencies. Similarly, women could justify their position as independent entrepreneurs within a view of the precolonial period in which men usurped their long-established privileges. Thus it should not be surprising that my informants had more vivid recollections of an earlier period than they did of a period of more subtle change chronologically closer to the time of their interview.

Much of the detail my informants provided on the precolonial industry, however, was framed in normative terms. It was based on how they thought the industry *ought* to have functioned, not necessarily as it actually did. James Scott encountered a similar social construction of meaning in his study of the impact of double-cropping on the Malaysian village of Sedaka.

As we listen to the rich and poor of Sedaka attempting to make sense of the massive changes they have all experienced over the past decade, we find ourselves in the midst of an ideological struggle, however small in scale. It is a struggle over facts and their meaning, over what has happened and who is to blame, over how the present situation is to be defined and interpreted.... As in any history, assessing the present forcibly involves a reevaluation of what has gone on before. Thus, the ideological struggle to define the present is a struggle to define the past as well.[40]

Both Scott and I encountered a normative bias in the oral record of a period anterior to a socially transformative event or process. In Scott's case, this was caused by the impact of double-cropping and the use of combine harvesters. In my case, it was because of the transformations associated with colonial conquest and the end of slavery. Both male and female informants shared this normative bias. I am concerned, however, that the normative accounts of the handicraft textile industry may be based on a "remembered economy," which contains only a refracted vision of what actual lived experience may have been.[41]

Just as my informants' understanding of their contemporary situation influenced how they recounted the past, the actual circumstances of the moment of recording the oral record are a crucial part of the production of knowledge. In his critique of the biases in the Works Progress Administration program of collecting slave narratives in the American South, Paul Escott argues that

in the 1930s, when former slaves were interviewed ... southern blacks lived in the grip of a system of segregation that was nearly as oppressive as slavery. Old, poor, and dependent, they were trying to stay alive while the nation's economy lurched sickeningly through its most serious crisis. They could not afford to alienate local white people or agents of the federal government, which might provide them with vital relief or an old age pension. All the rules of racial etiquette had to be observed, and the informant had to give priority to appeasing his interviewer rather than telling the truth about the past.[42]

My being a white male historian collecting data in Mali on the heels of the Sahelian drought in the late 1970s and during a period of severe strains on the national economy and politics in the 1980s must have influenced the context in which I sought to reconstruct the past using oral history.

For whatever reason, my informants' silence on the social changes in the production of handicraft textiles during the early colonial period is disconcerting. I know that these changes occurred; I had collected evidence to that effect in the archives. Why didn't my informants provide me with the answers to questions I needed to complete my study? The simple answer is that reversible social processes are difficult to reconstruct using oral sources. But the larger answer goes beyond oral sources and research design to the nature of the production of knowledge itself.

Historical memory is not like a sponge, soaking up experiences indiscriminately. Instead, historical memory is culturally determined. "The memory of a man's name," writes Paul Irwin in his study of Liptako oral traditions, "tends to have a longer life than other sorts of memories: genealogies are so inextricably bound up with notions of identity that no one neglects them entirely." Moreover, historical memory and its forms of expression are intimately linked to what David Cohen calls the "reservoirs of holdings of intelligence upon which social life is contingent."[43] How to gain access to those reservoirs, how to privilege our informants' own histories, and how to proceed with questions of interest to academic historians are the future challenges of African social history.

In this book, I have tried to make clear to the reader how my position in the interview process shaped the outcome of the session. For this research project, I asked leading questions.[44] My questions shaped the larger cognitive arena in which my informants responded. They did not always answer as I would have liked, providing me with the rich reservoirs of intelligence I assume they controlled. Nor was my questioning rigid and formulaic. I encouraged my informants to range broadly over the issues I was concerned with and pursued tangents when they raised new issues or different perspectives. Nonetheless, the objectives of my research remained the same. I more or less determined the questions. I needed informants to provide me with evidence to fill out the historical processes I had identified. Despite the variety and flexibility of my interview design, the interview revolved around my position as interviewer. The give-and-take of the actual interview accounts for the somewhat awkward way in which I present the oral evidence in this book: it reflects the rough and direct way in which the oral transcript was made. My questions are followed by my informants' responses.

Despite my efforts to empower my informants and to listen to their history, this book has been deeply shaped by what I would like to have found out but was not told. The archival record, in contrast, is dense. Its density testifies to the importance of cotton to the colonial program of economic development. Since I began this study, my project has shifted in relationship to the evidence I collected and to the issues of concern to historians of Africa. Although I may not have been able to satisfy my original research design, I remain convinced that the story I have is worth telling.

The *Politique Cotonnière* in French West Africa

The French described what they were doing to develop the colonial economy of the French Soudan around cotton as the *politique cotonnière*. The term *politique* means policy, so *politique cotonnière* translates as cotton policy. But the term *politique* also refers to politics, as in the practice of political power, thus suggesting a wider context in which to understand the development and challenges to the French cotton policy in colonial West Africa. Indeed, there was no unified or coherent cotton policy in French West Africa or even in the French Soudan, which became the French West African colony dedicated most fully to cotton production. Thus the notion of a politics of cotton production makes sense only if we understand it to operate within an environment of contending social, economic, and cultural forces. Various groups of French administrators, agronomists, entrepreneurs, and merchants and African producers, consumers, and chiefs aligned themselves differently along the three core categories of cotton policy: labor, markets, and quality.

The earliest application of a cotton policy and its attendant politics of production occurred in Senegal in 1817. On the eve of retaking Saint Louis and Gorée from the British, Governor Julien Schmaltz wrote to the king and notables of Galam urging them to "produce as much cotton as possible."[45] French colonial cotton policies evolved significantly from this early exhortation, although each policy iteration involved some mix of labor, markets, and quality control. As policy was elaborated, each of these core categories had its own politics. French colonial cotton policy can be understood as a tool kit containing three compartments. From each compartment colonial administrators drew out versions of these core categories and combined them to "fix" the linked problem of inducing a growing supply of good quality cotton to satisfy metropolitan demand and of fitting the changing notion of Africans and of colonization. Each different combination of labor, markets, and quality control changed the shape of colonial cotton policy and reflected a different vision of colonialism. Moreover, colonial administrators' understanding of the problem of inducing cotton supply for export also changed over time as different mixes failed to yield the expected results. The high point in the debate over colonial cotton policy occurred in the period from 1918 to 1932. The debate was not only about cotton production; it centered on who was to control the entire colonial economy. The French could exhort, cajole, coerce, and punish, but they could not control the decisions and intentions of Africans, who as peasants or as laborers determined the success of colonial policy.

Both the proponents of peasant cotton and of irrigated cotton understood that Africans were to be the producers, although they were to produce under very different labor systems. For those promoting peasant cotton, the key policy issues involved encouraging Africans to cultivate more efficiently on their own farms. For those supporting irrigated cotton production on plantations, Africans were to supply labor in exchange for wages. The supply of wage labor, however, depended upon the development of a labor market and the one that developed in the French Soudan favored instead migration to Senegal and the Côte d'Ivoire. To operate within a labor market unfavorable to wage labor, employers turned to the state to assist them in recruitment. The colonial state's response to cotton plantations' request for wage labor was deeply ambivalent. On the one hand, colonial administrators were under considerable pressure to make their colony yield cotton for export; on the other, some senior administrators were reluctant to supply labor for enterprises that could not attract labor because they were not willing to make their offers sufficiently attractive. Many senior administrators were committed to the ideas of free labor and free markets, and they considered state recruitment of labor a "lazy solution." Nonetheless, when the Soudanese remained unwilling to come forward at the prevailing wages, the state assisted in generating a supply of labor to the struggling cotton enterprises.

Reluctant laborers and racist managers led to labor scandals on two European-managed cotton plantations, the Société auxiliaire africaine and the Compagnie cotonnière du Niger, in the 1920s. These scandals forced the colonial administration to reappraise its commitment to the European-managed cotton plantation and to its assistance in recruiting labor. Out of these failed efforts to recruit wage labor, the managers of irrigation turned to forms of internal colonization, relying on Africans to settle in the irrigated cotton zone.

Perhaps in no other area were the contradictions between ideology and reality more apparent than in the colonial administration's commitment to a free market in cotton. As cotton came to represent colonialism in the French Soudan, administrators needed to prove the viability of their policies—and the viability of their colony itself—measured by the volume of cotton exports. Debates about the colonial cotton market and solutions to its imperfections are a constant theme running throughout the entire history of French colonial cotton policies. Administrators were almost always frustrated because the performance of the Soudanese cotton export market was constrained by four factors over which they had little control. First, because French spinners and weavers were part of a highly competitive world market, they would use colonial cotton only if the price and quality were competitive with those of other cotton available on the world market. Second, the export market for cotton in the Soudan competed with a robust domestic market for cotton, feeding a thriving handicraft textile industry. Cotton prices in the domestic market were almost always higher than the export market could support. Third, the colonial state was committed to free markets, which meant that it could not simply expropriate cotton from African producers. And fourth, the colonial state was obliged to delegate the trade in cotton to the private sector, which, operating in a narrowly defined arena of profit and loss, was prepared to support cotton exports only if they made money. These constraints yielded lively debates about what constituted just returns for both African peasants and expatriate merchants.

Frustrated with the performance of the cotton market, administrators turned to increased surveillance and compulsion. Governor-General Marie François Joseph Clozel in 1912 captured the paradox of linking compulsion to free markets when he stated that Africans have a "strict obligation" to cultivate cotton but complete freedom to sell it.[46] In 1924, Governor-General Carde justified the use of force in cotton cultivation as a form of "benevolent intervention," which was needed to develop African societies even against their own wishes.[47] In Chapter 8 I examine the policy of official cotton fairs, which in the 1920s and 1930s were the only sites where cotton could legally be bought and sold. Peasants were obliged to bring their cotton to these markets, have it weighed and graded, and then, if they were not pleased with the prices offered by the assembled merchants, they could carry the cotton home again. The administration's commitment to free markets took many bizarre forms throughout the history of French efforts to promote cotton for export.

But the French did not want just any cotton. They wanted a cotton that was competitive in price and quality with the American medium staple, which was the industry standard. A central part of the politique cotonnière thus revolved around quality control. Some forms of quality control could be exerted at the level of ginning, when seeds could be sorted, the best retained, and the others discarded. Some projects to improve quality simply involved distributing imported varieties of cotton; others required painstaking scientific efforts to breed new cotton varieties from the best of indigenous and imported cottons. But quality control also meant intervention and micromanagement of African production and marketing decisions. Colonial administrators and extension agents worked with and often coerced peasants into using different planting techniques. Because cotton was readily subject to cross-fertilization, peasants were obliged to pull up all old cotton plants and cultivate their fields of imported cotton far from their fields of indigenous varieties. Administrators introduced the hated *champs du commandant* as a means to "instructing" Africans in cotton cultivation and assuring a supply of cotton. In their efforts to promote cotton for export, colonial cotton policies involved changing mixes of coercion and control at the conjoined levels of labor, markets, and quality control.

Although the Soudanese were not called upon to help define colonial cotton policy, their actions nonetheless determined its outcomes. And French cotton policy in the Soudan failed in its intentions of generating vast supplies of cotton for metropolitan mills. Who, then, were the actors in the drama of colonial cotton production? First and foremost they were the African men and women who for centuries had been cultivating cotton, ginning, spinning, weaving, dyeing, trading, and wearing it. In this book, I often lump together under the term *Soudanese* Africans who would define themselves as Maraka, Bambara, Fulbe, Somono, Bobo, Minianka, Malinke, Senufo, and so on, whose local histories would reveal many

variants to the general patterns described here. Even if colonial officials defined Africans as rational economic actors, Africans lived in
complex social worlds in which market incentives were only one of
many factors influencing production and marketing decisions. As
they produced cotton, Soudanese peasants also reproduced culture
and struggled over the meanings of family, marriage, labor, wealth,
and power.[48] Men and women from all over this region engaged in
complex and changing social relations to produce cotton textiles.
Soudanese cotton textiles, especially from the Middle Niger Valley
during the nineteenth century, were highly regarded commodities.
These textiles figured prominently in the assortment of goods traded
with the people of the desert edge and those of the forest. Demand
for handcrafted textiles throughout the colonial period remained
strong. Because local spinners and weavers consistently paid more
than the export sector, most of the Soudanese cotton harvest flowed
into regional circuits of production and trade.

Colonial administrators played a prominent role in the politique
cotonnière. Senior administrators may have determined the policy,
but their junior colleagues in the bush were the ones who implemented it. Senior administrators were by no means agreed on the
best means of enhancing the quality and increasing the quantity of
cotton exported to the metropole. Sometimes they favored peasants,
and at other times they favored capital-intensive European-managed
irrigation projects. No matter which of the two policies they favored, most shared two assumptions: first, they believed—some more
strongly than others—in the inherent responsiveness of African
peasants to market stimuli. They were convinced that given the right
incentives, whether in wages or in prices for their commodities, Africans would respond favorably and produce vast quantities of cotton. Second, senior and junior administrators alike harbored deep
resentments against French expatriate merchants. Most dedicated
their careers to public service from which they would gain only
through more or less rapid promotions. Few moved laterally into the
colonial commercial sector upon retirement, as their colleagues in
the Belgian Congo did.[49] Thus they defined themselves largely in opposition to the self-interest of merchants and saw themselves as the
protectors of naive Africans unable to defend themselves from un-
scrupulous manipulations of market forces. Although administrators were obliged to rely on merchants to provide the market incentives so necessary to the politique cotonnière, they distrusted the
merchants sufficiently to doubt whether the merchants were willing

and able to carry out their share of colonial development work. The merchants, for their part, keenly resented any infringement on their right to free and unfettered play of market forces, shaped largely by their own actions. This tension was captured by the essayist Albert Londres during a tour of the French Soudan in 1928.

Silent Africa is nothing but a football field.
There are two teams, always the same teams, both white.
One wears the government colors; the other the colors of the business man.
The Negro is the ball.
The game is fiercely played for the possession of the ball.
The white official protects the Negro against the business man, but uses him for his own purposes. The business man accuses the official of doing with the Negro precisely what all the others are forbidden to do.
The official treats the business man like a margouillat.
A margouillat is a little lizard with suckers in its paws, which is always dying of hunger and catches all the mosquitoes within reach on the wing.
The business man says the official is another Denys, the tyrant of Syracuse.
The official insists that, except for him, the business man would rob and exploit the Negro; the man of affairs retorts that if the official forbids him to exploit the Negro, it is only so that he may do so himself without interference.[50]

Expatriate French and Syrian merchants were thus central players in the drama of colonial cotton development. They sought to defend their interests through fierce opposition to efforts to fix prices as part of the debate on just prices, and they fought against tightly controlled cotton fairs as an infringement on their rights to free markets. Expatriate merchants harbored deep resentments against colonial officials, whom they blamed for their own personal difficulties.

African merchants were also crucial to the private sector's engagement with colonial cotton. But their role was more ambiguous. On the one hand, African merchants and agents of the expatriate French commercial firms were crucial intermediaries between producers and the big French import-export houses. On the other hand, African merchants also plied the domestic and regional cotton and textile markets, buying cotton only to sell it elsewhere in the colony for higher prices, buying cotton textiles, whether handcrafted or imported, and selling them throughout the West African continental market. The demand for Soudanese textiles reached from Senegal and Mauritania down to the Côte d'Ivoire and the Gold Coast.[51]

Sitting somewhere midway between the commercially disinterested nature of the administration and the self-interest of the merchants was the Association cotonnière coloniale (ACC). As I discuss in Chapter 4 and develop in Chapters 5, 8, and 11, the ACC was formed by a group of French industrial spinners and weavers to promote cotton production in France's new colonies. The ACC was chartered as a nonprofit agency and as such was eligible for government subsidies. Using both government funds and monies donated from the metropolitan textile sector, the ACC played a pivotal role in the formative period of French cotton policy in the Soudan. Because it saw its role in the immediate improvement of cotton exports, the ACC aligned itself, however unintentionally, with the propeasant camp. In order to promote cotton production for export, the ACC became the principal supplier of new varieties of cotton seeds. Because seeds were removed at the ginning stage, the ACC also became the primary reservoir of cotton seeds and thus central to the renewal of the cotton program each year. The ACC, however, was not content to be a junior partner in the politique cotonnière and used its relationship with the colonial state to promote its interests.

Although cotton grew widely throughout the West African savanna, local varieties tended to have short, spindly fibers not favored by industrial spinners. To make colonial cotton more attractive, agronomists were charged with making scientific studies of local cotton varieties, with acclimating exotic varieties imported into West Africa, and with developing long-term programs of hybridization designed to merge the best of the local and exotic varieties of cotton. Agronomists were thus called upon to play a central part in the politique cotonnière. For example, the agronomist Yves Henry played a crucial public role in generating support for a commitment to West African cotton; Robert H. Forbes, an American expert in rainfed cotton cultivation, was central to the debates surrounding irrigation, even if his advice was not always heeded; and Budichowsky's hybridization program at the experimental farm at M'Pesoba resulted in a new cotton variety, which promised to rescue the proponents of peasant cotton from the juggernaut of the pro-irrigation camp. Untold other agronomists, their African assistants, and agricultural extension agents played crucial roles in the quality control side of the politique cotonnière.

And finally, there was a group of public works officials and a handful of French entrepreneurs with some real and much presumed expertise in irrigation. In contrast to the British, whose public works engineers had firsthand experience in India, few Frenchmen had skills or knowledge of massive irrigation works in tropical and semitropical areas.[52] None had experience with cotton irrigation, which

helps to account for the prominence of the analogy to cotton irrigation along the Nile, which, as we shall see, was deeply flawed. Yet
one public works official, Emile Bélime, rose to command tremendous power and authority as a consequence of his successful efforts
to introduce irrigation into the debate on cotton policy. With a won-
derfully astute sense of colonial politics and an immense capacity for
self-promotion, Bélime recognized, furthered, and rode a wave of interest in "massive development projects" into virtually unrivaled
power in the Soudan.[53] Bélime was not, however, unchallenged.
These struggles among competing interests to capture the cotton
harvest and to capture the resources of the colonial state were intensified precisely because cotton colonialism failed in its stated goals.

This book is organized into three periods. The first covers roughly
a century, from the earliest French efforts to promote cotton in Senegal in 1817 to the end of World War I in 1918. Chapter 2 provides
background to the encounter between two worlds of cotton, one
emanating from industrial Europe and the other one deeply inter-
twined with the dynamic of West African regional economies. Chapter 3 examines early French cotton colonialism in Senegal as a prelude to the more sustained cotton development programs in the
French Soudan. Chapter 4 examines the first dozen years of cotton
colonialism in the Soudan, which was to become the site of the most
ambitious efforts by the French to develop cotton production for export. It also explores how colonial cotton programs were thwarted by
the Soudanese, who preferred to participate in the domestic market.
The cotton policy experiences of this period were important to the
debates that took place from 1918 to 1932, which forms the middle
period of this study. Indeed, before he promulgated his important cotton program in 1924, Governor-General Carde of the French West
Africa Federation admitted to reading the "archives" of French colonial cotton policy in Senegal and the Soudan.

The second part covers 1918 to 1932, a period in which the most
sustained debates concerning cotton development occurred. In his
1924 program for cotton development, Governor-General Carde created space for both the pro-peasant activists and the proponents of
irrigation. The period from 1918 to 1932 should be considered the
high point in the struggles between the two opposing views on colonial cotton production. The chapters in this section explore change
over time, but they are organized thematically. Chapter 5 briefly surveys the impact of World War I on French colonial cotton policy,

largely from the metropolitan perspective. In Chapters 6 through 9, attention returns to the Soudan. Each chapter explores in turn the politics surrounding the core ingredients of cotton development: labor, quality control, and marketing. The policies applied during this period were usually understood to be technical solutions to problems of imperfections in markets, incentives, and the culture and work ethic of the Soudanese. Chapters 6 and 7 explore the forces promoting irrigation under European management. Labor control was a crucial issue. Chapter 8 examines the increasing surveillance of and intervention in peasant cotton growers' production and marketing decisions. Chapter 9 is concerned with the dynamic of the domestic cotton and cotton textile industry. It explores the domestic industry by examining the elasticity of demand for cloth, the operation of dual cotton markets, and the processes of change in the handicraft textile sector. Most of the earlier chapters allude to the handicraft textile industry to explain the little success of the politique cotonnière. In this chapter, I move the handicraft textile industry to center stage and examine its organization and its historical dynamics. Although this study uses the French Soudan as its unit of analysis, many of my examples—especially those drawn from oral evidence—stem from my regional studies of the Middle Niger Valley. Additional research is needed to assess whether the patterns of social change varied elsewhere in the Soudan and in West Africa more generally.

The third period, 1932 to 1946, witnessed the rapid ascendancy of the irrigation model of cotton production, but also its collapse. Chapter 10 focuses on the Office du Niger, the massive public works project designed to make the Soudan into the cotton center of West Africa and Soudanese peasants into happy, efficient farmers. Chapter 11 explores the efforts of the pro-peasant camp to respond to the apparent hegemony of the irrigation model of colonial economic development. Indeed, a new hybrid cotton introduced in 1932 revitalized the pro-peasant cotton policy. Despite this revitalization, those promoting peasant cotton still failed to capture the cotton harvest of the Soudan precisely because of the resiliency and dynamism in the handicraft textile industry.

I end this study in 1946, when, following World War II and the Brazzaville meeting, compulsion was declared illegal throughout French West Africa. Without compulsion, the irrigation model of cotton production collapsed. Without compulsion, Africans could no longer be forced to cultivate cotton or to bring their harvests to the central cotton fairs and ginning stations. Cotton, however, did not disappear from the Soudanese landscape. On the contrary, a revived and reconfigured pro-peasant program in the southern tier of the Soudan in the late 1940s and 1950s began to yield phenomenal cotton harvests. Cotton remains to this day independent Mali's most important export earner.

PART I

Two Worlds of Cotton

Cotton, the European Cotton Textile Industry, and the Western Sudanese Handicraft Textile Industry

The first sustained encounter between two worlds of cotton addressed in this book occurred at the beginning of the nineteenth century in West Africa. Cotton and handicraft cotton textile production had long been part of the economies of West Africa, especially those of the savanna, and cotton textiles catered to both domestic needs and regional markets. The other world of cotton emanated from Europe, which was undergoing rapid industrialization of its cotton textile production. In the process of procuring raw materials, the world of European cotton linked itself to the Atlantic economies and other semitropical and tropical regions producing raw materials. When the French returned to the two colonial towns of Gorée and Saint Louis in 1817, they set about shaping their colony along new economic and political models. First under Governors Julien Schmaltz and Jacques-François Roger and later under Louis Faidherbe and Jean-Marie Emile Pinet-Laparde, the French sought to build colonialism on production of agricultural commodities for export to the metropole. The ubiquity of Africans cultivating small plots of cotton caught their attention and they raced to the facile conclusion that cotton was ideally suited to the economic future of their colony.

West Africans had long been familiar with European and Indian textiles. Europeans, however, were not interested in West African cotton until the end of the eighteenth century. Then demand for West African cotton made Europeans aware of the dynamic handicraft textile industry of the Western Sudan. These two worlds of cotton—the regional world of West African cotton and cotton textiles and the world of the European cotton industry—came increasingly into contact and occasionally into collision during the course of the

nineteenth century. This chapter provides background to the historical geography of cotton, to the industrialization of the cotton textile
industry in Europe, and to the production and commerce of cotton
and cotton textiles in the Western Sudan.

The Historical Geography of Cotton

Cotton was one of the eight main groups of natural fibers widely
used to make clothing as well as tents, floor coverings, wall coverings, cordage, and containers, to mention only a few of the hundreds
of uses of textiles. Although there is some overlap, wool, silk, flax,
and cotton were used widely for clothing, and hemp, jute, abaca, sisal, and henequen were used more in commercial and industrial processes.[1] Of the fibers used for making clothing, cotton emerged as
preeminent only in the nineteenth century.

No one in the fifteenth century could have imagined that cotton
would become king of the fibers. According to Fernand Braudel, "a
geography of textiles" is revealed by taking a global view of production and exchange and linking the slow work of weavers to regular
crises in access to raw materials. Europe had wool, but not in sufficient quantity; it lacked cotton and silk. China had silk and wool but
lacked cotton. India had cotton and some silk but lacked wool. Black
Africa, according to Braudel, bought foreign fabrics with gold or
slaves. "That was how poor peoples paid for their luxury purchases."
Because of periodic and recurring supply crises, textiles were "always
on the move, taking root in new regions."[2] Originally guarded jealously by China, silk was introduced into the Mediterranean by Jus-
tinian in the sixth century. Byzantium, too, guarded the secrets of the
silkworm, although cracks in control allowed silk to expand to Sicily
and Andalusia around the eleventh century and from there to Tus-
cany, Venetia, and into the Rhône Valley by the fifteenth. Flax was
not as mobile, spreading eastward only as far as the Baltics and Russia. Wool found a home in South Africa and Australia, especially in
the nineteenth century. Cotton, however, eventually dominated the
world of textiles.

Cotton cloth appears earliest in excavations at Mohenjo-daro along
the Indus River valley, where it was dated to around 3000 B.C. Cotton
appears to have been independently domesticated and woven in Peru
around 2500 B.C. By 500 B.C. cotton was being grown and woven in
the Meroitic kingdom along the fourth cataract of the Nile River.
Between the eleventh and sixteenth centuries, some cotton was be-

ing cultivated in the Iberian Peninsula, southern Italy, Greece, Cyprus, and especially Turkey.[3]

All cotton varieties belong to the genus *gossypium*. They divide into two families based on the number of haploid chromosomes. The Old World family, consisting of thirteen haploid chromosomes, contains two broad species: *G. arboreum*, which is a perennial shrub colloquially known as tree cotton because the plant grows upward to six feet, and *G. herbaceum*, a lower-lying shrub, two to four feet high. Until the nineteenth-century transformation in world cotton growing, *G. arboreum* was produced in a broad arc from the Indian subcontinent through Southeast Asia into China, where it found its most important commercial home. *G. arboreum* was likely the variety grown in ancient Meroe, from where it spread southward into the Shire and Zambezi river valleys. *G. herbaceum* seems to have spread predominantly westward; it is found from south India through Persia into Afghanistan and Turkestan, but it also spread into Iraq, Syria, and Turkey to eastern Mediterranean islands. From there, *G. herbaceum* took hold of North Africa, possibly drifting southward to West Africa. *G. punctatum*, widely found in the Western Sudan, was related to this species. Varieties of *G. herbaceum* also found homes in parts of China and in southern Africa.

The other family of cotton, consisting of New World cottons, contains 26 haploid chromosomes. As in the Old World family, the New World cottons also fall into two broad species: *G. hirsutum* and *G. barbadense*. Perhaps originating in highland Peru, *G. hirsutum* spread over the semitropical and tropical areas of the New World, moving northward from Central America into the American Southwest. *G. hirsutum* found its widest distribution as American upland cotton. In contrast, *G. barbadense* spread through tropical South America and into the Antilles, from where it took hold of the South Atlantic coast as the famous Sea Island cotton. *G. barbadense* traveled eastward across the Pacific into Polynesia and the East Indies. In the 1820s, *G. barbadense* became domesticated as Egyptian (or Jumel) long-staple cotton.

Old World and New World cottons divide not only along the lines of the number of haploid chromosomes but also by their characteristic fiber length. Fiber length was critically important only with the marriage of cotton to machine power.[4] Until the end of the eighteenth century, while cotton was still spun by simple hand- or human-powered machines, the length of fiber determined the convenience of spinning but was not critically important to the spinning process. Spinners preferred long cotton fibers because they were easier to use.

Cotton is classified largely by quality and length of fibers. Long-staple fiber consists of cotton whose fibers are between one and one-eighth to two inches long. These are all *G. barbadense* varieties. Medium staple, most of which are American upland varieties, have fibers from seven-eighths to one and one-eighth inches long. And short-staple cottons, mostly *G. arboreum* and *G. herbaceum*, have short, spindly fibers between three-eighth and three-quarter inches.[5]

Cotton has its own distinctive geography, growing predominantly in a wide tropical and subtropical belt between 37 degrees northern latitude and 32 degrees southern latitude. Depending on climate, sunlight, and ranges of temperature, cotton can be grown from as far north as 47 degrees (in parts of the Ukraine) to as far south as 32 degrees (in eastern Australia). When cotton spinning and weaving became mechanized in the late eighteenth and early nineteenth centuries, the demand for raw materials induced farmers to experiment with cotton even in conditions where late frosts could damage the crop or massive expenditures for irrigation were needed to assure needed moisture. Coincident with the dramatic increase in demand, agronomists experimented by adapting cotton varieties to a wide range of new habitats. Starting around the second quarter of the nineteenth century, agronomists, colonial officials, and agricultural engineers engaged in a worldwide but informal exchange of cotton seeds and studies.[6]

Generally, however, within this broad zone cotton requires 200 warm days with average temperatures well above 60 degrees. At least 60 to 70 percent of the days must be sunny, thus yielding an irregular isothermic line through this broad zone. Moreover, cotton is a thirsty crop; it can survive on as little as 29 inches of rainfall a year and as much as 52 inches, but the rain must be more or less evenly spread throughout the growing cycle. More than 60 inches of rain causes significant plant disease and harvesting problems. Rainfall should taper off during the harvesting season because once the cotton boll opens, excessive moisture leads to the deterioration of the fiber. The great expansion of irrigation in the last half of the nineteenth century and first quarter of the twentieth brought cotton to semiarid and arid regions of the world, where the sunshine and temperature conditions were adequate but rainfall was not. Cotton is demanding of the soil, especially in its need for phosphorus and nitrogen. The crop thus prefers certain soils, although the chemical balance of the soil can be altered by the application of fertilizers and manures.[7]

Cotton and Capitalism

Until the seventeenth century, most British and continental European textiles were composed of locally produced materials: wool, linen, silks. Even the coarsest clothing was expensive, and, with the exception of the most expensive silks and linens, European textiles were usually drab in color. This helps account for the steady demand for imported luxury textiles from the Orient.

In the latter half of the seventeenth century, the East India Company began importing into Britain and reexporting to the Continent inexpensive, lightweight, brightly printed cotton cloth from India.[8] These calicoes quickly became popular, resulting in a marked consumer shift away from woolens. Silks and linens remained strong competitors, but cotton cloth eroded demand among all contemporary textiles because cotton alone took and retained a variety of dyes.[9] To protect its domestic industry, France prohibited the sale of imported Indian cotton cloth as early as 1686 and the British woolen industry pressured Parliament to restrict imports of dyed calico in 1701. These restrictions stimulated the development of a domestic cotton textile industry in both France and Britain.

Developing a domestic cotton textile industry, however, involved significant technical and commercial problems. Cotton had been used in European weaving since the twelfth century, when it was first imported from the Levant. A little cotton could be squeezed from southern European soils, but yields were low and quality poor. Moreover, cotton had shorter and more fragile fibers than wool, silk, or linen. Thus to use cotton yarns, cotton had to be combined with another fiber, such as linen, to yield a hybrid yarn. When used as a weft, cotton hybrid yarn resulted in a cloth called *futaine* or fustian. Fustian cloth, however, remained expensive, was difficult to launder, and did not retain dye well. Thus when British and later French traders brought Indian cottons to European consumers, they were greeted with enthusiasm.

Most European textile production was tightly controlled by guilds and depended on highly regulated supplies of raw materials. Because of the scarcity of cotton in most of continental Europe, cotton textile production was not as tightly regulated as the wool, silk, and linen industries. Thus the new cotton textile industry could emerge within an environment in which labor and management could be organized in new and innovative ways.[10] As these new cotton textile industries developed, they confronted a problem not faced by the woolen, silk, and linen industries: the need to import raw materials from vast distances. Capitalist transformation of the cotton textile industry in Britain and on the European continent at the beginning of the nineteenth century led to worldwide inducements to expand cotton production and commerce.

Between 1697, when the first reliable statistics on cotton imports appear, and 1749, the imports of raw cotton into Great Britain were relatively stationary. In 1679, 1,976,000 pounds of cotton were imported, in 1749, 1,658,000 pounds. Imports of raw cotton fell in the ten years after 1701 to a low of 715,000 pounds. In 1748 an exceptional 4,853,000 pounds were imported. Throughout the first half of the eighteenth century, however, the annual average imports of cotton was just under two million pounds. The stationary level of cotton imports is remarkable given the demand for cotton yarns and cotton textiles in the domestic and export markets and in face of the technological changes in weaving and spinning. Indeed, until 1775, cotton was rarely used exclusively in textiles; most often it was spun together with wool or linen or used as the weft yarn for woolen or linen textiles.[11]

Most cotton imported into Great Britain in the first half of the eighteenth century came from Smyrna in the Ottoman Empire and from the West Indies. Some Indian cotton was imported between the last decade of the seventeenth century and 1708, but even when a baling press was used to compress the bulk of cotton for shipment, high transport costs limited the demand for Indian cotton. After 1708, Indian cotton no longer appeared on customs accounts. Instead, between two-thirds and three-quarters of cotton imported into Britain came from the West Indies, the rest from the Levant. West Indian cotton was preferred over that of the Levant, but there were significant differences in quality even within production regions. Although generally inferior to West Indian cotton, cotton from Cyprus was more highly regarded than that from Smyrna. From the West Indies, the most highly regarded cotton came from the French islands, particularly Cayenne, Saint Domingue, and Guadaloupe, followed by the British islands. Jamaican cotton fetched virtually the same price as that from the French Antilles, but Antiguan varieties were less well regarded.[12]

Despite the importance of West Indian sources for the total cotton imports into Britain before 1750, West Indian planters considered cotton a minor crop. Sugar was king. Planters grew cotton only where sugar would not grow, and they abandoned cotton for sugar when they could. Slave traders sold the sickest slaves for the lowest prices to cotton planters. Cotton dominated only the smallest islands, and even on Tortola, where cotton had been the principal crop until 1748, profits from its sale went to acquire more slaves to plant sugar.[13]

The American colonies contributed virtually nothing to the cotton trade. Small shipments of cotton from Charleston were made in 1748 and 1757, but these were probably West Indian reexports. The first recorded import of American mainland cotton took place in 1771 and consisted of three bales from New York, four bags from Virginia and Maryland, and three barrels from North Carolina. There is no further record of American imports until 1784, when eight bags were imported into Liverpool. That shipment caused considerable confusion because British customs doubted that the newly independent United States could actually produce that much cotton. Moreover, the shipment languished in a warehouse for several months thereafter, in part because the quality of the cotton was not considered adequate.[14]

Between 1775 and 1790 the technological innovations in spinning and weaving resulted in a capitalist reorganization of the British textile industry.[15] Increased productivity in spinning and weaving in turn generated intense demand-side pressure for raw materials. Between 1770 and 1775, an annual average of 4,800,000 pounds of raw cotton was imported into Great Britain. By 1782, seven years after the introduction of Arkwright's water frame and three years after Compton's mule, Britain imported 11,828,000 pounds, and by 1789, Britain was importing 32,576,000 pounds.

Despite planters' disdain for cotton, the West Indies supplied nearly 71 percent of Britain's demand for cotton in the period 1786–90. In 1781, cotton was first imported from Brazil. The initial shipments from Maranham were not well regarded, although the cotton from Pernambuco was classed as equal to the better West Indian varieties. From 1700 to 1750 the supply of cotton did not respond strongly to price changes. Cotton prices, however, rose steeply from 1776 to 1781, when they temporarily reached three and four times the 1775 prices. They eventually stabilized in 1787–88 at the low end of the 1776–80 range and supply rose again. The increased supplies came primarily from the West Indies, Brazil, and the Levant. In

1788, Manchester manufacturers urged the East India Company to promote exports of cotton.[16] The beginning of the French Revolution and the rebellion in Saint Domingue caused cotton prices to move upward again.

High prices for American Sea Island cotton stimulated efforts from 1785 to 1795 to extend its range on the mainland. Sea Island cotton did not produce well on the mainland, although the medium-staple upland varieties thrived. Upland cotton had fuzzy fibers to which cotton seeds clung tenaciously, thwarting the efforts of the roller gin to remove efficiently the seeds from the fiber. Even using slave labor, the cost of removing seeds by hand was much too high. In 1793, during a visit to the American South, Eli Whitney invented the cotton gin, which transformed the world cotton market. Whitney's cotton gin and Hodgen Holmes's improvements provided an inexpensive means of making American upland cotton commercially attractive. Supplies of American cotton to British spinners rose from 183,316 pounds in 1790 to 16,000,000 pounds in 1800.[17] Figure 2 shows the relative importance of different sources of cotton, using percentages for the annual average of five-year periods.

Data for the French cotton textile industry are not nearly as complete as for the British, but the patterns of technical innovation leading to demand-side pressure on cotton supply paralleled the British

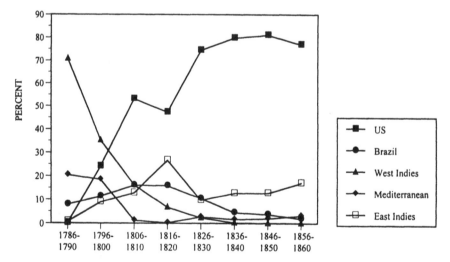

Fig. 2. Percent of Raw Cotton Imported into Britain, Five-Year Averages, 1786–1860. (Source: Ellison, *Handbook*, p. 86.)

model. Kay directly introduced his flying shuttle into France in 1753. Fearful of competition, Britain forbade the emigration of skilled artisans in the early eighteenth century, and from 1750 she enacted regulations banning the export of machinery. Despite British prohibitions on export of new technologies, Hargreaves's spinning jenny, invented in 1764, was introduced into France through the offices of the Lancashire native John Holker, who had established a cotton mill in Rouen in 1750. In 1754, Holker was appointed as the inspector of foreign manufactures, charged with royal efforts to introduce and expand industries in France which were more advanced in other countries. The Ancien Régime had an industrial policy that, under the banner of mercantilist ideology, sought to promote industrial development in France so as to minimize the flight of gold and to increase the exports of domestic production. Holker not only encouraged the migration of skilled Lancashire spinners and weavers, in direct contravention of British prohibitions, but also British entrepreneurs, who established manufacturing activities in Normandy region. Holker was also responsible for the introduction of Arkwright's water frame.[18]

France was therefore not noticeably behind Britain in the development and application of the new cotton spinning and weaving industries. As in Britain, the original cotton textile industry developed out of the well-established linen and silk industries. And as in Britain, cotton textile production was not subject to vestigial guild restrictions. French textile producers had used cotton since at least the early seventeenth century, mostly as a fiber mixed with linen and wool in fustian cloth. This, in part, accounts for the importance of Alsace, Vosges, and Mulhouse in the French cotton textile industry. The growth of the cotton textile industry in Normandy was favored by its proximity to France's main cotton port, Le Havre. By 1790, France had eight large spinning mills with nearly 10,000 spindles. By 1815, France had 50 spinning mills with more than 150,000 spindles. Nonetheless, France's cotton textile industry did not expand as dramatically as its counterpart across the channel.[19]

The relative backwardness of French industrial development has exercised economic historians for generations. Its causes have been variously defined as a general aversion to risk; a dislike of banks in favor of "auto-financing," which reduced the volume of capital available for industrial development; the persistence of restrictions on trade and commerce, including higher taxes and duties; lower per capita income; and social and political conditions, including the sustained disequilibrium of the revolution through the Napoleonic Wars.[20]

Mechanization spread first and fastest to spinning and more slowly to weaving. Mechanized weaving expanded only after 1820–25; by 1830 there were more than 2,000 mechanized looms in Haut-Rhin alone. Mechanization of weaving progressed faster in Normandy, where by 1860 between 30,000 and 60,000 workers tended the mechanized looms. By 1825, textiles accounted for 20 percent of the total value of French industrial production, although when the secondary manufacturing of textiles is included, the value of the entire textile industry in 1835–42 accounted for 42 percent of the total value of French industrial output. Within the textile industry itself (including the hand-loom sector), the rates of growth varied by product. For the industry as a whole, the rate of growth for the quinquennial average 1831–35 to 1876–80 was 1.7 percent annually. For the most dynamic sectors—cotton, linen, jute, and silk—the rate of growth was 2.3 percent annually. For the period especially germane to this study, the rate of annual growth in the cotton textile industry fell to 1.9 percent in the period 1871–75 to 1886–90, but it rose rapidly again after 1886–90 to 3 percent per annum and remained at that level until the outbreak of World War I.[21]

As in Britain, the demand-side pressure to find steady supplies of cheap and reliable raw material led to a rapid dependency on American upland cotton varieties. In 1849, France imported 64 million tons of cotton; by 1890, imports had risen to 146 million tons, and by 1912, France imported 346 million tons. Of this supply, 78 percent of the 1850 cotton imports came from the United States. Ten years later, on the eve of the American Civil War, 93 percent of cotton used in France came from American sources. During the same period, France more than doubled its production of cotton textiles, rising from 510 million meters in 1850 to 1,060 million meters in 1860. With the outbreak of the American Civil War, shipments of American cotton fell dramatically only to rise gradually during the first years of Reconstruction. Because of the huge store of raw cotton stockpiled in Britain and on the Continent, the impact of the reduction in American cotton supplies was delayed. In 1862–63, however, 97,000 textile workers were laid off in Seine-Inférieure alone. Hunger stalked all the mill towns of the Haut-Rhin, Vosges, Mulhouse, and Normandy. The outbreak of the American Civil War thus induced a crash in the world cotton supply, exacerbating the overproduction of cotton and cotton textiles during the exceptional harvests of the two previous years.[22] Interruption of supplies from the United States, industrial dislocation, and domestic unrest induced the renewal of the politique cotonnière in Senegal. I take this story up again in Chapter 3.

The revival of the politique cotonnière in Senegal in the 1860s and in the Soudan in the 1890s rested on the assumption that the French could capture the supply of cotton already being cultivated. Capturing the cotton harvest for export turned out to be much more difficult than it first appeared to colonial lobbyists and administrators. French efforts to make their West African colonies into France's supplier of cotton confronted Africans cultivating cotton for lively domestic and regional demand.

Cotton and the Handicraft Textile Industry in the Western Sudan

In the major sociohistorical study of cotton in French West Africa published during the colonial period, Charles Monteil advanced an important argument regarding the origins of cotton and clothing in the region. Islam, Monteil argued, made nudity embarrassing. "At the beginning of the eleventh century, there clearly appeared the decisive and growing influence of Islam in the expansion of cotton; even to this day, this influence continues unabated." Monteil drew on Abou Obed El Bekri's account of his voyage to the Upper Senegal in the eleventh century, when he had commented on the ubiquity of cotton in the region. Monteil further elaborated a set of connections between Islam, cotton, and commerce. "Islam and cotton are always side by side in the Soudan, without doubt this is due to Muslim morality which requires an exterior decency which cotton aids in achieving and for which commerce finds a profit in catering to this morality." Raymond Mauny's magisterial surveys of published and archaeological evidence for the medieval period of West Africa support Monteil's hypothesis linking clothing and Islam.[23]

Monteil admitted that his chronology suffered from the lack of source material for the period before the arrival of Muslim travelers. Indeed, relying on Muslim travelers probably distorted the picture of the origins of cotton in West Africa. Cotton leaves a poor archaeological record, which has confounded efforts to date its earliest domestication in Africa. Cotton is fairly reliably dated to the sixth century B.C. in Meroe, but there is some suggestive evidence from Nile Valley and Nubian sites that an independent domestication of cotton occurred between 4500 and 3000 B.C., which is earlier even than the accepted date for domestication of cotton in the Indian subcontinent. Plant geneticists have argued that at least two varieties of Old World cotton, *G. anomalum* and *G. africanum*, were native to Africa.[24] This would suggest a far earlier date for the use of cotton than Monteil permits.

The second problem with Monteil's chronology is the narrow functional linkage between Islam and cotton. Excavations at Jenne-Jeno along the interior delta of the Niger River have uncovered spinning whorls. Susan Keech McIntosh and Roderick J. McIntosh do not regard the inhabitants of early Jenne-Jeno site as Muslims so this evidence suggests that some qualification is needed before accepting Monteil's functional linkage of clothing and Islam.[25] Students of weaving in Africa maintain that by the twelfth century spinning and weaving of cotton were widespread in the Nile Valley, the Horn, and the Sudanic belt from Lake Chad to the mouth of the Senegal. Cotton weaving also spread deep into the West African interior well in advance of Islam. By the fifteenth century, Europeans observed Africans along the coast weaving.[26] Cotton spread to non-Muslim regions at least as early as to Muslim areas. Thus the link between cotton, clothing, and Islam appears far too simple.

Mauny, who combed accounts of tenth- through twelfth-century Muslim travelers who visited or wrote about West Africa and the Western Sahara, concluded that West African Muslims were observed to be clothed and non-Muslims naked. "Nudity . . . seems to have been the rule in the region prior to the arrival of the Arabs . . . although nudity was not always total."[27] Mauny thus added but did not elaborate another set of variables into Monteil's equation: fashion (as in the wearing or not of clothing) was related to aesthetics and social identity. Neither Monteil nor Mauny cited a very astute turn-of-the-century observation of Louis-Henri-Ernest-Edmond-Gaston Tellier regarding clothing and class in the Soudan: "As a general rule, the native dresses himself to the extent that he is wealthy. In truth, during three quarters of the year clothing is useless, more or less, against the cold. Thus, one displays his fortune, here as everywhere, in the multiplications of superfluous things. One may also find in this fashion another reason: to be dressed in three or four superimposed garments clearly indicates that one does not work himself; it is thus, a sign of wealth."[28] Monteil's functional linkage between Islam and cloth and Tellier's link between class, social boundaries, and clothing support Fernand Braudel's arguments that clothing and fashion form two of the five "realities of material life: food, drink, housing, clothing, and fashion." Braudel argued that food, housing, and clothing were human necessities (although clothing per se was not, apparently, a biological necessity in much of tropical Africa), "but [man] could choose to feed, live, and dress differently." To Braudel fashion and the social statements it makes (which he calls "languages" or "meanings") are as important as the material things to life. He concludes by arguing that "if luxury is not a good way of supporting or promoting an economy, it is a means of holding, of fascinating a society. And those strange collections of commodities, symbols, illusions, fantasms and intellectual schemas that we call civilizations must also be invoked at this point. In short, at the very deepest levels of material life, there is at work a complex order, to which the assumptions, tendencies and unconscious pressures of economies, societies, and civilizations all contribute."[29] Braudel is here raising important issues about aesthetics, the social functions of fashion, and their linkages to long-distance trade. Many of the materials that drove fashion and made the clearest social statements were acquired from afar. Fashion, aesthetics, and social boundaries are important elements in understanding the social construction of the African market for textiles, but they take us beyond the argument I wish to make here.[30] I am concerned here principally with demonstrating the dynamism in the domestic market for cotton and cloth and in establishing why knowing this is central to the collision of the two worlds of cotton in the nineteenth and twentieth centuries and to the explanation for why the French failed to capture the cotton harvest in the region.

In the absence of more precise dating on the origins of cotton cultivation in the Western Sudan, we can assume that the expansion of clothing coincided with the sharpening of social identities along with the spread of Islam and the consolidation of polities. Clothing along with scarification and hairstyles became important markers of social identity.[31] Because the spread of Islam facilitated long-distance trade, clothing as fashion, as an expression of Muslim modesty, and as a social marker likely proliferated after the eleventh century, as Monteil and Mauny suggest. But the relationship is more complex than either Monteil or Mauny understood. It was rooted in political, economic, and cultural change. By the time the French began to promote cotton colonialism, cotton cultivation in the Western Sudan had been established for at least eight centuries.

In this brief overview of the handicraft textile industry in the Western Sudan, I will argue that cloth and clothing should be considered necessities: whether they were biological or social necessities is unimportant as long as the wearers themselves considered them to be. Through clothing West Africans made social statements about themselves, their ethnic and religious affiliations, and their class, age, and social status. Poor people, as Braudel noted, do not often lead the change in fashion. But even the poor make social statements through their clothing. Moreover, clothing was a relatively inexpensive luxury. Beyond what was strictly necessary for social and biological survival, accumulation of extra clothing was, indeed, a luxury. We should consider Africans' demand for cloth highly elastic. When they had the means, Africans accumulated textiles lavishly; when times were bad, they made do with much less. This was clearly the case in the late nineteenth and twentieth centuries when statistical evidence is available.

Already by the time of his visit to the Western Sudan in the fourteenth century, Ibn Battuta remarked on the different capacities rich and poor had to make social statements through clothing. He noted that in preparing for attendance at the Friday mosque, the people "clothe themselves in beautiful white clothing and those that do not possess any, wash their old shirts in order that they be proper for the date to assist in the public prayer." Royal pages were dressed in red, probably of imported Magrebian cloth.[32] Indigo-dyed cloth was also in demand as a luxury. Some was imported from India; other varieties were produced in the indigo-dyeing centers of the Western Sudan. Gaspar Mollien in 1818 wrote that the "inhabitants [of Timbo in Futa Jallon] are rich. All the women have silver bracelets and large gold earrings, and wear cloth of blue guinée stuff, which is a sign of great luxury amongst these Africans."[33] In the 1860s, the ruling Massassi family of Kaarta, staunchly non-Muslim at the time, wore cloth dyed so blue that it was virtually black.[34] Clearly, indigo-dyed cloth was a form of conspicuous consumption and served to mark its wearers apart from the mass of white-clad agriculturalists.

Clothing was certainly one—if not the major—use of cotton. Cotton was also used for shelter, especially for the nomads of the desert and the desert edge. Ibn Battuta observed that the nomads' "tents are constructed in a singular manner; they cover the poles with mats help up by a wooden grid and everything is covered with leather or with cotton cloth."[35] Cotton was also used in making blankets—a form of shelter against the chill of the dry-season nights. Cotton also had a wide variety of other uses including wicks in lamps and fishing nets, although other fibrous plants could yield more specialized fibers.[36]

Cotton grew widely throughout the savanna and sahelian belt of the Western Sudan, wherever rainfall and temperature conditions were conducive. Cotton was cultivated mostly on small plots and served the domestic needs of the household. Once domestic needs were met, there was little interest in harvesting or storing the surplus. Almost every village had its own sources of cotton. Cotton was usually sown interspersed within fields of millet or sorghum. Cotton ripened later than grain and thus did not usually compete for labor with the vital grain harvest. This may help explain Eugene Mage's comment that "the Malinke villages are regularly surrounded by cotton fields which are half-harvested."[37] In some communities, however, cotton was cultivated on a much larger scale, feeding regional circuits of trade and textile production. A colonial administrator from Segu captured the contrast between the domestic and commercial spheres of cotton production in his 1897 report:

In the district of Segu, almost all the Bambara villages cultivate cotton. On the left bank of the Niger and in Gueniekalary in particular cotton is usually cultivated separately. Only when labor is lacking, is cotton sown in other fields, usually millet. The fields are usually sown toward the end of the rainy season using seeds retained from the previous harvest. No selection is made of the seeds planted. The size of yield varies with atmospheric conditions, especially the onset of the dry season, but also by heat and humidity. The cotton plants are not the object of special care. The fields are weeded only when the plants are threatened.[38]

This comment and similar remarks made by other nineteenth-century observers point to the existence of two superimposed systems of cotton production. At the base of cotton production in the Western Sudan was a form of production designed to supply the domestic unit with what was strictly necessary for biological or social survival. Most households were largely self-sufficient in cotton, and the transformation of cotton into clothing followed a well-established gender division of labor. Among the Malinke, Bambara, and Maraka, men farmed. Cotton fields were prepared and sown by men; weeded by men, women, and children; and harvested mostly by women and children. Women carded and spun the yarn. Men wove. In 1847 Anne Raffenel described the processes of carding and spinning, which remained virtually unchanged throughout the century: "Ginning is practiced by the women, and takes place on a flat stone; on a small part of the surface one puts well dried cotton. This is forcibly pressed between the stone and a small metal rod (made by the ironworkers) held in the hand. This primitive technique makes the operation very long. After that, the cotton is placed on a [hand held] carder (usually of English origin) and then transformed into yarn of different thicknesses."[39] Using simple, narrow-strip double-heddle looms, men wove the yarn into long but narrow bands of cotton cloth which were ten to fifteen centimeters wide. Men then sewed these bands into larger cloth: four or five strips for a simple wrap, called a *pagne;* eight to fifteen for a large gown or *boubou* or for a blanket. Men's and women's work thus combined to make strong, durable cloth.

In 1847 Raffenel also remarked that weaving was a socially degraded occupation. Unlike ironwork, leatherwork, and praise singing, weaving was not restricted to castes, except among the Fulbe. "Weavers, herders, and cultivators are not united into castes, and their industry is not exercised by special men. All the inhabitants compete together, free men and slaves. Weaving is a little esteemed industry."[40] Developing at variance, but by no means incompatible, was the second form of cotton production designed for commerce and accumulation. Where this form of production prevailed, the cultivation of cotton was given considerably more attention. In 1897 Captain Kibes, commandant of Bamako district, described the cotton of the seven Maraka towns of Beledugu as "the best cotton in the country. The cultivation of cotton is conducted with much care and the articles manufactured are in great demand by the natives."[41] The crucial distinguishing features of this form of production were market demand for its products and the availability of labor to permit the production of cotton beyond what was strictly necessary for survival. This helps account for Raffenel's observation regarding the low prestige of weaving. Certainly not all weavers were slaves, but the social degradation of weaving evident to Raffenel was probably linked to the expanded system of cotton and cloth production in the nineteenth century. Especially in regions where cotton and cloth were produced on a commercial level, weaving became associated with low social status because much of the work was done by slaves.

Commercial production of cotton benefited from the economic implications of the broad ecological belts that traverse West Africa laterally. These broad zones encouraged forms of human adaptation to the environment in which most inhabitants pursued similar types of livelihood. These zones also created conditions favorable to exchange and commerce across ecological zones based on comparative or absolute advantage. For the purposes of explaining the concentration of the expanded form of cotton production within the savanna and sahelian zones, we need to return to Ibn Battuta's remark regarding the desert nomads' tents. Because of their adaptation to the desert and desert edge environments, nomads relied on sedentary farmers for a supply of grain (especially during the summer months when their herds' milk supply dwindled) and cloth for their clothing and tents. Both grain and cloth were necessary to their subsistence.

Sedentary farmers along the desert edge or at the northern termini of the transhumance routes benefited from exchange with the nomads who brought with them livestock, salt from desert sources, and imported luxuries from across the Sahara. Nomads' herds also grazed the harvested fields and deposited green fertilizer in the process. Out of this exchange of ecologically specialized products arose a complex production and commercial system, which led to the investment in slaves to expand the production of grain and cloth to cater to this desert-side trade.[42]

Using the desert-side trade as a foundation for their production and commercial strategies, the Maraka of the Middle Niger region and other commercial groups of the Western Sudan expanded their commercial connections with southern ecological zones as well. Still operating within the principles of comparative advantage, Maraka traders carried with them desert salt, which they had received from nomads, plus locally produced indigo-dyed cloth and dried fish in their trading expeditions to the forest and forest edge, where they received kola nuts, slaves, and imported European goods in exchange. A crucial component in this southern trade was cloth, especially indigo-dyed cloth pagnes referred to as *tamba sembe* and cotton blankets known as *kosso*. Emile Baillaud captured the dynamism of this cotton textile industry at the turn of the century.

From Bamako to Mopti, this is the region *par excellence* of cotton weaving. The cloth woven in this part of the Niger carries the generic name of blankets and pagnes of Segou. Without doubt, this is because Segou is the city which had the most commercial relations with markets of the [West African] interior. But this city can hardly claim a monopoly of production; indeed, it is the point on the Niger where the least cloth is produced. Instead, it is on the left bank of the Niger where most of the blankets and pagnes are produced. The centers where most of the weavers are found are Banamba, Nyamina, and Sansanding. These so called Segou cloths are all dyed with indigo.[43]

The production of indigo-dyed cloth fed demand generated by wealthy consumers, eager to distinguish themselves from the ordinary people clad in simple white garments, and by women, especially in the southern savannas, who preferred to wear the *tamba sembe* while they worked in the fields.[44] In 1897 Félix Dubois noted that demand for the Segu blankets and pagnes was widespread throughout the Western Sudan. "These are in great demand in Senegal, in the market of Timbuktu, and throughout the Soudan. Even the people of Senegal and the coasts prefer this cloth to European textiles."[45] Dubois's comment is important not only in defining the scope of intracontinental trade in West African cloth but also in indicating consumer preferences from among a range of cloth, including imported European textiles.

Indigo, however, was not the only color added to plain white cloth. The Bambara dyed some of their cloth yellow-brown and black, known as *bokolanfini*, or mud cloth. The region of Kong was an important center for the production of pagnes dyed red as well as indigo blue, although other regions also produced red cloth. A wide range of other natural dyes was also used.[46] Of dyed textiles, however, indigo-dyed cloth reached farthest in part because dyeing was linked to the same expanded sphere of production as cotton.[47] Throughout the nineteenth century, the commercial towns of the Middle Niger Valley and the desert edge became centers of production and trade in indigo-dyed cloth and in Segu blankets. In the Western Sudan, dyeing was considered women's work, although in the massive indigo-dyeing industry of the Central Sudan, men both dyed cloth and beat indigo into it after dyeing.[48]

To achieve the scale of production necessary to feed their commercial strategies, the Maraka among other groups in the Western Sudan returned some of their commercial profits back into production. Many of the slaves they brought back from their trading expeditions found themselves in the expanding plantations that ringed the seven Maraka towns of the Middle Niger region. Increased investment in slave labor permitted the expansion of production of cotton and grain, so crucial to the desert-side commercial strategies of the Maraka. This expanded form of production was characterized by different cropping strategies (separate cotton fields), intensified capacity for carding and spinning (because female slaves spun), and increased output of cloth (because male slaves wove). Female slaves also contributed to the increased scale of dyeing. Expanded production of cloth fed both the desert- and forest-side demand for cloth.

The Maraka were not alone in their appetite for slaves. Indeed, the nineteenth century generally saw an increase in enslavement and slave use throughout Africa as a consequence of the end of the transatlantic slave trade. In the nineteenth century, slaves probably became more widely accessible than before and, because of the demand for African commodities both internationally and regionally throughout West Africa, there was also greater demand for labor. Moreover, the political economies driving enslavement—formation of warrior states and predation—persisted throughout the nineteenth century. Paradoxically, persistent warfare was not always inimical to commerce and production. It often fed regional circuits of commerce by providing slaves and by generating demand for weapons, horses, and luxuries for the warrior elites.[49] Thus the nineteenth-century Western Sudan as a whole witnessed an unevenly dispersed era of expanded commodity production in which the production and demand for cloth fed local and intracontinental demand. Demand for cloth was linked to biological and social survival, but it was also marked by demand, which was highly elastic.

The men and women of the Western Sudan in the nineteenth century operated within a world of cotton and cotton cloth production that consisted of two superimposed systems: one for subsistence and one for expanded, commercial production. West Africans were prepared to consume large quantities of cloth. They were also prepared to do without when their incomes did not permit. This, then, was the world into which the French arrived in their quest for cotton.

CHAPTER THREE

The Beginning of French Cotton Colonialism, 1817–1896

French efforts to define a cotton program for West Africa began first in Senegal. In the 1820s, the French elaborated policies on the assumption that theirs was a colony of European colonization, although it was one in which Africans would labor for Frenchmen. Africans, however, chose to work for themselves, and they produced groundnuts, not cotton. Faced with disappointing results in the fields and with ever-increasing supplies of cotton from United States sources, the French let their efforts to promote Senegalese cotton production for export lapse in the late 1820s. In the 1860s, the politics of cotton production in Senegal were revived. They now reflected changing notions of colonialism and an awareness of the need to secure tropical sources of raw materials. Cotton colonialism in the 1860s also stemmed from the fear that the American Civil War would interrupt supplies of cotton, result in increased prices, and cause social chaos in the mill towns of France. During the 1860s the French renewed their attempts to promote cotton through direct efforts at production and to tap into existing circuits of production and trade in cotton.

French efforts to make their African colonies secure sources of vital raw materials for metropolitan industry failed in the 1820s and again in the 1860s. French colonial efforts to develop cotton in Senegal thus form a central piece of the historical record of cotton colonialism in Africa. The policies and their failures foreshadowed the subsequent policies and failures in the French Soudan in the twentieth century.

The politique cotonnière first developed in Senegal reflected the same assumptions about Africans and about their capacities for work, and it contained virtually the same policies that were later applied with greater effort in the Soudan. In the late 1890s, the French simultaneously discovered that they had an immense colony in the interior of West Africa and that the voracious boll weevil and the rapid industrialization of textile production in America threatened their established supplies of cotton. The politique cotonnière came into its own in the French Soudan just as the century was ending.

There were differences between cotton colonialism in Senegal and in the Soudan. In the late nineteenth and twentieth centuries, the politics of neomercentilism were more sharply drawn in France, which influenced policies in the colonies. The mix of policies was more complex and the struggles for control over the politique cotonnière more intense in the Soudan than in Senegal. The geographical shift in this book—from Senegal in the nineteenth century to the Soudan in the twentieth century—is appropriate because cotton and the politique cotonnière regained prominence not in Senegal but in the French Soudan. Nonetheless, it was in Senegal in the 1820s and 1860s that the French first elaborated their politique cotonnière and set in motion assumptions and policies that guided French cotton policy until 1946.

The Prelude to French Colonial Cotton Policies: Senegal, 1817–1865

Under the 1814 Treaty of Paris Britain agreed to return to France the two Senegalese towns of Gorée and Saint Louis and their affiliated trading posts along the coast and up the Senegal River, which they had captured earlier in the war. Although the treaty stipulated that the British were to return these towns in the condition in which they had found them, the reality was quite different. Not only did French officials find the physical condition of the administrative buildings and forts in advanced disrepair (doors, windows, and even the administrative library in Saint Louis were removed), but economic conditions were also profoundly changed. The Treaty of Paris had stipulated that French nationals could no longer participate in the slave trade, which had been one of the main pillars of the tiny French colony.[1]

Thus when the French regained possession on Gorée and Saint Louis in 1817 they were obliged to define a new colonialism. Gum arabic remained an important staple of commerce, although its trade was encumbered by complex commercial practices. During the period 1809–17, the volume of Senegalese exports declined by over

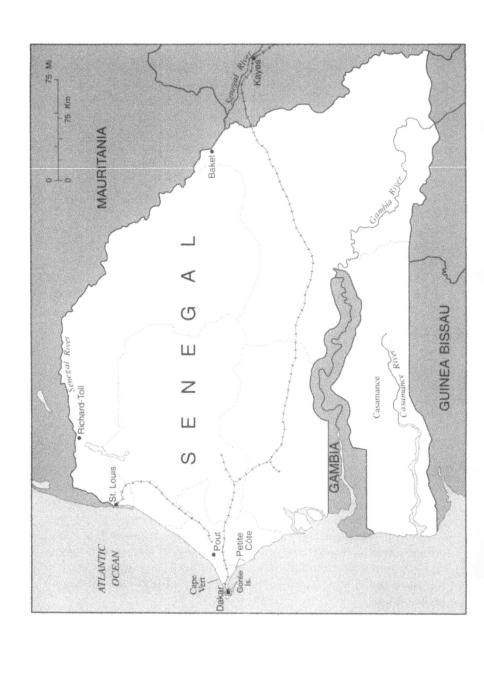

two-thirds and the value by half. With future revenue from both the slave and gum trades in question, metropolitan and colonial officials sought new sources of wealth and new foundations for the colonial economy of Senegal. Instead of bringing African labor to the Antilles, they planned to bring crops and European colonialists to what they considered to be the underused labor in Senegal.[2] Cotton was a central part of this new colonialism in Senegal. To encourage cotton, the minister of colonies and the new governor of Senegal, Colonel Julien Schmaltz, pursued several policies. The first was to make African notables aware of French intentions and to direct their attention toward cotton. To the king and notables of Galam, Schmaltz wrote in 1817 that "I wish to alert you that the King of France will shortly retake possession of Senegal, which at this very moment is occupied by his troops. In view of developing the means of exchange and in extending commerce, I urge you to produce and gin as much cotton as possible, which will serve as a new branch of the economy and which will become as important to the people of Galam as the gum trade is to the Maures of the desert."[3] The second was to encourage metropolitan mills to shift from American sources of cotton to colonial varieties. Schmaltz pursued two strategies. The first was to assure that the volume of exports would be sufficient to compete with the annual imports of 80,000 bales of American cotton. He thus wrote to the minister of colonies that "Dargou variety of cotton is widely cultivated in all the lands [of Senegal] and I believe that before long we can procure considerable quantity for our textile manufacturers."[4] Schmaltz added that cotton could be obtained in exchange for blue guinée and other imported merchandise, thus further benefiting metropolitan industry and colonial commerce.[5] Second, Schmaltz sent Senegalese cotton to France for evaluation by Rouen manufacturers. The results were promising. "Dargou cotton is a very good variety and is capable of replacing advantageously Georgia and Louisiana varieties. . . . Casamance cotton is superior to those and equal to the best of Brazil. Once improved, it will be able to replace even Georgia long staple varieties. Moreover, these varieties are capable of supporting a strong dye, which gives them a marked superiority over American cottons."[6] Schmaltz was also interested in indigo, which together with cotton seemed ideally suited to the climate and soils of Senegal. Cotton and indigo, Schmaltz argued, would easily repay the efforts and costs of promoting large-scale enterprises. Schmaltz also propagated a view of the fertility of Senegal River valley, which he compared favorably to that of the Ganges.[7]

Not content with the promise of Senegalese cotton varieties, Schmaltz urged the minister of colonies to organize shipments of exotic varieties of cotton. Between 1819 and 1820, several shipments of Georgia long-staple cotton seeds arrived in Saint Louis.[8] Cotton seeds and a handful of French colons did eventually arrive, but Schmaltz's facile assumptions linking the ubiquity of cotton in Senegal to successful French cotton plantations proved more difficult to put into reality. Waalo and the Senegal River valley were convulsed by wars, and Africans chose not to work for Europeans. Schmaltz left Senegal in 1820 with little to show for his efforts to promote cotton or colonization.[9]

Schmaltz did, however, set in motion an interest in cotton production which was pursued more energetically and systematically by Governor Jacques-François Roger. Roger served in Senegal from 1819, first as attorney general and then as director of the royal garden at Koilel, where agronomic experiments were conducted. When he became governor in 1821, Roger established an agricultural service designed to explore and acclimate crops capable of supporting French colonization and to teach Africans to use European agricultural technology.[10] In 1822, Roger appointed the agronomist Richard to head the new agricultural station on the Senegal River at what became Richard-Toll. Under Roger, Richard-Toll became part of an intercolonial and international exchange of seeds, technology, and development concepts. Cotton seeds arrived from the Americas and India. Roger also sought ministerial assistance in procuring the latest ginning machinery because he was fully aware that Senegalese cotton could not easily compete with American varieties unless the cotton arrived at the market in the best condition possible.[11] By the beginning of 1824, an official remarked that the farm at Richard-Toll was "remarkable for its very impressive cotton fields."[12]

Roger's support for agronomic experimentation at Richard-Toll was part of a more comprehensive plan to encourage agricultural colonization. Roger wanted Frenchmen and the Euro-African *habitants* of Saint Louis and Gorée to seek government concessions surrounding a handful of French posts on the several islands in the mouth of the Senegal River and along its banks. To promote these private ventures, Roger received ministerial approval to allocate subventions and prizes. In 1822, Roger awarded 10,000 francs to the Saint Louisian resident who cultivated more than 20,000 cotton plants. Several smaller prizes were also awarded to those introducing the most efficient production techniques. In addition, subventions of 30 frances per hectare of cotton were offered. In 1827, Roger shifted his strategy from encouraging cotton production to encouraging commerce in cotton. Subventions of 20 percent of the value of cotton exported were awarded in an effort to encourage Saint Louisian merchants to seek their cotton among African producers. Roger anticipated that some of his subventions would find their way into the hands of African cotton producers. He expected that within a few years over one million cotton plants would be cultivated for export.

Between 1822 and 1825, Senegal exported just over 50,000 kilograms of cotton or an annual average of 12,500 kilograms.[13] This was a tiny portion of France's annual consumption of cotton. Despite the minister's insistence that the colony pay its own way, total agricultural exports returned only 188,000 francs against more than one million francs invested in promoting agricultural colonialism.

Neither Schmaltz nor Roger had understood the difficulties of cotton cultivation. By 1826–27, it became clear that the climate and soils did not suit certain imported varieties of cotton. Securing labor to work the cotton fields proved more difficult than they had anticipated. Roger had tried several forms of labor, including importing workers from the Canary Islands, using convict labor, and promoting long-term apprenticeships.[14] Labor was also recruited from neighboring African communities, but in all cases the cotton concessions were sites of serious problems of discipline. Hostilities between the fledgling French colony and its African neighbors created long-term disincentives to invest in agricultural improvements. Moreover, the shift in 1827 from subsidizing the costs of production to the costs of commerce led to the abandonment of the cotton concessions supervised by Europeans and Euro-Africans.[15] By 1829, cotton was all but abandoned except for the experimental plots at Richard-Toll. "Before long," wrote Richard's successor, "we recognized that cotton was established in chaotic and tumultuous [political] circumstances and in a soil poorly studied, where the climate, the land, the effects on one's health, and the bad attitude and carelessness of the population all had to be combated." Although cotton remained "rich in expectations," it was progressively abandoned as an export crop produced by Frenchmen and Euro-African habitants directly on agricultural concessions.[16] When Roger was recalled, colonization efforts lapsed, and by 1831 there was no longer any budgetary provision for European colonization. Senegal had returned to its role as an entrepôt.

The Revival of a Politics of Cotton Production
and the American Civil War, 1858–1865

The rate of industrial expansion in French textile manufacturing rose considerably through the second quarter of the nineteenth century. The number of spindles in operation increased dramatically from the end of the Napoleonic Wars. In its process of industrializing the textile industry, France became increasingly dependent on American sources of cotton. The average annual imports of cotton into France between 1827 and 1836 were 33,000 metric tons; by 1847–56, the volume had nearly doubled to 65,000 tons. By 1860, it had nearly doubled again, reaching 123,700 tons. During the same period, the share of United States cotton in the total French cotton imports increased as well. In 1820, France imported 50 percent of its cotton from the United States; by 1833, the United States provided 70 percent and by 1860, 93 percent.[17] The growing reliance on American cotton worried senior French government officials. Although the balance of trade between France and the United States was roughly equal, the heavy reliance on one main source of cotton was seen as a liability.

In 1857, Manchester cotton textile industrialists created the Manchester Cotton Supply Association with the intention of encouraging cotton production in Egypt, India, and British West African colonies

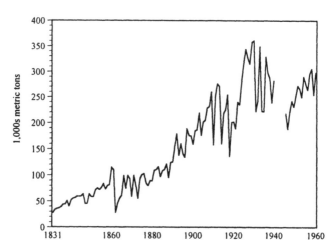

Fig. 3. Imports of Raw Cotton into France, 1831–1960. Source: Mitchell, *Historical Statistics.*

and protectorates.[18] The English initiative stimulated the minister of Algeria and colonies to urge the governors of Algeria and Senegal in 1858 to examine ways of promoting cotton production in their areas.[19] Between 1859 and 1860, the political climate in the United States deteriorated even though the American cotton harvests broke all records. In 1861, 64 percent more cotton arrived in France than during the annual average of 1851–53.

Writing just before the beginning of the American Civil War, Louis Reybaud described the dependence of France's cotton textile industry on slave-produced cotton thousands of kilometers away.

During normal times, the material which feeds our industry arrives at its appointed destinations from sources far away. Suppose, however, that there is some disturbance in the provision of cotton. If the disturbance is mild, then only several thousand workers will lose their jobs; if it is severe, it will push millions of laborers from their work. A poor harvest would thus be calamity, but that is nothing compared to the two terrible events which one day could impose themselves on our industry: a maritime war and a modification of the system of slavery.

"Sad and fatal," Reybaud concluded, "has been the coupling of cotton and slavery."[20] When civil war broke out in April 1861, President Abraham Lincoln declared a blockade of the Confederate States and proved true Reybaud's worry.

Civil war and the blockade sent the price of cotton on the Le Havre cotton exchange upward, although gradually at first. Because the 1859 and 1860 harvests were exceptionally large, cotton spinners and weavers in France had considerable supply on hand. By December 1861, however, the price was up 22 percent, and it rose steadily each month until it topped out in November 1862. A bale of American cotton then cost four times what it had less than two years before. With record high prices, the volume of French cotton imports in 1862 dropped to 40 percent of their annual average in 1851–53. Cotton prices moderated after November 1862, fell back somewhat over the next few months, but climbed again in the middle of 1863 following Northern military victories at Gettysburg, Vicksburg, and Port Hudson.

In 1862, France imported only 24,595 metric tons of cotton from the United States, either directly or via Liverpool. The fall in imports and the rise in prices led to massive layoffs in the cotton textile industry and extreme hardship in the textile zones of France. After the record high cotton prices in November 1862, merchants and manufacturers sought other sources of cotton. A significant supply of

American cotton arrived in France via blockade runners traveling first to Liverpool and then directly to French spinners, thus bypassing the cotton exchange at Le Havre. Cotton merchants tapped other sources, including those from Egypt, Algeria, India, and Senegal.[21] Despite the high prices, the volume of cotton imports began to climb in 1863. By 1865, France was importing 37,400 tons, nearly 92 percent of its 1851–53 annual average. By 1866, just after the end of the Civil War, the volume of cotton imports to France reached 85,500 tons, which was 48 percent larger than the 1851–53 average, although it was still below the record 1860–61 imports.

Although the 1858 ministerial instructions to Governor Louis Faidherbe of Senegal were framed by colonial rivalries with Britain, the deteriorating political situation in the United States in 1860 made efforts to promote colonial sources of cotton even more pressing. In 1860, the minister provided Faidherbe with the first of a series of credits designed to encourage the production of new crops and, in particular, cotton. Faidherbe had commented to the minister in June 1860 that he was making considerable efforts to propagate export crops. Groundnuts, he noted, were daily becoming more important. "I have not forgotten cotton," he wrote, "but encouraging this crop will be more difficult."[22] The minister, however, wanted the governor to take special initiatives in regard to cotton and urged that cotton bought for export be subsidized. He cited the example of groundnuts to prove that Africans would respond favorably to remunerative prices and turn to new crops, although he neglected to say that groundnut production had never benefited from subsidies. The minister also bought the latest in ginning machines from New Orleans and Edinburgh, arguing that properly ginned cotton increased its price threefold. Many plans were floated concerning how to stimulate cotton production in Senegal; one envisioned encouraging Americans of French origin in Louisiana to migrate to Senegal to help establish cotton there.[23]

Jean-Marie Emile Pinet-Laparde, who succeeded Faidherbe in 1860, argued that with "a little perseverance" agriculture in the colony could be developed and made to serve the interests of all concerned.[24] In May 1861, Pinet-Laparde became a cotton enthusiast, spinning a grandiose vision of cotton productivity.

Almost no one between Cape Vert and Sierra Leone is foreign to the culture of cotton, but until now commerce has ignored this product and it is sown only in the amount strictly necessary for [local] needs. Concerned only about their needs, producers take no special precautions to assure the abundance and quality of the cotton harvest.

Despite this, it is easy to prove that cotton will give both natives and commerce profits at least as great if not greater than they receive from groundnuts. One hectare planted with groundnuts returns on the average 100 bushels, which are sold at 2.75 francs maximum and give natives a return of 275 francs. One hectare cultivated in cotton produces a minimum of 1,600 kilograms of raw cotton. If our traders would buy this cotton at 0.20 francs per kilogram, the native would receive a sum of 320 francs for his effort, which is even less painful than that expended for groundnuts.

The source of Pinet-Laparde's figures is not clear, but hopes for a yield of 1,600 kilograms of cotton per hectare were profoundly unrealistic. Nonetheless, Pinet-Laparde's description of the untapped potential of cotton production in Senegal quickly became a central tenet of the revived politique cotonnière.

Pinet-Laparde was, however, not as sanguine about the future as his simple calculations suggested. "It would be wrong," he continued, "to believe that there will be no difficulties to overcome in convincing natives [to sell us their cotton]. Cotton has for them a market price much higher than the price we are able to afford, if we desire to export." He went on to describe the case of Saint Louisian traders in the Casamance, where they could buy cotton for 0.50 francs per kilogram. Instead of taking the cotton to Saint Louis, they took it to the lower Casamance, where they traded it for rice. Among the Diola, cotton was worth twice what it was in the upper Casamance, allowing traders to double their investment. The traders took Diola rice back to the upper Casamance factories, where they sold some and used the rest to feed their commercial personnel. In describing this situation, Pinet-Laparde raised for the first time the issues of the dual markets in which West African cotton was sold and the disequilibrium between domestic and export prices.[25]

Pinet-Laparde's report circulated widely in Paris. The director of colonies was impressed by the potential earnings per hectare of cotton compared to groundnuts, and he sought to argue away the problem of higher domestic than export prices. These higher domestic prices reflected, he said, the very restrained supply of cotton because Africans produced only what was "strictly necessary" for the needs of the land. Unstated in his argument was the belief that domestic cotton prices would fall once production for export supplied more cotton than could be absorbed locally. Moreover, the latest assessment of Serere cotton indicated that the best Senegalese cottons could fetch as much as 1.50 francs per ginned kilogram on the Le Havre exchange.[26]

Pinet-Laparde's report and the discussion it generated revolved around several unresolved issues. Who should cultivate cotton in Senegal? Which cotton should be cultivated? And how should cotton production be encouraged? Two different solutions were advanced, both reflecting deeper debates about the nature of the colonial economy and the role of the colonial state. Coincident with the renewed interest in Senegalese sources of cotton was the debate surrounding the long-established commercial practices of the gum trade. Essentially, these practices favored the suppliers of gum, particularly Trarza notables of the desert edge and the large merchant houses based in Saint Louis, which dominated the bulk purchases of gum through the intricate arrangements of advances and agreements. The small African and Euro-African traders of Saint Louis and Gorée might play minor roles as agents of these large commercial houses, but they were excluded from the most remunerative side of the trade. These small merchants fought against the restrictive nature of the gum trade under the banner of free trade. Free trade issues logically flowed from the debates about the gum trade into discussions surrounding means to encourage the expansion of cotton production and trade.

Faidherbe, as governor from 1858 to 1860 and again in 1863, championed free trade issues.[27] The colonial ministry in Paris, however, was not ready to abandon cotton to free traders at exactly the time when a national industry was being threatened with strangulation and when hunger and potential social unrest stalked the cotton mills of France. The other argument promoted direct state efforts to encourage cotton cultivation for export. The debates and policies designed to encourage cotton production in Senegal thus accommodated free trade practices, which focused on the commercial side of cotton, and direct state intervention in the production side, especially through concessions to Europeans, model cotton farms to induce Africans into cotton production, and supplying seeds.

As the price of cotton rose and the volume of imports from the United States declined from 1861 to 1863, industrialists and their legislative representatives put increasing pressure on the Ministry of Colonies to have the colonies yield cotton for their hungry mills. Louis Drouet, the representative from Seine-Inférieure, an important cotton textile region of France, drew the minister's attention to his long experience as a trader along the West African coast. From first-hand observation, he was convinced that cotton had a bright future. "Everywhere," he wrote, "one finds cotton, even where it is not cultivated. There the natives simply gather it, spin it, and then dye it."

An important market for cotton was there to be tapped, the representative was convinced, but to obtain results "one must employ simple means to give immediate satisfaction to the black." The exact mechanisms Drouet proposed remained vague, but they involved government guarantees to support the export market. "It will be necessary, at the outset, to buy small lots and to continue for some time. . . . But after some days, the quantities presented at the market will increase. . . . The assurances of an advantageous outlet will encourage the natives to plant many fields of cotton." The trader turned political representative insisted that once the government opened a market for cotton, trade must be free to permit commerce to "exploit this magnificent commercial lode."[28]

The prosperity of Rouen, one of the textile centers in the Seine-Inférieure, depended to a large extent on access to cheap cotton to manufacture cloth for Algerian and Senegalese markets. Leading textile manufactures of the region took several direct initiatives during this period of severe cotton shortages. A consortium of Rouen and Mulhouse industrialists sent representative Drouet to Senegal to report firsthand on the extent and condition of cotton production. Part of his mission was to encourage natives to produce cotton for export.[29] Rouen and Mulhouse industrialists also sought to promote cotton production in Senegal by supporting European concessions. Antoine Herzog, Fritz Koechlin, and Gustav Dollfus advanced funds to several large Senegalese cotton plantations established during the Civil War era. These included a 1,000-hectare missionary farm at Saint Joseph under the direction of Monsignor Kobès, a 1,000-hectare concession owned by a consortium headed by Fritz Koechlin and supervised by Louis Drouet at Pout, another 1,000-hectare concession owned by Antoine Herzog—all on the Pétit Côte, Cape Vert peninsula, or slightly inland—and one by Ardin d'Elteil at Richard-Toll on the Senegal River. A concession of 1,500 hectares on Cape Vert was run by a stock company, La Compagnie agricole de la Presqu'île du Cap Vert.[30] Cotton united these four concessions, although the motivations driving them were different. Monsignor Kobès saw cotton production in Senegal as satisfying both the immense need of French industry and the larger mission of civilizing the natives, especially young Africans who would till the cotton by day and toil with good books afterward. "By providing an example of [remunerative] work given to natives, it is one of the most powerful means of assuring the propagation of civilization and French influence in these semi-barbarous countries."[31] The Koechlin-Drouet enterprise sought the concession at Pout with the goal of introducing cotton and developing it on a "vast scale" in Senegal. The Herzog concession near Saint Joseph was similarly inspired.[32]

At the Saint Joseph concessions, two forms of labor were used. The first involved gangs of 30 to 40 men who worked large plots and were supervised by an overseer, a system that resembled slave cotton production in the Antilles and the antebellum American South. Brunil, an employee of the agricultural service who spent a year at Richard-Toll, described another form of gang labor used primarily for harvesting. "No one discusses harvesting, even though it is one of the most important operations of cotton production. . . . Here a woman can pick 5–6 kilograms per day. However, it is much more difficult to organize and coordinate a large number of women at the same location because they quarrel continuously: with 15 women, they pull each others' hair and with 20, they do nothing other than fight. To obtain peace, one has to offer very frequent rest periods."[33] The second form of labor was composed of "men of confidence," who were given individual plots to farm. Each farmer received one plot for cotton and another for millet and other subsistence crops. The Herzog concession nearby followed the same labor organization.[34] The central problem was to find Africans willing to work under these conditions.

The Compagnie agricole de la Presqu'île du Cap Vert, founded a year after the Saint Joseph and Herzog concessions, could barely get any cotton planted because of labor problems. The president of the company asked rhetorically, "Are the natives, whose aversion to work is invincible and established since time immemorial, capable of pulling from their soil the wealth which is hidden there? If we answer in the negative, then Senegal has been, is, and will forever be a dead letter for the metropole."[35]

The Cape Vert agricultural company had more than its share of labor problems. The company complained of raids by local residents, who pillaged the buildings and destroyed the crops. The Koechlin-Drouet concession was also victim of "too frequent thefts by natives." Lack of labor discipline and pilfering were not the only barriers to successful cotton cultivation. Grasshoppers ruined what little remained at the Cape Vert concession; Koechlin and Drouet threw in the hat after four years because the annual ravages of yellow fever became progressively worse and it was virtually impossible to maintain a supervisory staff of Europeans.[36]

Worse still was the impact on cotton of the savanna climate with its sharply alternating wet and dry seasons, especially on exotic varieties imported from the Americas and from Egypt. During the first year at Saint Joseph, cotton planted early in the rainy season initially grew well with an abundance of capsules, but once into the dry season, 90 percent of the capsules did not mature. During the second year, the rains were more regular, and Monsignor Kobès expected a better harvest. Brunil was more skeptical about the future for cotton in the sandy soils of the coastal zone, where most of the concessions were located. Instead, he pointed to the Senegal River, where the "water was sweet and the soils deep and muddy." This was ideal country for Louisiana and Georgia cottons, as well as tobacco. "One hectare planted in Louisiana will yield 2,000 kilograms, but irrigation is indispensable." In contrast, Brunil was convinced that no amount of effort would make indigenous cotton very productive. Brunil concluded his assessment by adding a new idea to the tool kit of the politique cotonnière in West Africa: "without irrigation, no remunerative cotton."[37] Governor Pinet-Laparde did not challenge Brunil's claim for irrigated cotton, but he could not ignore the net results of three years of direct European cotton planting. He concluded that "it appears that native procedures of cotton cultivation are likely to be more successful [than European methods] in this country where irrigation is not practiced. Under these conditions, it would be preferable to encourage natives to cultivate cotton by means of the market."[38]

The problem was to induce Africans to produce cotton for the market in addition to groundnuts—or instead of them—and then to sell it to the export market at prices competitive with supplies on the world market. During the American Civil War, world prices rose high enough to make the export sector attractive, or so it seemed. Governor Jean-Bernard Jauréguibéry described in 1862 the nature of the domestic market in Senegal and estimated its size.

To this day, natives do not harvest more cotton than is necessary for their needs. The cotton fields surrounding their villages are badly neglected and the cotton they harvest they sell to weavers at 60 to 80 centimes per kilogram.

We estimate that the entire annual cotton harvest is no higher than 140,000 kilograms, of which 90,000 are transformed into pagnes in villages and in Saint Louis, Gorée, Bakel, etc. A considerable number of cotton capsules are left to rot on the plants or on the ground.[39]

According to Jauréguibéry's estimate, 36 percent of the cotton harvest was wasted. This assessment fit the prevailing colonial notion that cotton grew everywhere and with little effort. All that was necessary was to find some means for tapping into the existing production of cotton and direct it toward the export market. After all, at least 50,000 kilograms of cotton were left to rot in the fields.

Late in 1861, a French entrepreneur, Bertrand Bocande, approached the minister of colonies with a proposal to conduct commerce in cotton in the Casamance. The minister was favorably disposed to this proposal because cotton in Casamance was reputed to be "in abundance, but in a savage state." Bocande received an advance of 400,000 francs to purchase trading goods and cotton gins and to open shop to stimulate the production of cotton and to encourage its exportation. Bocande arrived in the Casamance, but the cotton gins did not work and he was obliged to send to England for replacement parts. The archival record reports no further news from Bocande's expedition, although it does indicate that cotton production in the Casamance was part of a well-established regional system of production and trade in which cotton sold for 0.50 francs per kilogram locally. French commerce needed to pay at least 0.60 frances to attract any cotton. Around Saint Louis and Gorée, merchants would have to pay more than the 0.60–0.80 francs paid by local weavers.[40]

But any cotton at all was what the metropolitan industry wanted. Cotton left to rot was not suited to mechanized spinning and weaving, nor indeed were the short-fiber cottons planted by the Senegalese for their own needs. Throughout the first half of the 1860s, the minister of colonies together with the governors of Senegal orchestrated a worldwide exchange of exotic varieties of cotton, including Jumel from Egypt, Georgian varieties from the Confederate States, and Indian varieties. Efforts to acclimate the imported varieties of cotton were conducted by the agricultural service under the head gardener Lecard, who also experimented with irrigation. These, however, were long and laborious processes ill-suited for an industry in need of immediate supplies. The minister also ordered cotton gins sent to Senegal to prepare the cotton for export.[41] The success of imported cotton on the French concessions was not promising, however.

In 1865, the American Civil War ended. Although the volume of American cotton imports in 1866 was not yet back to what it had been in 1861, it was sufficient to let the frantic search for colonial sources of cotton lapse. Against the ravages of the grasshopper, yellow fever, and the predations of their neighbors, efforts to promote direct European cotton farming in Senegal waned. Moreover, groundnut production exploded in Senegal from the mid-1850s, fueling what has become known as the peasant revolution in Senegal and making groundnuts the premier export from that colony.[42] The colonial administration under Faidherbe turned its attention to consolidating its precarious hold over its colony and to building the institutions needed to launch a more aggressive campaign of territorial conquest later in the century. As a tool of colonial development, the politique cotonnière was laid to rest until 1897, when Governor Louis de Trentinian again sought to promote cotton for export from the new colony of the French Soudan.

Trentinian's interest in Soudanese cotton coincided with a renewed fear of a contraction in the American cotton supply to French mills. Trentinian also believed, like his counterparts earlier in the century in Senegal, that the production of cotton and cotton textiles was ubiquitous throughout the new colony and that it would be relatively easy to direct Soudanese cotton toward metropolitan needs. Trentinian, as his Senegalese predecessors had done, underestimated the complexities of cotton and textile production in West Africa.

La Politique Cotonnière in the French Soudan and the Handicraft Textile Industry, 1896–1918

With the resumption of steady supplies of American cotton to French mills after 1866, cotton again receded from the archival record. Between 1879 and 1898, colonial politics in the Soudan were the politics of conquest led by the French military. In 1898, the French stormed Sikasso and captured Samory, effectively destroying their two remaining African military opponents. Military skirmishes persisted well into the twentieth century, but African opposition to French conquest no longer had a centralized military expression. The military had simultaneously fulfilled its goal and undercut its mandate to rule.

Colonel Trentinian became lieutenant governor of the Soudan in 1895. As a military man he understood the need to fulfill the goals set forth by Colonel Louis Archinard, the architect of conquest, and he assisted in the final military victory. He was also an astute administrator, and he understood that conquest was not sufficient to continue to lay claim on public legitimacy for empire and metropolitan financial support. Conquest of the vast areas of the West African interior coincided with renewed worries about the reliability of the American cotton crop and increasing competition from European as well as American and Asian cotton textile producers. The new colony of the Soudan needed to have a mission. During the course of conquest, several European traders and planters had become interested in the cotton of the Western Sudan. By 1896 samples of local cotton were in the hands of cotton brokers in Le Havre.[1] Between 1896, when preparations for the final conquest were being made, and 1898, when victory was at hand, Lieutenant Governor Trentinian sponsored several scientific and commercial missions to survey the economic potentialities of the new colony. One of these missions included an industrial spinner from Le Havre, who came to study the commercial prospects of Soudanese cotton for metropolitan needs.[2]

Trentinian's solicitation of Le Havre's cotton interests was timely. The depression of 1873–96, the rapid expansion of the French textile industry after 1886, and the world cotton supply crisis of the end of the century revived the possibility of colonial solutions to raw material needs of metropolitan textile industries, which had been dormant since 1865.[3] The vocabulary Trentinian used about the Soudan's fulfilling the metropole's needs for secure sources of raw materials was shared by many French politicians and industrialists.

The ubiquity of cotton in the Soudan—every village had its cotton fields—provided substance to the French colonial search for a way of tying the new colony economically to the metropole. Moreover, because the Soudan was a new colony, it was not hindered by entrenched interests as Senegal was, so a new approach to constructing the colonial economy could be tried. It was for this reason that the struggles between colonial administrators, agronomists, French industrialists, representatives of metropolitan commercial houses, and African peasants were so charged. What was at stake was nothing less than control over both the colonial state and its economy.

This chapter examines the first twenty years of French colonial cotton policy in the Soudan. The results of French efforts to transform the Soudan into la France cotonnière were uneven. Some progress, however, was made. Trials of American long-staple cottons proved disappointing. More attention was drawn to the agronomy of cotton production, which increased the importance of long-term hybridization experiments. The volume of cotton exports, though only a fraction of metropolitan needs, demonstrated to French industrialists that Soudanese cotton had metropolitan applications and that African peasants could produce satisfactory cotton. If progress were measured in terms of the homogeneity of cotton fibers and in the volume of exports, however, it demonstrated how feeble French control over the cotton fields of the Soudan actually was.

In contrast, the French were much more successful in the ideological field. Beginning around 1895 with the creation of the new French West African Federation, the senior administration in both the federation and the Soudan revived and modified a set of assumptions about Africans, about colonialism, and about the tasks of the various actors in the program of cotton production. During the first twenty years of la politique cotonnière, senior colonial administrators were committed to promoting peasant cotton production in opposition to the countervailing models of direct European colonization and large concessionary companies. Their position was built on the experience

French Soudan

of Senegalese peasants and the groundnut market. The fantastic success of groundnut exports convinced the colonial administration that African peasants were capable of producing vast amounts of cotton and that they were rational economic actors responsive to positive economic incentives. The tasks of delivering these economic incentives and of evacuating the cotton harvest were to fall to the commercial sector, composed of metropolitan commercial houses and their African agents. The colonial state would assist in providing the infrastructure of railways, wharfs, and roads. Moreover, the colonial state put its local administrators behind policies to encourage Africans to plant cotton and bring it to market. This division between the public and private sectors of the colonial economy reflected prevailing assumptions about the metropolitan state and economy. Assisting the peasants and the private sector in making Soudanese cotton conform to metropolitan expectations fell primarily upon a semiofficial nonprofit enterprise founded by French industrialists in 1903. The task of the Association cotonnière coloniale was to promote cotton production for export by assisting in seed distribution, agronomic outreach, and erecting ginning and pressing stations. The ACC pursued both practical and quasi-scientific policies to promote cotton exports. Its policies reflected prevailing assumptions about European modernity and African backwardness. In the period under study in this chapter, the most dramatic initiatives came from the ACC.

Significant struggles over control of these protected economic spheres emerged during these first twenty years. Concerned that the private sector was not fulfilling its share of the burden in promoting cotton exports, the ACC entered into direct cotton purchases. The private sector responded to this assault on its prerogatives by accusing the ACC of monopolistic practices. The colonial state reasserted the boundaries between the actors' roles but shared with the ACC a resentment against the private commercial sector for wanting the profits from successful commercial transactions but being unwilling to accept the risks of nurturing them. Because of their ideological commitment to free trade, however, administrators had limited means to promote market incentives in the absence of sustained participation by the private sector.

The first twenty years of the politique cotonnière in the Soudan marked France's first sustained commitment to colonial cotton development. The onset of World War I prematurely ended this phase of the struggles to shape and control the colonial economy of the Soudan. The war revealed how easily the world supply of cotton could be disrupted. It also underscored yet again the potential of the colonies to provide metropolitan economies with secure supplies of crucial raw materials.

The meager results of the first twenty years of colonial cotton programs in the Soudan, however, revealed how difficult this task actually was. French military conquest of the Soudan ushered in a period of significant social and economic change, characterized by social mobility and a willingness to invest land and labor in surplus production. The regional economy of the Soudan expanded largely along its precolonial foundations. African peasants and African plantation owners responded to increased demand for African commodities. With more income to spend, African consumers bought more cloth, both imported and handcrafted. Increased demand for local cloth pushed up cotton prices. Higher prices for cotton on the domestic market undercut efforts by the colonial commercial sector to encourage a flow of cotton to France. Moreover, as the war interrupted the flow of imported cloth into the Soudan, the female and male workers of the handicraft textile sector seized a greater share of the domestic cloth market. The resiliency of the handicraft textile industry was a central factor in the uneven results of the first twenty years of France's effort to make the Soudan into a secure supplier of cotton for the metropole.

Practical and Ideological Beginnings, 1898–1907

In 1898, Trentinian ordered local administrators to buy large quantities of cotton to provide metropolitan industrialists with sufficient stock to assess the value of Soudanese cotton. The industrialists were favorably impressed. Trentinian was now convinced that cotton was the way of linking the new colony to France economically. He believed that the single biggest obstacle to opening Soudanese cotton to metropolitan France was transporting bulky raw cotton to the Senegal River, where it could be loaded onto boats and sent to the coast for shipment to France. To reduce transport costs of bulk cotton, he ordered ginning machines and presses from France and erected them in Bamako.[4] Moreover, the railway linking Kayes on the Senegal River with Bamako on the Niger was inching its way eastward and would arrive in Bamako in the middle of 1904. The railway promised further reductions in transport costs, thus opening the floodgates of Soudanese cotton exports.[5] In 1899 Captain Charnet, the administrator of Bamako, also saw cotton as the future of the colony but with a different configuration. Instead of bringing Soudanese cotton to French mills, French mills should come to the Soudan. "Despite everything, native industry without capital or tools will always remain insignificant. The future is in the association of native workers with European tools and capital. And the Frenchman who establishes a textile factory to satisfy the needs of the Soudan and uses local cotton and local labor will make a brilliant affair."[6] The colonial state had other ideas about cotton, and developing a mechanized local industry was not one of them.[7]

After all, cloth was the leading French manufactured good imported into the Soudan. By 1891, for example, an average of 15,000 meters of cloth was imported into Bamako each month, and the volume increased thereafter.[8] Sponsoring the development of a local textile factory, as Captain Charnet of Bamako proposed, would undermine two important areas of the colonial economy: importation of French manufactured goods and the export of raw materials suited to the needs of French industry. Colonial policy sought to encourage demand for imported cloth and the export of cotton.

Such policy resonated well in France itself. In March 1901 delegates from the regional cotton syndicates met and formed the Industrie cotonnière française under the leadership of Albert Esnault-Pelterie. Esnault vigorously pursued a colonial raw materials policy, and by November 1902 the manufacturers' association had formed a branch designed to encourage cotton production in the colonies. The Association cotonnière coloniale came formally into existence in 1903. "Following the example of Russia in Turkistan, England in Egypt and the Indies, and Germany in Togo, these men want to encourage cotton production in Africa, notably in the Soudan," lauded the *Dépêche Coloniale* in 1903.[9] "It is in the valley of the Niger," wrote Captain Eugène Lenfant to a Le Havre merchant and vice-president of the Association cotonnière coloniale in 1903, "that you will create la France cotonnière."[10] The Association cotonnière coloniale was established as a semiautonomous colonial arm of the French textile manufacturers' syndicate. Its nine-point charter defined its mission in scientific and practical terms. The ACC was to identify colonial regions where cotton useful to French industry was cultivated; buy sufficient stock to assess its qualities; stimulate purchases of cotton; subvene French colonists' efforts to propagate cotton cultivation; find the means to assist natives in the amelioration of their farming practices; compare experimentally selected indigenous and imported varieties of cotton; compare the practical value of different ginning machines; locate sites for purchasing, ginning, and pressing centers; and work with the metropolitan and colonial states to extend communication and transport facilities.[11] Because the ACC received government subventions—and thus had a "public character"—it was legally barred from engaging in commercial activities for profit. The ACC, however, was invited to aid the diffusion of seed and technology and to erect and maintain ginneries with the purpose of encouraging cotton production for export. Ginneries served the dual purpose of preparing cotton for use and of separating out the seed. The seed was then culled to eliminate poor quality cotton and to provide a reservoir for the next planting season.

In the 1904–5 cotton season, the first in which the ACC participated in the Soudan, it distributed some 20,000 kilograms of imported cotton seed, mostly Sea Island and other American long staples, to village chiefs in designated cotton regions. "Each village," remarked Lieutenant Governor William Ponty in his annual report that year, "has its fields of cotton." He anticipated that cultivators "will bring their next harvests to the ginning stations, [just] as our peasants bring their wheat to the mill."[12] The French continued to think extravagantly: they saw the future bringing 400,000 hectares under cultivation of American cotton varieties without special projects and with the existing population. At the very least, the agronomist Jean François Vuillet expected to have an annual yield of 60,000 metric tons.[13]

The first tasks of this politique cotonnière, in which both the colonial administration and the ACC participated, were to convince producers to plant American cotton seeds, cultivate cotton using "modern" methods, and then part with their harvest. "It would be of little value," wrote Captain Charnet, "to clear new land and to use new plants if the methods were to remain the same and the yields inferior." As early as 1899, 1,500 delegates from neighboring villages came to the colonial agricultural experimentation center at Kati near Bamako. These chiefs and notables were divided into groups of 50 to 100 and were shown various plants and European agricultural techniques. "They took turns guiding the plow, preparing the soil, fertilizing, and seeding. For cotton, they chose for themselves the best seeds and put them in water to germinate them."[14] Although the trainees seemed to be serious about experimenting with imported long-staple varieties of cotton, the results were not encouraging. The plants did well initially, but with the onset of the dry season they suffered dramatically. Termites and other insects ravaged what remained of the cotton fields.[15]

The administration had several options to counter these disappointing results. It could devote more attention to seed selection, locating other long- or medium-staple varieties, which were better suited to regional conditions and which also satisfied the needs of metropolitan spinners. Indeed, the colonial state through its agricultural service experimented with hybridization, trying to retain the best of the local *G. punctatum* while breeding in the characteristics sought by metropolitan users. It could encourage producers by paying higher prices, thus compensating them for lower yields. And finally, it could force them to grow cotton.

The administration tried all of these options. In 1899, the acting governor of the French Soudan decided to abandon the state's sponsorship of Sea Island cotton in favor of efforts to ameliorate local species and to promote agricultural extension programs.[16] In 1899, the administration began to assess local agricultural resources with the objective of collecting part of the 1900 tax in cotton. Administrators also discussed "punishing" villages "convicted of laziness" by not expanding cotton cultivation.[17] Although coercion might yield an immediate supply of cotton, the administration was aware that it was not a viable solution to the long-term problems of encouraging a steady supply of good quality marketable cotton. "Because of the heavy charges that have been placed on natives, from requisitions of workers for public projects and porterage to obligatory furnishing of millet," warned the Bamako commandant, "it is to expect acts of undiscipline by requiring natives to bring all their cotton to the headquarters of the district. This will certainly risk losing their goodwill."[18] Despite these warnings from within its own ranks, the administration never fully abandoned coercion from its repertoire of solutions to the problems of fulfilling the state's goals.

Finally, the administration tried to stimulate production of cotton by offering what it thought was an attractive price. After consultation with Etienne Fossat, the Havre cotton courtier who had come to the Soudan in 1898 with one of Trentinian's scientific missions, the administration began the 1899–1900 cotton purchasing season with a price of 0.20 francs per kilogram. "In the event that the producer villages are not satisfied with this," wrote the Bamako commandant, "I will raise the price to 0.30 francs/kilogram. . . . because it is important not to discourage the goodwill [of the natives] and above all to encourage the natives to plant cotton on a large scale."[19] What constituted adequate compensation for producers, however, remained a central problem in the debates surrounding the shape of the colonial economy.

In 1899, Lieutenant Governor Trentinian floated the idea of swapping French cloth for Soudanese cotton. "Several commandants," he wrote, "have asked me to provide them with white cloth to pay for their [cotton] purchases. This way of payment is to be encouraged: the Service Local makes a profit, and besides the native prefers this type of payment because it replaces the cotton which has been sold."[20] Some producers might have been happy to exchange their cotton for imported cloth, but not all. By February 1899 peasants in the Bamako district were complaining about the incessant demands made on them for labor, grain, and now cotton.[21] Local administrators cautioned the administration against pushing the producers too far, too quickly.

The administration was also unwilling to bear the costs of long-term subsidies to the supply of cotton exports through purchases and direct exchanges of cloth. Moreover, at 30 centimes per kilogram, the price of cotton rose beyond what the export market was willing to bear. In Segu, the commandant thus lowered the price offered for cotton to 0.20 francs per kilogram and then to 0.10 francs per kilogram. The result was hardly surprising. "The native," he wrote, "always retains a very large part of the [cotton] harvest. . . . What he wants most of all is to pay his annual tax and to satisfy his desires and fantasies with the product of his labor. . . . If we offer a price which permits this, then we shall have large areas cultivated." Here we have a clear statement of the "rational peasant" position held by many local administrators in the Soudan. The commandant also underlined the separation of tasks between the administration and the commercial sector in the goal of encouraging cotton production for export. "It belongs to traders to augment [the peasant's] needs, by making him aware of the products which are more and more appreciated by our natives. We could organize a series of regional fairs in which our manufactured objects would be exposed side by side with local products."[22]

In 1903, Governor-General Ernest Roume of the French West Africa Federation firmly committed his administration to the peasant option in his speech to the banquet of the ACC. The speech was significant because it is the first unambiguous statement by a governor-general of the pro-peasant cotton position. But it was also important

in squashing the Industrie cotonnière française's proposal to establish large European concession companies, following the colonial
model applied in the Congo.

You must brush aside the idea, that seductive but often deceiving (and certainly so in this case) theory of large territorial concessions, where gangs of
regimented blacks work for the account of powerful financial societies. All
who know the real economic conditions of production in West Africa, who
know the spirit of the blacks and the power they can bring to bear—almost
all are unanimous on this point—and I believe that you will adopt a wise,
just and humane solution, which has the object of stimulating production
and also the moral and material development of the worker himself.

There remains to you, gentlemen, without doubt, still a large domain to
explore all the questions of economic and industrial order. If you will allow
me this counsel, you should direct your attention first to establishing a system of purchases, which will permit the black cultivator, during the first few
years at least, to be assured the disposal of all his harvest. It is the price and
the price alone that will give [the African peasant] confidence and which will
let him devote himself to this culture out of which he will be assured of a
profit.[23]

Putting the colonial administration's commitment to promoting
peasant cotton into practice, however, posed serious problems. Cotton was unlike groundnuts, which undergirded the French West African peasant model. Senegalese peasants responded with alacrity to
the market demand for groundnuts, and Senegalese supply dominated the French market.[24] American cotton, however, dominated
both the French and the world markets. Thus those favoring a colonial cotton development policy had to find a balance between the
need to stimulate production through market forces and a price
that made colonial cotton competitive in world commodity markets.
Metropolitan spinners would be interested in Soudanese cotton only
if the quality and the price were right. Finding this balance led the
lieutenant governor in 1906 to lower the official price for seed cotton
to 0.15–0.18 francs per kilogram.[25] Lowering the price did not necessarily dissuade Africans from producing cotton; it only encouraged
them to redirect the harvest to the parallel domestic market of local
weavers and artisans, which offered more. West African cotton producers thus provided support for Roume's conviction that they
would respond positively to market stimuli, but not necessarily as
the French intended. In contrast, given the constraints it imposed on
itself, French colony policy was irrational, if only in the sense that it
established unrealistic expectations for the outcome of policy.

In its efforts during these formative years, the Association cotonnière coloniale's participation in la politique cotonnière ran more or

less parallel with the colonial state's. The ACC targeted the Middle Niger Valley as the preliminary center for its activities. It erected a ginnery at Segu in 1904, although it did not commence operations until 1905 and was not running at full capacity until 1906. In 1905, the Segu ginnery produced 2,000 kilograms of cotton fiber. Doubting whether this quantity would be sufficient to induce metropolitan industrialists to switch to Soudanese sources of cotton, the ACC representative decided to send samples of the fiber to France and to sell the rest of the ginned cotton locally. Without understanding the paradox of his actions, the representative wrote to the governor of the Soudan that "I would find it advantageous to sell our cotton to the local trade, which presently offers a price superior to European markets at 2 francs per kilogram [ginned cotton]."[26]

The ACC also directed its energies to selecting new varieties of cotton seeds. In a generally enthusiastic letter to Governor-General Roume in 1904 concerning initial reports of producers' responses to the new varieties of seed, president of the ACC Esnault-Pelterie stressed that the administration and the ACC "should not lose sight of the fact that the French spinners are the only judges of the qualities of the cotton purchased on their account."[27] In that regard, the ACC was beginning to attract attention in the metropole. Industrial experts in France gave their approval to Soudanese cotton sent by the ACC. Walter-Scitz, an industrial spinner and weaver in Vosges, conducted rigorous tests of these samples and pronounced himself convinced that Soudanese cotton was easier to use than Indian varieties and that it could replace American cottons for coarser applications.[28] Cotton courtiers of Le Havre classified Soudanese cotton as "fully good middling."[29]

In response to encouraging signs in both the colony and the metropole, Lieutenant Governor Ponty declared that for the 1905–6 cotton season "the moment has arrived to enter into the path of industrial exploitation. Experiments made possible by the ACC and the administration have proven that the natives are ready to develop the culture of cotton and that they have adopted and planted the new seeds given to them."[30] At the 1906 international congress of industrial spinners and weavers, Esnault-Pelterie stated that the "union, each year more intimate" between the colonial administration and the ACC, marked a new era. Whereas before a "sort of antagonism existed" between the administration and private enterprise, now both proceeded with goodwill and "we have the firm conviction that we will succeed" in our task.[31] Both the colonial administration and the

ACC, however, underestimated the difficulties of transforming the French Soudan into la France cotonnière. Even if they could unleash the entrepreneurial inclinations of producers, they still had to contend with natural and economic forces over which they had no control. They also had to contend with logistical and transportation difficulties in Africa, which impeded their progress.

Despite the widespread conviction that the French Soudan was a naturally endowed cotton zone, imported American long-staple cottons did not perform as well as expected. The unreliability of the rains was particularly harmful to the gestational cycles of these imported plants. The 1904–5 season was hit by an exceptional drought. The season of 1905–6 was good, but seeds were distributed too late. Indeed, because the ACC based its early program on the use of American cotton, seeds had to be sent from across the Atlantic. The twenty metric tons of American seed the ACC expected for the 1905–6 season arrived in Kayes in July, far too late for planting in the cotton zone of the Middle Niger.[32]

Although the rains in 1906–7 were abundant, they fell sporadically, and the cotton plants in the Segu area were deprived of water just at the crucial point of maturation. Scientific studies at the colony's experimental fields were beginning to yield data which indicated that American cottons were very sensitive to the reliability of the rains and the fertility of the soil and excessively vulnerable to local insects.[33] Moreover, ginning and pressing machinery arrived in poor condition and local representatives of the ACC were forced to rebuild them, often improvising and scavenging parts from other agricultural machinery just to get some ginning and pressing capacity on line.

Besides these initial technical and logistical problems, the politique cotonnière launched by the ACC and the administration had to confront the reluctance on the part of French commercial houses to participate. The alliance between the colonial administration and the ACC was but part of the triad envisioned by Roume. For Roume's peasant model to work, market forces needed to be harnessed to the task of encouraging producers. Because of its semiofficial capacity—and because it received government subventions—the ACC was barred from engaging in commerce. Buying cotton for initial trials of the machinery and to provide adequate samples for metropolitan spinners was within its jurisdiction. To make the colony perform to metropolitan expectations required the active engagement of French merchants. In 1904, Esnault-Pelterie approached the commercial houses of Bordeaux, which traditionally dominated the commerce of French

West Africa, but they "remained distant to our task, despite the advances we have made [to them]."[34]

Frustrated by the continued lack of response on the part of the colonial commercial community, in 1906 Esnault broached the idea of establishing a consortium to buy cotton. Admitting that the consortium was but a "temporary means for buying cotton," Esnault launched the Compagnie française d'études et d'entreprises coloniales with a capital of a million francs later that year.[35] The success of Esnault's company was short-lived, for several years later the ACC launched another company, the Compagnie du coton colonial (CCC), with the same aims. The ACC's incursion into the protected sphere of commerce raised important ideological and practical questions about the politique cotonnière as envisioned by Roume and the senior colonial administration.

Retrenchment and Revision, 1907–1915

Within three years of establishing itself in Africa, the ACC was aware that its expectation of transforming the French Soudan into a large-scale supplier of raw material for metropolitan industries had been too naive. Its initial agenda had relied on a facile assumption that if it imported and distributed American cotton seeds, producers would cultivate ever-increasing fields of the cotton metropolitan spinners and weavers were accustomed to. When these anticipated results did not materialize, the ACC turned to four other methods for fostering production and commercialization of cotton. First, the ACC abandoned its exclusive commitment to American cotton. Industrial users in France had, after all, expressed an initial interest in Soudanese cotton, especially if the fibers had greater "homogeneity."[36] To achieve greater homogeneity, which was critical to the mechanized spinning industry, and quickly, which was central to the ACC's perception of its role, the ACC pursued an aggressive policy of extending its ginning centers and diversifying its geographical focus. Using subventions it received from the National Assembly, the ACC built ginneries in Kayes and in Koutiala to augment the one in Segu. In the 1907–8 cotton season, the ACC bought more than 130 metric tons of native cotton in the region of Kayes. The next year it acquired 45 tons in Koutiala.[37]

The ACC was now convinced that the development of cotton exports lay in ameliorating local cotton varieties. Rather than planning long-term hybridization programs, it let the administration's agricultural service pursue them. The colonial agricultural service began to breed cotton varieties better suited than the American cottons to the Soudanese savanna.[38] These were, however, long-term programs that could not solve the immediate goals of the ACC or the immediate needs of metropolitan industry. The ACC wanted results quickly.

Instead, the second track the ACC followed was to generate better quality by changing production techniques. The ACC pursued a policy of agricultural extension by concentrating on practical experiments using model fields under its direct supervision based on the assumption that trickle-down effects would occur. In 1903–4, the ACC established model fields under its direction, although the practice was expanded in the period after 1907. It continued this policy until 1915, when most of its employees were conscripted into the military and returned to France. These were not experimental cotton fields in the sense of those of the colonial agricultural service; they were cotton fields worked by the ACC and its salaried laborers using mechanical cultivators and plows. They were designed to test the quality of agricultural machinery and to demonstrate their utility to Africans.[39]

The ACC also sought to alter cotton production through sharecropping arrangements. Sharecropping emerged as a means of extending the model field concept without direct intervention. Africans, usually chiefs, contracted with the ACC to cultivate a specified acreage using seed supplied by the association and to deliver a minimum yield per hectare at a prearranged price. Sharecroppers agreed to have their fields supervised by the representatives of the ACC and to cultivate these fields with "more care than they ordinarily give their own fields." On its side, the ACC advanced the shareholder 25 francs and agreed to buy all cotton produced on a sliding scale, increasing the rates if the yields were over 200 kilograms per hectare. The ACC hoped that African producers would realize the commercial value of sharecropping because it minimized risks of market fluctuations. ACC officials also hoped that these sharecropping contracts would encourage producers to devote more care to production and, in the process, diffuse European technologies among the wider peasant community. Even at the high end of the scale, however, the ACC's prices for cotton were at or below the prevailing domestic market prices.[40]

Third, the ACC began to voice support for large-scale irrigation as the solution to the failure of American cotton to survive the starkly defined rainy and dry climate of the French Soudan's savanna. In a letter to the lieutenant governor of the Soudan at the time of the retrenchment of the politique cotonnière, Esnault-Pelterie did not abandon his vision of la France cotonnière. Instead, he promoted an alternative route. "I see an immense future for cotton in your region with irrigation," he wrote.[41] In 1909 the ACC began experimental irrigation in the lower Senegal River valley near the colonial agricultural station of Richard-Toll and at Podor. Their experiments, which used significant inputs of chemical and natural fertilizers, indicated that Egyptian long-staple cotton performed best. In 1913, the ACC began its first foray into irrigated cotton along the banks of the Niger.[42] Although irrigation was not seriously considered before World War I, a group of Parisian financiers and merchant brokers, led by Marcel Hirsch, had already petitioned the Ministry of Colonies and the governor-general of the AOF with its plan to make the Niger into the Nile of West Africa. Hirsch's entry into the politique cotonnière added new intensity to the debate on the shape of the economy, which I shall address in Chapter 6.

The fourth prong of the ACC's revised policy focused on the commercial side of the politique cotonnière. Through its agreement with both the metropolitan and colonial states, the ACC was barred from entering the market to deal in cotton for profit, but the ACC saw the success of its cotton program resting on its ability to attract sufficient cotton to convince metropolitan users of its commercial value. Frustrated by the continued reluctance of the colonial commercial sector to carry its load—the profitability of cotton trade had yet to be determined—the ACC ventured boldly into the commercial cotton market. The ACC founded a subsidiary, the Compagnie du coton colonial, to act as a cotton broker within the private sector. The nature of this new commercial company was never clear; yet the personnel of the ACC were identical to those of the CCC. For all intents and purposes, the CCC was equivalent to the ACC's commercial activities. Throughout the cotton zone of the French Soudan, local administrators understood their role to assist the ACC to the point of forcing producers to carry their cotton to the central market or ginning facility for the account of the ACC.[43] The CCC thus received considerable assistance from the colonial administration.

By the time the French commercial houses established in the Soudan first seriously participated in bulk cotton purchases in 1911–12,

they were confronted with the predominance of the ACC and its subsidiary, the CCC, in cotton commerce.[44] Several European merchants
in Bamako filed a complaint with the governor-general. "The cotton
buying season has arrived," wrote the firm of Carrié and Dabrigeon.
"The ACC has forced the natives to grow cotton and we feel that its
task is finished, and that it should cede its place to merchants wanting to export this product. . . . If the ACC continues to buy, we would
like to know if we can receive the same favorable terms."[45] Because
the ACC was receiving substantial subventions from the colonial
state, favorable freight terms, porters recruited by local commandants, and quasi-official authority to require Africans to sell it their
cotton, the ACC obviously had an unfair advantage in the marketplace. The ACC was forced to dissolve its subsidiary. Governor-General Ponty admitted that the ACC exceeded its jurisdiction by trading
in cotton. But he also argued that these legitimate complaints should
not detract from recognizing the value of the services the ACC had
rendered to cotton development.[46] In responding to the commercial
houses' complaints, the senior colonial administration reaffirmed its
commitment to a "free market" in which the producer was absolutely free to sell to whomever he wished.[47]

Although this commitment to a free market might slide easily
from the pens of the colonial administrators, it posed serious policy
constraints. First, the Ministry of Colonies in Paris wanted results.
Yet the operation of the market rested on the gradual give-and-take
of market forces. Second, a commitment to free markets prevented
the application of compulsion, which the administration never fully
abandoned. Finally, the administration never fully trusted French
commercial houses to carry their share of the responsibility for colonial development. The colonial administration feared that commerce would abandon cotton without hesitation when profits were
slim and would thus undercut the long-term strategy of encouraging
cotton production by offering peasants market incentives.

In his defense of ACC activities, Administrator Colliaux of Koutiala touched the heart of the administration's ambivalence between
its ideological commitment to free markets and its mandate to resolve the practical problems of making the colony conform to models
determined in France. Colliaux's report written in 1910 also revealed
the administration's resentments against the private sector:

We have often heard [the argument] that the administration should let the
producer and the buyer debate the price. . . . Certainly we do not now con-

sider granting monopoly privileges to the ACC. But the objective which it pursues is concerned with a much higher goal: the future of the colony and the future of our national industry.

Were it only possible for competition and a [higher] rate of cotton production to emerge naturally! If competition is not born naturally, it is precisely because the parsimonious commercial companies judge the price of cotton too high to realize a serious profit from export. What is necessary now is to assure commercial activity. This is another reason to support the activities of the ACC.[48]

Colliaux's remarks underscored the uncertainty surrounding the boundaries between incentives, compulsion, and profits and therefore the ambiguities surrounding the mandates for each of the actors in the colonial cotton program. This ambiguity was reaffirmed in 1912 when Governor-General Clozel wrote that the administration's cotton policy implied "for the native a strict obligation to cultivate cotton," even though he was ostensibly free to sell it or not as he chose.[49] In San and other cotton districts along the Niger River, Soudanese cotton growers were obliged to bring their harvest to a central fair, where ACC representatives bought their produce.[50] Large European merchant houses might hesitate to deal when profit margins were small, but African traders, juula, responded rapidly to the steady, if not substantial, profits that could be made from buying cotton in outlying areas and selling it to the ACC. Juula in the Koutiala district bought cotton for 0.14 francs per kilogram in the countryside and sold it to the ACC at M'Pesoba for 0.17–20 francs per kilogram. Of the 50 tons of cotton they delivered to the ACC ginnery, the juula collectively earned between 3,000 and 6,000 francs. Most of the cotton—172 tons—however, was brought by individual producers. "The inhabitants, pressed by the need to have money for tax purposes, understand rapidly that it is in their interests to bring the cotton directly to the factories for ginning."[51] Thus the combination of long-term price stability, even at relatively low rates, and administrative compulsion provided the ACC with steadily increasing stocks of native cotton.

Figure 4 demonstrates the changes in the cotton stocks held by the ACC in Segu. A similar situation prevailed in other districts in the cotton zone. By 1915, just as the war broke out, the French could point to some success in encouraging an expanding export market for cotton. At the same time, however, the other world of cotton—the regional economy and the handicraft textile industry—continued to expand. When the effects of World War I began to be felt in the Soudan with the decline in manufactured cloth imports, shrinking ex-

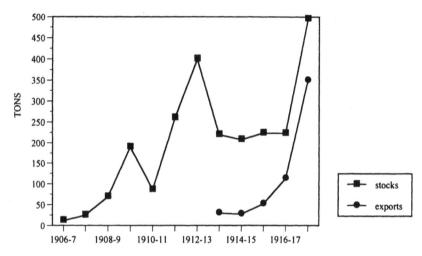

Fig. 4. ACC Cotton Stocks in Segu and Cotton Exports from Haut-Sénégal-Niger, 1906–1918. 1913–14 was a drought year. The war years, 1914–18, witnessed a decline in textile imports that encouraged an expansion of local handicraft production which absorbed large quantities of local cotton. Sources: Total de la recolte du coton mat (fibers), 4 May 1907, ANM 1 R 90; Chef de Service d'Agriculture, Revue des grands produits et examen des principaux facteurs du développement économique, Pays du Segu et régions voisines, 1920, ANM 1 R 232; Lieutenant-governor, Haut-Sénégal-Niger, letter to governor-general, 14 Aug. 1918, Kouluba, ANM 1 R 118.

port sector demand for cotton, and fewer colonial administrators and cotton experts, the men and women of the handicraft textile sector expanded production to meet the demand of consumers.

The Handicraft Textile Industry and La Politique Cotonnière

Colonial conquest and the first twenty years of la politique cotonnière led to changes in the handicraft textile industry of the French Soudan, although these changes were not necessarily the ones the administration had anticipated. The most dramatic changes in the social organization of the handicraft industry occurred before 1911 and coincided with the end of slavery. Less dramatic and reversible processes of change were occurring at the level of the household during this period as well.

In the Western Sudan, ethnicity and occupation were directly correlated, and access to many economic resources presupposed membership in the given ethnic group which dominated that economic resource.[52] These ethnic boundaries were, however, permeable and besides marriage, enslavement was the primary method of recruitment. Enslavement usually required the slave to pass through a long period of acculturation before becoming assimilated into the host society. In the process, slaves learned the tasks associated with the ethnic group's bounded economic resources.

With the general increase in commodity production and commercial activity after 1890, producers began to test the social boundaries surrounding economic resources. By 1905, the Segu commandant wrote that "trade, agriculture, herding, monopolies long recognized [as belonging] to this or that race, are today contested by all and make rapid progress."[53] Between 1905 and 1911, slaves throughout the French Soudan began to leave their masters. In so doing, the slaves participated in yet another transformation of the handicraft textile industry, for their leaving altered the relations and organization of production they had helped to establish. Many freed men and women, who as slaves had learned to weave and to dye, established themselves as independent craftsmen and entrepreneurs. By 1906, inhabitants of the district of Bouguni were producing indigo-dyed cloth where previously only locally woven white cotton cloth was produced. It is not surprising that Bouguni was one of the centers to which a significant number of former slaves from the weaving and dyeing centers of the Middle Niger went.[54] In some districts, particularly Segu and Kita, the numbers of independent weavers now exceeded demand. Between 1908 and 1909 weavers from both these districts migrated to neighboring regions—some as far away as Fada N'Gourma—in search of work.[55] Because the costs of entry into weaving and dyeing industries were relatively low and demand for locally produced cloth was increasing, former slaves were better able to survive the first few years on their own.

To respond to new economic opportunities, weavers and spinners redoubled their activities. Weavers, as noted in Chapter 2, were dependent on the productivity of spinners. Spinning was one of the bottlenecks of increased production of handcrafted cloth. Paradoxically, the politique cotonnière actually contributed to increased output of handspun yarn and handcrafted cloth. Already by 1904, Marcel Quesnel, a local representative of the ACC, noted the producers' positive response to the new varieties of long-staple cotton. He drew attention to the women, who, "when they see this beautiful cotton, so long, so easy to spin, they want to retain it for themselves."[56] While Quesnel viewed women's attraction to exotic cotton with curiosity, the president of the ACC saw it as contributing to his organization's poor results in fostering cotton exports. "A curious happening is to be remarked: if the quantities [of cotton] which arrive in France are small, it is because the women, who spin for themselves, have been taken in by the superiority of the new cotton and they supply themselves with it before it leaves for France."[57] Cotton varieties introduced for the export market were being used to augment the production of handicraft textiles. Women had traditionally reserved for themselves the best cotton capsules, and yarn spun from these new cottons may have been used to produce cloth better able to compete with imported manufactured cloth. Thus, far from contributing to the collapse of local industry and to the decline of women's status and condition, the establishment of colonialism in the Soudan led to new opportunities for economic growth and new ways for women to enhance their autonomy and their income.

The ginning factory erected by the ACC in Segu also contributed to the circulation of ginned cotton. In 1905, the ACC sold the bulk of its ginned cotton locally and in 1906, after the supply of long-staple cotton was exhausted, the ACC ginned native cotton without charge.[58] Even paying the estimated rate of 11.67 francs per 100 kilograms of cotton ginned, the possibility of obtaining ginned cotton outside the context of the household may have contributed to the changes in the handicraft textile industry. Certainly, the ACC ginning factory lessened one of women's time-consuming tasks—carding—and it may have also contributed to increases in productivity because access to ginned cotton gave women more time to devote to spinning. According to one of my male informants, the mechanized ginneries "made women lazy."[59] Instead of being a statement of fact, my informant's comment may have refracted more significant change through romanticized cognitive categories. He may have perceived women as becoming lazy because they no longer worked as hard for the household and, especially, the male household head.

In Koutiala, a district adjoining Bouguni, where the politique cotonnière began in 1908, the ACC managed to buy only three tons of cotton. In explaining the apparent scarcity of cotton on the market, the commandant noted that "the ginning of cotton is confided to women, who sell [yarn] to local weavers, who make natural or colored bands, used in making clothing. The money made by the women from the sale of cotton [yarn] serves to build their own nest eggs. This is one of the causes, we think, of the scarcity of cotton in the [French] Soudan."[60] This report's emphasis on selling yarn to weavers suggests that the textile industry was being gradually extracted from the household. A description of the commodities available in the markets of the Segu district in 1908, which was more or less identical to those of other markets in the cotton zone of the French Soudan, provides additional indication that the factors of textile production were now circulating outside the household. "Different markets of the cercle are well provisioned in millet, rice, groundnuts, indigo, tobacco, karite, honey, dried fish, carded cotton, uncarded cotton, yarn, and bands of cloth locally manufactured."[61]

The availability of yarn outside the bounded, gender complementarity of the household was indicative of the changes in the social organization of the textile industry itself. Between 1910 and 1913, industrially spun yarn, known as *boloti* among the Bambara, arrived in significant quantities. Of all the factors of production in circulation, the presence of industrial yarn represented perhaps most dramatically the changes in the household handicraft textile industry. The availability of boloti lessened the two very time-consuming tasks women engaged in and weakened the centrality of women's carding and spinning work for the household. Boloti freed women from reliance on the household or the market as sources of raw cotton; boloti freed weavers from reliance on women. "Women," noted one of my informants, "had ceased to card and spin cotton. They bought the yarn from the whites."[62] As represented in Figure 5, the initial surge in demand for boloti coincided with marked social mobility following the end of slavery. The end of slavery witnessed the sometimes dramatic but often subtle change in relations of production. Many former slaves moved away from their masters; some returned to their homes; others settled close to the burgeoning towns along the Niger River and other important commercial centers. The end of slavery also marked a period in the decentralization of the textile and dyeing industries, hitherto concentrated in the Maraka towns of the left bank of the Niger. Many male former slaves continued to weave, but they did so for their own accounts. Many female former slaves, trained as dyers, pursued their craft independent of their former masters.[63]

Whether the reduction in boloti imports after 1913 forced women back into household relations of production is not clear. When the ACC ginneries closed or operated only erratically during the war years, women certainly resumed carding and spinning by hand to meet weavers' requirements for yarn for increased local cloth production. Women continued to seek labor-saving opportunities, and dur-

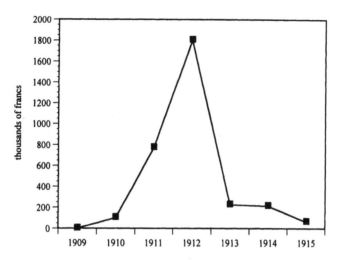

Fig. 5. Imports of Yarn into the French Soudan, 1909–1915. See Fig. 6 for sources.

ing the war women increased their use of hand carders. Measured in the value of imports, hand carders were among the nine most important commodities imported into the French Soudan in 1917.[64]

One of the most vexing problems for the social historian of the handicraft textile industry is the silence in the oral record regarding social processes of change evident in the archives. The availability of yarn on the market to both weavers and dyers is indicative of profound restructuring of the precolonial social organization of production. The household was no longer the obvious locus of production. These changes did not mean that the household textile industry was dead. It suggests only that men and women could now engage in textile production more easily outside the social relations determined by the household. Increased demand for local cloth during World War I provided new opportunities for men and women to redefine their relations of production and to control the social product of their labor. Whether individual producers were the predominant form of textile production remains unclear. With the available data, we can, unfortunately, do little more than suggest the contours of those changes. An analogous problem faces the historian interested in assessing the impact of French cotton colonialism on the production and disposition of the cotton harvest.

The entry of the ACC and the colonial state into the domestic cotton market caused at least a momentary disequilibrium in the supply of raw materials to local artisans. In 1907, just after the ACC ginning factory in Segu began full operation, the commandant reported that local weavers were finding it difficult to provision themselves with cotton.[65] The commandant of San, an important cotton region in the Middle Niger, noted that the obligation that producers bring their cotton to the central market where the ACC bought it "has not been conducted without a certain perturbation among the weavers and dyers. The impact on the industry of making cotton bands and blankets is an ill-understood consequence of the bulk purchases of cotton."[66] But the increase in the volume of cotton available in both Segu and Koutiala coincides with evidence from the monthly commercial reports that while producers were bringing more cotton to the ACC ginneries, weavers were increasing their output, and local textiles continued to dominate the regional commercial circuits between the savanna and the forest zones. In 1908, the commercial report from Segu noted that the textile industry was very active and "particularly prosperous," exporting a considerable amount of cotton bands, blankets, and pagnes to neighboring districts and colonies.[67] The textile industry throughout the cotton zone was prospering.

As long as the export sector was willing to pay the prevailing domestic prices for cotton, as long as cheap and plentiful manufactured cloth was imported, and as long as the colonial state could force producers to bring their cotton to central markets, local spinners and weavers were at risk. But this did not occur. The export market could not better the prices paid domestically. Administrators could occasionally force Africans to bring their cotton to market, but they could not effectively control whether producers brought all their harvest or just a fraction. Even if administrators were so inclined, they could not use their coercive powers because the higher administration had committed itself to "free markets." And finally the French commercial sector's hold over the cloth market was tenuous at best. In some districts, imported cloth had displaced some local varieties, but not all. And in others, it had taken no hold at all, as Colliaux, the administrator from Koutiala, made clear in his report on the 1909–10 cotton season. "Imported cloth is not for sale in the district, because it is too expensive and without use. The native searches above all for strength in his cloth and prefers naturally the white cloth of the land."[68] The decline of cloth imports during the war further eroded the place of imported cloth on the domestic market.

Many cotton growers found the new market for cotton to be in their interests, and many increased the scale of their production. The

increase in cotton exports shown in Figure 4 is indicative. In normative terms (that is, when the household was in its developmentally
ascendant form and when agronomic and market conditions were favorable), the household was organized on a two-field system.[69] Because it was based on overlapping collective and individual obligations and property rights, the two-field system could be harnessed to
increase productivity. This was the basis behind a report on the
1912–13 cotton campaign. "The cotton fields are of two kinds: first,
that which is worked by the whole family under the direction of the
head of the family and whose profit is for the benefit of all; and second, the individual fields, much less extended than the above, and
cultivated by individual members of the family during the days that
are by custom attributed to their own use."[70] The administrator did
not suggest what proportion of the cotton supply was derived from
which source, although he could have ventured an educated guess.
Because the colonial administration identified the household as the
basic African social unit, the household became both the unit of
taxation and the object of agricultural extension services. If local
administrators sought to require minimum cotton deliveries, they
would most likely do so at the level of households. The household
head was thus empowered by these new responsibilities but also the
victim of changing political economies in which the collective identity and functions of the household were at risk. Particularly for
those living far from the riverine transportation system of the Niger,
which could drain the grain harvests, cotton was the crop most likely
to offer household heads a commercial return. Moreover, the size of
the cotton crop could be increased without fundamentally altering
the agricultural calendar. It was in the household head's interests to
find a balance between the subsistence functions of the household
and the commercial opportunities available to earn cash.

The household head thus had to offset the increased work required
of the household's members to produce commercial crops against
their right to their own time. This had become a delicate task. Colonial conquest had introduced new economic opportunities for producers. Through their work on their *sanforo* (Bambara: fields of the
night), individuals could earn income which was theirs to spend.
Moreover, the market for labor expanded, particularly in coastal cash
crop regions, and building the railway. Especially for young men, this
may have eroded some of the power their elders had over them. The
end of slavery also contributed to the lessening of patriarchal authority.[71] Household heads therefore had to balance their fiduciary re-

sponsibilities with the newer forms of autonomy available to members of the household. The increased volume of cotton likely came from both collective and individual fields, with producers spending more time on their individual fields than they may otherwise have. Indeed, the administrator from Koutiala supported this contention when he stated that "the cotton produced on the individual fields is never brought to the ACC, but always sold on the markets, bought most often by the juula who bring the cotton to be worked on in neighboring districts."[72] Because the product of their field was their own, it was in the interests of individual producers to sell it to the highest bidder, which was almost always the domestic rather than the export market.

The commencement of hostilities in Europe profoundly altered the politique cotonnière and its impact on the handicraft textile industry in the Soudan. In 1915 the momentum of ACC activities stopped abruptly. Most ACC personnel were mobilized for the war. Cotton purchases for export lapsed and the ginneries shut down. The commercial sector hesitated to acquire colonial commodities because of the uncertainty of transport and the instability in metropolitan markets and prices. Yet the administration felt committed to support cotton producers even under these conditions. Because "cotton culture has made rapid progress over the past few years," wrote the governor of the Soudan, "it is in our political and economic interest not to let the 1914–15 harvest remain in the hands of producers."[73] The administration thus stepped in and bought all the cotton available on the market. The administration was prepared for some financial loss, but to its surprise, it made a profit of nearly 15,000 francs.[74]

The most noticeable effect in the Soudan of the deepening war in Europe was the decline in imported cloth and the consequent reduction in the activities of the French commercial houses. Textile manufacturers in France and England refused to guarantee prices and delivery. The stock of imported cloth on hand in Bamako at the end of 1916 and early 1917 fell dramatically. Because textile sales drove a majority of all commercial transactions, declining stock had significant repercussions throughout the Soudan. Figure 6 indicates the trends in cloth and yarn imports from 1909 to 1916.

The peak years of cloth imports, 1911–12, coincided almost exactly with the 1911–12 cotton harvest, as measured by the stock of cotton the ACC had on hand (see Figure 4). Producers faced an exceptionally severe drought in 1913–14, which reduced both the cotton

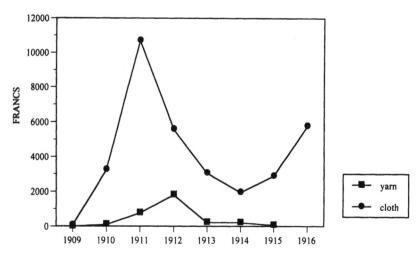

Fig. 6. Imports of Yarn and Cloth into the French Soudan, 1909–1916. Annual data used for 1911, 1912, and 1913. Fourth quarter data used for 1909,
1910, 1914, and 1915. Sources: Haut-Sénégal-Niger, Rapport sur la situation
de la colonie pendant le 4ième trimestre 1910, ANS-AOF 2 G 10-?; Haut-
Sénégal-Niger, rapport sur la situation économique pendant l'année 1911,
ANS-AOF 2 G 11-9; Haut-Sénégal-Niger, rapport sur la situation économique pendant l'année 1912, ANS-AOF 2 G 12-13; Haut-Sénégal-Niger,
rapport sur la situation économique pendant l'année 1913, ANS-AOF 2 G 13-
11; Rapport sur la situation économique de la colonie du Haut-Sénégal-Niger
pendant le 4ième trimestre 1915; Rapport commercial, 4th Quarter 1916,
Bamako, ANM 1 Q 44.

harvest and the demand for imported cloth. Demand for imported
cloth recovered somewhat from 1914 to 1916, only to collapse during
the second half of the war. Although I do not have complete data for
the cotton imports from 1917 to 1918, the quarterly commercial reports from the Soudan indicate a sharp drop in the volume of cloth
imports. Because European and Indian textiles formed fully half of
the total imports into the Soudan, a serious decline in the volume of
cloth stocks reduced the commercial activities of both French and
African merchants. Prices of most varieties of imported cloth rose
between 50 and 100 percent. By 1918, calico had increased in price
by nearly 400 percent and guinée from Pondicherry by 650 percent,
putting that cloth out of the reach of most consumers.[75] Despite the
administration's efforts to keep cotton flowing into its hands, it lost
the initiative. With the decline in the volume of imported manufactured cloth and the coincident rise in prices, weavers and artisans

increased their production and offered more for local cotton. Because the administration would not raise its purchase price, producers sold a large portion of their harvest to the local trade.[76]

As weavers increased their production to meet demand, prices for cotton on the parallel domestic market rose. "The price is established by free competition between European buyers, native traders, and local consumers who have their women spin the cotton," wrote the head of the Soudanese agricultural service. "The primary cause for the rise in the price of cotton is not the change in the rate in Europe, but the rise in the price of imported cloth."[77] Although the colonial administration had been committed to creating and supporting a "free market," it was not pleased with the results. The declining volume of imported cloth stimulated demand for handcrafted cloth.

World War I and the Handicraft Textile Industry

The war made clear just how resilient the handicraft textile industry was. It also demonstrated that the first quarter-century of colonialism had not significantly altered the foundations of the regional economy of the Soudan. African cotton growers had proven themselves responsive to market incentives, and they sold their cotton to the highest bidder. The problem was that the highest bidders were the local artisans. By 1918, a metric ton ginned of Soudanese cotton sold for 2,500 francs; the rate for ginned cotton on Le Havre's commodity market was only 1,200–1,500 francs. Governor-General Joost Van Vollenhoven warned the governor of the Soudan that cotton exports, which had risen more than tenfold between 1914 and 1917, were in danger of falling rapidly.[78]

The French were not willing, however, to let cotton exports they had nurtured for nearly two decades slip through their fingers. Mobilization for the war in Europe had led to greater state intervention in the economy, and the free play of market forces was not permitted to interfere with the supply of materials deemed critical for the war effort. In the midst of the war metropolitan administrators and industrialists were forcefully reminded of the value of their colonies, which the commercial interests of Bordeaux and Marseille and the colonial lobby had known all along.[79] The Ligue coloniale française redoubled its efforts to make the French public aware of the colonies' importance to the metropole. "Despite the present difficulties," wrote the president of the league to the governor-general of AOF, "we have not ceased to pursue our propaganda to cultivate in the French public the idea that our colonies should in large measure supply the needs of the metropole."[80] The war also provided French manufacturers with an opportunity to rethink the role of the colonial market for their products. In their submission of a draft program on postwar reconstruction, the delegates from the textile manufacturers attending the Union coloniale française meeting were convinced that they could supply more varieties and greater volume of cloth to the African market and thus displace their English and Dutch competitors.[81]

During the war, the Ministry of Colonies came to play a more important role in the war cabinet's decisions concerning the metropolitan economy. As part of a more general effort to control the supply of raw materials and production for both military and civilian needs, all colonial commodities deemed critical for national defense were imported under the direct authority of the Ministry of Colonies.[82] Between the middle of 1916 and 1918 imports and distribution of oils, jute, paper, and cotton were controlled by the Ministry of Colonies or by interministerial committees in collaboration with metropolitan manufacturers and dealers. In 1917 the minister of colonies instructed the governor-general of French West Africa, "in view of the supply of the metropole, to incite the native by all appropriate means to extend his crops and to establish in West Africa direct requisition of products which will be effected by the administration directly without the intermediary of the private sector." Governor-General Van Vollenhoven argued strongly against imposing on administrators yet another task for which they were at best ill-prepared. Because of their experiences with the many and varied markets of the colony, he preferred to leave to the colonial commercial interests the tasks of buying the harvests, transporting them to the ginneries, administrative centers, or embarkation points, and the supply of imported goods which formed the counterpart to the sale of crops. This was, Van Vollenhoven argued, the private sector's raison d'être and its social mission. But the governor-general was not prepared to leave the supply of the metropole totally in the hands of the private sector, whose performance in that regard had not been consistently above reproach. He defined a more constrained task for the private sector. The commercial sector was to procure the crops from producers and deliver them into the hands of the administration, which would then reimburse the merchants the prices they paid producers—which were to be determined by prior agreement between the administration and the commercial sector—plus the costs of transport and an "appropriate remuneration." But he warned the assembled delegates of the commercial sector that he could resist the minister of colonies' requisitional order only if the commercial sector would constitute itself in a "union of all the commercial houses of the AOF," which would then be considered the colonial administration's "intermediary" for the purchase of the next harvest.[83] The minister of colonies did not oppose Van Vollenhoven's "commercial consortium," although he voiced his concern that this consortium should not exclude the role of African merchants and he stressed that the "profits" guaranteed by the state should not be abnormal.[84] Although the war was over before the commercial consortium envisioned by Van Vollenhoven could be tested, the policy indicated a renewed willingness on the part of both the metropolitan and colonial states to intervene in the structure of the colonial economy to make the colonies conform to goals established in France.

Although the exports of Soudanese cotton to France increased sixfold between 1916 and 1918, Lieutenant Governor Charles Brunet of the French Soudan explained to his superior in 1918 the peculiar difficulties of turning his colony into la France cotonnière as envisioned only fifteen years earlier. At the same time he stressed the differences between the economic situation in the Côte d'Ivoire and in the Soudan:

I will explain the reasons why the rise in prices [paid] to cotton producers, following the procedures in the Côte d'Ivoire, does not seem to have a simple result [here]. These reasons are the following: the commerce in cotton has always been free in this colony; a very active competition over this product exists between European buyers with a view toward export and weavers who prepare a large part of the cloth used to make local clothing. Direct sales of cotton between producers and weavers escape our attention, and in recent years, their importance has increased as a result of European cloth being offered at higher and higher prices. The result of this situation created by the difficulties of making and importing European cloth is that the current prices have attained a rate superior to the normal value of the product. Given these conditions, it is hard to foresee the application of those happy measures applied to Baoule, because the circumstances themselves encourage the cultivator to develop his production. . . . The problem seems more complex in the Haut-Sénégal-Niger than in the Côte d'Ivoire, where [cotton] commerce has been to some degree channeled by the local government. Few artisans there work with cotton and the producer thus has no other openings except the sale to the administration.[85]

In his report, Lieutenant Governor Brunet concluded that the central obstacle to the politique cotonnière was the existence of the handicraft textile industry, which continued to produce cloth for local and regional consumption, absorbed a large share of the annual cotton harvest, and competed with European traders for cotton.

During the first 25 years of colonialism, the various lieutenant governors of the Soudan and the governors-general of the French West Africa Federation had identified the colonial economy of the Soudan with cotton. Operating together with the semiofficial Association cotonnière coloniale and with the private sector of the French metropolitan commercial sector, the colonial state sought to make the Soudan into France's premier colonial supplier of cotton. In the process of putting these visions into practice, the colonial state, the ACC, and the private sector struggled to control the shape of the colonial economy and to define the economic spheres in which each was to perform its special roles. Undergirding the entire program were ideological assumptions about Africans and about the economy, which profoundly shaped the forms of intervention in the economy each actor could engage. The colonial cotton program rested on the assumption that Africans were rational economic actors who would respond positively to market incentives and on the ideological commitment that the economy be "free." Africans proved these assumptions to be true; they did produce more cotton and they did sell it to the highest bidder. The problem for the success of the politique cotonnière was that African cotton producers sold their cotton to local artisans and not to the export sector. The meager success of the colonial cotton program provided opportunities to colonial interests with different assumptions about Africans and about the colonial economy to reopen the struggle over the shape of the politique cotonnière and by extension over the colonial state and the colonial economy in the Soudan. These struggles dominated the period 1918–32.

PART II

The Struggle to Control the Economy

CHAPTER FIVE

World War I,
Postwar Reconstruction in France,
and Colonial Cotton Production

The war made French industrialists and state officials acutely aware of their dependence on imported raw materials and of the importance and potential of the colonies for the reconstruction and development of the metropolitan economy. Cotton was considered a commodity of national importance. The war also left a legacy of direct state intervention in the economy, represented as a set of institutions that interceded within the free play of market forces. This willingness to intervene more forcefully in the economy was also manifested in the colonies, where the revival of the politique cotonnière centered on the roles of the colonial state and Africans in the shape and performance of the colonial economy and in the provision of cotton to metropolitan users.

This brief chapter examines the impact of the war on the French textile industry as a prelude to a more detailed study of the dissonant voices proposing solutions to the problems of the colonial supply of cotton for metropolitan needs. The debates on colonial development and the practical accomplishments of managing European enterprises on the banks of the Niger between 1918 and 1932 indicate a gradual coalescence of colonial cotton development advocates into two competing camps, each of which sought to impose its ideological models of the economy on cotton policies.

The debates on colonial cotton development surround fundamentally divergent beliefs about the role of African peasants and the place of metropolitan capital and European management. At the core of the revived debates about cotton development were contradictory assessments of Africans' capacities to work, of their responsiveness to market incentives, and of the meager results of the first twenty years of la politique cotonnière in the Soudan. Between 1918 and

1932, new voices within France and within French West Africa participated in this debate, calling for increased cotton production for export by investment in irrigation. Others called for encouraging African producers through amelioration of seed and technology, changes in commercialization, and the introduction of price supports. Despite the intensity of the public and administrative debates about cotton development policy, French efforts to control the production and supply of West African cotton had very uneven results. In the end, all the efforts of the French to make their colony conform to the needs of the metropole foundered on the actions of the Soudanese. Despite French policies to capture cotton production for export, the handicraft textile industry persisted and used most of the annual cotton harvest to service the needs of the domestic Soudanese economy and a wider regional one.

The period 1918–32 constitutes the second major phase in French colonial cotton policy in the Soudan. World War I had left deep scars on the industrial landscape of Europe. Postwar reconstruction operated within renewed debates about the economic protection of national industries and securing safe supplies of crucial raw materials. Europeans began to examine their colonies more seriously as a way to solve metropolitan problems.[1] Indeed, this fourteen-year period should be considered the second European colonial occupation of Africa because it entailed more sustained efforts to develop colonial economies and make them serve metropolitan needs.[2] Many of the ideological positions taken during the first phase of colonial occupation regarding the economy and Africans were revisited and revised in light of the war and postwar changes in metropolitan political economies. The struggles between the colonial administration, the colonial commercial sector, the agronomic and public works "experts," and African peasants were realigned and renewed with special vigor. What was at stake in these struggles was control over the power and policies of the colonial state.

Within this period 1918 to 1932, 1924 formed an important watershed. From 1918 to 1924, those supporting the European-managed, capital-intensive irrigation model of cotton development were ascendant. In 1924, Governor-General Carde issued a major policy statement about French West African cotton development, which provided support for both the irrigation model and the pro-peasant, rain-fed model of cotton production. From 1924 to 1932 deep cracks were becoming evident in the application of the irrigation model: irrigated cotton did not perform as expected and African labor did not come forth willingly to work the irrigated fields. From 1924 to 1932, the pro-peasant camp pursued with renewed vigor its vision of the Soudan's cotton future, although it too had to confront serious problems of quality control and marketing as well as the domestic market for cotton.

Despite the reinvigoration of the debates about colonial development, those programs, which did not consider Africans as strategic actors in the colonial economy, were doomed to fail. In this period, as in the previous phase of colonial cotton development, Africans calculated their interests within a range of domestic and colonial forces and acted to maximize their well-being. This policy often took the form of producing cotton, using it for their own needs, and selling it to the highest bidder. As we shall see, Africans sold their cotton to the export sector sometimes because they were attracted by market incentives and sometimes because they sought to minimize the pain of colonial control and punishment.

After a brief reprieve during World War I, the two worlds of cotton collided again in the French Soudan and even more intensely than before. Again colonial cotton policies foundered because the French did not fully control the economic life of the men and women who lived there. The economy of the Soudan remained characterized by a relatively small import-export sector and a much larger, although more difficult to measure, domestic economy that catered to local and intracontinental demand. Within the larger domestic economy, African demand for cloth remained one of the pillars of everyday life. The French failure to transform the Soudan into la France cotonnière was caused in part by their failure to capture the market for textiles. The decline of imported cloth during the Depression revealed just how little the French actually controlled the economic life of the region.

No one in France had prepared for a war of the intensity and duration it actually had. Although the state had reserved for itself powers to requisition transport and matériel and rights to conscript men for the military in time of war, neither the military command nor the commanders of state had made provisions for the mobilization of the national economy. Following initial confusion and hesitation, the state began to intervene more systematically and energetically in the economy. As it intervened by inserting itself between buyers and sellers, albeit without an overall plan, the state effectively preempted the principles of economic liberty upon which French industrialists and merchants had operated. The state sought to control the supply of transportation, labor, fuel, and raw materials and to allocate these factors according to priorities determined above all by the Ministry of Armaments, which directed the supply of goods and services for the war effort.[3]

By the middle of 1916, the state had elaborated a system of control over raw materials and the provision of labor so that even where it did not requisition factories outright, it effectively imposed its commands on most French industries.[4] The state often exercised control over production with the active collaboration of industrialists and businessmen by creating consortia. Consortia were associations of dealers and manufacturers interested in the same category of goods. Once combined as official consortia, they exercised monopsony powers. They centralized demand, purchased raw materials from abroad, and distributed the imports to members of the association in proportion to shares held in the consortium and at prices previously agreed upon. These consortia were constituted under direct state supervision as capitalized companies, shares of which were determined by the relative shares individual firms had of the market.

The elaboration of consortia was just one example of a change in the prevailing conceptions of the economy shared by those who grappled with solutions to wartime shortages. The economy was seen more clearly than ever as something to be managed, and those best able to manage it were the "technocrats." Although the technocrats came to power most fully in the postwar reconstruction, their imprint on the new role of the state and the economy can be seen from this period of wartime management. It is not surprising that many of these technocrats were originally trained as engineers, and they helped, as Richard Kuisel put it, to "give French management a peculiarly strong engineering outlook, one that stressed high technology and production."[5] These shifts in metropolitan thinking about the economy were to find resonance in the irrigation model of colonial cotton development.

Members of the consortia met regularly with officials from the interested ministries and planned for both military and civilian needs. With state approval and with a commitment from the state for the provision of transportation, the consortia approached international sellers of commodities. This was the model for the consortium of cotton, established at the end of 1917. Consortia of jute, oil, hardware, glassware, and paper among others were similarly constituted.[6]

Although the free play of market forces was obviously constrained, members of the consortia made profits according to previously deter-

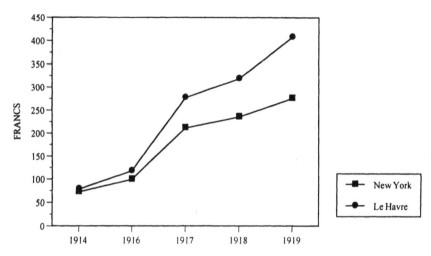

Fig. 7. Prices for Cotton Bales in New York and Le Havre, 1914–1919.
Source: Aftalion, *L'Industrie textile*, p. 30.

mined wholesale and retail prices and in accordance with the volume of material each dealer or manufacturer was allocated. In principle, the consortia could not realize profits, although consortia occasionally reaped windfall profits from changing world market prices. Such a situation existed in the market for cotton, the price of which initially fell with the onset of hostilities but rose dramatically between July 1914 and August 1918. As German submarine warfare began to take its toll, the price differential for cotton in New York and Le Havre began to reflect the increasing costs and risks of maritime transport. In 1914, the price differential between cotton in New York and Le Havre was 8 percent; by August 1918, it had reached 48 percent.[7] Figure 7 illustrates the price movement of cotton during the war.

By taking advantage of price fluctuations of both currencies and commodities and because of their monopsonic character, consortia often controlled significant reserves of capital. Because of the public, semiofficial nature of their activities, these consortia could use their profits only to pay for operating expenses.[8] Whatever capital remained after the end of the war was to be reserved for the state to use in projects that benefited the "general interest of that branch of commerce."[9] Thus the liquidation of the Consortium of Cotton after the war provided the state with considerable resources to implement policy decisions derived from the renewed discussion surrounding the politique cotonnière.[10]

Although the French textile industry was sufficiently dispersed to avoid catastrophe, the war and German occupation of the industrial north and east led to a sharp decline in French textile production. In 1919, production was only 60 percent of its prewar level. The war had undercut French industry's dominance over a protected domestic market, and the fall in domestic production during the war led to a growing reliance on imported cotton cloth and ready-made garments, particularly for men, to meet the army's needs. Moreover, because the textile industry had been the largest single industrial employer in France, declining production threatened significant unemployment at the time when demobilized soldiers were being reincorporated into the work force.[11] "At first glance," wrote Senator General Adolphe Messimy in a report presented to the National Assembly in 1924, "in seeing the colossal industrial organization of metallurgy and of the mines, one is tempted to consider them as the masters of industry. But that is not the case; the textile industry constitutes the principal element of production."[12] In 1906, 36 percent of the total industrial labor force in France was engaged in textile production compared to 12 percent in metallurgical and engineering industries. By 1924, those employed in textile production had shrunk to 20 percent of the total labor force, but there were still nearly 620,000 workers engaged in the cotton, linen, and silk industries.[13]

Actual war damage was limited to the industrial plant in the north and east, and even there it was slight. Only 20 percent of the power looms and slightly more than 13 percent of the spindles had been damaged or destroyed. In addition, the postwar return of Alsace-Lorraine contributed nearly 25 percent more spindles, 33 percent more power looms, and doubled the number of calico printing machines for the French textile industry. The demobilization of the economy thus provided an opportunity to modernize industrial technology and to reorganize labor and management. Following the armistice, the Ministry of Armament quickly transformed itself into the Ministry of Industrial Reconstruction and directed capital to those industries damaged by the war and to those that needed to be retooled for civilian production. Funds from the Ministry of Industrial Reconstruction were unevenly distributed: more flowed into capital goods than into consumer goods industries such as textiles. The Ministry of Industrial Reconstruction did not, therefore, direct significant capital to the French textile industry.[14]

Postwar reconstruction of the metropolitan textile industry, however, had to confront two linked problems. First, from 1919 to 1926, the French franc fell dramatically in relationship to British pounds and American dollars. During the war, the French state had borrowed heavily and taxed less thoroughly, running up massive debt. The Allies had assisted the French war effort through loans and by fixing the value of the franc to American dollars and British pounds at relatively stable rates. In March 1919, the Allies stopped supporting the franc, and it started a fall that lasted into 1926. By 1926, the franc was worth only 17 percent of its prewar value in dollars. Second, the declining value of the franc translated into increased cost for raw materials purchased on the world market and in particular for cotton. French industry was completely dependent upon imported cotton. In 1923, France acquired more than 62 percent of its cotton from American sources, 17 percent from British Indian sources, 7.5 percent from Egyptian sources, and the rest from smaller suppliers, including West Africa. Because of the devaluation of the franc after 1919, the three major suppliers accepted only gold in payment. In 1923, French spinners spent nearly 2.9 billion francs on cotton, and the government anticipated a 30 to 40 percent increase for 1924.[15]

As the French textile industry regained its prewar production levels in 1924–25, managers of the French state and captains of French industries were becoming uncomfortably aware of the growing bill for importing cotton and the growing drain on their gold reserves. Prices for American cotton showed no indication of declining. As the franc declined, the bill for cotton kept rising. By 1926, consumption of cotton was nearly 20 percent above prewar levels. The fall of the franc and the rise in consumption of cotton had three consequences. First, it resulted in a high domestic price for cotton textiles. The cost of domestically produced calico, for example, was 50 percent higher than the wholesale price index for consumer goods. If textiles were not so expensive relative to other consumer goods, thus depressing demand, and if the costs of raw materials were not so high, thus leaving more capital for investment and modernization, the recovery of the French textile industry might have occurred even earlier than it did.[16]

Second, as industrialists and officials had warned, France had become a tributary of the Americans, for there were no significant alternative sources of cotton for the French industry.[17] The National Assembly considered this unfavorable balance of payments a national calamity. And third, the renewed call for the protection of national industries was paralleled by a revival of colonial development programs to serve national interests.

The debate surrounding colonial cotton development was renewed in this context of the "national calamity" of French dependence on imported cotton. The renewed debate drew on many old issues and protagonists, but by 1924 it had congealed into two opposing camps: those who favored the peasant option of rain-fed cotton cultivation and those who favored the development of massive irrigation projects. Proponents of the peasant option had dominated the senior administration in French West Africa, at least from the time of Governor-General Roume in 1903. Others, like Governor-General Carde, who came to power in 1923, sitting at the head of a loose and unwieldy confederation during the time of the renewed debate on colonial sources of raw materials, tried to balance support for both positions. In the period immediately after the war, however, the raw materials shortages and the balance of payments problems confronting metropolitan industry favored those with new solutions. Proponents of the irrigation model included actors from the colonial agricultural services, engineers from the public works division, and private enterprise. Many of these players had not been active participants in the debates between 1896 and 1918. All, however, were united in their belief that the colonies, and particularly French West Africa, held the solution to France's cotton requirements. Although the debate had been festering for years, wartime raw material shortages, postwar reconstruction, and evidence that American mills were absorbing ever-increasing amounts of American cotton brought home the seriousness of the problem and the meager results of the previous twenty-five years of the politique cotonnière in the Soudan. The period 1918–32 witnessed the sharpening of the debates surrounding colonial development in general and the politique cotonnière in particular, and the debates over implementing policies needed to give substance to the various development programs.

By 1932, the forces unleashed by those favoring massive irrigation as the solution to both metropolitan raw materials needs and colonial development led to the establishment of the Office du Niger. Proponents of irrigation seemed unstoppable. By 1932, however, a new hybrid strain of cotton—Karangani–Garrah Hills, also called Budi—was undergoing final testing. Budi was resistant to local parasites, hardy enough to withstand irregular rains, and capable of yielding a vast quantity of cotton for metropolitan mills. It promised a bright future for peasant-produced rain-fed cotton.

The following chapters focus on the struggles over colonial development and their consequences for Soudanese cotton producers and handicraft textile workers during the period 1918–32. These chapters illuminate the uneven impact of the capitalist world economy on the regional economy of the Soudan, the cultural side of colonial economic development, the ways in which the debates over cotton fractured the colonial state, and how a study of colonial cotton development can provide insights into the social history of this period. Chapter 6 deals with the revival of plans for cotton irrigation and the articulation of a model of colonial development in the period 1918–24. Chapter 7 examines the period 1924 to 1932 from the standpoint of the growing concern over labor. After all, those proposing cotton irrigation needed steady supplies of workers. Chapter 8 examines the twin issues of quality control and price. French metropolitan spinners wanted a high-quality product at a good price. The cotton quality issue, as I shall argue, was critical to colonial efforts to make colonial cotton acceptable to metropolitan users. Using quality control as a pretext, administrators put Africans under much greater surveillance, both at the point of production and at the point of sale. Within the context of the struggle between those supporting the European-managed irrigation model and those supporting the pro-peasant model, the debates over prices paid for Soudanese cotton and whether to fix prices had a politics of their own. Most important, the debate about prices reflected assumptions about Africans as rational economic actors and permitted administrators to vent their disdain for the commercial sector. The final chapter of this part, Chapter 9, examines the period 1918–32 from the perspective of the handicraft textile industry and argues that despite state and private efforts to control the production and supply of cotton, the local handicraft textile industry expanded to meet growing domestic demand in the Soudan, in Senegal, and in the Côte d'Ivoire. The failure of French colonial cotton policy to capture the cotton harvest of the Soudan is directly linked to the robust nature of the handicraft textile industry.

Colonial Cotton Development, Irrigation, and the Illusion of a New Egypt, 1918–1924

The postwar debates on colonial cotton policy began with a critical assessment of the previous twenty years of the politique cotonnière. During this period, those favoring new, ambitious solutions to the metropole's raw materials needs were ascendant. The initiative in French West Africa was taken by a private entrepreneur, Marcel Hirsch, who represented the capital-intensive European management solution to the metropole's raw materials crisis, and by Emile Bélime, an employee of the colonial Public Works Department, who became the most eloquent advocate of irrigation. This chapter examines the articulation of a colonial development model which had been neglected in the first phase of the French colonial cotton program in the Soudan and some of the forces seeking to shape it. This chapter also explores the core cultural assumptions undergirding irrigation as a model of colonial cotton development. Central to the emerging program of irrigation were the assumptions of France's technical power to control both nature and labor.

In 1918, Yves Henry, perhaps the leading French expert on colonial cotton and an official of the Service d'agriculture in French West Africa, launched a critique of the past performance of the ACC.[1] He argued that the ACC's mandate was too vague. Because it lacked focus, the ACC dissipated its resources, encroached on areas reserved for other participants in colonial cotton development—including the private commercial sector and the colonial agricultural service—and made enemies. Henry's most damaging criticism concerned the ACC's lack of agronomic expertise. Because the ACC represented metropolitan interests that wanted results quickly, the association did not respect "scientific" principles. The experimental procedures the ACC followed in the field were, according to Henry, fundamentally flawed. "On the one hand, imported seeds were distributed without knowing their agronomy; on the other hand, distribution was conducted under poor conditions of execution and the total absence of technical agents to control the experiments. From the point of view of experimental results, nothing was gained from these trials. . . . Because of the lack of personnel [and their lack of scientific training], it was impossible to sustain the trials using the same seeds. Thus, the yields from imported cotton were virtually the same as local varieties of cotton."[2] Moreover, Henry argued that the ACC's cotton trials were deficient in preparatory tilling, fertilization, and basic crop rotation. Despite these flawed practices and meager results, Henry was convinced that France should pursue cotton development in French West Africa. "Need," he wrote in his 1918 study of irrigated agriculture, "will be the genitor of initiative and effort." Henry went on to argue that France's pressing need for raw materials could be satisfied through realizing the potential of her West African colonies, and particularly "our grand African river valleys."[3] Irrigation, he argued, had the potential of increasing cotton yields ten times over rain-fed cultivation.

In developing his argument in favor of irrigation, Henry established a vocabulary that gained a wide currency in the subsequent debates, and he established an analogy that was often used as a substitute for more careful scientific research. "Irrigated agriculture," Henry wrote, "will be a task in the public interest and it will be socially uplifting. . . . [Irrigation] will put into the native's hands the means to regularize his staple food crops . . . and it will prepare for a future time when he will produce export crops, especially those which are of most interest to us: cotton and jute. Irrigation will also lead to the progressive transformation of the primitive state of herding."[4] Such a transformation of agricultural production and the evolution of the native would require considerable time and effort. But the effort, Henry was convinced, would be worthwhile.

Henry developed his argument by analogy to the Nile Valley in Egypt. Whereas it has taken centuries to tame and transform the Nile Valley, French West Africa could pass through the same stages much more rapidly. Especially in the Senegal River valley, Henry wrote, one would find conditions closely approximating those of Egypt for the production of long-staple Egyptian cotton. In this task, Henry argued, there was an important place for private European initiative. Intensive agriculture under the direction of Europeans would expand

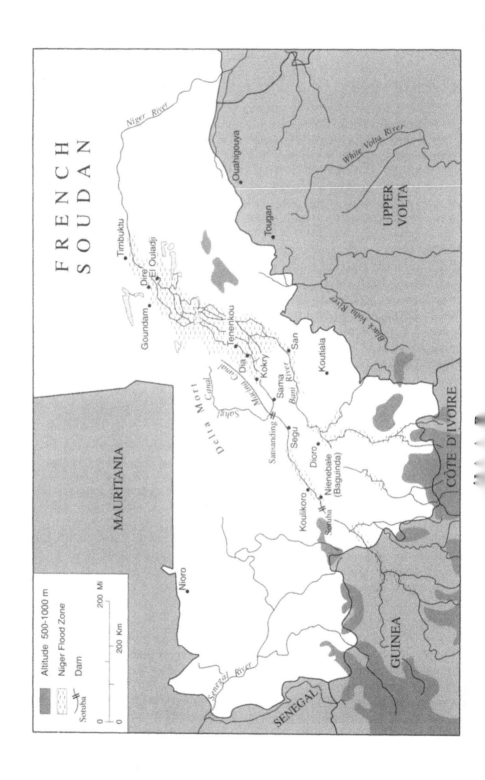

faster and more quickly lead to a steady supply of raw materials for the metropole.[5]

In 1909, a Parisian banker and entrepreneur, Marcel Hirsch, toured Algeria and French West Africa with the idea of encouraging irrigated cotton production. Just before the war, he approached the governor-general in Dakar through his contacts with the Union coloniale with a proposal for private initiative in cotton irrigation. Because of the administration's preoccupation with the war, Hirsch had to wait until its end was in sight before he renewed his contacts with the senior administration in West Africa. In October 1917, Hirsch presented a preliminary proposal for a massive irrigated cotton project to the division of public works in the Ministry of Colonies. Henry Simon, then minister of colonies and a personal friend of Hirsch, agreed to pass the proposal on to Governor-General Gabriel Angoulvant in Dakar, but he did so with only lukewarm support. In his turn, Angoulvant wrote to Hirsch that he was favorably disposed to enter into the path Hirsch had indicated, but he sent the proposal on to the director of the division of public works in the AOF and to the lieutenant governors of Senegal and the Soudan without recommendation. An agreement between Hirsch and the governor-general was not concluded until the end of 1919, and the Compagnie de culture cotonnière du Niger (CICONNIC) came into being in 1920.[6]

As Hirsch's proposal was making its way through the administration, Governor-General Martial Merlin commissioned Emile Bélime to conduct a major study of the suitability of irrigation in the Niger Valley in 1919–20. The results of Bélime's mission, published in preliminary form in 1921 and in a fuller version in 1925, fit directly into the renewed debates on the politique cotonnière.[7]

Bélime was an extremely ambitious government official with a checkered past and somewhat dubious technical credentials. He was also eloquent and a quick learner of both the technical and political situation, and he brought boundless enthusiasm to the debates on cotton development. Bélime's project was grandiose—to irrigate over one million hectares in the Soudan using three canals—and it was subject to vigorous debate. Bélime built on Henry's argument of the twofold benefits of irrigation. Using Indian analogies, Bélime argued that irrigation would help alleviate the social consequences of recurrent and disastrous droughts such as the one of 1913–14. Large-scale irrigation, Bélime continued, "could not be financially remunerative unless it has as its goal the cultivation of exportable products capable of supporting the heavy costs of hydraulic works and administrative control over the cultivation. Cotton is one of these products."[8] Whereas Henry had favored the Senegal River valley as the site for irrigation, Bélime favored the Niger River valley, and he made a compelling case by linking the annual cycle of cotton to the annual flood cycle of the river. Controlling the floodwaters would provide necessary moisture to the fruiting cotton at just the right moment.[9]

Developing the analogy to the Nile Valley first coined by Henry, Bélime argued that the "Soudan of the Niger River, equally favored by nature as Egypt and Mesopotamia, has remained the inverse of these countries; it has remained savage and unorganized. Until this day, man has never exerted, by the association of land to water, the effort necessary for the production of this agricultural wealth, which, since antiquity, has been as celebrated as the Nile and the Euphrates rivers."[10] His 1921 study proposed a massive three-canal system feeding over one million hectares. It developed in detail only the Segu canal and the derivation dam at Sotuba. The Segu canal was audacious enough, for Bélime argued that it was capable of irrigating 750,000 hectares in the region between the Niger and the Bani rivers. The Segu canal, which Bélime called a "prestudy," became the center of the controversy, which I deal with later in this chapter.[11]

Although Bélime was a man who respected order, he was also a man of action, who chafed at the slow pace of administrative decision making. Irrigated cotton production was such an obvious solution to the pressing needs of French industry that delay was unthinkable. "Another cause of inertia is the result of our penchant for total solutions, hierarchical and orderly, in which everything is known and anticipated and which is less troubled by the current realities." Bélime looked favorably on British practice in India in the middle of the nineteenth century, when they began their irrigation projects. According to Bélime, they too lacked technical expertise at that time, but they had extraordinary vision. France, Bélime admitted, was not endowed with cadres of hydraulic engineers familiar with agricultural conditions in the colonies. We are all students, he concluded, and what we know is derived from the accumulation of local solutions.[12]

The leap of faith from men of action, which Bélime called for, was taken by Albert Sarraut, minister of colonies, in his April 1921 presentation to the National Assembly of his ambitious plans for the economic development of the colonies. Sarraut fully incorporated in his plan Bélime's vision of a cotton future through irrigation. Sarraut prefaced his development agenda with an overview of colonial assistance to the metropole during the war and postwar reconstruction. "Colonies," Sarraut argued,

long regarded with casualness as an onerous luxury, but indispensable for the prestige of a great nation, demonstrated in an exalted fashion, at the moment of peril, that they can bring useful assistance to the defense of the metropole. . . . Colonies are not just distant lands where the dreams and fantasies of writers run free. They are lands overflowing with intense activity, rich in men and rich in natural resources, which manifested their vitality at the hour of our greatest need. By these positive results, the colonial endeavor has demonstrated that it pays for itself.[13]

The link between current and future metropolitan needs and colonial development was thus easy to make. Invoking the imbalance of payments for cotton and the prospective of declining supply as a grave danger to the national economy, Sarraut argued that "the hope of our textile industry, threatened in its supply of cotton, is currently turned toward our colonies." But colonial development was not a one-sided process. Colonial development, in Sarraut's terms, had the same twofold quality Henry had established: "development of natural resources and development of human resources." Colonial development should not be regarded as "fiscal sponges," draining metropolitan capital. On the contrary, Sarraut argued, colonial development does not oppress, it liberates; colonial development does not exhaust, it enriches; colonial development does not exploit, it shares.[14] The colonies, particularly French West Africa, could provide the solution to the raw material needs of the French textile industry. The key, Sarraut concluded, lay in intensive cotton production with the assistance of irrigation. The model was Bélime's. Sarraut brushed aside the issue of the costs of the proposed irrigation schemes by arguing that if only one-tenth of the capital used to purchase cotton from foreign countries each year were directed toward colonial public works, France would recover its expenses and rectify the balance of payments deficit within five or six years.[15] Sarraut's computations could not have been more naive, but his program was certainly attractive in the face of the drain of gold from France.

The transmission of authority on irrigation from Henry to Bélime to Sarraut indicated more unison than dissonance in colonial development thinking of the immediate postwar period. But this was not the case. Former governor-general Angoulvant had his own ideas about solving the national cotton crisis. In contrast to the massive expenditure irrigation required, Angoulvant's proposal seemed cost free and promised an immediate rectification of the past performance. He drew on his experience in the Côte d'Ivoire when he was lieutenant governor and cotton exports rose from zero in 1912 to 350 tons in 1916. In a letter to the minister of colonies, he argued that the Côte d'Ivoire's success was due to a mix of requiring Africans to grow cotton, fixing prices at remunerative rates, offering subventions to producers far from collection points, and directly overseeing the collection of cotton.[16] In 1924, in the midst of the national cotton debate, Angoulvant again added his Côte d'Ivoire model to the dissonant voices.

If we want to attain the result which I have indicated [50,000 tons of cotton], we can do this by requiring that each inhabitant of French West Africa, from Senegal to Oubangi-Chari, provide ten kilograms of cotton. We should not hesitate to remember that this is the method of obligation I used in the Côte d'Ivoire for the extension of cocoa and cotton production. Obligation, when it is used for the sole profit of the state, as in the case of the Dutch Indies, or of private societies, as in the case of our own Congo, is not acceptable. But obligation is laudable when it is limited solely to profit the native producer, who remains the master of the fruits of his labor.

The obligation to produce should not shock us more than the obligation to learn, to which we are subject. One thus establishes among the improvident native a "laboring capital," just as we constitute among Europeans, more or less, an "intellectual capital," when we impose an obligation to attend schools between two determined ages. The obligation we impose on natives to work is often indispensable for the development of colonies. It quickly provokes in natives a taste for labor by the resources that they can procure and which the natives appreciate as a just reward. . . . [By way of conclusion] I repeat that ten kilograms destined for sale represents, in local production, a tiny surface—a third of a hectare at the most—and a very small effort.

The success of Angoulvant's program, however, depended upon a commensurate effort on the part of the administration. Properly selected seeds had to be distributed to native producers, the number of ginning factories increased, and permanent cotton markets established to which producers would transport their crop. Angoulvant stressed that permanent markets and ginneries had to be erected at logical points within the cotton zones to minimize the distance natives would be obliged to transport their cotton. He argued that subventions would also be paid for those who had to transport their cotton beyond specified distances. "During the war," Angoulvant concluded, "we found 200,000 soldiers among our West African populations. It depends on our national will to find there, during peace, 50,000 tons of cotton, which today furnish only 500 tons."[17]

The ACC, whose politique cotonnière had lapsed in West Africa during the war, was not silent during this period, nor was it lacking in supporters. Angoulvant defended the ACC against Yves Henry's attacks. "Without any other goal than the noble ambition to raise the production of cotton, the ACC has put at my disposition, spontaneously and liberally, all that was necessary to the success of the task. This is to say that the results obtained in the Côte d'Ivoire are for the large part its work."[18] Under the leadership of the incumbent president, Gustave Roy, and the incoming one, Arthur Waddington, a Rouen textile industrialist, the ACC launched an aggressive effort to renew and to expand its activities in the field.

In its effort to lay claims to a share of the new politique cotonnière, however, the ACC had to confront the meager results of its previous experience, its meager success in relationship to the oft-compared British Cotton Growers Association, and the virtual elimination of budgetary allocations during the war. Between 1918 and 1921, the ACC reached an agreement with the West Africa Federation's Service d'agriculture over the division of the politique cotonnière, and the ACC underwent an administrative reorganization from which it emerged newly aggressive. The agreement with the Service d'agriculture reiterated the ACC's support of rain-fed cultivation, essentially the pro-peasant position it had always maintained. In response to the negative comparisons with its British counterpart, Roy wrote that "we are exclusively and we will remain an association of propaganda and vulgarization. Our statutes and the prescriptions of the ministerial departments which provide us with subventions, prohibit us from engaging in commercial and financial operations which could result in profits. . . . Our task is essentially disinterested and this is what distinguishes us from the British [Cotton Growers Association]. Moreover, our budget is one hundred thousand francs whereas that of the British association is 70 million francs."[19] To permit the ACC to pursue its action in the field, Gustave Roy convinced industrial spinners to impose a voluntary tax of one franc per bale of imported cotton.[20] The ACC also applied to the Committee on the Liquidation of the Consortium of Cotton for additional funding.[21]

The postwar debates on colonial development were directly linked to metropolitan raw materials needs. The solutions proposed, as I shall examine in this and the following chapters, were aligned along two divergent axes: one school maintained its conviction that metropolitan users of cotton could best be served by assisting African peasants to work in their own interest; the other school, looking at the little success of this peasant model over the previous twenty years, demanded a new departure and a new investment in irrigation with agricultural production under the control of Europeans either directly in the case of private enterprise or indirectly through state supervision. The next section explores more fully the arguments in favor of irrigated agriculture by examining the enterprise of CICONNIC. The experience of CICONNIC is central to the history of the politique cotonnière because many of the policy considerations concerning massive irrigated cotton production, which the Office du Niger was to confront, were played out first there.

The New Egypt: Private Enterprise and Irrigated Cotton Production in the Niger Valley, 1919–1924

Irrigated cotton production in French West Africa had been a seductive dream since the 1860s. Already in 1864, the chief colonial gardener in Senegal, Lecard, compared cotton yields of indigenous, American, and Egyptian varieties in both rain-fed and irrigated plots at Richard-Toll on the Senegal River. The 1864 crop was destroyed by locusts, but the 1865 crop indicated that irrigation increased the yields of all varieties by a factor of ten and, in the case of American cotton, by as much as thirteen. Interest in Senegalese sources of cotton, however, faded in the face of the return of American cotton to pre–Civil War levels. Further interest in irrigating cotton along the Senegal River had to wait until 1903, when a Saint-Louisian trader, Rabaud, returned to Richard-Toll. With a subsidy from the ACC, Rabaud conducted cotton trials. In 1904, the government took over the experiments and placed them under the supervision of the Service d'agriculture. Convinced of the similarities between the Senegal and the Nile river valleys, Yves Henry planted only Egyptian varieties. With generous fertilization and adequate irrigation, three varieties of Egyptian cotton yielded the equivalent of well over one ton of cotton per hectare, a phenomenal increase over rain-fed cotton yields. In 1905–6, the extraordinarily high waters of the Senegal destroyed the experimental cotton crop.[22]

Despite these positive experimental results and despite its proximity to the export termini of Saint Louis and Dakar, developing massive irrigation works in the Senegal River valley posed serious technical and political problems. In the words of Inspector general Julien Barois of the Division of Bridges and Causeways, an "archive of the river" was gradually, if somewhat superficially, being assembled.[23] The data were disconcerting. They indicated that the Senegal River valley was not susceptible to irrigation by gravitation, by far the most efficient method. Moreover, the floodwaters of the Senegal did not correspond to the cycle of cotton. And perhaps most troubling of all, the population of the Senegal River valley was dispersed, it had developed complex property rights regulating access to uplands and river basin, and it had manifested over the past century a certain "hostility" to the colonial endeavor. Interest in the Senegal River valley declined as the ACC and the colonial state shifted their attention to the Soudan and to rain-fed cotton cultivation.[24]

But the dream of irrigation was not completely abandoned. Reports favorable to irrigation were filed by administrators in the lacustrine region of the Niger River from 1907 onward. In 1909, agricultural engineer Vitalis of the Service d'agriculture assessed the possibility of irrigation in the lakes region, downstream from Mopti. In 1910, the lieutenant governor of the Soudan authorized public works engineer Aron to study irrigation along the Niger basin. Although he filed only a cursory report, Aron contributed to the allusion to Egypt. "One day," he wrote in a generally favorable assessment of irrigation, "the Niger will have its Aswan, which will collect a vast reservoir of water and will release it gradually." Aron warned, however, that such a project required enormous temerity, might be impossible to build, and in any case could not be used by the existing population of the region, which was too thinly distributed.[25] The next year, the director of public works in Senegal was dispatched to assess Aron's findings. Amid those trumpeting the glorious future of irrigated cotton along the Niger, Hardel sounded an alarm. Hardel cautioned against making a commitment to such a vast program without first conducting detailed studies of hydrology and agronomy. He also urged that a pilot project be started. Indeed, Hardel was shocked to discover that despite the long years of debate, he could not find one detailed study of irrigated cotton production along the Niger. Instead, Hardel called for a more practical solution centered on raising the shores of Lake Debo, thereby creating a vast reservoir in an existing floodplain.[26]

Engineer René Younès was next commissioned to study both the Senegal and Niger rivers. The outbreak of the war interrupted his mission. After a delay of five years, Governor-General Clozel renewed the studies on irrigation. He commissioned Vitalis to conduct cotton experiments using Egyptian long-staple varieties under irrigated conditions in 1917–18 at El-Oualadji agricultural station in the lacustrine region of the Niger River. By irrigating at critical points between July and November, Vitalis managed to squeeze out nearly three tons of cotton per hectare.[27] The allusion to the Nile was now complete: not only were the climates of the two areas and the hydrology of the rivers apparently analogous, but Egyptian cotton seemed to thrive under the right conditions. This was the evidence that tipped Marcel Hirsch's interest to the Niger River.

In 1917, Hirsch submitted to the Ministry of Colonies a proposal for a massive cotton irrigation project in both the Senegal and Niger valleys. In support of his project, Hirsch drew upon somewhat dubious evidence generated by Younès, Vitalis, and "Egyptian personalities, experts in cotton production" he had commissioned. Despite his efforts to make his project conform to the debates on cotton and to place it within the "national interest," Hirsch's project was in trouble by 1918. Marius Etesse, director of the Service d'agriculture, argued that Hirsch's project was too vast and that it would result in "the abandonment of all progress [in the Senegal River] valley to the monopoly of a private company. Such a monopoly does not strike me as the best way to develop a country."[28] The administration of French West Africa was nearly unanimous in its concern that Hirsch's project would undermine the authority of the state and compromise the future of irrigated cotton. Minister of Colonies Simon was concerned that the cotton experiments thus far conducted were far from conclusive and suggested that Hirsch limit his enterprise to a "société d'études."[29]

Hirsch returned to French West Africa late in 1918 to salvage his project and pursue negotiations with the administration. The Ministry of Colonies and the administration in French West Africa could not long ignore the emerging debates on metropolitan industrial reconstruction. Under the new governor-general, Martial Merlin, Hirsch entered into an agreement with the government of French West Africa for the establishment of a scaled-down irrigation project on the banks of the Niger at Dire, some ten kilometers downstream from the El-Oualadji, where Vitalis had just had such fantastic success with Egyptian cotton. To cement ties with the administration, Hirsch appointed Vitalis and Desbandes, both of El-Oualadji, and de Loppinot, the administrator of Goundam in which Dire was situated, to senior administrative posts in the new company.[30]

The convention concluded between Hirsch and the government of French West Africa conceded to the role of private capitalist enterprise in cotton production, but it severely constrained the powers of the company over a more limited concession. The convention also stipulated specific financial and performance conditions, which had to be met before more land would be granted. Hirsch had to invest 300,000 francs of his personal funds in a corporation that was initially to have a capital of 2 million and eventually 20 million francs. The government of French West Africa committed 800,000 francs to Hirsch's company, particularly to the task of "managing the waters," but to be paid in four equal payments, which corresponded to the four-stage increase in the company's capitalization. The company promised to repay this interest-free loan from the profits remaining after deductions for capital development and after paying shareholders a maximum of 8 percent per year.

The convention granted CICONNIC rights to 100,000 hectares, although access to this land was pegged to the company's performance. First, title to the land was provisional until the company had developed cotton production within the context of stipulated crop rotations. Second, the company had to produce 500 tons of cotton from the initial concession of 2,000 hectares within six years in order to claim further land. Third, from each subsequent concession of 1,000 hectares, the company had to produce 75 tons of cotton. And fourth, the company had the right to request noncontiguous concessions within the broadly defined zone of the lakes region.[31] Following the signing of the convention, Hirsch also received a significant grant from the liquidation of the funds of the Consortium of Cotton.[32]

Hirsch moved quickly. Within less than one year, Hirsch founded the company, assembled its management, hired Egyptian engineers, chose the initial concession, bought tractors, pumps, ginneries, and other equipment, shipped them to Dire, and constructed dwellings and buildings on site. Moreover, plowing the fields and leveling the concession were under way in preparation for planting.[33] Formidable as this task was—Dire was 800 kilometers from the railhead at Koulikoro—it paled in comparison to the subsequent tasks of assembling a labor force and of cultivating cotton profitably. In these two areas—labor recruitment and cotton production—the experiences of CICONNIC lay at the heart of the debates surrounding the future of cotton in the Soudan.

Although the government of French West Africa had agreed to support Hirsch's project of irrigated cotton production under the direction of European management, lower-level administrators were far from unanimous in committing themselves to subordinating African labor to European capital. Many still harbored an ideological commitment to the notion that Africans were inherently rational in their economic choices and that given the right conditions, they would act to satisfy European demands, whether for labor or for crops. Recruiting labor for CICONNIC put these assumptions to the test as the new director at Dire made clear. De Loppinot, the former administrator of Goundam and probably never a partisan of the pro-peasant option, wrote to the lieutenant governor in the Soudan:

Permit me first of all to thank you for the moral support which you have offered our enterprise, which is even more precious to us than the 800,000 francs which the governor-general gave us so liberally. But 800,000 work days would help us even more for capital has no value unless it can be transformed into labor power.

You know the native perfectly well and you know that he will not exert himself beyond what is strictly necessary. Once he has paid the tax and assured his existence for several months, he will not work except under pressure from the authorities. . . . I am also aware that the local government does not furnish workers indiscriminately to all the enterprises, especially as a result of the recruitment drive of 1915–16 which occasioned the theory, current in certain circles, concerning the "return to slavery for the profit of capitalism."

Do we, however, want to develop our colonies and have them produce that which we have a right to expect of them? If yes, then it is necessary to assist those companies, which rely on natives and which are incapable at the moment of engaging in large-scale agriculture. If, on the contrary, one wishes to abandon these enterprises to their own devices, would it not have been better not to have encouraged them in the first place? [34]

As a former administrator, de Loppinot was certainly aware of the recent decisions enacting minimum compensation for labor recruited for public works projects.[35] "Our conditions of employment," he noted, "are actually more advantageous than those of the public works gangs. . . . I respectfully point out, that a monthly salary of 35 francs in Kayes cercle, where the tax is very high and where the cost of living is double what it is here, means that the 22.50 francs per month prevailing at Hirschville corresponds to 40 or 45 francs at Kayes."[36] De Loppinot concluded with a request for government assistance in securing labor for the activities of CICONNIC, by requisition if necessary.

Although Marcel Olivier was lieutenant governor of the Soudan from 1919 to 1924, Jean Henri Terrasson de Fougères acted as lieutenant governor during Olivier's absences. Terrasson succeeded Olivier in 1924 and remained as lieutenant governor until 1931. He was an able administrator with strong convictions. It is not surprising that Terrasson's opinions and actions during his extraordinary tenure loom especially large during this critical period in the history of the politique cotonnière. In response to de Loppinot's request for requisitioned labor, he wrote that "it is not possible for me to enter into the path you indicate. . . . If that solution were taken, all the agricultural concessions and industries installed in the colony would make similar requests." Terrasson was committed to the idea of a free labor market, and he was convinced that Africans would respond positively to attractive economic inducements.

You must know that the lakes region is particularly well placed for the native to work under excellent conditions. The lands are rich and abundant, and the producer can always find a market for his commodities at profitable rates. Moreover, the river offers a means of transport at low cost. It is thus evident, that with the salaries you offer, and given the cost of living, you will find only a few workers in the villages near your concession. There are, however, regions further away where the population is denser and where natives are prepared to hire out their services. But the people of Koutiala, Sikasso, or San will never accept to travel to the district of Goundam, whose name they are unfamiliar with, whose climate is different from their own, where there has never before been one of their own, for 22.50 francs per month. If you want the administrators of these districts to find voluntary labor for you, I think that the salary offered should be 30 to 35 francs per month with a daily ration at the very least.

De Loppinot's request for labor was nothing new to the administration. Terrasson had already established an *embouchage*, a kind of recruitment office, organized by district officers, for those seeking work. Each district fixed its own rate of pay, and administrators informed the African recruits what the rates were in different regions, although wage labor was in demand almost exclusively in Kayes. "It is only the offer of salaries," Terrasson stressed, "which induces them to leave their villages. The largest number of workers actually come from the districts of Koutiala and Nara, where the native finds it difficult to sell his products."[37]

Not finding the administration receptive to his original argument, de Loppinot pursued his case for requisitioned labor on a different track. He argued in correspondence with the lieutenant governor that the irrigation works, to which the governor-general contributed significant capital, would eventually revert to the colony. It was, by its very nature, a commercially disinterested endeavor that warranted labor requisitioned along lines similar to projects in the public interest.[38] Terrasson would not accept this argument either, and he responded that even if certain projects were eventually part of the public domain, that was not sufficient to categorize the spirit of the entire enterprise.[39] With considerable tenacity, de Loppinot pursued the same argument with Governor-General Merlin. Merlin had, after all, been a signatory to the original convention with Hirsch. And indeed, Merlin overruled Terrasson. He wrote to Camille Maillet, who was chosen as acting lieutenant governor in 1920, that he "wished to see the local authorities give their support to enterprises which have as their goal the cultivation of cotton," and he ordered the administration of the Soudan to recruit sufficient labor to satisfy de Loppinot's needs. By the end of September 1920 convoys of recruited labor were making their way to Dire.[40]

When Olivier returned as lieutenant governor at the beginning of 1921, he took the middle ground between Maillet and Terrasson on the issue of labor recruitment. Olivier could not ignore Merlin's orders, but he instructed administrators first to assemble voluntary workers for CICONNIC and only then to resort to impressment. Few workers were willing to work for CICONNIC; no volunteers were forthcoming from the districts of San, Sikasso, Bandiagara, or Timbuktu; of the 220 workers from Bamba, only 6 were volunteers; only the district of Gao furnished 234 volunteers between 1921 and 1922.[41] As late as January 1927, even with monthly salaries running at 52.50 francs, only 63 of 1,624 contractual workers at CICONNIC were voluntary.[42] Throughout its history, CICONNIC was never able to satisfy its labor needs within the play of free market forces.

Faced with the need to maintain a performance schedule determined even before construction began, management had little leeway in its labor demands. In 1921, de Loppinot floated the idea of moving an entire village to Dire as a means of alleviating the disinclination of workers to sign on to long contracts far from friends and family. De Loppinot had in mind the rebellious village of Tabi in Bandiagara, whose move to Dire would send a signal to other potentially rebellious villages and whose labor could be disciplined as a punitive measure. Lieutenant Governor Olivier would not agree, but he did squeeze out of the company a commitment to subvene the costs of transport for each worker who came with his wife and to provide her with reduced rations during the tenure of her husband's contract. Inspector General Kair lent authority to the concept of internal colonization when he wrote that "the best farmers are the Bambara, who are not satisfied at Dire because of the distance which separates them from their home villages. . . . The company has started to attract and above all retain workers by establishing villages where they can live with their families and where they can engage in herding and farming using the waters from the irrigation canals. . . . A school will be built which the children of the workers can attend as well as the adults."[43]

Especially after 1926, the company would turn increasingly to internal colonization, but because of the nature of working conditions, voluntary recruitment and internal colonization did not solve CICONNIC's labor needs.[44]

In his official inspection of CICONNIC in 1923, Kair uncovered management's strategy to retain labor by erecting a company store. CICONNIC management contracted with the French commercial house of Danel to establish a retail outlet in Hirschville, where both "European and native personnel can provision themselves." The establishment of a Danel outlet caused a series of complaints, both from other merchants and from workers. The merchants, who had been attracted to Dire in anticipation of the commercial opportunities servicing the new community's needs, complained to Kair that the company store violated the principles of commercial freedom. Workers complained because part of their salary was paid in coupons, redeemable only at Danel. Hirsch responded that the Danel outlet was only a service rendered to the company's employees, in which he had no commercial interest. Although Kair was generally sympathetic to Hirsch's enterprise, he rejected this argument and said that the store was reminiscent of the system of company canteens prohibited by metropolitan law.[45]

Management's reliance on forced labor meant that desertion by workers was commonplace. Management tried to dissuade workers from leaving before the end of their contracts, and it tried to control work on the job. De Loppinot was accused of beating workers. But the central tactic management employed was to restrict salary payments by establishing a "nest egg." Management justified withholding 43 percent of all workers' salaries under the guise of enforced savings, arguing that otherwise they would waste it before the end of the contract and have nothing to show for their efforts.[46] But management also imposed discipline by deducting wages. Thus management's efforts to discipline labor in response to the difficulties of labor recruitment made recruitment even more difficult. But labor was only one of the problems CICONNIC faced in the years between 1920 and 1926.

The Nile allusion, so useful to the politics Hirsch and CICONNIC pursued, carried hidden costs. The first was the assumption of an abundance of labor. Unlike the Nile delta, the Soudan was not densely populated. Labor was thus not freely available, and labor costs were high. The second problem was the choice of cotton variety. Henry's yields at Richard-Toll along the Senegal River and Vitalis's at El-Oualadji demonstrated the potential of irrigated production of Egyptian cotton varieties. Egyptian cotton, however, accounted for less than 10 percent of the total supply of French industrial needs. Egyptian cotton was a long-staple variety, which catered to users at the upper end of the metropolitan market. The bulk of French requirements were for medium staple supplied by American cotton farmers. Because Egyptian cotton was among the world's most expensive, its potential for substituting for the American staple was extremely limited.

For a project such as CICONNIC, whose management used the vocabulary of "national interest," the decision to plant Egyptian cotton would seem a contradiction. CICONNIC, however, was a private enterprise, whose success or failure was measured in profit and loss. Because Dire was far from coastal embarkation points, costs of transport and production were high. Hirsch needed a product that could carry these extra costs and still return a profit.

In late spring 1921, CICONNIC was ready to plant its first crop. On an 80-hectare plot, CICONNIC planted Mitafifi, Sakellaridis, and Zagora, all Egyptian long-staple varieties. The harvest yielded 40 tons, of which ginning produced 14 tons of fiber. This was a start, but CICONNIC was far from reaching the performance goals stipulated in the 1919 convention. In 1922–23, the company planted 267 hectares and in 1923–24, 848 hectares. In 1921–22, the average yield per hectare was 600 kilograms; in 1922–23, it fell to 468; and in 1923–24, it rose to nearly 900 kilograms per hectare. Although these yields did not compare to those of the experimental farms, they were respectable and encouraging.

The commencement of production brought new difficulties. By the time the harvest and ginning were completed, the waters of the Niger near Dire had receded and the cotton could not be exported until the next flood. Management was also finding it increasingly difficult to provision the pumping machines with easily accessible wood because in the dry sahel region of Dire, trees were few and widely scattered. The pumps consumed more than 700 tons of wood each year.[47] These logistical problems help account for Hirsch's pursuit of three additional concessions further upstream. In 1924, CICONNIC claimed an additional 8,000 hectares in Saga, Dioro, and Senenkou, between Sinsani and Mopti on the southern fringes of the interior delta. Without more than a cursory examination by Hirsch's Egyptian "experts," the company began preparations for planting Egyptian cotton there.[48]

The 1924-25 crop at Dire, however, was a disaster. Although 960 hectares were planted, yields per hectare fell to 219 kilograms. After ginning, the company had only 68 tons of cotton fiber. The collapse of the 1924-25 harvest was the result of a combination of faulty management and unsound agronomic practices. The company had opted for extensive cultivation, but it did not invest in adequate fertilization and did not rotate crops annually to regenerate the soil. Moreover, the company often left cotton plants in the ground for a second year, thus jeopardizing the quality of the entire crop. Plants left in the ground for a second year spawned cotton parasites and led to degeneration of the cotton strain because of uncontrolled cross-fertilization with indigenous varieties. Later studies also revealed that the company had not conducted adequate soil analysis, for the region around Dire was composed of heavy colloidal clays, which when submerged during irrigation became even denser and choked the plants. A study conducted by the agronomist Vuillet in 1923 also indicated that to give the impression that Egyptian cotton was a correct choice CICONNIC management inflated the yields by underrecording the acreage planted. According to Vuillet, yields per hectare were about half what the company reported.[49]

The company was thus in serious trouble, although the yields for 1925-26 of 366 kilograms for each of 934 hectares were the best yet and provided a brief reprieve. Evidence on CICONNIC's performance was not yet public knowledge when the Comité du Niger sponsored a public scrutiny of Bélime's model of irrigated cotton production.

The Bélime Controversy

At center stage in the debate surrounding the irrigation model of colonial development was the publication in late 1923 or 1924 of a slim volume, *Les Irrigations du Niger: Discussions et controverses*, in which Bélime provided eloquent rebuttals to selected critiques. These critiques were taken from the published record of 1921 and 1922, and they addressed Bélime's 1921 study. The volume was published by the Comité du Niger, founded in 1921 to provide a forum for those supporting the irrigation model.

The controversy centered on Bélime's proposals for the massive irrigation of the Niger River valley. All the protagonists—Julien Barois, whom we encountered earlier, Auguste Chevalier, a leading colonial agronomist, François Bernard, an advocate of colonial development, and Yves Henry, whose postwar studies on irrigation helped shape the language of the debate—were sympathetic to colonial development in general and to irrigation in particular. Their disagreements with Bélime's project were usually technical in nature, and they addressed issues such as the scope of the actual project, its appropriateness, and the supply of labor. Those supporting the alternative pro-peasant position were not represented at all.

Bélime's program for irrigation was audacious in its scope and scale, but it fit directly within the metropolitan debates on raw materials and on colonial development. Bélime and his project became the unifying element of one group of a larger pro-colonial faction within metropolitan politics. The Comité du Niger, a political action and propaganda group favoring irrigation along the Niger, was founded in 1921 with a leadership drawn from former colonial administrators and military heroes.[50] The committee found in Bélime an articulate spokesman, whose mastery of the literature on irrigation and colonial development was impressive. But Bélime was also impetuous. He was a man of action, who was intolerant of what he considered lack of national will. In response to Barois's and Bernard's concern that the data on the Niger River were not yet adequate to permit the investment of massive capital, Bélime responded that "for more than twenty years we have examined the question of cotton in French West Africa and yet we are still in the stammering phase of our early infancy, because of the time we have lost discussing and doing nothing. The verdict of the history of this period of inaction will one day be written. . . . Nothing counts but action, nothing is possible without a persevering faith allied to a unity of view and a taste for action."[51] Bélime's project, however, did not meet with universal approval.

The Comité du Niger privileged three dissenting voices in its volume. They were those of Chevalier, Henry, and Bernard. Chevalier established the agenda for the debate when he identified five points of disagreement with Bélime's project: scope, time frame, manpower, technical qualities, and crop choice. "For a project this vast," Chevalier wrote, "we are tempted to say grandiose, one has to consider the capacities of the country." Such massive irrigation, Chevalier warned, entailed heavy reliance upon Europeans to oversee construction and subsequent management. It also entailed a virtual transformation of agricultural practices for which the Africans were not prepared. Chevalier doubted whether the eleven-year time frame Bélime had anticipated was realistic. Bélime had argued that an initial trial on the right bank of the Niger between the Sotuba rapids could be completed within three years and that an additional eight years were needed to construct the remaining dam at Sansanding and to build the Nyamina and Sansanding canals. Bélime expected that the Segu canal would irrigate fully 750,000 hectares between the Niger and Bani rivers—virtually half of the entire region—of which one-third would be in cotton. Such an expansion of production, Chevalier noted, would require significant immigration of workers, most likely from the more densely populated Mossi region, for example. But Africans, he argued, would not willingly leave the homes of their ancestors permanently.

In a cursory manner, which Bernard later developed more fully, Chevalier noticed Bélime's tendency to describe the program as a whole without paying adequate attention to technical detail. In particular, Chevalier accused Bélime of underestimating both the costs of construction and time to completion. In what was probably the strongest attack on the project, Chevalier described an alternative model of irrigation developed by public works engineer Hardel, which was presented at the 1918 Congrès d'agriculture coloniale. In contrast to Bélime's 1921 project, Hardel proposed to take advantage of the natural geographic endowments of the lakes region of the Niger's inland delta. Hardel described how, for an expenditure of a mere 250,000 francs, a dam at Gande-Tama would feed a reservoir capable of irrigating nearly 11,000 hectares. Hardel also proposed a grander project, to irrigate nearly 250,000 hectares by raising the banks of Lake Debo and creating a reservoir of 1,000 square kilometers. In contrast to Bélime, Hardel framed his program in terms of the resettlement of nomads and the development of beef exports to the metropole. Hardel also warned that the Nile analogy was simplistic and that significant differences in demography, hydrology, and location vitiated the utility of drawing on the Egyptian experience.[52]

Chevalier concluded his critique of Bélime with his worry that massive investment in irrigation in the Soudan was misplaced. The distance to the ocean was far and, more important, cotton was not a crop that necessarily repaid the initial investment. Cotton, he argued, could be grown successfully in the rain-fed regions of Togo, Dahomey, and the Côte d'Ivoire without recourse to irrigation. Chevalier ended with a nod in the direction of the pro-peasant development model: "The most urgent task in the Soudan at this time is to assist the African to improve his agricultural practices and to ensure that he will be able to sell his products at higher prices."[53]

Although it is not clear whether he was aware of Chevalier's attack, Bernard vigorously pursued the same issues. "At the limits of the Sahara, in a desiccated and nearly desert land, Bélime evokes a new Egypt . . . an enormous granary, created in one simple action by a magnificent effort of French genius. The belief is so marvelous, the appearances so seductive that one does not ask if the task is realizable." According to Bernard, the problem with Bélime's project derived in part from analogies. "It is the Nile, due to the regularity of its flood and the utilization of its waters that created Egypt. The Soudan possesses, as does Egypt, a large river, subject also to regular floods. Therefore, why do we not realize a parallel project in the Soudan?" The test, Bernard added, ought to be how well the utility of an enterprise compared to the sacrifices involved.[54] And in this matter, he found Bélime's project fundamentally deficient. The subtext of Bernard's argument was an effort to demonstrate that the Nile analogy did not fit the Soudan, but it did apply to another part of the French empire.

Bernard demonstrated that Bélime's basic preparation of technical data was faulty. Plans for the Segu canal, for example, were drawn without having adequate survey data. How, Bernard asked, could an engineer plan construction by gravitation without access to such basic data as contour lines? Bernard also accused Bélime of seriously underestimating construction costs. The Segu canal, for example, would enter an irrigable zone at kilometer 200 and the costs per hectare would therefore have to include expenditure for this unusable distance. Moreover, Bernard accused Bélime of using data on irrigation costs derived from one project in India. Bernard demonstrated that when this one case was compared to other irrigation projects in India and those in Java, Turkistan, and Afghanistan, the costs per hectare were considerably higher. Thus the costs of the Segu canal should be calculated at three to four times that which Bélime estimated.[55]

Bernard argued that instead of being analogous, Egypt and the Soudan were very different. Egypt's rich delta, where irrigation was practiced, was close to the ocean, which facilitated the evacuation of agricultural products. In contrast, Segu was 1,700 kilometers from the ocean. The densely populated Nile delta contained 450 people per square kilometer compared to 4 or 5 in the Segu region. Moreover, Egyptian peasants were accustomed by many centuries of irrigated farming to the meticulous tasks of production and management. The farmers of Segu were, according to Bernard, inept and unskilled. From his calculations, derived from similar ones conducted by Henry, Bernard estimated that irrigated farming required a minimum of two farmers per hectare, which meant that the 750,000 hectares fed by the Segu canal would require 1,500,000 workers to produce 100,000 tons of cotton per year. With only 150,000 people in the entire Segu district, how, Bernard asked, would this miracle be realized? Bernard was critical of Bélime's facile belief that within 20 or 30 years the Niger Valley would be densely populated by natural growth and colonization.[56]

Despite his criticism, Bernard did not abandon Sarraut's colonial development model or the Nile analogy. He merely shifted its focus. "In order to obtain rapidly a considerable production, we must find more favored regions, which are more densely populated and where the native has for a long time been accustomed to relatively complex agricultural tasks and where transport is relatively inexpensive. In all our colonial domain, Indochina is the only area which currently fits these conditions. At this time, six million hectares are cultivated; even if one-tenth of this area were devoted to cotton, within a short delay, the region could furnish the metropole with one-half of its raw cotton currently bought on foreign markets."[57]

Although sharing a basic consensus on the future of irrigated production in French West Africa, Yves Henry's criticism of Bélime's project also touched on areas ranging from agronomic to financial. The controversies book contained extracted parts from several of Henry's voluminous publications on cotton. Most appropriate, however, were those derived from his 1922 book, based on a prestudy of the Segu canal. Henry was fully in accord with the efforts of the Comité du Niger to open Bélime's project to the fullest scrutiny. "An enterprise of this scope, which lies at the very heart of the political and economic life of a land, which depends heavily on the credit of France, and which will be passionately discussed in all circles and in parliament, must be prepared in minute detail and in good conscience, lest it fall into certain disaster." Besides the array of technical issues Henry raised, none of which were fundamentally contradictory to the basic premises of Bélime's project, he privileged the issue of labor. "The importance of irrigation systems is a function of the factors of production, of which one is determinant: manpower." Henry estimated that if the Soudan were to supply all the needs of metropolitan spinners, it would need to produce 300,000 tons annually. Based on a good average yield of 300 kilograms per irrigated hectare, at least one million hectares of cotton needed to be cultivated under irrigated conditions. And because cotton cultivation under irrigation required considerable inputs of fertilizer and given the paucity of available fertilizers, a three-year crop rotation was needed to ensure the fertility of the soil. If at least one million hectares needed to be in cotton at any one time, then three million hectares had to be irrigable. Next, Henry assumed that if each hectare required three workers, three million hectares would require nine million workers living exclusively from cotton and from the crops rotated in. When considering also the diverse occupations necessary to assist irrigated production, the total population envisioned was more than eleven million. Although Henry admitted that the resources in land and water were probably adequate for Bélime's project, he doubted whether the manpower resources were. Henry speculated that even with the most optimistic demographic projections of an emigration from the most densely populated districts and a quadrupling of the population within 60 years—as had the population of Brazil—only three and one-half million workers would be available to work 900,000 hectares of which only a third would be in cotton. At best, Henry conceded, the Soudan could provide 100,000 tons of cotton for metropolitan use.[58]

Henry also argued that the projections of the amount of land the Segu canal could irrigate were vastly inflated. Instead of the 750,000 hectares Bélime envisioned, Henry demonstrated that the terrain through which the canal would run was considerably broken and that at best only half of the acreage Bélime anticipated would actually be irrigated. Moreover, most of that would be in smaller, scattered parcels. Henry, like Hardel, preferred the potential of the interior delta with its already existing lake reservoirs and its richer alluvial soils. Development in the lakes region, however, had to confront the disadvantage of distance from the railhead. And in that regard, Henry suggested, the Senegal River valley, which he had always favored, presented even more advantages. Henry concluded his assessment by reiterating his conviction that French West Africa was capable of satisfying France's requirements for cotton but that informed decisions must be made only after exhaustive preliminary studies.[59]

Bélime responded to these criticisms in *Discussions et controverses*, which he then incorporated into his 1925 volume, *La Production du coton*. Taken together, these books represent the fullest defense of irrigation in the Soudan and became the intellectual blueprint for the Office du Niger, which was constituted in 1932. In response to public scrutiny, Bélime argued eloquently in favor of his solution to the supply of cotton to France, but he was shrewd enough to realize that he must reduce the scope of his project lest he risk losing it altogether. By 1927, he jettisoned the Nyamina canal. The Segu canal never delivered the waters of the Niger beyond the cluster of new agricultural villages surrounding Nienebale and Baguinda.[60] Only the dam at Sansanding and the several canals it fed remained part of the scaled-down but still immense irrigation project.

In response to criticism by Bernard and Henry, Bélime developed a more thoughtful defense of the labor issue in the development of irrigated cotton production. In *Discussions et controverses*, he responded to the numbers game by figuring the manpower requirements differently. Instead of assuming labor needs per hectare, as Henry did, Bélime cited labor inputs per ton of cotton produced in the major irrigation projects in India, Turkistan, the western United States, and Egypt. By dividing the tonnage produced by the population resident in the irrigated districts, Bélime came to a set of labor estimates considerably smaller than Henry's. Instead of the eleven to fourteen million inhabitants Henry estimated, Bélime demonstrated that the labor needs were actually one-third of Henry's calculations. Bélime concluded by asserting that the Soudan already had sufficient labor to assure an irrigated cotton harvest equal to the needs of metropolitan industry.[61] The only problem, he admitted, was the current distribution of that population.

The distribution of population was not the result of natural selection but of "wars which bloodied the land in the nineteenth century and devastated and depopulated the Soudan and the valleys of the Niger. The numerous ruins along the shores of the rivers from Felou to Bandiagara are irrefutable testimony to the long years of devastation, dispersement, and carnage."[62] Bélime was convinced that once opportunities existed, workers would return to the Niger Valley.[63] This was, he argued, how workers had responded to the construction of irrigation projects in the United States, India, and the Anglo-Egyptian Sudan.

Bélime had changed his mind on the methods of labor recruitment since his 1921 study, in which he had made a case for both agricultural wage labor and indigenous colonization. His 1925 study stressed indigenous colonization. Bélime drew his inspiration from Governor-General Carde's important circular of 1924 and from the current difficulties CICONNIC and the Société auxiliaire africaine encountered in recruiting and retaining labor. In 1924 Carde identified two preexisting African models of labor mobilization for agricultural work: the recurring pattern of forming agricultural hamlets on the fringes of cultivated land because of the long periods of fallow and the annual cycles of migration to the groundnut fields of Senegambia and to the cocoa groves of the Ivory and Gold coasts.[64] Bélime expanded Carde's cursory remarks into a major argument favoring internal patterns of migration and resettlement. "One of the most striking aspects of colonization, which takes place throughout most of the Soudan, proves that the native is susceptible to powerful driving forces, which are capable of dividing his village, which is the only political and economic unit of these primitive societies able to resist all domination. Generally as a consequence of the rule of survival, but also as a result of conflicts within families, a group of inhabitants settles elsewhere. . . . This form of colonization can be easily applied to the development of the Niger [irrigated] lands and it is easy to imagine how to adapt it to these purposes." Bélime also developed a case for assuming that the inherent rationality of the seasonal agricultural workers to move annually to Senegambia or the southern forests could be applied to the Niger Valley cotton development. "If centers of intense economic activity are created and prosper in regions more accessible to the Soudanese population, and if the workers are offered similar advantages, there is no reason to doubt that the same phenomena of attraction and the same patterns of immigration would not be oriented to the new areas of production."[65]

In contrast to the rationality of these indigenous patterns of labor mobilization, Bélime attacked forced recruitment of labor. Although he was convinced that CICONNIC enjoyed a good reputation among workers—witnessed by the number of contract renewals—Bélime argued that forced recruitment was justified only for public works projects. As a system of labor organization, forced recruitment was absurd, archaic, and reminiscent of the corvée of the pharaohs of ancient Egypt. Well-regulated and supervised recruitment could prove to be immensely popular, however, especially with young male workers assured of returning home with 300 or 400 francs. Central to the success of voluntary recruitment was the "nest egg," a guaranteed form of savings. "This formula," Bélime wrote, "unassailable in theory, has given only mediocre results in practice."[66]

Throughout the section of his 1925 book on labor and colonization, Bélime maintained fundamentally contradictory arguments. On the one hand, he was convinced of the inherent rationality of indigenous methods of labor recruitment and supply; but on the other hand, he disdained the qualities of African workers. "There are things," he wrote, "that the Bambara and the Bobo just do not easily grasp." He favored European-managed cotton plantations but worried about the costs to workers' morale in the face of discipline on the job and the new social circumstance of living outside the confines of the native village. "Numerous are the requisitioned workers who died of simple neurasthenia." Given the right conditions, the black could and would produce and reproduce sufficiently to satisfy the needs of the metropole and the goals of economic development. "In Virginia, Georgia, Florida, Louisiana, and in the other states along the Mississippi, the black imported from Africa has multiplied, accustomed himself to work, and in the course of 150 years, he has become a human type with a rare vigor. If his intellectual and moral qualities are less well developed, his role in the economic order is incontestable. It is in effect the American Negro who produces three-quarters of the cotton consumed in the entire world."[67] Bélime rested his case on his unshaken belief in the future of the irrigation model for cotton production in the Soudan and on his general disdain for the practical side of colonial development planning.

Despite the accumulating evidence that irrigated cotton production under European management was ill-suited to the agronomic and labor conditions of the Niger Valley, proponents of irrigation rode a wave of ministerial and public support which effectively blocked public debate and scrutiny of the assumptions and calculations upon which the irrigation model of cotton development rested. Following a favorable assessment of the Segu canal by the Compagnie générale des colonies, a consortium of French banks and engineering and public works companies, work began on the derivation dam at Sotuba and an experimental portion of the canal in 1925. The dam and the canal were opened in 1929.

In this chapter, I examined the renewal of the politique cotonnière during the period from 1918 to 1924. This was when the initiative in colonial development thinking was held by those favoring irrigation, and in particular by Marcel Hirsch, the entrepreneur, and Emile Bélime, the ambitious colonial official. Bélime, in particular, was responsible for articulating and justifying a model of cotton colonialism which expressed the seductive allure of the big, technically sophisticated development project. The big project rested upon a belief that the managers could actually control the forces of nature and the actions of Africans. Land and water along the Niger River seemed readily at hand. Labor, however, was not. The next chapter develops more fully the politics of labor recruitment within the context of the debates to promote cotton production for export. The debates about labor and labor recruitment reveal deep tensions within the colonial state and between the proponents of the irrigation model and those who remained pro-peasant.

CHAPTER SEVEN

The Problem of Labor, 1924–1932

In recruiting labor for CICONNIC, the colonial state rendered private enterprise an invaluable service, for without direct state assistance European-managed cotton enterprises would never have acquired the labor they needed. But not all administrators were comfortable with this task. The senior administration in the Soudan was generally cool to the labor demands of private enterprise, and by 1926 it was no longer willing to serve European cotton concessions without extracting from them safeguards and guarantees for African workers. As the administration became reluctant to recruit labor for these private enterprises, it pressured them to develop alternative models of labor use. Between 1926 and 1932, the colonial state and private enterprise experimented with several forms of sharecropping and internal colonization.

In this chapter, I examine the colonial state's major cotton development policy statement—the Carde program of 1924—and in particular the role of African labor within it. The Carde program conceived of cotton development in much broader terms than did the proponents of the European-managed capital-intensive irrigation model. Under Carde's 1924 program, labor was one of a handful of "problems" that had plagued the goal of making West Africa the supplier of the metropole's cotton needs. From finding itself a servant to private enterprise's demands for labor in the early 1920s, the colonial state began to engineer alternative conceptions of African labor organization on irrigated cotton fields. As I develop in Chapter 8, the colonial state also supported the role of Africans as primary producers of cotton under rain-fed conditions. Under these conditions, the state did not see its role as a manager of the labor supply; instead, it saw its task as managing the quality of cotton by influencing production decisions at the level of the cotton fields and managing the marketing of cotton.

A central issue in the Carde program and in the subsequent policy debates was the divergent assessments of the African as a worker and as a rational economic actor. Positions on this issue had already been taken in the Bélime controversy, and they remained critical in this period as the administration's efforts to help private cotton enterprises meet their labor needs resulted in a labor scandal. The scandal at the Société auxiliaire africaine (SAA) concession in 1925 was bound to happen, for the labor system organized on the European-managed cotton plantations pitted racist managers against reluctant workers in the context of a crop whose return on investment was dubious. The scandal revealed clearly that the program of cotton development rested on cultural representations of Africans as workers which bore little resemblance to the reality of work in the Soudan and on the illusions of national necessity which did not conform to the economic calculus of metropolitan manufacturers. The scandal at the SAA cotton concession at Kenenkou in the Segu district converged with the deteriorating financial condition of many of them and undermined the mix of factors central to the ideological justification of the irrigation model.

The year 1924 stands as an important benchmark in the history of the French colonial cotton program. Through Carde's policy statement of 1924 and in the years thereafter, the colonial state reclaimed some of the initiative it had lost to private enterprise, but it proceeded slowly. Carde's policy statement outlined a broad and ambitious plan. It provided colonial state support for irrigation. It could do no less, especially because of Colonial Minister Sarraut's 1921 statement in support of irrigation and because of the publicity surrounding the Bélime controversy. It also provided support for those who continued to believe that the future of cotton lay with African peasants. This chapter begins with the Carde program of 1924 and then examines the problems facing European-managed cotton plantations and in particular their problems of labor recruitment and meager cotton harvests.

The Carde Program: Cotton and the African Worker

In 1923, Jules Carde replaced Merlin as governor-general. From Merlin's impetuous and inchoate effort to promote cotton production in West Africa and thereby demonstrate the colonies' utility to the metropolitan economy, Carde hammered out a more cautious but also a more ambitious policy. Carde, however, benefited from the

results of Merlin's contract with the Compagnie générale des colonies, a private sector consortium of banks and public works enterprises, to test the agronomic potential and to assess the technical
problems of irrigation in the Niger River valley.[1] Because of the
dearth of qualified cotton experts in France, the company hired an
American, Robert H. Forbes, who had long experience in Arizona and
was also familiar with Egyptian cotton cultivation. Forbes arrived in
the Soudan too late in the spring of 1922 to undertake experiments,
but he was ready in 1923. He coordinated experiments in both rain-
fed and irrigated cotton in Baraweli, Banankoro, and Soninkoura,
which ranged from the heartland of Segu to the shores of Lake Debo.
Forbes's experiments demonstrated the relative inappropriateness of
Egyptian cotton to the Soudanese environment. Because of its long
growing cycle, Forbes noted, Egyptian cotton was not adapted to the
climatic conditions upstream from Lake Debo. Moreover, even under irrigated conditions, yields from Egyptian cotton were less than
220 kilograms per hectare. In contrast, several American varieties
yielded between 1,300 and 2,000 kilograms per irrigated hectare and
were judged "fully good middling" by the cotton brokers of Le Havre.
Forbes had also experimented with several indigenous cotton varieties, whose results were promising. He concluded that "once acclimated, indigenous cotton under irrigation is probably more productive even than recently introduced American varieties."[2] Forbes's
results provided the government of French West Africa with the technical validation it needed to launch an ambitious state-sponsored
cotton program in 1924.

Following two tours of the interior and a careful reading of the
25 years of accumulated evidence on hopes for and trials of cotton,
Carde issued on 15 March 1924 a policy circular addressing the future of cotton in French West Africa. The governor-general avoided
the "doctrinaire discussions, which have sterilized the research and
discredited the conclusions" of so much of this accumulated documentation.[3] Instead, Carde saw a future for both rain-fed and irrigated cotton cultivation.

Carde acknowledged that the task of directing Africans to produce
a better and larger harvest for export was formidable indeed. Most
cotton, he admitted, was consumed locally, and the little that was
exported was not consistently well received by metropolitan users.
Some of the problems in producing better quality and greater quantities of cotton were susceptible to technical solutions, including
wider distribution of light plows, more instruction on crop rotations

and fertilization, better seed selection, and more roads to ease the burden of transporting crops to market. Others were more intractable. The cost of 25 years of failed efforts to promote cotton production for export, Carde noted, was peasant disdain for cotton export markets.

On the one hand, seeds were not distributed at the best time; on the other, no measures were taken to assure that the harvest would be purchased at a price which would leave the producers sufficient profit. It is thus understandable that the peasant would rapidly lose interest in this task, which offered nothing in return but the loss of his time and his money. Thus, the latest reports signal uniformly the abandonment of the "cotton of the whites" which the producer had consigned to the worst fields and had offered the least effort capable of concealing his disinclinations.

But Carde did not consider African producers blameless. "The Soudanese farmer," Carde noted, "is not, in the actual sense of the term, a producer." Even if exports of agricultural commodities had increased since French conquest, this was only the result of the need to have cash to pay taxes and to satisfy his desires for European merchandise. And even if the African producer sold an ever larger part of his harvest, he had not modified his habits and his agricultural practices. Thus, Carde concluded, "the African producer's capacity to work, which was mediocre at best, has not in any significant measure increased." Although Carde modified the pro-peasant bias of some elements of the colonial administration, he remained consistent with the administration in his refusal to countenance forced labor, which, he noted, collided directly with French ideas concerning individual liberty. Forced labor also posed significant practical problems, and it would exacerbate the already troubling situation of emigration from French border regions into British zones. Instead, Carde concluded that in "a goal which is strictly within the humanitarian defense of the native against his own nature, the actions of the administrator no less than those of the scientist and the doctor will be justified if they result in an increase in work which will result in an increase in money necessary to ameliorate his current standard of living."[4]

Besides the sterile debates he so abhorred, Carde recognized that errors in choice of terrain were made during the early years of crop trials. Because of the ubiquity of native cotton throughout the French West African savanna, the early protagonists of cotton paid too little attention to climate. They were ignorant of the recurrent droughts in that zone. With bold strokes, Carde divided French West Africa into two zones: a rain-fed cotton belt composed of territories on the right bank of the Bani River, including San and Bouguni, neighboring cercles, and the areas of adequate rainfall of Guinée, Upper Volta, Dahomey, and upper Côte d'Ivoire; and a zone of uneven and irregular rainfall where irrigation was practicable.

Following Yves Henry, Carde argued that "irrigation has as its first advantage the regularization of production." It also has, Carde quickly added, the capacity to increase yields considerably. Drawing on the transmitted authority of Henry, Bélime, and Sarraut, Carde used the Nile allusion. "The [interior] delta of the Niger," he wrote, "will become, as is the delta of the Nile, a privileged area for large-scale irrigated agriculture." Moreover, recent crop yield data indicated that the Niger's inland delta had the capacity to outperform irrigated cultivation in the Nile delta, Arizona, and Turkistan. Carde acknowledged two possible objections. The first, financial, he dismissed in a manner reminiscent of Sarraut. "From the financial point of view, the objection has no value. Currently the object of a careful study, nothing now indicates that the management of the interior delta cannot be accomplished at the price of a short-term effort, which the finances of the colony can support without difficulty."[5] The second, the supply of labor, required a more considered argument.

Carde admitted that future cotton plains of the Niger Valley were not densely populated, but he argued—and Bélime would elaborate—that two well-established indigenous models of labor supply for agricultural activities already existed. The first was the age-old pattern of creating agricultural hamlets on the outskirts of villages in response to declining fertility of the soil. The second model was the annual migrations of Soudanese farmers to the peanut fields of Senegambia and the cacao groves of the Gold Coast. Carde was convinced that both these models of internal colonization could be channeled to provide labor for the irrigation works along the Niger. Anticipating criticism on this point, Carde argued that nowhere in the arid and semiarid tropics did colonization precede hydraulic works. Labor was attracted to these areas precisely because of new opportunities. To prove his point, Carde pointed to the example of CICONNIC, which he argued had "without difficulty" secured 2,000 voluntary workers. Although Carde's use of the CICONNIC example raises questions about his reading of the available documentation, he used this example to make a political point in opposition to the suggestion that the Niger Valley should become a target for European colonization. European colonization, Carde argued, would not only pose a "dangerous constraint," but it would be unnecessary given Africans' experiences in providing labor and migrating to areas with new agricultural opportunities.[6]

Having charted a general program of political economy for both rain-fed and irrigated cotton production, Carde created a new government agency to oversee these layered tasks. The Service des textiles et de l'hydraulique was designed to coordinate the various administrative, scientific, and technical efforts to encourage cotton production, which had hitherto operated at cross purposes. Not surprisingly, he named Emile Bélime as the new director. Under Bélime's authority would be the farm schools, the experimental stations dealing with cotton and other fiber products, the temporary missions sent to examine various agronomic, zoological, and hydraulic aspects of the production of fibers, and the offices for the classification of export fibers. The costs of many of these new enterprises would be borne from a loan of 3,500,000 francs from the Consortium of Cotton, which was committed to aid the establishment and operation of research on cotton cultivation.

In a more practical vein, Carde elaborated a sixfold program, which he delegated to the lieutenant governors to implement. First, he noted the government's fruitful collaboration with the ACC and indicated that he supported completely its efforts to upgrade and expand ginneries and packing factories. Second, he directed the lieutenant governors to create a network of roads and wharfs to facilitate the transport of cotton to the ginneries. Third, he directed the experimental stations to examine the possibilities of ameliorating native cotton varieties and to expand their extension services. In no case, he warned his subordinates, should producers put their subsistence crops at risk. Fourth, he underlined his belief that American cotton varieties held the most promise but warned that quality and quantities depended upon adequate control over seed selection and protection against unwanted hybridization. Fifth, Carde noted the encouraging results from preliminary studies concerning irrigation at Nienebale, which was to be part of the Segu canal Bélime had proposed. Carde also commissioned further studies of irrigation in the delta region and of internal colonization. Finally, Carde stressed the importance of cotton classification, for only adequate classification would provide industrial users with assurances of the quality of Soudanese sources.

Carde concluded his program with a call for the mobilization of a common effort, reminiscent of the language of wartime France. "The military conquest of our colonial empire has not been the work of a single day. We have hardly started the economic conquest. . . . In developing our textile production, we will assist also in the economic liberation of our land."[7]

Carde's program provided new incentives to the politique cotonnière. It did so, however, as the problems in the irrigation model were becoming increasingly evident. The further financial decline of CICONNIC and a labor incident at the Kenenkou plantation of the Société auxiliaire africaine severely tested—and then snapped—the administration's willingness to provide labor for European-managed private cotton plantations. These events also discredited the ideological supports upon which the model was erected, although, paradoxically, supporters of the massive state-sponsored irrigation of the Niger Valley in the form of the Office du Niger escaped this outcome.

The Problem of Labor

Marcel Hirsch may have been at the forefront of the private sector's initiative in the renewed politique cotonnière of the postwar period, but he was not alone.[8] A consortium of French commercial houses, French West African banks, the Dakar–Saint Louis railway, a merchant shipping company, and individual French planters was formed in 1920 to take advantage of the opportunities to expand irrigated cotton production in the Soudan. The Société auxiliare africaine was established on three concessions: at Samanko in the Bamako district and at Kenenkou and Sassila in the Segu district. In 1922, the company had access to 2,800 hectares, of which 600 were in cotton. By the 1925–26 season, 1,200 hectares were in cotton. As Hirsch had done, SAA management asked the governor-general for subventions to expand production, but the request was rejected.[9]

Despite this setback, the company renewed its effort in 1924 to bring the largest possible area under cultivation. Following CICONNIC's lead, the local director of the company turned to the state for assistance in recruiting labor. "We would like to solicit your help in executing as soon as possible our work," he wrote to Terrasson, the lieutenant governor of the Soudan, "by recruiting 75 workers who would arrive here 15 March and another group of 75 workers on 15 May. . . . While we cannot designate the region of recruitment, we would prefer workers from Koutiala, who have rendered us the best work and who do not readily desert." Terrasson agreed, but only after the company promised to abide by a contract modeled on the protections hammered out of the experience of recruiting labor for CICONNIC.[10] But Terrasson was not satisfied with the protections offered workers in the 1920 CICONNIC contract, and in April 1924, just as the new workers were beginning their contracts, he instructed the management of the SAA plantations to deposit half the workers' salaries, which was to constitute their "nest eggs," into the coffers of the administration. By taking the nest egg out of the hands of management, Terrasson hoped to reduce the abuses associated with it in Dire. He was convinced that this would assist in the recruitment and retention of labor.[11]

Cotton, however, was an unforgiving crop, and unless certain tasks were completed at just the right moment, the entire harvest was put in jeopardy. Labor troubles continued to haunt the SAA's operations. Primel, director of the Kenenkou plantation, complained to the governor-general about the late arrival of the second contingent of workers, the continued desertions of contracted labor, and the lack of responsiveness by the local administration to his labor needs. With only thinly disguised contempt, Battesti, the Segu administrator, urged SAA management to use temporary agricultural labor until the contracted labor arrived "without waiting for weeds to invade his concession." The workers from Koutiala, who had probably delayed their departure until they had put their own crops in, eventually arrived.[12]

For its part, SAA management sought greater control over labor by lengthening the contract. Instead of the six-month contract in force in the 1924–25 season, Primel asked the administration to recruit labor on a one-year basis for the 1925–26 season. The six-month contract, Primel argued, left management with serious seasonal labor shortfalls, particularly if workers arrived late at the critical points of planting and harvest. Primel also sought to increase the number of workers on his concessions, in part to work the extra acreage but also to absorb absences and desertions. Terrasson was reaching the end of his limited goodwill toward the SAA when he noted that "Primel asks too much when requesting [another] 300 workers when he already has 400." Moreover, the administration was finding it increasingly difficult to recruit labor, and it felt that it could not condone the lengthening of contracts of those workers already employed. Terrasson argued that the company was bound to honor their promise that workers could return to their villages in the rainy season.[13] The administration's refusal to accede to the company's demands put pressure on management to retain and control the labor it currently employed.

This was the context at the end of December 1925 when Madec, the European overseer of SAA's Kenenkou cotton plantation, beat N'Tji Koulibali unconscious. Koulibali died the next day without regaining consciousness. The Kenenkou management did not inform the Segu administrator of the incident for more than a week, and when he arrived with the local doctor, Koulibali's body was badly decomposed. The doctor's report attributed death to a severe pulmonary infection, although the report described two extremely large bruises on the deceased's spine and neck. "If there was a correlation between the victim's death and the beatings," concluded the doctor, "it is not clear." If the medical report hesitated in assigning cause, Battesti was convinced that Madec had intensely disliked the workers, "who complained, with cause, that he frequently beat them. . . . Let the courts decide." All 25 workers from Koulibali's village deserted.[14]

Cebarama Dembele of Banankoro remembered working for the SAA plantation at Kenenkou when Madec was there. Although he did not recollect the incident with Koulibali, he described labor relations at the Kenenkou and Sassila plantations and the problems of recruitment and desertion.

Question: A white was at Kenenkou, Madec, do you remember him?
Response: What did you say? Madec? I suffered under him. He sprinkled the peanut seeds with gasoline to stop us from eating them. He told us that gasoline kills. We worked for an entire year without being paid. We received a daily ration of millet. [Recruits from] each village designated a cook, who cooked for all of us for fifteen days; we took turns. Workers came from all the villages of the canton. There were eight of us from Banankoro, five from Koukoum, nine from M'Peba. We were 250 workers who worked for a whole year without receiving a penny of our salary. Those who deserted were returned or replaced by their villages.
Question: Did any of the workers come voluntarily?
Response: No. The chief of the canton called all the village chiefs and told them how many workers each had to send. Each village chief, in his turn, called all the household heads and told them what the authorities wanted. After consultation, the desired number were designated from those who had not been called since the last demand for workers. The household head made a choice among the young men of his house, but he did not take the same one twice in a row.[15]

Desertion troubled management and the administration, but the director of the SAA was also concerned about the impact the administration's response to the Koulibali incident would have on labor relations.

Primel wrote to Battesti with copies to Terrasson and the governor-general protesting the administration's response to this unfortunate incident. He wrote that the company would make no formal comments so as not to interfere with justice, but he stressed that he considered the accusation false. He also stressed that the ways in which the administration handled the incident, when one white "mocked" another white in front of African workers, seriously undermined the authority of all Europeans. He concluded by reiterating his request that the administration send additional workers to make up the shortages created by the desertions. Terrasson responded by halting all further administrative recruitment for the company.[16]

In April 1926, 49 workers from the SAA plantations presented themselves to the district administrator in Koutiala, having deserted six months before their contracts expired. They provided additional testimony to the poor working conditions on European-managed cotton plantations. The administrator listed their grievances: "1. they were beaten; 2. they were too frequently punished by withholding their pay; 3. they were made to work even when sick; 4. they were obliged to prepare their own meals after working; and 5. they were refused permission to leave their positions to drink, even during the hottest time of the day."[17] What these workers neglected to say was that late April was when they had to make final preparations for their own crops if they had any expectations of reaping a harvest that year.

In 1927, Terrasson reluctantly resumed recruiting on behalf of the SAA. In a series of letters to management between 1927 and 1928, he told of several new conditions of employment. Wages were to be raised from 1.75 to 2 francs per day and 1 franc was to be retained daily for the nest egg. Daily rations were to be increased to include one kilogram of millet or maize or one-half kilogram of rice, 250 grams of fresh meat or 75 grams of fresh fish, 50 grams of animal or vegetable oil, 20 grams of salt, and 2 grams of condiments. Terrasson also sought to limit how management could discipline workers. "Several of your workers claim to have been brutalized. Even the smallest physical punishment is prohibited; withholding salaries is an unacceptable procedure if this applies to anyone but a man who was absent all day; it is not applicable to a worker whose work is judged insufficient. Daily work must be fixed in a measure that is possible to execute." Management was stunned by the "severity" of Terrasson's tone but agreed to abide by these principles.[18] Desertions, however, continued to plague SAA and other European-managed cotton plantations along the Niger. Justice in the Madec-Koulibali case was eventually rendered. Madec was fined 100 francs for his complicity in the death of N'Tji Koulibali.[19]

From the beginning of European efforts to erect cotton plantations on the banks of the Niger, the administration in the Soudan had been reluctant to use its offices to recruit labor for private enterprises. It disliked the private sector's attitude toward African workers and was uncomfortable with management's expectations that the administration would rectify the problems of a flawed labor market. But the failure of European-managed plantations to secure adequate labor without recourse to administrative coercion indicated that a labor market had not developed in the Soudan and that Africans retained viable alternatives to selling their labor power to Europeans. By 1928, it was obvious that neither the European cotton plantations nor the administration had been able to capture and redirect the long-established seasonal migrations to Senegambia and to the forest zone, which had been a central premise of Carde's 1924 program and of Bélime's model of intensive irrigation. As these shortcomings in the labor market and in European management were becoming obvious, the further deterioration of CICONNIC's cotton harvests and finances made the alternative model of internal colonization more attractive.

The Financial Collapse of CICONNIC
and the Rise of Internal Colonization

In 1924, CICONNIC claimed an additional 8,000 hectares in Sama, Dioro, and Senenkou on the southern fringes of the interior delta in the Segu cercle. Elaborate management charts were drawn up for what appeared to promise rational exploitation of the new delta concessions. Plans were under way to plant Egyptian long-staple cotton there, notwithstanding the results of Forbes's 1923–24 cotton experiments, which indicated beyond question the unsuitability of Egyptian cotton to delta soils. Recruitment and retention of labor remained serious problems for the CICONNIC plantations in the delta just as they did for their SAA neighbors. Desertions were rife and less than 1 percent of the contract workers recruited by the colonial state agreed to renew. Lieutenant Governor Terrasson thought that CICONNIC directors in Paris were using the new concession as a means of squeezing additional capital from sharehold-

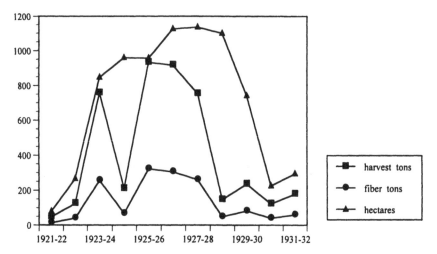

Fig. 8. CICONNIC Cotton Results, Dire, 1921–1932. Source: Direction des Services Economiques (AOF), Note au sujet de la Compagnie de Culture Cotonnière du Niger, Dakar, 18 Aug. 1932, ANS 1 R 73; Inspecteur de 3ième classe de Colonies Bargues, Rapport sur les conditions d'exploitation, par la Compagnie de culture cotonnière du Niger, du domaine de Dire, Dire, 22 Apr. 1935, ANF-DOM Aff écon 107 bis-3.

ers to compensate for the poor returns at Dire.[20] Although the 1925–26 cotton harvest at Dire was respectable, those of 1926–27 and 1927–28 demonstrated that the best the company could hope for was to hold back declining production. The 1928–29 harvest was a disaster from which the company never recovered. Figure 8 displays CICONNIC's performance from 1921 to 1932 in hectares planted in cotton, the size of the harvest, and the yield of fiber.

By the end of 1927, CICONNIC had virtually exhausted its capital reserves. Harvests at Dire remained far below expectations, and the considerable investment in the delta concessions drained what little remained in the company's coffers. Many of the same technical, financial, and agronomic mistakes made at Dire were replayed in the interior delta concession, and the company found itself unable to make payments to its creditors.

Early in 1927 Terrasson had recognized that the company was in trouble and suggested to the governor-general that in exchange for any further assistance the company should renounce its claims to land upstream from Lake Debo. These claims were part of the original 1919 convention between CICONNIC and the government-general of French West Africa. Terrasson hoped that renouncing its land claims would ensure that the company would not interfere with plans and execution of the state-run irrigation of the Niger Valley.[21]

In March 1928, CICONNIC reached an agreement with the governor-general in which the company transferred its assets in the delta concessions to a new company, the Compagnie agricole et industrielle du Soudan, which would pursue mixed agriculture and herding activities. The agreement stressed that the new company would experiment with textile crops other than cotton, such as sisal. CICONNIC also agreed to turn over a considerable part of its Dire holdings to another new company, the Compagnie d'élevage du Niger, which would pursue herding and livestock management. A year later, in the face of continuing decline in cotton production, the governor-general moved forcefully to reorganize the management of CICONNIC. On 25 November 1929, the governor-general and CICONNIC entered into a new convention, in which the management of the company was placed in the hands of its principal creditors, who combined to form the Société d'études et de colonisation. The governor-general agreed to provide 500,000 francs annually for three years so that the reorganized company could maintain the infrastructure of the concession and pursue diverse agronomic and labor organization studies. In exchange, the company agreed to deliver its entire cotton harvest to the colonial state.

The promise the governor-general extracted from the new company to pursue alternative labor arrangements had a major impact on the future of the irrigation model. The administration now considered private enterprise's reliance on state recruitment to have been "a lazy solution."[22] Already in 1927, CICONNIC management at Dire felt obliged to redesign labor organization. In place of Europeans supervising African workers, the company promoted several long-term workers to gang foremen over sections of the plantation, paid them a base salary, and offered them profit-sharing incentives. Each section leader was to receive a quarter of a centime for each kilogram of cotton harvested. Management also flirted with the idea of sharecropping, based on what it described as an "Egyptian" model. The company would furnish the soil, water, seeds, and plowing; the sharecropper would provide the labor. The harvest was to be divided, although by the beginning of the 1927–28 season the shares had not yet been determined.[23]

The form of sharecropping that emerged at Dire in the 1927–28 season was derived instead from a metropolitan model of an agricultural cooperative. Sixty-eight African farmers recruited from current and former workers constituted themselves as a formal agricultural association under the 1926 agricultural credit program in French West Africa. The two parties, the association and the company, then entered into an agreement under which the company ceded to the association 204 irrigated hectares at 1,000 francs per hectare payable over ten years. The company also promised to supply water, deep plowing, and seed. In addition, the company ceded to the association at no cost 100 low-lying hectares, which were not currently irrigated but were susceptible to flooding, for subsistence crops. The agreement stipulated exactly how many irrigated hectares would be planted annually in cotton, peanuts, and forage crops and that this land would be worked under the supervision of agents of the company. The shares of the harvest depended on the fields and the crops. For cotton, the association received three-fifths and the company two-fifths. For peanuts, the crop was divided in half shares. And the entire harvest of the nonirrigated plot belonged to the association.

The company did not, however, enter this sharecropping contract willingly. Because it was near bankruptcy, the colonial state effectively imposed these alternative models of labor organization on a management that had been trained to measure success according to immediate returns—and not the "patient and disinterested" efforts required of fostering innovations—and resented the intrusion of the state into the authority of its "domain." In his assessment of the 1927 colonization scheme at Dire, Comptroller Dongier noted three other errors made by CICONNIC at this time. First, the company was under considerable pressure to put this alternative model of labor into practice quickly, and it enticed individuals to join by offering spectacular cash advances, averaging 75 francs per month initially. Members of the association considered these advances to be their salaries and therefore failed to understand the debt burdens they had unwittingly accepted. Second, the company imposed no qualifications on the members of the association. "They belonged for the most part," Dongier wrote, "to the most questionable element of the population: bellahs who had fled their masters' tribes and vagabonds of different races. All were without their families. They were attracted by the allure of advances in cash and in food and without an exact understanding of their new situation. There was no common ethnic bond, capable of forming a homogeneous collectivity and of organizing life around ancestral customs, which could permit them to establish ties to the land." And third, Dongier thought that for an experiment such as this, the number of initial colons was too high. It would have been preferable, he argued, to have a smaller number over whom tighter control could have been exercised to ensure the success of this first experience.[24] The agricultural cooperative barely survived until 1930, when the agreement was abrogated. By then, the company had embarked on another colonization scheme.

Although CICONNIC later claimed to have been the initiator of colonization programs in the Soudan, Inspector Bargues in 1935 argued that Bélime was the originator of the concept and that colonization on irrigated cotton land was first refined on the state experimental farm at Nienebale.[25] The experimental station at Nienebale, some fifteen kilometers downstream from Koulikoro on the right bank of the Niger, was established in 1921 as the location for the experimental study of Bélime's Segu canal. Governor-General Merlin had commissioned the agronomists Henry, Jean Vuillet, and Edouard Lavergne to select the best location. By the end of 1921, they had submitted their report, cleared 200 hectares, and started construction of the administrative buildings and sheds. In 1922 planting started under Vuillet, who was appointed the first director. In 1924, following the announcement of Carde's program, Nienebale was selected as a center for experimentation in colonization.[26]

Carde had stressed as central to his 1924 program the need to train Soudanese farmers in modern agricultural methods. The Nienebale scheme was predicated upon attracting families to this new area, where they would be trained in rational European farming technologies and encouraged to relocate permanently. In April 1926 the first group of fourteen families, containing 66 people, was recruited. They were not yet considered colons; instead they were apprentices, who received salaries and rations for their entire families. In addition, small plots were made available to the families as kitchen gardens. At the end of the first year, Vuillet weeded out one-third of the families, whom he considered ill-suited to modern farming. The nine remaining families were given irrigated plots, seed, water, and the free use of agricultural machinery and draft animals. By the end of the 1927–28 season, these families had tripled the output of the previous year, and each family pocketed between 6,000 and 10,000 francs.

Even as the first group of nine families were working on their own plots, Vuillet's staff was training fifteen new families, who worked as apprentices as the first group had done. For the 1928–29 agricultural season, both groups were given plots, seed, water, and access to agricultural machinery, and the value of the harvest doubled yet again. The colons' new prosperity, wrote Inspector Chastenet de Gery, "manifests itself in their satisfaction of unanticipated needs and in a definite air of contentment. . . . Among their former villages, the colons' unexpected fortune excites considerable envy."[27]

Governor-General Carde considered the Nienebale experiment a revolution in the doctrine of colonization.

> It had been universally admitted that intensive cultivation of the colonies was the prerogative of European enterprises in which the native plays a role similar to that of a machine. But we have seen that this same native can familiarize himself with methods of work, which if not the latest word in technology, entail nonetheless a total transformation in his agricultural practices. If this result has been obtained in a very short time and under a reduced European supervision, then it is but the first stage in an evolution which we cannot yet completely discern.

Carde considered the Nienebale success owing to the careful training and preparation of the colons, and he anticipated that it would serve as a model for the colonization of Macina after the completion of Bélime's project. In contrast, Carde thought that the colonization experiment at Dire failed because of the lack of adequate planning.[28]

Carde was not completely sanguine about the long-term implications of internal colonization, however. One of the unanticipated consequences he identified was the legal problems surrounding the ownership of the land. "The idea of private property," he wrote, "seems to be nearly completely foreign to the Soudanese native and to this day he manifests not the slightest desire to establish his rights to the land he cultivates. The colons of Nienebale would like to retain the land they occupy, but they demand only that they not be dispossessed. They do not have a notion that it is possible to establish rights which can guarantee against eventual eviction." Duthoit, the director of the Office of Economic Affairs in the Soudan, cautioned against a too rapid application of ownership rights to land. The question of ownership of the irrigated land, Duthoit wrote, "implies a profound modification of the economic situation in this colony and of native custom in terms of property rights. [The colon would] in effect become the proprietor of the land and of rights to water, he would then possess the two sources of wealth, which are separable but difficult to negotiate separately." Duthoit preferred that colons be given long-term usufruct rights to irrigated land and water and that these rights not be transferable or alienable without the consent of the governor. Otherwise, he warned, the administration risked seeing the colons dispossessed and becoming a landless, wage-earning class. "Such a class does not currently exist in the agricultural population and it will come into existence only at grave danger to the social order."[29]

The success of the state-run Nienebale project contrasted sharply with the experiments conducted by private sector plantations. The Société d'études et de colonisation, the group of creditors who took over CICONNIC management in 1929, was under obligation to the governor-general to explore alternative forms of indigenous colonization. In the 1929–30 season, management entered into individual sharecropping contracts with eleven former overseers of the company. Each sharecropper received nine irrigated hectares divided into three sections based on triennial rotation (cotton/millet-legumes/forage). In addition, each sharecropper was entitled to one or one and one-half hectares for his kitchen garden. The company provided all the heavy mechanical preparation of the three hectares designed for cotton and the water payable at 250 francs per hectare. Sharecroppers were responsible for all further agricultural work and for all the labor on noncotton fields. Only the cotton harvest was shared, with the sharecropper retaining two-fifths and the company three-fifths. All other crops belonged exclusively to the sharecropper. The results of the first year were not unsatisfactory, but neither did they offer practical solutions to the problems of cotton production and colonization. The company found itself with a continual labor shortage, and it was forced to draw upon its sharecroppers for work on the company's fields. And as it had done earlier, the company advanced its sharecroppers considerable capital, which reduced their end of harvest earnings considerably.

Only six of the original eleven sharecroppers and their families remained at Dire for a second year. Instead, the company recruited, with the assistance of the local administration, 60 new families for the 1930–31 season. All the new families were recruited from the canton of Bourem in the Goundam district, whose population had a reputation for good work habits. The families were selected on the basis of the numbers of males they contained. None, however, came willingly. A regional drought provided some incentives to relocate, but the administration gave them an extra shove. Those who moved to Dire, however, found themselves without resources and dependent on company advances of food and cash. "It was with considerable mistrust that the colons [of Bourem] began to work," wrote Comptroller Dongier. The nine-hectare family plot remained the model for the new colons. Dongier, however, criticized the company for failing to recognize the immediate needs of the colons, and in particular for refusing to assist the colons with their food crops.[30] Despite the company's initial lack of success in fostering colonization, by 1937–38 415 families had resettled on CICONNIC's lands in what the administration conceded was a relatively prosperous center of colonization.[31]

The failure to recruit and retain adequate labor for the European-managed capital-intensive irrigation projects on the banks of the Niger discredited the ideological foundations of the irrigation model. European managers and colonial administrators experimented with sharecropping and internal colonization schemes in response to the difficulties in the supply of labor. These experiments provided a justification for the development model of the Office du Niger, but it also foreshadowed the problems this model would face.

While the European-managed capital-intensive irrigation model was under siege by creditors and the administration, the pro-peasant camp was making considerable effort to capture and control the supply of cotton from rain-fed cultivation. In the following chapter, I examine the linked problems of quality control and commercialization of peasant-produced cotton.

Incentives, Surveillance, and Control: The Promotion of Peasant Cotton, 1924–1932

In his 1924 program, Governor-General Carde privileged irrigation as the long-term solution to the problems of colonial cotton production, but he argued that in the short term, cotton exports depended upon peasants. Carde recognized that indigenous cotton was of uneven quality and that the cotton brokers of Le Havre had equated the Soudanese varieties with mediocre Indian cotton, for which metropolitan spinners expressed little interest. With the decline of American cotton on the world market during World War I and in the immediate postwar period, French cotton spinners were more inclined to accept fiber that was somewhat shorter and irregular. Carde admitted that some progress had been made in ameliorating the quality and presentation of Soudanese cotton; this was, however, the historic opening administrators and exporters had been waiting for, and even greater effort in assuring quality control and promoting production was called for.[1]

Ameliorating cotton quality and intensifying production were understood to be technical problems for which there were both technical and managerial solutions. Former lieutenant governor Hesling of Upper Volta, who also served as director of the Association cotonnière coloniale, captured the sense of the colonial state's role in cotton development when he argued that the problem of improving colonial cotton production for metropolitan use had a political and administrative as well as a purely technical character.[2] Under the guise of technical intervention, the colonial state and the semiofficial ACC intervened in Soudanese peasants' cotton production and marketing decisions. Such intervention was consistent with Carde's position that the colonial state had the right *and* the obligation to intervene at all levels in the lives of Africans "to protect the native against his own nature." The colonial state and the ACC launched a four-pronged effort to manage, to improve, to control, and to encourage the production of rain-fed cotton. Through these efforts the colonial state reclaimed its initiatives within the broader politics of colonial cotton development.

On one level the politics of cotton development from 1924 to 1932 was characterized by a new language of management and the willingness to intervene more aggressively to shape the production and marketing of cotton. On another level, efforts to grapple with the imperfections of the Soudanese cotton market in these years revealed just how fragile were the bonds holding together the constellation of actors favoring peasant cotton.

The ideological and programmatic edifice of the pro-peasant model of colonial cotton development rested on the assumption that African peasants would respond positively to market incentives. Governor-General Roume had defined the administration's position on this point in 1903, when he stated that "it is the price and the price alone which will give the African peasant confidence and which will let him devote himself to this crop out of which he will be assured a profit." Governor-General Carde reiterated this principle in 1924, when he asserted that cotton development could proceed only if the producer was fairly compensated for his labor. Because Soudanese cotton was to feed French mills, it had to perform within the constraints of the world cotton market in which quality, yield, and supply determined price. Carde also ordered that the expansion of cotton production not intrude on African peasants' subsistence. Instead, it had to operate alongside the well-established food production strategies. Roume and Carde thus narrowed the parameters under which the cotton development in French West Africa could operate.[3]

The belief in the economic rationality of African peasants was hardly sufficient to keep together the congeries of actors supporting peasant production of cotton. Each group laid claim to a share of policy and programs, which became a privileged space in which it alone would function. Each group pursued policies that promoted its privileges and interests. The commercial sector of French commercial houses and their African agents laid claim to the marketing of cotton and to the application of market incentives. The Association cotonnière coloniale sought to monopolize ginning and classification as a way of ensuring its instrumental position in colonial cotton development. And though the colonial state seemed to be the one determining "policy," it did so within narrow limits shaped by the division of labor among the actors promoting peasant cotton and by ideological assumptions regarding free labor and free markets.

When world market and regional conditions were favorable, as they were in 1923–24, this alignment of forces yielded increasing cotton exports. When all the conditions were not perfectly congruent—they were rarely so from 1925 to 1932—cotton exports declined and the politique cotonnière was thrown into crisis. As the colonial state grappled with the recurrent crises facing its cotton development program, it began to intrude into the privileged spaces jealously guarded by the various actors. Because it never fully trusted its belief in peasant rationality or the commercial sector's commitment to apply satisfactory market incentives and because it needed to show results, the colonial state enveloped its cotton programs in surveillance and control. If market forces would not "naturally" provide the incentives and institutions necessary to the flow of cotton exports and to the improvement of quality, then the colonial state would impose them. Mandating market forces led to ever-increasing interventions in the production and marketing of cotton. The ensuing politics and resulting policies reveal ideological and programmatic limitations of those promoting peasant cotton.

Because each of the three major actors addressed in this chapter— the ACC, the commercial sector, and the colonial state—pursued policies promoting both cotton exports and its own interests, the chapter explores in turn the politics and policies designed to improve quality and yields (ginning and classification; amelioration of production) and those to organize and sharpen market incentives ("legitimate" prices; cotton fairs). Each section examines responses to crises affecting the promotion of peasant cotton over roughly the same period, 1924 to 1932. These crises also reveal the unrealistic expectations and irrational assumptions of colonial development held by French protagonists of Soudan's cotton future.

The first crisis occurred in the spring of 1925. In April reports of a poor millet harvest in Senegal circulated through the French commercial community in Bamako. By May it became clear that the 1925 Senegalese millet harvest was a disaster. The French commercial houses sensed a rich opportunity, and they quickly abandoned cotton for millet. Bélime, director of the Service des textiles, described the events of 1925.

Throughout [the Soudan] cotton transactions are deficient and it is necessary to add that it is the commercial houses which must bear the responsibility. Their first error was to offer natives an absolutely insufficient price. Then, Senegal announced a bad millet harvest and the orientation of their commercial campaign was abruptly modified. . . . . The extraordinary increase in the price of a staple food crop has had serious repercussions.

Today, the warehouses of the commercial houses are overflowing with millet which cannot be evacuated. Considerable capital has been immobilized, which would have been incontestably better employed in buying the cotton harvest, a far less perishable product. The cotton harvest has remained to a large extent in the hands of the producers. . . .

We must guard against [the consequence of these events]. Cotton production cannot develop if we cannot assure the purchase of the crop each year and if we cannot assure that these transactions take place in the best conditions. Commerce has proven its ineptitude to furnish these guarantees.[4]

Bélime did not hide his resentment of the commercial sector's failure to uphold what he and other senior officials had considered its share of the politique cotonnière.

The second and more severe crisis facing the politique cotonnière was heralded by the bumper cotton crop of 1925–26 in the United States. That of 1926–27 was even bigger. These harvests pushed down world cotton prices for the first time since 1914. Except for 1927–28 and 1928–29, prices remained below 1914 levels into 1941. With abundant supplies of inexpensive cotton of the preferred industry standard available on the market, metropolitan users were less willing to pay premium prices for mediocre colonial cotton. To compound matters, the rapid devaluation of the franc in the middle 1920s played havoc with the commercial sector's ability to juggle prices and supplies.[5] Merchants were loath to invest their capital in commodities whose value declined quicker than they could unload them. District officers and canton chiefs, however, exerted considerable pressure on producers, regarding both collective labor on the commandants' fields and the propaganda they spread, to expand production. In meetings throughout their districts, administrators exhorted peasants to increase production and promised that cotton would become a significant genitor of household income.[6] Not surprisingly, cotton producers were confused by the contradictory signals they received. Confronted with wide fluctuations in cotton prices and a marked decline in the value of their harvest, some cotton producers refused to sell their crops, some directed their harvest to the domestic market, and others planted food crops.[7] In February 1927, Lieutenant Governor Terrasson wrote to the Bamako Chamber of Commerce that "the abundant harvest in the United States and the rapid revalorization of the franc has resulted in a considerable depreciation of the value of [Soudanese] cotton. This decline constitutes a serious setback for the development of African cotton."[8]

Both the metropolitan and colonial states responded to this crisis in a variety of ways. In France, the National Assembly slapped a sur-tax on each bale of imported cotton that did not originate in French colonies and used those funds to support the promotion of colonial cotton. In West Africa, the colonial state intervened more aggres-sively into what had been commerce's protected sphere by fixing prices and controlling sales. Senior colonial officials began to ques-tion whether Soudanese peasants were capable of producing high-quality cotton in sufficient quantities. Already in 1924 Bélime ex-panded on the cautionary note Carde had expressed in his circular concerning the limited potential of the Soudanese producer. Bélime was convinced of the economic rationality inherent in the produc-tion logic of peasants, but he framed it as a zero-sum calculation.

The increase in cotton production in this colony will have as its corollary the reduction in the volume of grains normally sold to commerce and prob-ably a net diminution of these harvests. The agricultural labor of the black will be thus allocated differently, but will not vary. . . . The stagnation of total agricultural output in the Soudan is very characteristic. It demonstrates that a rise in the purchasing prices of primary industrial products, which com-merce is seeking to acquire, will meet its limits in the producers' capacity to work, which is mediocre, and in the insignificance of their needs.[9]

The solution to this zero-sum equation was to capture the entire har-vest for export by controlling the commercialization of cotton and to improve agricultural productivity through technical innovations.

The protagonists of peasant cotton had, moreover, seriously over-estimated the attractiveness of cotton in relationship to other crops. The assumption of a positive linkage between increasing prices and increasing supply was thus flawed. In 1931, Inspector Mérat com-pared the returns on one hectare of cotton with other crops in the northern Côte d'Ivoire. Although the same alternatives were not nec-essarily available to Soudanese peasants, the range is indicative of the income derived from crops that competed with cotton for the peasants' attention. His calculations are as follows:

yams	1,250 francs
dry field rice	350 francs
cotton	250 francs
groundnuts	236 francs
corn	200 francs

Mérat's estimate of cotton yield was based on the fairly high price of 1.70 francs per kilogram of cotton. When offers for cotton in the ex-port sector fluctuated between 0.25 and 0.70 francs per kilogram, as they did in 1931–32, planting cotton for export hardly repaid the effort.[10]

"One of the obstacles [to the expansion of peasant cotton]," Carde admitted in 1924, "lies in the inferior financial return of rain-fed cotton cultivation in relation to other crops. In the Soudan, for example, within the region drained by the railway, groundnuts provide higher returns and cotton cannot compete. Cotton ceases to be an industrial crop and reverts as in the past to a domestic product. Amelioration of peasant-produced cotton must be pursued, for the future of this mode of production depends on those solutions."[11] The essential problem was how to ameliorate the quality of cotton and to bring increased returns to peasant producers within the constraints of a free market economy. Carde proposed a twofold solution. The first was to change the nature of the cotton plant itself, through both the long and tedious process of scientific hybridization and the adaptation of exotic (American) varieties to Soudanese conditions. The second and linked solution was to change the producers' farming methods.[12]

As a plant, cotton was especially susceptible to what Carde called "a rapid deterioration of the strains."[13] Efforts to combat unwanted hybridization could be taken at the level of ginning, when seeds producing inferior strains could be eliminated. They could also be taken at the level of the cotton field, ensuring that local varieties were kept distant from the chosen ones.[14] Carde thus linked the success of higher-yielding and higher-quality cotton strains to changes in farming practices. Carde called upon his subordinates to exert "a vigilant surveillance of the crops" and to expand their efforts to diffuse modern agricultural machinery and modern farming practices.[15]

The final crisis of this period flowed from the cycles of worldwide commercial deceleration stemming from the New York stock market crash of 1929. Although France escaped the pressures until 1930–31, it entered into a severe depression that deeply affected market demand for Soudanese cotton. Colonial officials feared that producers would lose interest in cotton production if they left the cotton market to the free play of market forces. Colonial officials thus became cotton brokers, buying, ginning, and selling cotton on the export market. The following sections explore the politics and policies of those promoting peasant cotton production during a period of sustained crises.

Control over Quality and the Politics of Ginning

The lack of homogeneity in Soudanese cotton and its improper preparation and packaging posed serious technical problems for metropolitan spinners. Improper ginning and packaging led to a deterioration of fiber and required reginning in France. The lack of homogeneity, however, was the most serious problem, as Inspector of Agriculture Etesse noted in his description of French West African cotton. "The bales [shipped to France] contain fibers of all lengths. This is a serious defect, for the spinning machines work with a high precision and losses due to fibers which have different lengths are serious."[16] Improvement of ginning thus lay at the heart of the effort to make Soudanese cotton more attractive to metropolitan spinners because it exerted control over cotton in three ways. First, it prevented deterioration of fiber by removing seeds and debris. Second, it allowed ginners to classify fiber at the moment of ginning, thereby facilitating the marketing of cotton in France. And finally, because ginning separated seeds from the fiber, it exerted control over what was planted by sorting seeds and removing those that yielded inferior strains. Seeds retrieved from ginning served as the major source of new cotton seeds.

In face of a critique of its past performance in the immediate postwar period, the ACC sought to justify its continued participation in the politique cotonnière by claiming a monopoly over ginning and cotton classification. During his tour of the Soudan in 1923–24, the director of the ACC, Arthur Waddington, assured the French merchants of the Soudan that the ACC's goal was to provide a necessary service, which it would eventually cede to private industry. He urged the merchants to form a "consortium of buyers" which would assemble all cotton traded, permit greater control over classification, and send the cotton to a single designated broker at Le Havre, who would cater to their needs. Waddington's strategy was to separate each of the tasks of cotton commercialization and to insert the ACC squarely in the center. Several merchants distrusted the ACC, especially those who remembered its monopsonistic intrusion into the commercial sphere with its affiliate the Compagnie du coton colonial before the war. Moreover, several ginneries were in private hands and the owners were reluctant to part with them.[17]

Put on the defensive by the harsh attacks of Henry and others favoring irrigation, the ACC slowly reorganized and began to petition the Ministry of Colonies, the Consortium of Cotton, and the government-general of French West Africa for significant new subventions to assist the modernization and expansion of ginneries in the Soudan and the employment of qualified classifiers to oversee quality control. By 1923, the ACC was back in business. The Consortium of Cotton agreed to subvene the ACC's activities to the tune of 5.4 million francs over five years. The minister of colonies was favorably disposed to the ACC's efforts to divide the tasks of the politique cotonnière and wrote to Governor-General Carde in 1923 that the "ACC assures the ginning, classification, pressing, and stamping [of cotton] without these operations constituting a formal monopoly [*monopole de droit*] but tending to become an actual monopoly [*monopole de fait*], because of the benefits which derive from uniformity of method."[18] Governor-General Carde, in turn, decreed in January 1924 that all agricultural products for sale and for export were subject to classification at departure points throughout the federation and at cotton ginneries.[19]

In 1923, the ACC was ready to embark on a plan to modernize its existing ginneries, which had lapsed into disrepair during the war, and to expand into the new cotton zones south of the Segu heartland. Construction was started on the ACC ginnery and experimental farm at Koutiala and in 1924 at Bouguni, Sikasso, and Bobo Juulasso. Building these ginneries required considerable effort. The administrator of Koutiala estimated that he needed 800 porters to transport the ginning equipment and building materials to erect one station.[20]

Despite its strategy to insert itself in the center of cotton commercialization and despite official support, by the end of the 1925–26 harvest, the ACC controlled only five of the twelve ginneries operating in the Soudan and its ginneries serviced only 29 percent of the total cotton ginned. In 1926, the ACC even sold its ginnery at M'Pesoba to a private concern. This was a far cry from the monopoly position the ACC had sought for itself.[21]

In response to growing complaints about inefficiency and mismanagement, the government-general refused to renew its annual subvention of one million francs until the ACC could demonstrate accountability.[22] The government-general asked all lieutenant governors to assess the ACC's performance. The report compiled by the Direction des affaires économiques in Dakar and submitted to the governor-general concluded that "in the whole, the responses of the lieutenant-governors were very close . . . that insufficient results [were] obtained."[23]

Even as the colonial government and private enterprise were voicing doubts about the ACC's ability to perform the central tasks of classification and ginning, supporters of colonial cotton development in France were moving ahead with a bill that would provide the ACC with even more revenue. Edouard Daladier, the minister of colonies, together with his counterparts in the ministries of Finance and of Commerce and Industries, drafted legislation that had as its logic the reduction of French dependence on imported American cotton and an increase in the amount of colonial cotton used. "We found ourselves [after the war] with the necessity of redoubling our efforts to liberate ourselves in the largest measure possible from foreign imports [of cotton]. . . . Given the important and [commercially] disinterested goal pursued by that association, the minister of colonies has sought to procure permanent and indispensable resources for it." The legislation, which became law on 31 March 1927, imposed for ten years a surtax of one franc on each 100-kilogram bale of cotton imported into France from foreign sources and on each bale of colonial cotton exported to a foreign country. Revenue from the special tax was to be divided among "subventions and reimbursable advances to enterprises or organizations, public or private, which have no commercial character and which operate in the general interest for the creation and extension of cotton production." The ACC was not the only beneficiary, but it was a large one. In 1927, the new surtax added an additional 1,890,000 francs to the ACC budget; in 1928, 2,551,000 francs; in 1929, 3,700,000 francs; in 1930, 3,401,000 francs; and in 1931, 3,400,000 francs.[24]

The directors of the ACC in Paris were understandably ecstatic for their newfound revenue gave them a certain independence from the colonial authorities in West Africa, just as their former patrons were expressing misgivings. The ACC also sought fresh—and potentially more welcoming—areas. "Our task in French West Africa," reported the director of the ACC to the annual meeting of members in 1927, "is to finish our [ginning] installations. We must still develop them, make them modern, increase their capacities. . . . Thanks to the new resources that the law gives us, we will become independent of French West Africa, which is not the only cotton region in our colonies, and we will bring our activities to bear wherever cotton promises to give good results."[25]

The ACC used its new revenue to expand its operations in French Equatorial Africa, Madagascar, and Indochina. Despite this diversification, French West Africa remained the core region for French hopes to develop cotton production for metropolitan needs. By 1931–32, the ACC controlled twenty ginneries throughout French West Africa, which represented a fixed capital investment of over seven million francs. Although in 1932 Lieutenant Governor Louis de Fousset and Governor-General Jules Brévié could argue that the ACC had fulfilled its 1923–24 promises to erect ginneries and to classify cotton, the association never realized the monopoly role it had sought nor had it enabled colonial cotton to capture the metropolitan market.[26]

World prices for cotton, which had started to tumble in 1926, plunged further with the onset of the Depression. Although by 1930–31 producers in Bouguni increased threefold the size of their cotton fields, the ACC closed its ginneries in Koutiala and Bouguni for lack of cotton.[27] By 1931 it was clear that the first prong of the strategy to control the quality of cotton at the ginning stage had failed. Simultaneous efforts had also been under way to control the quality of cotton at the production and marketing ends.

Champs du Commandant: Surveillance, Persuasion, and Compulsion in the Cotton Fields

Former governor of the Côte d'Ivoire and governor-general of French West Africa Angoulvant's clear and simple solution to the colonial supply of cotton to the metropole proposed in 1924[28]—that each and every inhabitant provide ten kilograms of cotton for export—was to have no place in Carde's 1924 cotton development program. Although Carde did not completely abandon the role of administrative authority, he situated it within the complex interplay of competing groups and ideologies of the pro-peasant camp. Carde was convinced that the African peasant would produce cotton, but only if it were in his interests. Carde was also aware that only by ameliorating the quality of Soudanese cotton did it stand a chance of capturing the metropolitan market. But at the same time he was critical of the African's capacities to produce.

But how, given the constraints of their commitment to free markets, could administrators encourage peasants to produce strains of cotton better suited to metropolitan needs in the absence of direct price incentives? Carde was clear in his refusal to countenance direct compulsion, but he was vague in defining an alternative. "In order to enhance [the agricultural abilities of Soudanese producers], it has often been proposed to institute administrative regulations obliging natives to produce. The least one can say about such legislation of compulsion is that it does not work. First, because it flies in the face of the ideas we hold concerning individual liberty, and second, because those who propose it too often omit to discuss the geographical context. The Soudan is not an island . . . [and we risk] stimulating a vast emigration toward the Gold Coast and Nigeria." Carde pushed this argument further: "It is not the legislation of compulsion which will lead the African to observe more than he does now the universal law of work. Our intervention will not be equitable nor will it be justified unless it has as its immediate and direct object the interests of the black people."[29]

Faced with the contradictory goals of meeting metropolitan needs and respecting individual liberty, Carde permitted himself a sleight of hand. He allowed the administration a transformative role in the protection of the African "against his own nature," which would take the form of benevolent intervention in his medical, economic, and social practices. This was particularly pronounced in a section of health and welfare of his 1924 program, which sought the expansion of both population and production. Carde argued that "to strengthen the native and to render him more active and to repopulate the land, the authority of the administrator is thus at least as necessary as the science of the doctor. A large part of the future development of West African production depends on their combined action."[30] Within the context of the politique cotonnière, the substitution of the "science of the agronomist" for the "science of the doctor" was easy to make. The colonial administrator together with the agricultural extension agent were to assist the African to work in his own interest.

The focus of their joint enterprise was a collective field, also called the *champs du commandant*, the field of the administrator. Cotton producers around the Middle Niger called the collective cotton field *faama foro* (Bambara: king's field), an ironic play on the term used to describe the huge fields of the Bambara king worked by his slaves. Each village was to have one, although those villages unfortunate enough to be the residences of the commandant, the *chef de canton*, or the extension agent were subject to closer supervision. The logic of the champs du commandant was the concept of trickle-down effects, wherein a single convincing case could assist the rapid diffusion of new technologies of production. In many ways, the champs du commandant bore a striking resemblance to the model field tried by the ACC and the administration in the Segu region in the early

years of colonial cotton development. Based on his firsthand observations in 1923–24, Waddington described how the champs du commandant operated.

Although the native has long cultivated cotton, it is in our interests to research the means to assist him, to guide and to instruct him, and we will
raise significantly his production. The natives are like large children, pos-
sessing the qualities and the faults of children, one of which is a certain degree of laziness. . . . It seems likely, however, that we can obtain from them
an even larger effort when we combine a judicious mix of compulsion and
persuasion, brought to bear by the administrators, all of whom I have found
during the course of my tour to have a good disposition in this regard. The
champs du commandant demonstrate the appropriateness and the wisdom
of this opinion. The administrator pushes the chief of the tribe to establish a
supplementary field, which is cultivated in cotton by the inhabitants. At the
end of the harvest, the administrator sells the cotton by auction and returns
the proceeds to the chief of the tribe, who divides it among the members. All
are happily surprised when they realize that they did not have to work without pay for the administrator, and next year they are the first to occupy the
administrator's fields. Here is a powerful example of compulsion and persuasion combined.[31]

Linking production on a collective field to administratively controlled cotton sales was Lieutenant Governor Hesling's Upper Volta
model. Between 1925 and 1927, cotton exports from Upper Volta rose
from 60 tons to 1,300 tons. Despite this remarkable increase in production and commercialization of cotton, Bélime, in his capacity as
director of the Service des textiles et de l'hydraulique, was uneasy.
He felt that cotton production in Upper Volta had an "artificial character" because it was based on assisting the buyer and not the
producer.[32] He was also concerned that European merchants "will
develop the habit of realizing the maximum profit with the least effort." Moreover, Bélime believed that the command model of cotton
production was possible only in hierarchically organized societies
like the Mossi, "where the authority of the chief permits the expansion of industrial crops without the genuine commitment of the
population." He worried that when these practices were stopped, a
decline in production was inevitable. Moreover, Bélime was convinced that the expansion of production based on the Upper Volta
model was based on fundamentally wrong agronomic assumptions.
Sustainable exports depended on increasing yields as well as acreage,
not merely expanding the cultivated surface.[33]

In contrast, the administrator of Bouguni was convinced that collective fields were "the only effective means of yielding important

results." He developed a formula in which each canton chief, each village chief, and each household head would oversee a cotton field. Based on his calculations, he anticipated that the 160,237 inhabitants of the district could deliver 400 tons of cotton fiber, or roughly 12.5 kilograms of raw cotton each.[34] For the system to work, however, the canton chiefs, village chiefs, and household heads had to have sufficient authority to command production. Giving them such authority led to abuses, particularly among canton chiefs, whose claims to authority were dubious at best. In Sikasso, where the canton chiefs in 1925 also controlled the sales of cotton, merchants threatened to boycott them in the future because the canton chiefs established prices based on their "fantasy" of profits.[35] One of my informants stated that for work on the champs du commandant, "there was never a question of salary. That was obligatory labor for the authorities. . . . Perhaps the canton chiefs received something. I don't know. The cotton was never weighed in our presence. We have heard that some canton chiefs received as much as 500 francs. We never saw anything."[36] Ko Togola of M'Peba, a village in the Segu district, explained in more detail how the champs du commandant operated.

Question: How did the French change the way cotton was cultivated?
Response: They ordered that cotton be cultivated in each village, not including the one cultivated by the canton chief.
Question: Who worked on these fields?
Response: Each village had its own and so did the canton chief. The authorities furnished the workers for him. Ten or fifteen people from the canton were assigned to cultivate his field. The field of the village chief was cultivated by all the male inhabitants of the village. For the harvest, everyone, men and women, worked.
Question: Were the proceeds from the canton chief's field paid to him?
Response: Yes. The money was given to him. Of course, he did not pay the laborers on his field; instead he might give them presents.
Question: How large was his field?
Response: He had two fields, which together equaled eight hectares. Each village chief had a one-hectare field.
Question: How were the proceeds from the village chief's field divided?
Response: The village chief received the money. He divided it among all who had worked. The eldest was in charge of supervising the work, not the chief.[37]

In response to a flurry of correspondence concerning the abuses associated with the champs du commandant in 1927, the administrator in Sikasso proposed that as far as he was concerned, "the canton chiefs will no [longer] intervene in [cotton] payments. But in regard to village chiefs, the prohibition should not be pushed too hard, because the latter are producers just as their villagers are."[38]

The senior administration came down hard on the excesses of the champs du commandant, which smacked of the forced labor they opposed. Adequately distinguishing between compulsion and incentives in their effort to raise the volume of cotton exports was difficult to do, however. During the rainy season of 1927, the Bamako administrator toured his district and held meetings with village chiefs and notables to explain the administration's new cotton policies.

Attention of the population was very energetically brought to the necessity and *obligation* that will be applied this year, and for the years which follow, to furnish greater effort for cotton cultivation. I explained that the mediocre results of the 1926–27 cotton harvest could not continue and that for the current campaign and above all for the future, larger harvests will become an important source of profits and a larger element of the prosperity of the land.

I also explained that there was a minimal area to be planted, that is, three hectares for each one hundred inhabitants. I urged them to follow intercalary seeding [*sémis intercalaires*], which would double their harvests. The disadvantages of the collective cotton fields were also discussed, and I explained that in the future the commandant's cotton field—where everyone worked more or less assiduously and the proceeds were divided more or less equally—will no longer exist. Instead, cotton cultivation will be individual. Each family will henceforth possess its own cotton field, just as it does its fields of millet and corn, and in the degree to which it devotes its energies, so will that family derive the legitimate returns on its work.[39]

The administration was convinced that the Soudanese peasants' disdain for the commandant's cotton field in no way indicated their aversion to cotton. Former lieutenant governor Georges Spitz wrote that "if the black cultivates cotton voluntarily for himself, he loathes to cultivate cotton for the demands of the administration, which the natives call the 'cotton of the commandant.'"[40]

Carde had not considered the champs du commandant to be a direct solution to the cotton supply problem. Instead, he had considered it to be a model field, which could be used to demonstrate the rewards of modern farming methods. This was a central part of the persuasion administrators were to bring to bear. Chief Abderramen in the Sikasso district was exactly the kind of modernizing indigenous leader Carde had in mind. He requested from the Sikasso administrator the assistance of a Soudanese agricultural agent, with whose help he prepared and planted a cotton field using a plow and harrow exclusively. By 1927, graduates of the farm school at Baraweli, under the direction of the Service des textiles, were already established in the districts of Mopti, Kita, Bouguni, Sikasso, Bafoulabe, and Segu, where they established model fields using modern agricultural machinery. The best results in 1927 were reported from Sikasso, where fourteen peasants assisted by agricultural agents and using plows given them by the administration had excellent results. By 1929, administrative propaganda and financial assistance were having visible results. Five hundred plows were distributed throughout the Soudan. By the end of 1930, colonial officials boasted that 8,500 natives had been given instruction in using plows and harrows and were prepared to use them.[41]

The abuses of the champs du commandant did not end with the reassertion of the primacy of persuasion over compulsion in 1927–28. The immediate and tangible benefits for chiefs and for administrators seemed to outweigh the long-term benevolent intervention that underlay Carde's conception. Again in 1937, residents of Bamako and Bouguni districts fled their villages to escape what they considered a supplementary labor tax on the cotton fields.[42] But just as in the case of the ACC's efforts to control the quality of cotton by controlling ginning, the administration's efforts to control the quality of cotton at the production end confronted the barrier of declining world prices. Administrators could persuade, cajole, and coerce their subjects, but unless the price was right, Soudanese peasants either abandoned cotton for other crops or directed their harvest to the domestic market. To prevent cotton growers from losing interest in cotton, the colonial state intervened in the marketplace to assure producers a "legitimate" return on their labor.

Legitimate Profits and Fixed Prices

In the midst of the 1923–24 bumper cotton harvest in the Soudan, Arthur Waddington of the ACC made his tour of the Soudan and held discussions with administrators and merchants. At the Kayes Chamber of Commerce in December 1923, Waddington signaled his concern that merchants not forget their responsibility to ensure that producers received the maximum return from their cotton harvests. The minutes of the meeting record Waddington's suggestion that minimum prices for cotton be fixed. "Finally it was remarked that merchants have a major interest in understanding the [implications] of the purchase price for cotton and not to let these transactions operate to the detriment of the producers; it is absolutely necessary that they receive the maximum possible for their harvest. Otherwise, the same will happen as before: the native will become disinterested in cotton and produce only enough to satisfy his personal needs."[43] Merchants, however, could offer peasants the maximum return on their harvest only if they were prepared to accept less than maximum profits for themselves. But their commitment to cotton, as was demonstrated in their response to the 1925 millet crisis in Senegal, was less than absolute. Although the quality of Soudanese cotton was improving, it nonetheless sold for a discount against the American staple on the Le Havre cotton exchange, which narrowed even further the profit margin under which merchants operated. In 1925, for example, the best Soudanese cotton harvested in 1923–24 sold for 25 francs per 50-kilogram bale below the American staple. The most common Soudanese cotton with irregular fibers was discounted at Le Havre's cotton market by 150 francs.[44]

In Paris, the ACC took up Waddington's call for assuring producers maximum profits and chided colonial merchants for their selfish claims on profits. At its annual meeting in 1924, Marande, vice-president of the association, suggested that the market price of cotton from each colonial region be calculated as closely as possible to permit an equitable division of the profits among producers, importers, and users of cotton.[45] Waddington and Marande thus raised the difficult issue of what constituted "legitimate" profits and how to assess them. The concept of a legitimate profit, however, harked back to an earlier era in the development of capitalist economies and it assumed that the economy operated—or ought to operate—according to ill-defined but implicit moral criteria.[46] The notion of legitimate profits nonetheless fit the pro-peasant camp's conception of Africans as rational economic actors and permitted a fine-tuning of market incentives. But given the larger political economy in which the politique cotonnière operated, how to determine an equitable division of profits pitted administrators against merchants, merchants against producers, and producers against administrators. Moreover, it put colonial interests in conflict with the interests of metropolitan industrialists, whose commitment to colonial cotton was lukewarm at best.

Bélime shared with Waddington a concern to protect the level of existing cotton exports by ensuring that producers were adequately—but not, he stressed, lavishly—compensated for their efforts. In 1924 he wrote that "we must consider fixing a very remunerative, but not excessive, local rate for cotton."[47] The 1926–27 cotton harvest in the United States, however, plunged the politique cotonnière into crisis.

By early 1927, prices in the official cotton markets had tumbled, and producers no longer sold their harvests. "Everywhere," noted the economic report for January and February, "natives refuse to sell because the price offered does not seem to them sufficiently remunerative."[48] In Paris, ACC directors worried that metropolitan users would abandon Soudanese cotton because it was too costly, and they worried that peasant producers would abandon cotton because it did not repay their labor.[49] By March and April, the circle of declining prices and peasants' refusal to sell their harvests led European merchants to abandon the cotton markets altogether.[50]

In response to this deteriorating situation, the administration moved on two fronts. First, it stepped in and bought cotton whenever the commercial sector failed to buy all that was offered. The administration took this step first in March 1927.[51] Second, the administration committed itself to establishing a minimum price for cotton at the beginning of each buying season. In March 1928, when it became clear that European commercial houses were only nibbling at the cotton harvest and that the price they offered was too low to induce cotton producers to sell their harvests, Terrasson stepped in again. When the administrator of Bouguni informed him that the prevailing price for cotton was 0.80 francs per kilogram, Terrasson considered that "the price is insufficient. Warn buyers that I will buy [cotton] myself if the price does not rise."[52] Both tactics marked a significant departure from the senior administration's commitment to a "free market" and marked its willingness to intervene in the commercial sector's protected sphere within the politique cotonnière.

By 1928, the administration introduced an official minimum price for cotton. But how did the administration determine what constituted a legitimate minimum price for producers? Robert Boussac, the senior agent for the Comptoirs de l'industrie cotonnière in Bouguni, protested the administration's intention of imposing minimum prices. "I request that you leave [prices] to the free play of competition and do not fix a minimum price, which may not correspond to the actual rates of cotton in France."[53] Because the administration had committed itself to colonial development through cotton, it would not permit commerce a completely free hand to determine the fate of cotton production. In his report on the 1927 cotton season, Bélime argued that cotton growing in the Soudan was a qualitatively different enterprise than groundnut cultivation in Senegal. "French

West Africa is a vast land and once one enters the interior, the factor of distance plays an important role. Distance aggravates the oscillations in world prices." He acknowledged that groundnuts were also subject to variations in prices, but because of the high costs of transportation from the Soudan to France, the world cotton price variations were effectively doubled for Soudanese cotton exports. Thus, though he acknowledged that the export sector had complete liberty not to buy the Soudanese cotton harvest as world cotton prices moved downward, such actions nonetheless left the politique cotonnière without the market incentives it needed. Something had to be done.

Bélime envisioned two scenarios. In the first, the administration would fix an average cotton price at the beginning of the cotton buying season, based on the prevailing rate for cotton at Le Havre and in consultation with the forecasts of the Fédération internationale cotonnière. Commerce, however, would offer a price equal to or higher than this average and acquire all the cotton. In the second, commerce would absent itself and the administration would buy, gin, and sell for its own account all cotton presented at the market. Bélime realized, however, that the administration's intervention would probably result in financial loss, so he argued for the creation of a special fund equal to the amount of the government-general's subvention of the ACC and drawn from the sum collected by the special metropolitan tax on imported cotton. "Commerce," Bélime concluded, "conserves its complete liberty to buy the harvest as long as it accepts the normal price. Finding a commodity concentrated in the [official] market, it therefore avoids intermediaries and shares the benefits with producers. . . . These measures will be completely accepted by commerce . . . and will act as a powerful stimulant to cotton production."[54] Bélime's proposal thus maintained both the fiction of free markets and the privileged space for French commerce, in which it bought and sold cotton only if it was assured of making a profit.

In April 1928 Lieutenant Governor Terrasson justified price fixing as a necessary response to the peculiar imperfection of markets in new colonial regions. He also reiterated the idea that cotton prices must include a legitimate return on labor. "The objection that price fixing," he wrote,

constitutes a diminution of commercial liberty has no doctrinal value. From the point of view of cotton development, commercial issues are entirely subordinated to those of production. . . . An active policy of cotton production thus creates a community of interests between commerce and the administration, and when the administration pushes the native to produce, it engages tacitly in assuring him a legitimate return on his labor. . . . In new lands where communication is not well developed a regulator is necessary in order to establish on solid ground the prices of a new product and to prevent special interests from actions detrimental to the growth of production. In the Soudan, in particular, unregulated commercial liberty of the cotton market will lead to complete anarchy. . . . It is not possible, in effect, to conceive of production of any importance without a well-organized market to permit selling.

Cotton, Terrasson reminded his reader, was a "poor" crop, which offered producers only inferior returns compared to millet and peanuts. "It is not certain that a priori a normal price of cotton would under all conditions be profitable for the producer." It was, Terrasson concluded, a step in the right direction. "Fixing minimum buying prices permits us to alleviate the imperfections I have identified. It will not increase competition between merchants, but it will establish a price floor and it will suppress the considerable price declines." In consultation with the ACC, the local Chambers of Commerce, and officials from the colonial and federation governments, the administration would annually establish minimum and average prices for each of the cotton regions following the rates of cotton fibers at Le Havre. Buying cotton at prices below those fixed was prohibited.[55] Since sales outside the official cotton markets were also prohibited, the administration seemed well positioned to control the price and the supply of cotton.[56]

According to administration estimates, as long as the prevailing price in Le Havre was 6,000 francs per ton, the most that buyers could offer in Segu was 0.60 francs per kilogram of raw cotton. In districts farther from the Niger, the costs of transport forced the purchase price down even further.[57] The following tabulation traces the cotton price range prevailing in Le Havre from 1927 to 1931:[58]

1927	8,300–12,200 francs/ton
1928	10,200–12,800
1929	11,300–12,600
1930	5,840–11,540
1931	3,360–7,180

In 1927, the fixed cotton price was relatively low to accommodate the low end of metropolitan cotton prices. In 1928 and 1929, the minimum fixed prices rose. Because international prices were relatively stable, European commercial houses bought all the cotton brought to the official markets and the colonial state did not intervene. In 1930–31, however, the effects of the New York stock market crash and the ensuing world economic crisis began to be felt in France and the Soudan and prices for cotton fell. The administration attempted to maintain 1929 price levels, but it was forced to abandon them. By 1932, the administration had largely capitulated to the market pressures of the Depression and dropped its fixed minimum prices to 0.30–0.40 francs per kilogram. Producers responded by funneling their harvest to the domestic sector or by planting less cotton. Exports of cotton between 1931 and 1932 fell sixfold, from 757 tons to 131 tons.[59] By fixing cotton prices, the administration intervened into what had been the preserve of commerce. Despite its actions, the colonial state proved unable to stem the flight of cotton from the export sector. The colonial state also tried to control peasant cotton through marketing.

The Cotton Fair: The Compulsion of Free Markets

Carde's 1924 program was singularly nondirective about how marketing could exert control over the quality of cotton. He lumped classification, packaging, and presentation together in a section describing the roles of ginning and marketing and described how his decree of 11 January 1924 established the means to exert control over exports at ginning stations, railways, and wharfs. "To avoid the danger [of uneven qualities], it is necessary that cotton, before it leaves the colony, be subject to assessment and classification of its value."[60] Carde must have recognized his uncharacteristic silence on marketing because later in 1924 he sent another circular to the lieutenant governors developing plans for regional cotton fairs. These cotton fairs, Carde wrote, "will assure strict classification and permit public weighing before [the cotton] will be presented to buyers." Carde instructed his subordinates to ensure that producers not have to walk more than 30 kilometers to these markets, to adapt them to local conditions using local materials, and thus to erect them quickly and inexpensively.[61]

The cotton fair was a variant of the more inclusive agricultural fair, which Governor-Generals Roume and Clozel had advanced in the first decade of the twentieth century. Both Roume and Clozel had sought to use their fairs to diffuse new technologies of production, to create lively competition among African producers by promoting higher quality, and to display metropolitan imports. In 1925, the annual agricultural fairs of Kayes and Bamako were held in February.

"These meetings," described the economic report of that month, "manifest a considerable progress over previous years. Beautiful specimens of cattle and horses are presented by the native herders. The market gardeners, whose industry is expanding, also exhibit superb vegetables, which can easily stand competition with metropolitan harvests." Cotton had a place in these general fairs, but its importance varied according to the district. In March, the Sikasso fair was well attended and the "natives have brought a large variety of products, but principally cotton."[62]

The cotton fair, however, was to be more than just another periodic market. It was an institution designed to exert control over the supply and marketing of cotton, to ensure quality, and to protect buyers and sellers alike. Because cotton prices in the export sector were determined by prevailing world prices, producers withheld supply from the market when the price was not right. When prices improved or when producers were burdened with too much stock, they unloaded their cotton. Unginned cotton, however, deteriorated during storage. Lieutenant Governor Terrasson instructed his district administrators at the start of the 1925 agricultural season to prohibit these practices, providing only that cotton for household use be retained.[63] Article 1 of the 1925 cotton quality decree prohibited the sale of mixed cotton, "that is to say, batches which contain white, brown, and stained cotton." Article 2 interdicted the sale of cotton stored over the rainy season. Article 8 empowered administrators to examine all cotton put into commercial circulation at both officially designated and unofficial markets, and Article 9 called for the application of the *indigénat*, the code of summary justice applied by administrators, for infractions of the decree.[64] The 1925 cotton quality decree served as the official basis upon which to build the formal cotton fair. More decrees were added through 1927. By 1928 cotton transactions outside the fair were prohibited. Responding to recurrent commercial imperfections, the colonial state had created a grotesque caricature of free markets.

The elaboration of the politique cotonnière provided a protected space for commercial activity, namely the buying of the harvest and the selling of imported goods. In their goal of expanding cotton exports the administration and the commercial sector were thus mutually dependent upon each other. Terrasson understood that the commercial sector required a legitimate profit, but he clearly resented commerce's efforts to build its profitability on the producers' equal claim to legitimate return and its failure to uphold their share of the implicit contract to further cotton production and exports. In 1928, he wrote a blistering critique of the commercial sector's performance.

From the point of view of cotton, the commercial question is entirely subordinated to that of production. If there exists in the French Soudan a certain tonnage of cotton available for export, that is due to administrative measures which have increased the surface area of the crop. The direct beneficiaries of this politics of production have been the traders. If this official intervention were to stop, the place of cotton in the exports would diminish year by year. A politics of cotton production thus creates a community of interests between commerce and the administration, but the latter, in pushing the native to produce, engages tacitly in assuring him a legitimate return on his labor.

Later in his report, Terrasson elaborated on some of the mechanisms, in particular the cartel, which traders used to undercut the legitimate returns to producers. He concluded this section by asserting where his sympathies ultimately lay.

Traders who frequent a market often wait to buy all the cotton presented at a single price and later divide it among themselves. This is the pure and simple suppression of competition. These combinations often result in difficulties, which in certain cases go as far as to threaten reprisals against buyers who hesitate to adhere to the agreement. In this case, the limitation of free trade is flagrant and we have the means to end it. . . .

These tactics would have a negligible impact if the natives knew how to defend themselves. But the reality is completely different, and one must consider that the producer is always the victim whenever the administration does not intervene to protect him.[65]

The cotton fair, as the physical location where cotton transactions took place, became an institutionalized mechanism for controlling the quality of cotton, protecting the African producer, and managing the freedom to buy and sell.

With the promulgation in 1924 and 1925 of the decrees controlling the quality of commodities destined for export and with increasing evidence of the failure of the commercial sector to uphold its share of the politique cotonnière, the program of cotton fairs was elaborated and pursued with greater rigor. Governor-General Carde's decree of 30 April 1926 transformed the cotton fairs into official regional cotton markets. By 1927, the Service des textiles anticipated that eighteen cotton markets would be functioning in the Soudan. For the 1928 campaign, 30 official markets were in operation.[66]

Bélime drew up a schematic plan for the cotton markets (Figure 9), which represented the physical expression of the control the administration wanted to exert over the cotton supply and cotton transactions. The initial response by both buyers and sellers to the official cotton markets was far from positive. African agents of the French commercial houses and independent traders opposed all regulation of cotton sales. They preferred to buy small parcels of cotton in the villages, where they could earn a small margin of profit by buying below the prevailing price and then selling larger parcels to the big export houses at premium rates. African producers resented the obligation to transport their cotton to the official markets. Producers in Sikasso were prepared to sell their cotton at a 10-centime-per-kilogram discount to avoid head-loading. The Bamako Chamber of Commerce was also cool to the idea of official cotton markets. Although its members thought the concept was "worth studying," they expressed their concern that the administration not move too quickly on the project. Some commercial houses, however, liked the idea of a cotton market as a means of avoiding the burden of purchasing small lots. Robert Boussac, agent for the Comptoirs de l'industrie cotonnière in Bouguni, felt that commercialization of cotton would be facilitated if the administration assembled lots of 20 to 30 tons of cotton but urged the administration not to set minimum prices, lest it hinder the commercial sector's flexibility to respond to world price fluctuations. To make matters worse, conditions were chaotic during the early years of the cotton markets. Official scales were often in disrepair; weighers and classifiers were poorly trained. Bélime promised that by the 1928 buying season all the official cotton markets would have scales that automatically weighed the cotton and imprinted tickets.[67]

Producers, however, remained reluctant to attend these cotton markets. Terrasson thus introduced legislation that prohibited all cotton sales outside these officially designated markets after the beginning of January 1928.[68] The monthly economic report around planting time in 1927 explained that the prohibition to sell cotton outside the official market did not really constitute an infringement on commercial freedom. "The producers will have to submit to the formalities of sorting and weighing but they will retain the freedom to sell at whatever price they want or not to sell if the price offered does not give them satisfaction."[69]

If there was a paradox in the obligation to attend the official cotton market and the right not to sell, it escaped the administrators who erected the cotton markets. The actual operation of the cotton market, which closely resembled Bélime's schematic model, became a

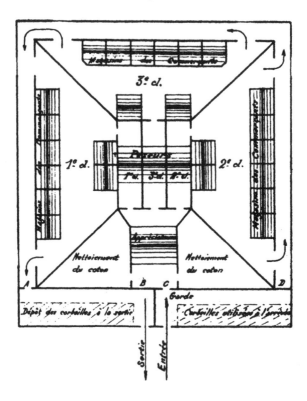

Fig. 9. Bélime's Schematic Drawing of a Cotton Fair, 1926. Source: Bélime, Rapport sur la production cotonnière de l'AOF en 1925–26, 15 May 1926, Kouluba, ANF-DOM Aff écon 72-4.

caricature of free markets. The contradictions in the administration's goals and ideologies coalesced in the cotton market as the colonial state sought to expand cotton exports, to increase the quality of the product, but also to operate within the constraints of a free market. Former lieutenant governor Hesling prepared a report on the cotton markets based on his firsthand observations of their operation in 1929.

These markets are organized and function in the following manner: they are constructed on a large square surface, bordered on four sides by shelters or places made available for traders to store the cotton they buy.

In the center are four weighing machines each one operated by a literate native. A fifth auxiliary is located between the scales and carries a *barème commercial* with weight and price correspondences. The market has one entry and one exit. Buyers are located around the weighing section, in front of their shelters.

Outside of the entry, each producer places his product in a large container put at his disposition by the administration. Under the supervision of a member of the constabulary, he enters the market and moves toward one of the weigh stations, where he places his container.

The weigher adjusts his scale. He inscribes the weight to the nearest kilogram on a ticket and announces it in a loud voice. The fifth auxiliary then announces the total to be paid and inscribes it on the same ticket. . . .

The ticket is returned to the seller, who then takes his container from the scale and is directed to the circle of buyers, each of whom tries to attract the seller by offering him kola nuts, a slightly higher bid, or by some other manner. The seller gives his container to the buyer of his choice and receives the sum printed on the ticket. He is then directed to the exit, where he finds another literate native auxiliary, who takes the ticket and assures that the price and weight actually correspond. The seller then retires with his money. The process continues in the same fashion from morning until night.

These markets offer serious advantages. They guarantee sellers an exact weight and a sincere price. The transaction is conducted individually between buyer and seller, and it does not matter whether the cotton is brought by a man, a woman, or a child. The native chiefs, whose previous intervention in cotton transactions has been self-interested, remain outside of the transactions. Also, this new mode of proceeding will certainly leave a favorable impression on the natives. It is not to be doubted that it will contribute to an increase in production.

On the commercial side, these markets offer no inconvenience. All buyers—larger or small, big companies or intermediaries—are placed on the same footing and work with the same means. It will, however, be in the general interest to stop the bidding, which troubles the native mentality and violent discussions often take place, especially in other markets and those where native chiefs are present. It is to be hoped that this experimental system, applied in two cercles of the Soudan this year with good results, will be progressively expanded throughout the cotton regions of French West Africa.[70]

The contradictions inherent in the compulsion of the cotton market could not, however, withstand the pounding of the declining world market price for cotton and the onset of the Depression. African producers responded positively to prices, just as the pro-peasant development model predicted. But instead of providing more cotton to the export sector, they sold it to the local handicraft textile industry. In 1931, the quarterly economic report noted that a very large part of the cotton harvest was circulating between natives outside the control of the administration and that it was servicing producers of local cloth. The administration's efforts to capture the supply of cotton by forcing producers to attend official cotton markets was clearly a failure.[71]

The colonial state intervened in the cotton market sporadically between 1927 and 1932. It intervened consistently only in the case of Allen cotton, a relatively high-yielding medium-staple cotton originally from Georgia, acclimated to the Soudanese conditions. The purchase of Allen cotton became the clearest test of the state's abilities to perform commercial functions. By 1931, however, the state was operating with a considerable deficit and the future of the colonial state's role as a cotton broker was seriously questioned.

The Colonial State's Cotton

The colonial state threatened to move boldly into the cotton market abandoned by the commercial sector in 1927. But despite its bluster and fury, it bought only eight tons of cotton that year. Cotton prices were relatively good during the 1928–29 and 1929–30 harvests, and with the exception of Allen cotton, the colonial state again did not intervene in the cotton markets. In response to the collapse of cotton prices in 1930–31, the administration bought eleven tons of cotton, which it ginned and sold locally.[72]

Allen cotton, however, was a special case. Between 1923 and 1926, the Service agronomique des régions tropicales acclimated Allen cotton to the northern savanna environment around Baraweli and Nienebale.[73] Yields were impressive: on a well-prepared and fertilized field, which was separated from local cotton varieties and planted exclusively in Allen, average yields on rain-fed farms were 300 kilograms per hectare. Under the supervision of agronomists, rain-fed fields yielded nearly 50 percent more, and on experimental irrigated fields, a hectare of Allen yielded nearly 1,500 kilograms. Allen cotton offered two additional advantages over local varieties. Its fibers were regular and of medium length, comparable to the American staple and thus ideally suited to the needs of metropolitan spinners. Its fiber yield after ginning was 30 percent, compared to an average of 20 percent for local varieties.[74]

Serious efforts to diffuse Allen cotton were undertaken by the staff and students at the farm school at Baraweli and by their trainees throughout the Niger Valley cantons of the Segu district in 1928. Because of the care necessary to cultivate this variety of cotton and because agricultural extension agents were obliged to supervise the crop, the new variety of cotton diffused only gradually. Seven tons of Allen were harvested in 1928–29 and 15.7 tons the next year. The administration felt that these quantities were not sufficient and that the current situation in the world cotton market was too uncertain to open an official cotton market in Baraweli. The administration thus decided to buy all the crop at a price considerably higher than that prevailing in the official markets to ensure its purchase and to protect producers' interests. In the 1929–30 harvest, the administration paid an average of 2.70 francs per kilogram for Allen compared to the high offer of 1.25–1.40 francs per kilogram for local cotton on the official markets. By 1930–31, however, producers' response to Allen was so good that the administration was obliged to buy nearly 200 tons in the Segu district alone.[75]

In cooperation with the ACC, the administration had its cotton ginned, prepared, and shipped to Le Havre. Soudanese Allen cotton was well received in France, but the small quantities did not rouse much enthusiasm among French industrial users. In 1929 and 1930, the colonial state neither turned a profit nor incurred a loss. Despite the collapse of world cotton prices in 1931 and 1932, the administration felt obligated to maintain relatively high prices for Allen and bought all that was offered. Although it dropped its offering price to 1.75–2.00 francs per kilogram, the cotton harvest was large enough so that the colonial state lost between 50,000 and 60,000 francs on the transaction. As the world economy contracted further in 1932, the administration dropped its offering price to 1.25–1.50 francs per kilogram. Nonetheless, Governor Fousset expected that the harvest of Allen cotton would double again and that the administration would incur a loss of between 100,000 and 120,000 francs. "In regard to Allen cotton," he wrote in 1932, "it is obvious that the administration cannot long continue this practice. If the economic situation does not improve, the administration risks having all its commercial operations, for which it is not in the least prepared and which are to a certain degree incompatible with its general organization, swept away by increasing deficits."[76]

As Governor Fousset made clear, the administration could not long continue to subsidize cotton prices and to run its budget on deficit spending. Fousset also argued that in its commercial activities, the colonial state, like the ACC, lacked the "suppleness" of commercial firms.[77] But this was not the only explanation for the dismal failure of the colonial state's cotton transactions. Because the colonial state entered the market only when conditions were unfavorable for private merchants, the state effectively subsidized not only cotton producers but also cotton merchants, who were able to participate in the market without risk. The colonial state lost money on its cotton deals precisely because it sought to protect the incentives of a market in which merchants were free to buy and sell only when they wanted and in which producers retained considerable market and nonmarket options. Because of its commitment to a particular model of colonial development, the administration felt obliged to ensure that market incentives were maintained even as merchants abandoned the market. This, then, was the central paradox of the politique cotonnière. If the incentives of a market economy did not operate naturally in the Soudan, then the political and economic policies of the pro-peasant model of economic development were also flawed. The economic contraction during the Depression made this commitment to "free" markets and to market incentives untenable.

The politique cotonnière in the Soudan operated under ideological and economic constraints determined both in the colony and in the metropole. What metropolitan users were prepared to pay for Soudanese cotton ultimately determined what could be accomplished on the ground in the colony. Despite metropolitan users' lukewarm commitment to colonial cotton—French metropolitan officials were much more enthusiastic—the colonial program of economic development in the Soudan and cotton came to be indistinguishable. Those promoting cotton also promoted their own interests. The administration continually exhorted producers and chiefs to expand cotton production, but they left to merchants the task of actually buying the crop and therefore providing market incentives. The commercial sector responded unevenly to this task. Merchants were victims of price fluctuations on the world market over which they had no control and they were committed above all to maximizing their own profits. Thus they dealt in cotton only as long as it was in their interest.

The politics and programs during this period also revealed just how fragile was the alignment of forces and actors that held together the various constituencies of those promoting peasant cotton. The period, especially after 1925, fractured the apparent unity among these groups, resulting in new initiatives that eroded the established boundaries surrounding the specialized labors of the various actors. In the next chapter, I will examine in more detail the role of the domestic market in determining the outcome of the politique cotonnière to 1932.

Local Processes and the World Economy: Imported Cloth, the Domestic Cotton Market, and the Handicraft Textile Industry, 1918–1932

French plans to build colonialism in the Soudan on exports of cotton to the metropole were a clear expression of the power industrial societies assumed they had to shape the world economy. The intervention of the colonial state in the production and marketing of cotton intensified during the interwar period. Whether it took the form of control over labor to work the vast European cotton plantations or surveillance, control, and management of peasant-produced cotton, the French could point to little success. Cotton was produced on both peasant fields and plantation lands, and some was exported to France. Most of the cotton harvest, however, remained in the Soudan, where it fed a dynamic regional economy. Sustained demand for handcrafted textiles bid up the price of cotton in the Soudan, creating a dual market system for cotton which favored local production of cloth rather than export of raw materials to France. Sustained demand for handcrafted textiles induced ongoing yet reversible change among the men and women of the handicraft textile industry.

This chapter examines three sides of the interplay of colonialism and dynamic local processes of the regional economy as they related to the disposition of the cotton harvest from 1918 to 1932: the demand for cloth, whether imported or locally produced; the emergence of dual markets for cotton; and the patterns of social change in the handicraft textile industry. To explain the persistence of the handicraft textile industry and the consequent demand for cotton in the Soudan, this chapter advances two linked explanations. The first explores the reasons for the persistence of demand for handcrafted textiles in the face of imported cloth. The second explores the emergence of dual cotton markets in the Soudan and the consequences of higher domestic prices for French efforts to capture the cotton harvest for export.

In this chapter, we move the handicraft industry from the shadows surrounding the debate between the pro-peasant administrators and those supporting European-managed cotton irrigation schemes to center stage. The peasant producers of cotton and the handicraft producers of textiles do not speak with the same clear voices as the protagonists in the colonial development debates. But their actions and their historical recollections—as represented by statistics on cotton production and the volume of imported cloth, in descriptions of cotton and textile production, and in oral history—speak loudly of the dynamism of the domestic market.

The French protagonists of colonial cotton development assumed a simple model of import-stimulated growth of raw material exports. They assumed that Africans wanted manufactured consumer goods and would produce and sell agricultural products to satisfy their wants.[1] Imported cloth had consistently figured as a major part of the assortment of goods imported into West Africa. Indeed, French officials considered imported cloth the "major regulator" of colonial commerce. This chapter demonstrates that the relationship between the volume and price of imported cloth and the volume of Soudanese cotton sold on the export market was complicated by two additional factors: first, the volume of the cotton harvest sold to the export market was determined by competition between the domestic and export cotton markets; and second, the market for imported cloth was directly linked to the output in the domestic sector of handcrafted textiles. There was no simple functional relationship among these factors. Instead, individual producers and households made complex calculations about how to dispose of their cotton harvest and their other resources based on prices offered for cotton, the volume and prices of imported cloth, administrative coercion, and demand for cotton by a domestic sector that produced local textiles. Colonial officials and modern scholars have sought to explain this relationship, but each understood only part of the equation. The colonial agronomist Marius Etesse linked the price of imported cloth and the supply of handcrafted textiles in his report presented at the 1923 Union coloniale française meeting.

Weavers are ubiquitous throughout West Africa. With their primitive yet easily transportable craft, they go from village to village, where with the assistance of yarn prepared by women, they make bands of cloth more durable than imported cloth. When imported cloth is amply and inexpensively available, then this industry is limited to ordinary clothing [*vêtements d'usage*]. The inhabitants love imported cloth not because of its value in relationship to handcrafted cloth, but because of its colors. Bright colors attract them and well dyed cloth is sought after by women.

Following the rise in prices for European cloth, however, the native is obliged to remedy the situation by fabricating cloth locally. The governor-general reported that throughout AOF there has been a very active revival of handcraft textile production and an equally rapid abandonment of purchases in imported cloth.[2]

Etesse's argument stripped producers' response to the lowest common denominator: if the price was right, Africans preferred imported cloth over locally produced varieties. Etesse assumed that Africans turned to more durable handicraft textiles only when imported cloth was not available at reasonable prices. By looking at price and consumer preferences, Etesse saw only some of the variables involved in the complex response of African consumers and African producers of handcrafted textiles to the enlarged market for textiles.

Marion Johnson, the historian who has devoted most attention to the impact of cotton imperialism on African textile producers, accepted price elasticity of demand as the principle of consumer responsiveness, but she also argued that the availability of cheap imported cloth was not sufficient to undercut the domestic African handicraft textile industry. Despite European cotton imperialism, domestic African textile production persisted because it was both cost effective and involved no opportunity costs.

For all but the wealthiest consumers, however, price is important. Only if the local weaver can produce cloth whose price, in terms of attractiveness and durability, can compete with imported cottons, can he hope to stay in business. How, with his slow rate of production on the hand-loom, can he compete with the mass-produced factory article? It is true that he has a certain protection in the cost of transport, but this has been declining with the years, and disappears with the establishment of local factories. The answer seems to lie in the economic organization of the industry. Apart from some working for elite markets, there are fewer weavers whose households do not produce their basic needs of food and most other necessities, and often his raw material as well. Often the weaver is himself a farmer, and weaves only in the non-farming season. . . . Under such a system, the marginal costs of production are virtually nil. The weaver receives his food whether he weaves or not, and pays nothing for his workplace; his yarn costs no more than the work, on similar terms, of his womenfolk. Only if there is an alternative employment in the non-farming season does his labour, or theirs, have opportunity cost. Much of the decline observed in various areas derives not so much from the direct competition of imported textiles, as from alternative employment opportunities, including seasonal migrant labour.[3]

In pointing to the costs of production, Johnson identified key variables in the persistence of the handicraft textile industry. Johnson, however, assumed that weavers were self-sufficient in cotton and did not, therefore, account for the lively demand for raw materials in the domestic market. Costs of production were not the only variables, nor was the labor of the weaver's "womenfolk" "costless." As we shall see later in this chapter, the reciprocity of household social relations was severely tested and strained in the course of the interwar period.

In comparison to Etesse, who recognized that the volume and price of imported cloth changed over time, Johnson missed a central aspect of the Soudanese textile industry. Handicraft textile production persisted also because of periodic disruptions in the supply of manufactured cloth and because the Soudanese market was linked to a wider West African continental market. Even if consumers in the Soudan were prepared to pay a premium for manufactured cloth, there were moments when none (or virtually none) was available. Thus production and consumption of handicraft textiles must be situated within the world economic situation in which colonial commerce operated. Nearly 50 years ago, Raúl Prebisch identified a simple functional link between what he called metropolis-satellite relations and economic development in the periphery. Andre Gunder Frank later developed and popularized these ideas into a schematic formulation of underdevelopment thesis. Frank argued that "satellites" experience economic development when their ties to their "metropoles" are weakest such as during economic depressions and wars.[4] Although Frank was concerned with capitalist economic development and his argument was overly reductionist, the persistence of the handicraft textile industry in the Soudan from the end of World War I through the Depression was linked to the decline in the supply of manufactured cloth resulting from crises in the economies of France and the world capitalist system. When the volume of imported cloth declined and prices rose, demand for local, handcrafted textiles increased. Moreover, the French Soudan was not an isolated market but one that sustained long-standing commercial contacts with a larger continental market. As a result, the handicraft textile industry in the Soudan responded not only to metropole-satellite relations in Frank's terms but also to market conditions within a West African continental framework.

In West Africa, demand for clothing was extremely elastic. In good times, Soudanese peasants had a virtually unlimited appetite for cloth; in bad times, they could make do with a few pagnes and a bou-bou. More cloth was needed for ceremonies, but the elaborateness of ceremonies could be adjusted to fit available resources. In the absence of aggregate population and production data, it is virtually impossible to estimate the size of the domestic market. Most of the local production, exchange, and consumption of cloth was never measured.

Prices of imported cloth were determined not only by demand and supply but by political and world economic conditions. Consumers' abilities to buy imported cloth also depended on their income, and their income depended on the prevailing prices for their agricultural commodities. When, for example, Soudanese peasants did not receive much for their harvest, they could not consume even if imported cloth was available at attractive prices. In such circumstances, Soudanese cotton producers sold their harvest to the domestic market, and weavers increased output for sale in neighboring colonies, especially the Côte d'Ivoire, Senegal, and the Gold Coast. Staple export production of rubber, cocoa, coffee, and groundnuts in these coastal regions often provided higher incomes than cotton producers received in the Soudan and stimulated demand for handicraft textiles.

Consumers did not merely turn to handicraft textiles in response to high prices of imported cloth. Consumers appreciated the durability of handcrafted textiles. More important, handcrafted textiles catered to market niches untouched by imported cloth, including demand for cotton and cotton-wool blankets, burial shrouds, durable work clothes, and ethnically distinct attire. Consumers were amenable to innovation, which provided workers in the weaving sector with opportunities to introduce new materials (imported, industrial yarn) and new patterns.[5] The point to be stressed is that the handicraft textile industry of the French Soudan remained a vital part of a domestic West African economy that was not destroyed by competition with imported cloth. Periodic interruptions in the supply of imported cloth ensured that the demand for handcrafted cloth remained strong and provided opportunities for Soudanese textile workers to escape direct participation in the colonial economy.

From the standpoint of the disposition of the cotton harvest, the robust domestic sector consistently offered between three and five times more for cotton than did the export sector. In 1927, the Segu district officer captured the paradox of the efforts to develop cotton production for export in competition with the domestic market.

French merchant houses hesitate to buy cotton, and even when some timid effort is made, at .50–.60 francs/kilogram, the price is of little interest to producers. There is, however, in this district, an extremely important trade in this textile, whether in its raw state or in the form of yarn and bands. . . . Local trade pays a price of 1.75 to 3 francs per kilogram. . . .

Above all, competition between commerce and the native consumers over cotton will naturally recur during the next harvest to the detriment of our exporters, because despite the increase in prices offered by the commercial houses, they will find it difficult to pay the producer the minimum price of 1.75 francs/kilogram offered by the natives.[6]

Given the alternative uses and markets for cotton, producers had considerable ability to respond positively to market incentives, although not necessarily as the French wanted.

Soudanese cotton producers did not calculate their profit and loss solely on the basis of the returns on cotton or alternative crops. Cotton producers were part of complex social and cultural systems, in which individual maximization may not have been a compelling force. Depending on how he calculated his well-being, the peasant cotton producer could sell his cotton to the export sector or to the domestic market of spinners and weavers, or he could use it within the subsistence functions of his household. Cotton prices were a significant factor in the cotton producer's decisions, but they were not the only one. His decision was shaped also by the prevailing market for imported cloth, the degree of nonmarket compulsion applied by the colonial state, and cotton prices on the domestic market.

In the absence of reliable production and productivity data for cotton and cotton textile production in the Soudan, I will advance a set of working hypotheses regarding the economics of dual cotton markets and handicraft textile production in the Soudan. Rain-fed cotton required hard work and sustained vigilance to squeeze cotton from the soil. Precisely because cotton was so labor intensive, most peasant households during the precolonial period produced enough to satisfy their own domestic needs. Normal surpluses fed a lively regional circuit of trade and handicraft production, but commercial cotton production was concentrated on slave plantations such as those the Maraka controlled during the nineteenth century.[7]

Low productivity in cotton production was linked to relatively high productivity in weaving. It was certainly not as high as industrial production, but weavers using simple double-heddle narrow looms could produce cotton bands sufficient for one pagne in one day's work, often in exchange for little more than their subsistence. Weaving was largely a dry-season activity, when there was little opportunity cost to devoting oneself intensely to weaving. As the market for handicraft textiles increased, the weavers probably bid up the price of their labor and cotton growers demanded more for their cotton. Nonetheless, the relatively low costs of production of handcrafted cotton bands assured that handcrafted textiles could maintain a hold on certain market niches at the very least. During times when the supply of imported cloth was interrupted, more weavers could be brought into production and a larger share of the domestic cotton harvest acquired.

As the architects of colonial cotton development were to discover, the existence of a dynamic production sector to supply the domestic market for cotton and cotton textiles coupled with the high elasticity of demand for both imported and domestic cloth drove the allocation of the cotton harvest more fully than did colonial policies. The Soudan was simultaneously part of a robust West African market and the world economy. The first section of this chapter examines the relationships between imported cloth and handcrafted textiles. The second section turns to the cotton growers' production and marketing decisions. No matter how they tinkered with prices and marketing, cotton slipped through their fingers and into the domestic market. What needs to be explained is how the export sector received any cotton at all. In the third section, I examine aspects of the social history of the handicraft textile industry during this period. And finally, the chapter concludes with an assessment of the Depression on the interplay of world economic forces and local processes.

Imported Cloth, Handicraft Textiles, and the Regional Economy

Manufactured cloth and imported guinée cloth had been part of the assortment of goods traded in the Western Sudan from the late nineteenth century. Conquest of the region in the 1880s and 1890s and the arrival of the railway from Kayes in 1904 opened the French Soudan more fully to metropolitan commerce. As noted in Chapter 4, the initial surge in cloth imports and purchases in the Soudan coincided with the commodity boom of 1911–12. Imports of cloth fell again as a result of the 1913–14 drought and did not fully recover before the onset of wartime hostilities in Europe. The war, however, caused the supply of manufactured cloth to the colonies to contract. Metropolitan weavers found themselves bound closely to the war effort and hence unable to guarantee deliveries or prices to the colonial market. What little imported cloth had been available in the early part of the decade virtually disappeared during the war and the immediate postwar period. By the end of 1921, some imported cloth reappeared in Soudanese markets, although it was still expensive. "Chiefs and notables," wrote agricultural engineer Costes in his annual report, "use imported percales, bazins, roume, etc., which they can procure at reasonable prices." The "humble class," noted Costes, continued to use local cloth.[8]

Economic recovery in France during the 1920s was hampered by the gradual pace of rebuilding the war-damaged physical plant. The wild fluctuations on the world commodity markets, however, obliged merchants to exercise extreme caution. In the Soudan, these conditions often meant that European commercial houses virtually abandoned buying, lest they be caught with expensive produce they could not unload. The administration encouraged peasants to grow cotton, yet the export market they had anticipated had not materialized. Consumers were thus faced with a triple burden: first, prices of imported cloth were high at least for the "humble class"; moreover, prices of imported cloth fluctuated dramatically, turning away the few consumers who had been interested in purchasing cloth.[9] Second, consumers had little cash because the commercial houses were unwilling to buy their produce. And finally, producers had their harvest of cotton. "Faced with the high prices of guinées, shandora, and imported cloth, the natives hesitate to provision themselves from the European commercial houses and address themselves to local weavers, who furnish for them at better prices cloth made of local cotton." Paradoxically, the model of cotton imperialism, in which imported cloth would undercut local artisans and yield a steady supply of cotton for export, operated in the reverse: "The sale of cotton bands, in regression for some time, had regained a certain importance and this article is much in demand."[10] In 1925, Bélime described the linkage between price and supply of imported cloth and demand for handcrafted textiles.

For a long time, the cercles of Segu and Koutiala, to cite only those where the culture of cotton has always been practiced on a large scale, have exported toward the territories of the south bands of cotton produced from local weaving. The sale of these products of this little local industry, however, has been very active recently. Since the war, and especially for the past two years, the increasingly high cost of European manufactured cloth has provoked a rapid extension of this commercial current, which now absorbs the largest part of cotton produced in the land.[11]

The price of imported cloth was a factor, but so was quality. "Natives find imported cloth too expensive and less durable than cloth made locally."[12] Faced with insufficient cotton prices offered by the export sector and expensive imported cloth, producers showed no interest in selling their harvests; instead, "to reap the largest profit, they retain their cotton in order to spin and weave cloth locally during the winter season."[13]

The handicraft textile sector increased output using both the domestic cotton harvest and imported, machine-spun yarn. Indeed, the value of imported cloth and yarn increased more than tenfold between the immediate postwar period and 1928–29, the years of peak imports. That the volume of imports increased at the same time as the handicraft industry increased output indicates a profound elasticity in consumption of textiles in the Soudan and in neighboring colonies. Figure 10 traces the changes in the value of imported cloth by category. The figure provides detail on consumers' preferences, indicating that consumption of manufactured cloth other than guinée was much more elastic than consumption of guinée and imported yarn. In 1928, Soudanese consumers bought manufactured cloth at a rate of nearly two to one over guinée, spending more than 36 million francs on manufactured cloth compared to 15.7 million

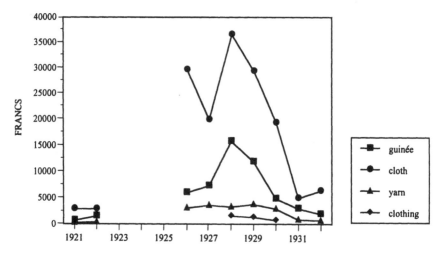

Fig. 10. Value of Cloth and Yarn Imports into the French Soudan, 1921–1932. Sources: ANS-AOF 2 G 23-5; ANS-AOF 2 G 23-45; ANS-AOF 2 G 27-1; ANS-AOF 2 G 27-7; ANS-AOF 2 G 28-6; ANS-AOF 2 G 29-4; ANS-AOF 2 G 30-31; ANS-AOF 2 G 31-37; ANS-AOF 2 G 32-9.

francs for guinée. Data on imported ready-made clothing are not good, but in the 1920s these imports accounted for a tiny fraction of total cloth imports. From the standpoint of the economic and social history of the handicraft textile industry, the imports of industrial yarn, represented in Figure 10, showed little elasticity. This suggests that the men and women of the handicraft textile industry were prepared to pay even the rapidly fluctuating prices to control the supply of yarn.

The increased volume of imported cloth did not satisfy all concerned, however. Despite disadvantageous tariffs, British cloth was more in demand than French manufactured cloth, especially at the lower end of the market where imported cloth competed most directly with local handicrafts. In 1922, for example, the value of British cloth imports into the Soudan accounted for three times the value of French cloth imports. Moreover, 91 percent of the total value of British imports was composed of cloth.[14] On the initiative of the Union coloniale française, a meeting in France was held between metropolitan industrialists and West African commercial interests to assess ways to pry the Soudanese market away from "Manchester industry, which in effect, controls the largest part of the African market." The Union coloniale and representatives of the West African commercial houses exhorted French industry to produce cloth "in the fashion of current demand in French West Africa." François Vézia, one of the leading Bordelais import-export houses, accused French manufacturers of disregarding colonial commerce. Vézia was convinced that French industry could easily furnish all the white cloth in demand in French West Africa, compete successfully with English producers for dyed and printed cloth, and undercut British prices.[15] By 1930, these predictions were borne out: Soudanese consumers were buying more French than English cloth, although England was close behind in total value of imported cloth with Belgian cloth in third place. France's share of the imported cloth market in 1930 was 32 million francs of the total import bill of 58.8 million francs or 54 percent.[16] But the victory was a Pyrrhic one, for French cloth captured a market that was about to crash.

Fluctuating world prices for both raw cotton and cotton textiles from the middle of the 1920s onward squeezed Soudanese producers and metropolitan commercial houses equally. Merchant houses avoided buying African cotton at high official prices as the American harvests boomed and world prices sank. "After the good years of 1924, 1925, and 1926, the native, surprised, refused to sell," wrote

Governor Fousset.[17] In response to continued declining cotton prices offered by European commercial houses for the 1928–29 cotton campaign, peasants withheld most of their crop from the official markets. "Native producers sell only what is strictly necessary for them to meet their needs and pay their [tax] obligations. This resulted in a marked reduction in the sale of imported merchandise."[18] Merchants found themselves saddled with stocks of imported cloth they could not sell.[19]

As the following report makes clear, trade in cloth was the "major regulator" of commercial transactions in general.

In the course of the year 1930, the low purchasing price of raw materials brought with it a significant decline in the natives' purchasing power. It is necessary to say that for the Soudan, commerce in cotton textiles is the major regulator of importations because imports of cloth represent nearly half of the entire value of imported merchandise. There is, however, a certain correlation between the decline of imported cloth and the production of handicraft textiles in the Soudan, which has undergone a veritable renaissance resulting in the local production of a very large quantity of native cloth.[20]

As the Depression deepened its hold on both metropolitan industry and colonial commerce, Soudanese cotton producers turned increasingly away from the export market.[21]

One nagging question remains. How, in competition with the higher prices in the domestic market, did the export sector manage to acquire any cotton at all? In the absence of aggregate production and consumption data, I can only suggest a set of hypotheses. First, given the administrative pressure on producers and the coercive power of canton chiefs and district administrators, producers may well have accepted cotton sales to the export sector as a form of tax, and they may have been willing to accept a lower price as one of the costs of extortion.[22] Second, producers may have been prepared to accept a lower price in the export sector as long as the cost of acquiring imported cloth was not too high. When imported cloth became more expensive, demand for handicraft textiles increased. And third, the domestic sector may not have had the capacity to absorb the entire cotton harvest, particularly in the higher-cotton-yielding southern savannas. The relatively undeveloped condition of the handicraft textile industry in that region probably meant that producers there had fewer alternative markets for their cotton. Nonetheless, the existence of the subsistence functions of the household and the domestic market constrained the abilities of the commercial sector to squeeze excessive profits from producers. In the same manner, the existence of these alternative markets for cotton constrained the flexibility of the commercial sector from responding positively to changes in the world market to maximize its own profits. In the end, the dual market for cotton undercut the administration's efforts to legislate market incentives.

Cotton Prices and Dual Cotton Markets

The 1923–24 cotton season was close to the ideal of the pro-peasant model of colonial cotton development. The harvest was abundant, export merchants paid high prices for cotton, and producers were able to buy relatively abundant and inexpensive imported goods.[23] Although world prices favored Soudanese cotton producers and exporters through 1926, the commercial sector was not always willing or able to take advantage of these conditions. In the summer of 1924, accidents cut the Thiès-Niger railway in three places. The railway was not fully operational again until later that year, which interfered with the 1924–25 cotton buying season. Merchants, unable to evacuate their cotton stocks, ceased buying.[24] In the course of the 1925 millet crisis in Senegal, merchants abandoned cotton for the quick profits of the grain trade. In 1926, excessively dry conditions hurt the cotton harvest, and despite high world prices the commercial sector was unable to acquire large stocks.

The rapid devaluation of the franc in the middle 1920s played havoc with the commercial sector's ability to juggle prices and supplies.[25] "The decline in the value of the franc and the uncertainty in the world price [of cotton] has resulted in a significant reduction in commercial operations," noted the monthly commercial report of April 1924. "The price offered producers is lower than before, demand is weaker, and in certain centers merchants have stopped buying completely."[26] Low prices and uncertain conditions continued throughout the 1924–25 cotton season. Thus, despite another abundant harvest, "the native shows no eagerness to sell his cotton, and he prefers, in the goal of getting the largest possible gain, to store his cotton in seed and to card and spin it during the rainy season in order to weave it locally."[27]

During the summer of 1926 merchants complained that Africans were no longer buying cloth, the staple item of commerce, because prices were too high. Because of the deepening decline in the value of the franc on international exchanges and the flood of American cotton on the world market, "prices offered natives for their products are significantly lower than last year at the same time. The producer, accustomed to having a higher rate over the past several years, does not understand the current price decline for groundnuts and cotton and hesitates to sell his crops in expectation of a better price."[28] A better price was not, however, forthcoming.

What the export sector was prepared to pay for Soudanese cotton clearly influenced producers' responses. Governor Terrasson argued that the only way to tell if producers were happy with the price offered was how much cotton they actually sold. Although production data for the Soudan are not very good, some global estimates made by officials provide evidence for Terrasson's "test." In 1927, 658 tons of ginned cotton were exported from the Soudan. Most of the total harvest of nearly 7,000 tons remained in the domestic sector. "Faced with the prices offered by commerce, producers prefer to sell their cotton to native buyers at prices ranging from 1.50 to 3.00 francs/ kilogram. These buyers come from regions where the cotton harvest has been deficient. One can without exaggeration estimate that at least two-thirds of the cotton production of 1926–27 remains in the colony and is used by local weavers."[29] Although producers did not always sell at the best prices, they were unwilling to sell their cotton at whatever the commercial sector offered.

Producers were, however, prepared to accept a certain loss in revenue because of the noneconomic pressures they faced. The archival record provides a glimpse into the threshold beyond which producers would not sell. In March 1925, following several years of increasing prices but in response to the commercial sector's rush to the millet trade, cotton prices averaged between 1.00 and 1.50 francs per kilogram. "The native hesitates to sell his cotton harvest at this price," noted the economic report for that month, "and having procured the small amount of cash necessary for his needs through the sale of millet at exaggerated prices, he conserves his cotton for family needs and brings only little quantities to market."[30] In December 1926, as the first wave of the large American cotton harvest was felt in the Soudan, producers refused to sell their cotton at the 0.70 francs per kilogram the commercial sector offered.[31] Mérat came remarkably close to this figure in his estimate of minimum returns necessary to make cotton profitable. "In that part of the Soudan where transport does not permit the export of peanuts, on the basis of labor costs alone, cotton must be bought at 0.75 francs/kilogram to be remunerative to the producer."[32] Cotton prices ranging from 0.75 to 1.00 francs per kilogram represented a fairly tight threshold beyond which peasants would not willingly sell their cotton. When prices in the export sector dropped below this threshold, as they did in 1932, exports declined dramatically. Some cotton was still exported, but most probably came from the administration's direct purchases and from the harvests on the champs du commandant.

No one has yet been able to measure the size of the Soudanese cotton harvest. The most reliable statistics refer to the volume of ginned cotton. From 1923 to 1929 more and more Soudanese cotton was ginned. Figure 11 traces the volume of ginned cotton exported annually from 1923 to 1932. Increased ginning capacity throughout the Soudan accounts for some of these increases. The decline in cotton exports between 1925 and 1926 was related to imperfections in the export sector's commitment to cotton, the decline between 1926 and 1927 to unfavorable climatic conditions, and the steeper decline after 1929 to the influence of world commodity prices.

Figure 11 is misleading, however, because there was no direct correlation between the volume of cotton ginned and the total size of the cotton harvest. For example, the fall in the volume of ginned cotton between 1925 and 1926 had less to do with the absolute size of

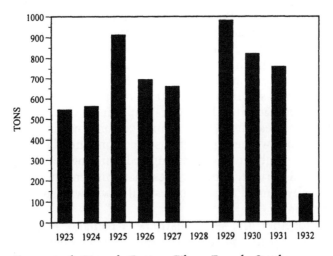

Fig. 11. Exports of Ginned Cotton Fiber, French Soudan, 1923–1932. Sources: Production du coton en 1925–26, ANS 1 R 102; ANS-AOF 2 G 26-33; ANS-AOF 2 G 27-41; ANS-AOF 2 G 30-31; ANS-AOF 2 G 31-37; ANS-AOF 2 G 32-9.

the harvest than with the decisions made by cotton producers about how to dispose of their harvests. "If one takes into account that trade in bands of cotton woven locally is increasing and that it absorbs an increasingly important share of the harvest from the year before, then one can conclude," noted Secretary-General Descemet, acting as interim governor, "that the cotton harvests of 1925 and 1926 are more or less the same with figures of about 2,000 tons of fiber."[33] With ginning yields of about 20 percent fiber, the total harvest for those years was 10,000 tons. The 1927 decline in total cotton ginned from 1926 was the result of a drought in October, which occurred at a critical time in the cotton cycle.[34] Data for 1928 are missing.

Although the data on ginned cotton are the best available indicators of the size of the Soudanese cotton harvest, two caveats are necessary concerning the evidence we can derive from them. First, the entire cotton harvest was not ginned by the ginning factories.[35] A significant amount was probably ginned by women using either long-established procedures or newer hand-held carders. This point was made clearly by Descemet in another report on the 1925–26 cotton harvest. "Local consumption of cotton has been seriously underestimated. Reports from all points of the colony indicate that native weavers are operating to full capacity; bands of cotton flow into the markets, where they are bought at a price higher than 25 francs/kilogram and then sent to the Côte d'Ivoire or the Gold Coast. This profitable price for worked cotton explains the general tendency for natives to conserve their harvests, and for the maximum amount to be ginned and spun by the women."[36] Second, not all the cotton ginned by the ginning companies flowed into the export sector. Depending on the district, a significant proportion of the total amount of cotton ginned flowed back into local consumption. In Chapter 4, I argued that one of the reasons so little ginned cotton flowed into the export sector was that women spinners used cotton ginned by the ACC to ease their own labor of hand carding and spinning. Table 1, based on the 1925–26 harvest, demonstrates that this tendency to consume mechanically ginned cotton domestically was widespread throughout the colony.

Taken together, the seven districts of Bamako, Bouguni, Kayes, Koutiala, San, Segu, and Sikasso produced 64 percent of the total cotton ginned during this period. If we subtract the cotton produced by CICONNIC in the districts of Goundam and Gourma—cotton produced expressly for export—these seven districts produced 73 percent of the total rain-fed cotton ginned. These figures are indicative

TABLE I

Ginned Cotton Exported and Consumed Locally, 1925–1926

(thousand kilograms)

Cercles	Local consumption	Exported	Pct. of total consumed locally
Bafoulabe	22.0	16.5	57
Bamako	80.0	131.9	37
Bandiagara	6.5	14.3	31
Bouguni	34.4	30.8	53
Gao	0.4	0.1	80
Goundam	4.5	9.9	31
Gourma	—	322.0	0
Issa-Ber	15.0	11.5	56
Kayes	40.0	179.0	18
Kita	14.0	73.4	18
Koutiala	67.0	110.7	37
Macina	6.0	15.4	28
Mopti	10.0	22.6	30
Nara	1.9	—	100
Nema	—	—	0
Nioro	26.0	15.5	62
San	35.0	59.4	37
Satadugu	10.0	10.0	50
Segu	115.0	113.7	50
Sikasso	130.0	50.9	72
Timbuktu	0.5	—	100
TOTAL	618.2	1,197.5	

SOURCE: [Descemet] acting lt-gov., Soudan, Production du coton en 1925–26, Kouluba, 24 Sept. 1926, ANS 1 R 102.

of the share of the total cotton harvest absorbed by the handicraft textile industry.

Some districts, such as Kayes, produced a significant amount of ginned cotton (219 tons) but consumed relatively little (only 18 percent of the total ginned). Kita produced 87.4 tons and consumed only 18 percent locally. Because of their positions on the major lines of transport, the agricultural production of both districts was easily evacuated. Kayes was the railhead and port on the Senegal River; Kita was an important town astride the Kayes-Bamako railway. Neither Kayes nor Kita was a significant center of precolonial textile production.

By contrast, in Bamako and Segu, the districts in the heartland of the Middle Niger Valley handicraft textile industry and well situated along the major riverine and railway transportation sectors, the local industry absorbed 37 percent and 50 percent respectively of the total cotton ginned. And because these were two of the three largest peasant cotton-producing districts, the proportion of mechanically ginned cotton consumed locally is significant. The districts of Bouguni, Koutiala, and Sikasso, located farther to the south and better situated to take advantage of rain-fed cotton production, produced significant tonnage for both export and local manufacturing. In the case of Bouguni, 52 percent of the total ginned cotton was consumed locally; but even more astounding is the case of Sikasso, where fully 72 percent of 180.9 tons of ginned cotton was consumed locally. Not surprisingly, all three districts abutted onto the Côte d'Ivoire, where demand for handwoven textiles remained strong.

Of the major cotton-producing districts, only Segu, Sikasso, and Bouguni absorbed half or more of the ginned cotton produced. How much hand-ginned cotton was absorbed in the Soudan remains guesswork. Observations by colonial officials provide a picture of the capacity of the domestic industry to consume large parts of the cotton harvest, which suggests that the industry was significantly larger than that represented by the local consumption of ginned cotton. In 1926, Acting Governor Descemet estimated that fully half of the harvest was consumed locally. In 1927, the official collecting data on the cotton harvest suggested "without exaggeration" that nearly two-thirds was retained locally.[37] In the 1929–30 cotton campaign, officials estimated that the total harvest was 14,400 tons.[38] The following account of cotton production and trade in San helps interpret the allocation of cotton between the export and the domestic markets. Writing at the end of the first quarter of 1931, as the steep decline in export cotton prices and the simultaneous contraction in the supply of imported manufactured cloth was being felt, the administrator from San noted:

What is striking is the decline in [cotton] tonnage traded, which seems to get smaller each year:

1926	587T	2.10F/kilogram
1927	35T	1.75F/kilogram
1928	431T	1.60F/kilogram
1929	301T	1.40F/kilogram
1930	211T	1.25F/kilogram
1931	100T (est.)	0.55F/kilogram

However, everyone will remark, and I will affirm, that the area cultivated in cotton this year at least is double that of 1929–30. What happens to the cotton?

I find it perfectly normal that at actual prices natives manufacture cotton bands, of which the price has also declined, but which still leaves them more profit than the sale of raw cotton.[39]

The probable solution to the discrepancy in the colony-wide statistics for the cotton harvest of 1929–30 lies in the two ways cotton entered the domestic market. The first was through sales between cotton producers and traders or weavers and the second was through nonmarket household production.

There was an active trade in raw cotton, in handspun yarn, and in cotton bands, much of it emanating from the old centers of production in the Middle Niger Valley. Administrator Aubin of Segu juxtaposed the dynamism of the domestic cotton and cotton textile sector to the lack of activity in the export sector. "There is, however, in the districts, an extremely important trade between natives in cotton in both its raw form and in the form of yarn and bands. In the first case, the buyers are the populations of the left bank of the Niger (districts of Bamako, Segu, Nana, Nara, Macina) who procure this product directly or through intermediaries to resell the product in different markets. In the second case, the yarn and bands are taken by traders to the region of Siguiri." Aubin also noted that at a rate of 0.50 to 0.60 francs per kilogram of raw cotton offered by the export sector, producers in Segu were little interested, especially when they could get between 1.75 and 3 francs per kilogram on the domestic market.[40] Demand for Soudanese handspun yarn and handcrafted cloth in Senegal, the Côte d'Ivoire, upper Guinea, and the Gold Coast remained strong, too. In 1925, for example, demand for cotton and cotton bands in the Côte d'Ivoire districts of Bobo Juulaso and Bouake drew off between 300 and 350 tons from Koutiala and Sikasso, some of it probably flowing into the Gonfreville weaving complex.[41]

The higher profits available on the domestic market did not escape metropolitan commercial houses. Just as they had always done, agents of the French commercial houses were quick to see local opportunities to turn a profit on domestic transactions. In a 1930 report, Lieutenant Governor Terrasson described with thinly veiled criticism how the colonial state's efforts to shore up minimum cotton prices and to control the marketing of cotton foundered on the actions of the commercial sector. "Almost all of the cotton of Koutiala and Sikasso was bought by intermediaries at official markets at minimum prices of 1–1.20 francs/kilogram fixed by the administration. These intermediaries sold it again locally or in very nearby centers for 1.50 francs. The [European] commercial agent of today has transformed himself into a sedentary agent surrounded by his intermediaries who, without exerting themselves, have developed into a singular contradiction to the efforts of the administration."[42]

The price of cotton alone does not explain satisfactorily the allocation of the cotton harvest between the domestic and the export sectors. Crucial to the decisions cotton producers made was the state of play in the supply and price of imported cloth. The supply and price of imported cloth thus constituted the other element in providing market incentives to cotton producers straddling two markets. Recurrent crises in the world and colonial economies provided new opportunities for the men and women of the handicraft textile industry to renegotiate their relations of production. In the next section, I will examine the available evidence on the organization of production within the handicraft textile industry.

The Handicraft Textile Industry

As the foregoing sections have demonstrated, the domestic market absorbed the vast majority of the Soudanese cotton harvest. But how was that raw cotton transformed into bands of cloth? "I have received data from all parts of the colony," wrote Acting Lieutenant Governor Descemet during the 1925–26 cotton season, "that weavers are working at fully capacity. Bands of woven cotton flood the markets, where they get a high price of 25 francs/kilogram and are then sent to the Côte d'Ivoire and the Gold Coast. This remunerative price for worked cotton explains the widespread tendency by natives to retain the maximum amount of their cotton harvest which can be ginned and spun by their women."[43] In his 1925 report, Bélime remarked on the tendency for Soudanese cotton producers to retain their harvest and to have their womenfolk work the cotton. Bélime's remarks anticipated Marion Johnson's comments about the costs of the household women's labor. "In February [1925], cotton yarn sold in Bouguni and Sikasso for 12–15 francs/kilogram. Ginning and spinning cost nothing for the native, because it is the women who do this work. The native sees that the sale of worked cotton is much more profitable than the sale of the raw material."[44] One of my male informants, Bamoussa Keita, made similar remarks about the costs of ginning. "Ginning by hand costs little in terms of effort, thus it is not expensive."[45]

The expansion of the handicraft textile industry during World War I and through the 1920s was based on long-established patterns of work and gender division of labor. But what did increased production actually mean to the men and women of the household and to the social tensions inherent in the household over control of social production? Did the men and women of the household simply renew their complementary tasks? Or did the increase in demand for handicrafts push production out of the household? Unfortunately, the oral data I collected are not adequate to provide more than a cursory and timeless view of the relations of household production. Nonetheless, there are enough variations in both the oral and the archival records to hint at the points of social tension within the household and how the expansion of the handicraft textile industry during the 1920s and into the 1930s contributed to yet another cycle of change in textile production. The most significant of these changes was the shift away from the household as the locus of production. I will explore these issues by examining changes in women's work in ginning, the imports of yarn, and relations established between entrepreneurs of yarn and weavers.

Descemet and Bélime described what appeared to be an unchanged household production system in which the household head organized the labor of his female dependents. But was women's work unchanged and did male household heads manage it? In 1932, Robert Gaffiot described and estimated women's productivity in ginning cotton.

As soon as the groundnuts have been harvested, the women begin the ginning of cotton. This is a very time-consuming and tedious task if one wants to avoid significant losses. These workers use a large flat board for this task, called *derrou*, or sometimes a flat stone. The cotton is placed on the surface and the seeds removed from the fibers by holding the cotton with one hand and passing a short iron rod or a stick over the cotton with the other hand. Using this technique, a woman can obtain 100–150 grams of cotton fiber per day. An especially able and hardworking woman can obtain 250 grams per day, conversations included!

In European enterprises, where motor-driven ginneries are used, the machines can gin 800–1,000 kilograms of raw cotton per day.[46]

At yields of about 20 percent fiber, the mechanized ginneries produced 200 to 250 kilograms of cotton fiber per day. At these rates, mechanized ginneries were one thousand times more productive than the most productive woman ginning by hand. Gaffiot, however, described an archaic form of ginning, which no doubt persisted, but it was not the only one used. Hand carders had been a staple part of the import trade into the Soudan since the 1890s. In 1924 the ACC redoubled its efforts to capture the cotton harvest by distributing hand carders without cost. The ACC expected that using hand carders would contribute to the profits cotton producers would realize when they sold their harvest to the export sector because they anticipated that carding cotton before bringing it to market would increase the amount of cotton peasants could transport.[47] What the ACC didn't anticipate, however, was that women would use hand carders to ease their labor and to increase their productivity in ginning. Nor did it anticipate that most of the ginned cotton would flow into the domestic sector.

Ginned cotton still had to be spun before it could be woven. In his research in Gumbu, Claude Meillassoux pointed to spinning as the bottleneck in the handicraft textile industry. He estimated that it took the labor of eight female slaves to provide the yarn necessary for the labor of one male weaver.[48] One of my informants, a woman who was active in the textile industry in the 1930s and 1940s, estimated that it took her fifteen days to gin and spin yarn sufficient for one pagne. She also estimated that the most efficient weavers could produce enough cloth for one pagne each day; on the average, weavers produced cloth for ten pagnes over twelve days. Unless the female ginners and spinners of Gumbu had much higher productivity (or the work of female slaves was more highly compelled), Hadja Toumata Contao's figures indicate a more severe bottleneck than Meillassoux described. Instead of the 8:1 ratio that apparently prevailed in Gumbu, in Segu's handicraft textile industry the labor of between fourteen and fifteen women was needed to satisfy the productivity of one weaver.[49]

Given the bottleneck in the handicraft textile industry, it is not surprising that so much ginned cotton flowed back into the domestic market. Based on the 1924–25 cotton season (see Figure 11), the amount of mechanically ginned cotton that returned to the domestic market was equal to 618,200 woman-days of labor devoted to ginning alone. Unfortunately, I do not have data on the productivity of female spinners, but this savings in labor no doubt contributed substantially to increased productivity of the handicraft textile industry in the 1920s. How much labor women saved by using hand carders is impossible to estimate.

Women, however, did not content themselves with the labor saved by spinning ginned cotton. They continued to spin local varieties of raw cotton, but increasingly they preferred the exotic long-staple cottons introduced by the ACC and the Service d'agriculture for the export market. Women had been very quick to recognize the advantages of these new cotton varieties. This was the case already in 1904, when the ACC representative in Segu first observed the widespread inclination of Soudanese women to gin long-staple varieties of cotton. Women's preference for these cottons, Bélime argued in 1926, contributed to mediocre qualities sent to market: "We must not forget that it is the native women, who are in charge of the cotton harvest, who gin and spin by hand the cotton, which is then worked by the village weaver. In order to ease their work, they use the very best cotton capsules and deliver to market only the mediocre and inferior varieties."[50] Dahou Traore, a cotton farmer and an agricultural innovator in the 1930s, noted the same tendency when he stated that "we retained a part of our cotton harvest for our own clothing. . . . That cotton was a variety called Allen."[51]

Far from capturing the cotton harvest for export, state intervention in seed selection and in cotton ginning contributed to the persistence of the handicraft textile industry by increasing women's productivity. But this is only the tip of a more complex process: what did increased demand for handcrafted textiles in the 1920s and 1930s mean for the gender division of labor in the household? For the household's subsistence functions? For the household head's ability to manage the labor of its dependents? How did the decentralization of the textile industry following the end of slavery contribute to the reorganization of the industry?

Neither the oral nor the archival records have provided me with the quality of insights I had anticipated finding. Instead, I am left with some anecdotal evidence, some cursory statistical data, and a few remarks by informants about changes in relations of production. In the normative reconstruction of the precolonial situation, provided by many of my male informants, women ginned cotton and spun yarn for the male weavers of the household, who then produced cloth for domestic use. Both the bottleneck in the industry and the points of friction over control of the social product, however, grew out of the complementarity of female and male labor. As I argued in Chapter 4, yarn was a pivotal factor in the organization of the handicraft textile industry. Control over yarn, therefore, lay at the heart of the social composition of handcrafted textile production in the Soudan.

Imports of manufactured yarn suggest that women's work would be easier because they were no longer spending endless hours ginning and spinning. The labor saved from buying ginned cotton and imported yarn did not, however, lead naturally to domestic harmony. Rather, as Tijani Sylla remarks, it led to the breakdown of established household social relations. His comments, of course, reflect an elderly male's longing for what he recollected the golden precolonial period to be like. Imported yarn and mechanically ginned cotton, he argued, "have made women lazy. They have thrown away their ginning stones upon which they had worked in order to buy ginned cotton. This has discouraged women from working with raw cotton. In the past, however, the women clothed the entire family from cotton grown by the family." Further in the interview, Sylla discussed the impact of imported yarn and of the availability of the factors of production outside the household.

Question: Can you explain what happened when a women bought yarn? Did she give it to her husband or to a weaver?
Response: Women bought the yarn; the husband knew nothing of this. Women would buy imported yarn [*boloti*], which they would give to weavers and then they sold the cloth. . . .
Question: If you needed cash, would you have turned to your wife? If she gave you any, would you have to reimburse her?
Response: Not today. Before, when you took money from your wife, it became your property and you did not return any of it. Now, anyone who gets money from his wife must reimburse it or divorce will follow. Before, women and men were equal and both participated in the maintenance of the family. Today, it is only the man who is responsible for the expenses of the family. Women do not help us at all.[52]

For social historians, Sylla's remarks reveal much of the juxtaposition between the "present" and the "past" and how history can be evoked to bemoan change; but these remarks reveal little of the historical process. A similar conflation of past and present is evident in the following excerpts from an interview with Bamoussa Keita.

Question: Your womenfolk used to gin cotton, then spin the fiber to have yarn to weave. What happened with the arrival of the yarn of the whites? Did everyone abandon their [handspun] yarn?
Response: The women stopped their work. They bought the yarn of the whites. Eventually, they abandoned weaving. It is now the weavers themselves who buy yarn and weave it for their own account.[53]

Both these interviews hint at profound changes in the organization of the handicraft textile industry, but neither provides detail on the process of change. To give some substance to the changes in the domestic handicraft textile industry, I will turn first to statistics on imported yarn and then to my informants' recollections about relations of production.

Figure 12 portrays the changes in the volume of imported yarn from 1909 to 1932 as far as the statistical data can provide. By appending data on imports from the earlier period, 1909–18, the figure better captures the dramatic rises and declines in yarn imports. As I

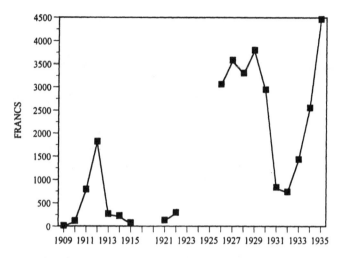

Fig. 12. Imports of Yarn into the French Soudan, 1909–1935. Sources: ANS-AOF 2 G 10-?; ANS-AOF 2 G 11-9; ANS-AOF 2 G 12-13; ANS-AOF 2 G 13-11; ANM 1 Q 44; ANS-AOF 2 G 23-5; ANS-AOF 2 G 27-1; ANS-AOF 2 G 28-6; ANS-AOF 2 G 30-31; ANS-AOF 2 G 31-37; ANS-AOF 2 G 32-9.

suggested in Chapter 4, the reversible nature of yarn imports created opportunities and strains for the household economy and for the organization of production. During times of increased imports, from 1910 to 1912 and from 1926 to 1929, the complementarity of gender tasks was no longer crucial to the production of handcrafted cloth. By buying imported yarn, both women and men could engage in production without recourse to household reciprocity.

Toumata Contao's description of her enterprise clearly indicates that she was producing yarn and cloth outside the bounds of the household:

Question: Did you have one weaver with whom you worked?
Response: I had eight under my tree. Three were solely in my service. The others worked for other people. We gave the weavers lodging and food and each month, each weaver wove five pagnes as payment.[54]

As I outlined in Chapters 2 and 4, the complementarity of gender tasks led logically to reciprocity of the household; but household reciprocity was not the only solution to bringing male and female tasks of handicraft textile production together. The subsistence functions of the household during the nineteenth century had clearly given way to the breakdown of both the male household head's authority and his capacity to manage the labor of all his dependents.

This helps account for Tijani Sylla's remarks that "before, women and men were equal and both participated in the maintenance of the family. Today . . . women do not help at all." The flip side of this process was evident in the household head's decreasing ability to call on the labor of his adult sons (see Chapter 11).

If the imports of manufactured yarn and the availability of ginned and raw cotton on the market contributed to the breakdown of the household as the locus of handicraft textile production, what happened during periods of declining yarn imports? From 1912 to 1913 imports of yarn declined precipitously, and they remained low (as far as the evidence suggests) until the middle 1920s. Without access to imported yarn, were female entrepreneurs of textiles forced back into the bounded gender tasks of the household? Imported yarn was only one of several means by which women gained access to their most important form of capital needed to produce cloth, but it was clearly the most productive avenue. The oral record, unfortunately, is silent on these issues. Although some women were no doubt forced by these circumstances back into household reciprocities, many women could still enter independent production of cloth by buying raw or ginned cotton on the market and by taking advantage of their "share" of ginned cotton. Cebarama Dembele reiterated the practice of one-fifth shares of cotton ginned. "Each time that a woman completed four baskets of ginning cotton, the fifth is hers. If you say that this work is not paid, then that which a woman could do in three days will take a month. If you announce a 'salary,' then you will be sure to be well served."[55]

Access to yarn, whether imported industrial or homespun, was only part of the calculus of production. Women still needed to get their yarn woven by men. In 1925 Acting Governor Descemet remarked that throughout the colony weavers were working at full capacity. This remark indicates that the handicraft textile industry was booming, but it also provides a backdrop for better assessing what changes were occurring on the weaving end of production. If women with access to yarn were progressively moving outside of the bounded relations of the household to have their yarn woven, then it is obvious that weavers, too, were moving outside the household to work. As I argued in Chapter 2, among the Maraka almost all male slaves were weavers. With the end of slavery, males former slaves became independent weavers, ready and willing to weave for pay. As Toumata Contao described in her interview, weavers were also willing to weave in exchange for food and lodging. Thus the increasing demand for handcrafted cloth accelerated changes in the organization of textile production which had been ongoing from the first decade of the twentieth century. Moreover, the decline in ethnic (and status) boundaries over economic spheres coincident with the end of slavery contributed to decentralization of the nineteenth-century textile industry and opened new opportunities to young men. The following exchange with Cebarama Dembele is indicative of these changes.

Question: In the time of the Bambara, were weavers free men or slaves?
Response: Some free men wove, but weaving was above all the task of the slave. . . .
Question: When the French arrived, everyone began to cultivate cotton. Did slaves remain the only weavers?
Response: Everyone wove; even I was a weaver. It was no longer a question of slave or free, everyone could now weave.

Dembele noted later in the interview that he began weaving in 1926, when he was 21, and stopped weaving five years later.[56] Dembele's experience as a weaver coincides with the period of rapid expansion of the handicraft textile industry, but his experience also hints at another side of the weaver's employment. Weaving was largely a dry-season activity and weaving provided nonfarm income. For a young adult male to have access to income outside of the household is indicative of the erosion of the bounded nature of household economic functions discussed above. Some weavers, as Toumata Contao described, established client relations with female entrepreneurs.[57] Others probably operated in a more free market context, attracting those with yarn depending on their reputations. Indigo-dyed pagnes (*ducouruni fin*) and white cloth were simple to weave. Other types of cloth, including the checkerboard pattern (*kosso-damier*) and other more traditional designs, provided weavers with some artistic independence. Cebarama Dembele described how women with yarn and weavers negotiated the design.

Question: When a woman brought her yarn to have woven, did she have a design in mind? Who determined the design, the women or the weaver?
Response: The weaver received a cutting of the pattern and he set the woof to that design.
Question: Did the weaver not have the opportunity to innovate the designs?
Response: Certainly. After seeing the cutting and having set the woof, the weaver reflected and developed a design of his own making. If I use three black threads and add one red one, then I will have a certain design. It is

not the owner of the yarn who defines that; rather it is the weaver, who finds inspiration. However, if a client had a model in mind, then she asked the weaver to make it.[58]

The checkerboard or *damier* design seemed to have become popular during the interwar period, particularly after Soudanese veterans returned from the war. The following sections of an interview with Dramane Kone pursue the issue of artistic invention.

Question: During which era did the weavers begin to use the *damier* pattern?
Response: Since ancient times. But those designs became more common [during the war].
Question: Did the weavers invent these patterns?
Response: Weavers copied designs which arrived from the East. Young people returned from their voyages with new designs.
Question: Who determined which design was woven into the cloth?
Response: The weaver wanted to satisfy his client who was the one who invented the designs. It is normal to want to please the client, some even gave additional presents in addition to the price of labor.[59]

The dynamic and resiliency of the handicraft textile industry was attributable to its position within the overlapping worlds of the world economy and the West African regional one, but the outcomes of struggles over production and control over the finished product stemmed from localized, long-term patterns of reversible social and economic change.

The Depression and the Politique Cotonnière

For almost two years following the New York stock exchange crash of 1929, France escaped the full effects of worldwide deceleration of economic activities. In 1931, however, France's exports collapsed and the value of its agricultural and industrial products declined.[60] Prices paid for cotton in France fell to their lowest level since 1894, which were well below the African producers' threshold. The ACC predicted that the cotton season of 1931–32 would result in "virtually nothing."[61] By the beginning of 1932, the effects of the economic crisis were felt in the Soudan. "An almost complete economic marasmus has characterized the commercial activities during this quarter," noted the economic report for the second quarter. "Many commercial houses have closed their shops. Those which remain open have been ordered not to make any purchases."[62] Without income from the export sector, peasants could not purchase imported goods, thus undercutting the assumption of export-led economic growth which undergirded colonial cotton development in the pro-peasant camp. Falling prices and declining incomes pushed peasants to direct their cotton harvests to the domestic sector or to weave the cotton themselves. This contraction in the export economy became a vicious cycle.[63]

Economic contraction spurred a renewal of debates on the nature of the economy in the Soudan and the colony's relationship to France. Some began to think of an economy organized by the needs of national defense and a return to the state's role in a command economy. Colonel Vallée, permanent secretary of the French West African bureau of the Défense Nationale, remarked that the colonies of the federation should be required to supply 4,400 tons of cotton fiber to France each year. Mérat, in his assessment of the politique cotonnière, responded by arguing that "the production of cotton cannot develop by simple administrative command. It can only develop if it is assured regular and normal outlets or those which have been artificially created and maintained." Mérat stressed that cotton could not yet be produced in the colonies at prices competitive with those on the world market. And he blamed the difficulties experienced in the colonies on the French textile industry. "Metropolitan industry," he wrote, "has through its purchasing prices severely encumbered the development of cotton in the colonies. . . . If, as is currently feared, producers of cotton in the United States begin to restrict sales, then prices will rise, rendering remunerative cotton production in new regions hitherto excluded." Juxtaposed to the "normal play of competition" in determining prices was a different organization of the economy, stimulated by the Depression and by newly prominent ideas about protecting national economies. "Closed economies," wrote Mérat, "are in vogue and protectionism has found its justification. This is a politics which has been elaborated and applied in France and on which the colonies have not been consulted, but yet they are subject, directly or indirectly, to the consequences. Economic autarky, however, carries with it the obligation for the metropole to assure the consumption of colonial products over those of foreign origin. . . . Once the metropole has consented to this obligation, then the development of regions until now separated and closed unto themselves is realizable." Bélime, director of the Service des textiles and soon to be the director of the Office du Niger, agreed with Mérat's conclusion.[64] Bélime was to apply a variant of the "closed economy" in the vast, irrigated lands of the Office du Niger.

Faced with the failure of the politique cotonnière to capture the cotton harvest of the Soudan during the 1920s and early 1930s as a result of the deflationary pressures of the worldwide Depression, administrators worried that their efforts to promote cotton production over the past three decades would be lost. Inspector Mérat, author of the inspection of the ACC in 1931, admitted that such fears were warranted given the failure of the export sector to maintain sufficient prices for producers. But he also recognized that cotton—as a crop— would not be lost because the domestic market for cotton would "assure the maintenance of cotton cultivation."[65] Throughout the Soudan, noted the fourth quarter economic report of 1931, "numerous weavers have made their appearance in the villages."[66]

The handicraft textile industry not only survived the politique cotonnière, but its persistence contributed to the failure of the French to capture the cotton harvest in the Soudan. Paradoxically, French efforts to exhort Soudanese to produce ever larger cotton harvests contributed not to increased exports but to increased production of the handicraft textile industry. The struggle to control the economy of the French Soudan between 1918 and 1932 was won by the Soudanese.

PART III

The Failure to Control the Economy

CHAPTER TEN

The Brief Victory of Irrigation:
The Office du Niger, 1932–1946

Relief from the worldwide Depression did not come in 1932. On the contrary, France, which had escaped the early effects of economic deceleration until 1931, found itself languishing deeper in the turmoil of economic distress even as some capitalist economies on the Continent and across the Atlantic were beginning to witness growth. As late as 1938, French industrial production had not yet returned to 1929 levels. The situation in the colonies was as bad, if not worse. Production of colonial exports stagnated after 1931, and for several crops, the value of 1935 exports plummeted as much as 90 percent from 1928 values. There was some recovery in colonial commerce after 1935, although in many areas of West Africa recovery did not occur until after World War II.[1]

It seems extraordinary that in such times the Ministry of Colonies in France would undertake a bold and costly commitment to irrigate nearly one million hectares in the middle of the Soudan. Constant lobbying in France by the Comité du Niger and the Union coloniale française throughout the 1920s and profound changes in the thinking of the managers of the French economy resonated with Bélime's model of massive yet technically sophisticated economic development. Investment in colonial irrigation, designed to provide French industries with raw materials, fit neatly into the renewed metropolitan interest in autarky. The result was the Office du Niger, a semi-autonomous government agency in the heart of the Soudan dedicated to the production of cotton and rice through massive irrigation. Bélime parlayed his political support into creating a personal fief, where he could, at least on paper, organize a new society according to his corporatist leanings.[2]

Just as the success of the European-managed irrigation model of colonial development was seemingly assured with the promulgation of a complex administrative and fiscal organization in 1932, incremental advances in plant breeding conducted at the colonial agronomic station at M'Pesoba yielded a new cotton hybrid, Karangani–Garrah Hills, able to withstand wide variations in rainfall and widely resistant to parasites. With Karangani–Garrah Hills, also called Budi after the colonial agronomist Budichowsky who developed the strain, the pro-peasant camp was rearmed with a new weapon to defend its besieged position: a cotton variety that promised to resolve all the limitations of rain-fed cotton production in the Soudan. As I shall discuss in Chapter 11, Budi would not become the hoped-for solution. It did prove remarkably resistant to parasites and to unintentional cross-breeding with other varieties of cotton, but it produced short fibers for an industry accustomed to medium-staple cotton. Budi was replaced by an improved strain of a local species, N'Kourala, which eventually gave way to a superior acclimated variety of Allen. This Allen cotton, with its regular fibers, high yields, and greater resistance to moisture, was eventually to prove true the vision of the pro-peasant camp. In the regions of Sikasso, San, and northern Côte d'Ivoire, cotton became king under the direction of the Compagnie française de développement textile (CFDT).

Despite these gradual advances in rain-fed cotton, Bélime was virtually unchallenged in France and in the Soudan until 1936. Moreover, despite accumulating evidence of abuses occurring within the Office du Niger and the enormous drain on metropolitan and French West African fiscal resources, there were no voices ringing out against Bélime and the Office du Niger until the advent of the Popular Front in 1936. Although the Popular Front seemed incapable of effectively reining in Bélime's autonomy and the pace of construction, it did empower dissident voices. The Popular Front's colonial reform was eclipsed by the tempo of war in Europe and the Front collapsed in 1938 before it could introduce legislation altering or halting the project. Nonetheless, under Colonial Minister Marius Moutet and Governor-General Jules Marcel de Coppet, the Popular Front managed to introduce greater protection for African laborers, including those engaged in building the massive irrigation system of the Office du Niger. With the fall of France and the rise of Vichy in 1940, Bélime found himself for the first time in a larger political environment that resonated nearly perfectly with his corporatist leanings and boosted his efforts to create a new society in the Office du Niger lands.

As cotton production in the southern tier of the Soudan took off in the middle and late 1940s, cotton production in the irrigated lands of the Office du Niger stagnated and then sank. By 1946, the Office du Niger began selling its cotton to the local domestic market instead of to the export sector. And by 1970, after nearly four decades of failing to face reality, the Office du Niger formally abandoned cotton.

This study ends in 1946, when, as part of the Brazzaville accords of 1944, compulsory labor in French West Africa was abolished. The end of compulsion was applied immediately to settlers in the Office du Niger, but it was extended to recruited construction workers only in 1948. Without compulsion, the managers of the Office du Niger could maintain neither its construction crews nor the African settlers who actually farmed the irrigated lands. The end of compulsion forms a fitting conclusion to this discussion of colonial development and, in particular, to the politics of massive irrigation.

This chapter takes up the story of irrigation in the Soudan with the opening of the Sotuba dam in 1929, some of which has already appeared in Chapters 6 and 7. But it is worth rehearsing some of these issues because they have to be set against the incredible, and sudden, success of Bélime's model in 1932.

The Sotuba Dam and the Constraints on Irrigation

Bélime's success in getting metropolitan and French West Africa Federation support for his major irrigation system in 1932 is all the more remarkable in light of the clear signals emanating from the ground in Soudan regarding the feasibility and practicality of massive irrigation. Bélime's 1921 project envisioned a massive three-canal system feeding over one million hectares, but he developed only the Segu canal in detail. By itself the Segu canal was audacious because Bélime claimed that it alone was capable of irrigating 750,000 hectares between the Niger and Bani rivers. Because Bélime privileged the Segu canal in his project, it was subjected to considerable debate and controversy in 1921–22. During the same period, Governor-General Merlin contracted with a private sector consortium with significant banking and commercial interests in colonial affairs, the Compagnie générale des colonies, to conduct an independent verification of Bélime's Segu canal project and to conduct technical studies on possible sites for a dam and irrigation work.[3]

The Compagnie générale did not deliver its report until late April 1924, one month after Governor-General Carde announced his major cotton program. By then, the Compagnie générale's report, which favored cotton production but not irrigation, came to a government already committed to irrigation. But Carde had changed the terms of the debate in subtle yet profound ways. Whereas for Bélime, irrigation along the Niger was to serve the interests of the metropole exclusively for cotton, Carde saw irrigation as fulfilling the dual role of regulating the production of food, especially rice—hence promoting the "welfare" of Africans—and production of industrial crops.[4]

Carde's support for the Sotuba dam and for a scaled-down version of the Segu canal came at a very opportune moment for the pro-irrigation camp. Irrigation was originally tied closely to Albert Sarraut's colonial development model of 1921, but its supporters along the Niger had seen their fortunes sink as metropolitan interest in colonial development waned. By 1924 Sarraut's plan was abandoned.

The Sarraut plan as originally proposed envisioned massive metropolitan support for colonial development. Governor-General Carde, overseeing the funds of the West Africa Federation derived from metropolitan advances and from taxes siphoned from member colonies, allocated some of his reserves to support parts of the Sarraut plan which fit his 1924 cotton program. Bélime, appointed in 1924 as the director of the Service des textiles et de l'hydraulique, rushed to provide Carde with a plan for a small dam at Sotuba and a very small experimental irrigation canal, a mere 20 kilometers long. Bélime clung tenaciously to his grandiose notions of what irrigation could accomplish: he expected that this small canal would irrigate 100,000 hectares, producing 50,000 bales of cotton and 100,000 tons of foodstuffs. In agreeing to the new vocabulary of what irrigation could accomplish—food as well as cotton—Bélime bent strategically to Carde's will, but he also kept alive the model of irrigated agricultural development. Work on the Sotuba dam began in 1925 and on the canal in 1926.[5]

Construction fell to requisitioned African labor under the direction of the Service temporaire des irrigations du Niger (STIN). Africans had been requisitioned for various forms of corvée labor in French West Africa for decades, but STIN differed because it was organized around the annual military recruitment drive. Compulsory military conscription in peacetime had been introduced in French West Africa in 1919. Each year, men in their twentieth year were assembled and given physical examinations. Those meeting the requirements were considered the "first portion" and liable to be drafted for a three-year stint in the Tirailleurs sénégalais. During peacetime, however, the colonial army recruited only 14,000 soldiers annually, leaving the rest of the physically fit free to return to their villages.[6] In 1926, Governor Olivier of Madagascar saw in the annual recruitment a powerful means of organizing labor for public works, especially for railway construction. He thus introduced a form of military conscription for public works projects, called Service de la main d'oeuvre pour les travaux d'intérêt général (SMOTIG). Under this "second portion" of the annual military draft, Malagasy recruits were originally liable to one year's conscription for railway construction, although this was rapidly extended to three years. Later that year, a similar decree organizing the second portion was enacted in French West Africa, although its implementation was left to the discretion of individual governors. In 1927, to help service the labor needs during the construction of the Sotuba dam and the Segu canal, the second portion labor recruitment was applied in the Soudan.[7] Cebarama Dembele recalled how the second portion labor grew out of military recruitment drives.

Question: Did the recruitment of workers correspond to the recruitment of *tirailleurs*?
Response: At the beginning it did, but afterward they [colonial officials] instituted the workers of the second contingent. The bottom of the paper was given to the recruit. Everyone received one. On each piece was written either second portion or military. Those who received the second portion were put into groups which were forced to go to the public work gangs as workers.[8]

In the face of resistance to a form of labor that resembled massive corvée in West Africa and in Madagascar and to protests from the International Labor Organization, René Mercier produced a defense of compulsory labor which resonated with the vocabulary of development embedded in the Henry-Sarraut-Carde model of colonial development. The African, Mercier described in neo-Malthusian language prevalent in colonial circles in the late 1920s and early 1930s, was the victim of malnutrition and of pandemic diseases, resulting in a dispersed population constantly suffering from high mortality and thus little inclined to exertion. Only by engaging in forceful efforts to develop the colonies would France be able to "drag [*arracher*] the native from his miserable existence, his ignorance, and his inertia." In these circumstances, then, "recourse to compulsion appears perfectly legitimate because it is indispensable and beneficial, and because it responds to a higher need, which may not yet be evident to the native." Compulsory labor in the public interest alone (he condemned compulsory labor for private enterprise), Mercier concluded, was good for the native and for the colony.[9] Similar language evoking a greater good had been applied in justification for several other institutions of the politique cotonnière, including the champs du commandant and the regulated cotton market. Moreover, in the absence of a developed labor market, recourse to compulsion appeared to colonial administrators as the only way to get the job done.

As I discussed in Chapter 7, administrators were disinclined to provide labor for private enterprise precisely at the time when labor abuses at the SAA and CICONNIC were making recruitment generally more difficult. Yet senior administrators had no such qualms about recruiting labor for public works projects. In 1927 the lieutenant governor of the Soudan ordered the first contingent of 1,000 men drawn from the second portion to supplement the labor otherwise recruited on the Sotuba dam and Segu canal projects. Labor was organized under the STIN, which itself was commanded by a military officer, Colonel Emile Doizelet, who had no formal experience with large-scale works projects, let alone hydraulic irrigation. Not surprisingly, given the conditions of labor and lack of adequate protection for workers, significant numbers of workers deserted (11 percent annually between 1927 and 1929) and were incapacitated by sickness or accidents (18 percent annually). Most of the abuses occurred during the second year of construction, probably as the pace of constructing accelerated. That year, desertions ran at 24 percent and incapacity at 32 percent of the 2,850 recruited laborers.[10]

In February 1929, André Maginot, the colonial minister, opened the Sotuba dam with considerable fanfare. Although the Segu canal was only fifteen kilometers long and capable of irrigating only 5,000 hectares, Maginot was sufficiently impressed with the success of the technical undertaking and with Bélime's tenacity to his project that he returned to France prepared to resurrect a version of Sarraut's plan (now under his name) and to provide 300 million francs to finance the larger Sansanding dam. Maginot's vision of irrigation shared more with Carde than with Bélime in that he saw irrigation as a means to make the veritable desert of the Soudan into the granary of West Africa.[11]

Maginot's support for irrigation and for Bélime in particular was critical to the realization of the irrigation model in the Soudan. But it also locked into place certain institutions and management proclivities that ultimately doomed the Office du Niger to failure. The first was the Office du Niger's reliance on forced labor. Until 1948, construction of the Sansanding dam, which was the cornerstone to the hydraulic system Bélime planned, and the two irrigation canals in the main part of the Office du Niger depended almost exclusively on coerced labor for construction. Because of the pool of cheap labor organized through STIN, management pursued construction through labor-intensive methods. The second was the practice of internal African colonization, started first along the experimental Segu canal at Nienebale. Exactly who was to work on irrigated lands and under what organization had always been fuzzy in Bélime's early conception of his project. Part of his vision originally included contracted African agricultural labor, but that experience had proved disastrous at CICONNIC's Dire plantation. By the time the Office du Niger began to recruit African settlers in 1934, it had committed itself to the Nienebale model. Although based on the notion of voluntary resettlement, the practice in Office du Niger lands was to reflect Bélime's corporatist and authoritarian inclinations. The third aspect of the Office du Niger's evolution reflected Bélime's tenaciously held view that he was absolutely correct in his assumptions about agronomy and hydrology, even in the absence of adequate data derived from careful agronomic, geological, and technical studies. And finally, given metropolitan and federation support for his vision of irrigation, Bélime used the complex administrative organization of the Office du Niger to create a personal fiefdom, in which his views remained unchallenged from within and largely unchallenged from without. These institutions and management organization generated a self-perpetuating momentum to the construction and development of irrigation works and colonization. Bélime managed to parlay this momentum into continued metropolitan support and to deflect criticism. Moreover, the project's momentum (and its fantastic costs) meant that all subsequent colonial ministries, including the Popular Front, were reluctant to question the principles or organization involved. After so much investment, no individual or group in authority was prepared to take responsibility for ending the project before its completion, especially when Office du Niger boosters argued that completion was just around the corner.

Bélime was eventually removed as director-general of the Office du Niger in 1943, when French West Africa sided with the Free French and when it was clear that the tide of war in Europe was turning. By then, however, Bélime's model of corporatist production in Office du Niger lands had been implemented—and had proven disastrous. With the end of compulsion in 1946, Bélime's new society crumbled.

Ascendancy of Bélime's Model
of Cotton Irrigation, 1932–1936

On 5 January 1932, the French National Assembly enacted laws establishing the Office du Niger as a "public enterprise belonging to the French state," funding for which the National Assembly had approved late the year before. The language of the legislation was critical to the evolution of the Office du Niger because it created what amounted to an island of administrative and fiscal autonomy within the colony of the Soudan. Until 1941, when it was subsumed directly into the Ministry of Colonies under the Vichy government, the Office du Niger was accountable to the government-general for its budget rather than to the colonial administration of the Soudan in which it was located. Administratively, it was accountable to a supervisory body that met irregularly in Paris.

The degree of administrative autonomy of the Office du Niger was truly unprecedented for colonial development projects. There was, however, an analogous metropolitan model for such a project. During the postwar era of state intervention in economic recovery, the national government had created "mixed companies" to pursue development for the public good. In 1921, for example, the French state created the Compagnie nationale du Rhône, which was designed to develop the irrigation, hydroelectric, and navigation potential of the Rhône River.[12] Even though Bélime did not allude to metropolitan models of hydraulic development, certainly the recent history of the Compagnie nationale du Rhône helped make his project intelligible to French parliamentarians. Bélime's model, encased in language representing itself as technically sophisticated and framing itself as a scientifically managed engineering endeavor, also appealed to the technocratic managers of the French government.

The 1932 AOF legislation created an otiose administrative council, appointed in part by the minister of colonies and in part by the governor-general, which was supposed to have jurisdiction over fiscal and organizational matters. Because of the cumbersome organizational structure, its irregular meetings, and because the majority of the administrative council supported the objectives of irrigation, the real power over the Office du Niger was wielded by the director-general. The legislation also created a local supervisory council, composed of the lieutenant governor of the Soudan, a representative appointed by the governor-general, and two notables. Neither council met frequently and neither exerted any influence over the daily operations of the Office du Niger. Moreover, in 1933, to facilitate the coordination of the many aspects of the project, labor recruited and organized under the STIN was placed directly under the authority of the director-general. In 1936, the STIN was dissolved, although its functions were reassigned to another division within the Office du Niger administration. As a consequence of Popular Front criticism, supervision of recruited labor returned briefly to the lieutenant governor of the Soudan. From 1932 to 1943, the director-general was Emile Bélime.[13]

In an era when colonial ministries changed hands with astonishing regularity, Bélime's tenacity to his vision of irrigation and his tenure in the Soudan provided him with an aura of authority and dependability. At one of its first meetings in Paris, Albert Sarraut, member of the administrative council and recently reappointed colonial minister, reiterated his position that long-term development projects such as the Office du Niger were undertakings much too intricate and delicate to be at the whim of rapidly changing personnel. Bélime thus managed to secure significant perquisites in the negotiations surrounding his contract with the government-general—he was never a regular employee of the colonial civil service—including a salary that virtually equaled that of the governor-general and the right to publish works of a technical, agronomic, and political character.[14]

In 1933, he used his newfound celebrity status to publish the first of several political tracts, *L'Heure de la France: Refléxions sur la crise*, in which he developed his solution to the deeply troubled politics of the Depression. For Bélime, the problems of France stemmed from disorder: France was caught between the raging radicalism of workers and the rising tide of Bolshevism on the one hand and the uncontrolled capitalism of big business, manifested by the ubiquitous crises of overproduction and massive unemployment on the other. The greatness of France was being eroded by weak and bickering politicians of the Third Republic. In condemning both liberal democracy and communism and in his call for a "return to order," Bélime shared much in common with French right-wing and continental corporatist thinking of the 1920s and 1930s.[15] Bélime continued his political activities and writings throughout the turbulence of the 1930s. He organized a study group called L'Ordre réel, which also became the title of his second political tract. Despite his obvious sense of his own importance, Bélime never played a significant role on the metropolitan scene.[16] It was only in the lands of the Office du

Niger that Bélime was able to build a version of the future he wanted for France.

Three aspects of this once and future world bear special attention. First, Bélime, who so disdained the myopic views and constant squabbling of colonial administrators and Third Republic politicians, managed to establish administrative "order" in the sense that he was unchallenged in charting the development of the Office du Niger. Second, he employed labor practices in building the hydraulic works on the Niger which reaffirmed his sense of the place of labor in his new social order. And third, he regimented daily life in the newly constructed agricultural villages to render production efficient.[17]

Crucial to Bélime's unchallenged position was his ability to situate the Office du Niger outside the normal ladder of colonial administrative authority. Instead of being accountable to the lieutenant governor of the Soudan, the logical point of supervision, Bélime used metropolitan support for his project to claim a special approach to administrative oversight. Bélime needed only to point to the inconclusive results of the past 30 years of colonial agricultural development. Only by ensuring that the direction of his project would not be interfered with by the local administration, he argued, would its success be assured. In this, Bélime received support from Governor-General Carde and his successor Jules Brévié. Both were keenly aware of the debates about cotton development, yet both felt that something different needed to be done to deliver on the promises of colonial development. Both were also aware that in the minds of the colonial ministry and the colonial lobby in France, irrigation in the Soudan and Emile Bélime were identical. In the course of hammering out the details of the Office du Niger's administrative structure, Bélime dictated the terms of his involvement.[18]

Moreover, Bélime remained absolutely convinced of the validity of all his assumptions about irrigation, agricultural output, and labor. Since he submitted his first version of irrigation in 1920, Bélime had lamented what he had described as the self-destructive caution of the colonial administration in the Soudan. Armed in 1932 with an administrative structure that favored the centralization of decision making in his hands and with a significant advance of capital from metropolitan and federation sources, Bélime commissioned work on the Sansanding dam in 1933. The engineering side of the project fell to a French consortium, composed of the Société nationale de travaux publics, the Etablissements Meunier-Cogez, and the Société de construction des Batignolles. Construction began in 1934. Labor fell to the STIN, reorganized into three "arrondissements" for work on the canals and embankments, for work on the irrigated lands, and for construction of the dam. The third group, construction of the dam, became the most labor intensive of all.

STIN was in 1933 still under the titular direction of a military officer, although in reality it was totally subordinated to the needs of Office du Niger construction. The third arrondissement, which was little more than a separately organized and administered labor camp, was headed by M. V. Bauzil, a civil engineer, who was also appointed by Bélime as his assistant director. Thus by the time construction of the Sansanding dam began, Bélime had created an oversight council in Paris that was woefully ignorant of events on the ground in the Soudan and rarely challenged Bélime's authority, he had bypassed the administrative reach of the lieutenant governor in the Soudan, he had personally commissioned a French engineering consortium, and he had established a virtually autonomous labor camp in Marakala, at the foot of the Sansanding dam. Bélime further solidified his personal power over the Office by using it as a vast system of patronage in which he did not tolerate dissent or challenge. Bauzil, his second in command, considered it "his study to defer to Bélime's authority." [19]

Equally crucial to Bélime's unchallenged authority was the profoundly inadequate system of financial accounting in the Office. Few officials of the Office du Niger and STIN conformed to standard accounting practices, leaving historians with a very confused record of the Office's finances and organization. Inspections into the Office du Niger's finances nonetheless revealed impropriety and mismanagement. [20] As a management strategy, however, deeply flawed accounting disguised mismanagement and abuses. It also reflected Bélime's disdain for the nuts and bolts of management.

The second aspect of Bélime's new world was his attitude toward and his organization of African labor. Constructing the Sansanding dam and the massive canals with their high embankments was an audacious task. Some earthmoving equipment was used in the period before 1946, but most construction fell to the coerced labor of the second portion because it was cheap, available, and could be disciplined. [21] Bélime's attitude to labor, which remained unchanged even after the scandals and inquiries of the Popular Front era, was largely to blame for the Office's complete disregard for the welfare of Africans. In 1950, well after he was forced to retire from the Office du Niger, he reflected on the role of African workers in the construction of the massive irrigation projects. Bélime believed that the African worker had to be disciplined because he was motivated neither by self-interest nor by the abstract goals of the project.

> Throughout the time of the labor gangs, when the big dam on the Niger was being constructed, when the canals along the river were being dug, and when the dikes along their banks were being raised, all this labor was strange, incomprehensible, even stupefying from their [Africans'] point of view. To them and to the other Soudanese, it was another example of the "manner of the whites," of which their only other example was the railway.
> But, one day, the waters of the Niger, brought by the sluice gates of the Sansanding dam, penetrated the big canals, and from there to the distributors, and then into the irrigation arteries and onto their fields. Then, the light entered their heads. . . . That will be the end forever of terrible famines and their resultant horrors. Then, the "manner of the whites" will be clear and it will make direct sense.[22]

Consistent with Bélime's desire for complete and unchallenged authority, he was willing to subordinate labor to the ends of construction. Not surprisingly, the regulations governing the use and maintenance of the second portion labor were all but ignored in the third arrondissement construction sites. Maintenance of minimum levels of food, shelter, and medical care were disregarded, leading to high desertion and mortality rates. Mortality rates were already 15 per 1,000 when construction of the physical plant at Marakala began in 1933; when work on the dam actually started in 1934, mortality rates nearly doubled to 27 per 1,000. Workers complained of constantly being hungry; a significant number were hospitalized for malnutrition. Absences because of viral and bacterial infections were high, and the one infirmary designed to support the construction crews was ill-equipped and understaffed.[23] An official inspection of the Office du Niger was undertaken by Inspector-General Bagot in 1934–35, but the report was buried bureaucratically until the Popular Front opened discussion about the Office du Niger once again in 1936–37. The abuses of labor led to new legislation empowering the lieutenant governor of the Soudan to take a more active role in Office labor policies after 1938.

The third aspect of Bélime's new order concerned the organization of labor to work the fields actually irrigated. The debate about agricultural labor had its roots in the failure of private agricultural plantations, but it saw its fullest expression in the agricultural colonization of Nienebale, discussed in Chapter 7. Nienebale and Baguinda succeeded because Africans willingly participated. Bélime's Sansanding dam and the two canals on the west bank of the Niger were to irrigate a zone known as the *delta mort*, which was once supposed to have been a major arm of the Niger. The region fit Bélime's vision of turning desert into farms, and he expected Africans to stream to these new irrigated lands.

Africans were, as the debate in the 1920s concerning the organization of African labor had concluded, willing to work in their own interests. One had only to look at the annual labor migrations to the groundnut fields of Senegal to see this propensity in action. Recruiters thus faced two challenges: the first was to capture this pool of willing agricultural labor and direct it toward the newly irrigated lands of the Office, which were, after all, much closer to these migrants' villages. The second was to encourage these migrants to invest in long-term agriculture, hence to move permanently to these new areas.

The concept of *îlots de prospérité* became the banner for the recruitment of Africans to Office lands.[24] Cohesive communities employing modern farming methods would be transplanted to these islands of prosperity. Their prosperity, for that is what had occurred in Nienebale, would draw ever more recruits as more and more land was brought under irrigation. In 1938, Bauzil, assistant director of the Office du Niger, described the Office's view of African colonization: "Irrigated agriculture," he wrote, "is a synonym of intensive agriculture. Hydraulic equipment by itself, however, does not suffice; labor is needed." Bauzil went on to argue that salaried labor was not the preferred solution. Instead, the solution was to establish "small rural properties, which alone will permit farmers to reap high yields that are possible from irrigated lands." The slogan for the recruitment of African settlers was "pas de salariat, un colonat."[25]

Recruitment for the experimental irrigated lands of Nienebale (Baguinda), placed under the authority of the Office du Niger, drew originally on neighboring villages. In 1934 officials began to recruit from several villages in the Baninko region, which the year before had suffered from a poor harvest. These villagers, it was assumed, would willingly move for they had little reason to stay in the region. When officials arrived, they found that the villagers had abruptly fled into the bush, leaving their cooking pots unattended over the fires.[26] Africans had responded to military recruitment and to corvée in much the same manner.

The model of African colonization for the irrigated lands of the Office du Niger—those islands of prosperity—was predicated upon Africans acting in their own self-interest. Officials, however, found few Africans willing to leave voluntarily for Office du Niger lands. News of the dangerous and unpleasant working conditions for STIN workers had spread rapidly throughout the colony, making recruitment for labor and settlement more difficult. Yet the Macina and Sahel canals were being dug and farmers were needed to cultivate the lands that could already be irrigated by waters captured from the annual flood. By 1936, 1,500 hectares along the Macina canal were irrigable, and the next year 500 hectares were opened along the Sahel canal.

Some voluntary settlers came forward, most of whom were drawn from the most marginal groups, just as the managers of CICONNIC's Diré plantation had discovered. Recruiters turned to three other techniques. First, they tried to induce volunteers through promises of free tools, land, and future prosperity. Some promised to exempt recruits from their annual taxes and from corvée labor. Second, they used compulsion, essentially forcing village chiefs to designate individuals and families for assignment in Office du Niger lands. And finally in 1935, Office du Niger officials turned directly to Yatenga Naba, titular leader of the Mossi, in an effort to have him lend credibility to recruitment of Mossi, whom colonial officials assumed were so numerous they could populate Office lands without difficulty. Indeed, in 1932, the colony of Upper Volta was parceled up and merged into the Soudan, the Côte d'Ivoire, and Niger. Two densely populated western districts, Tougan and Ouahigouya, were attached to the Soudan in an obvious effort to facilitate recruitment for STIN and internal colonization.

In November 1935, Yatenga Naba and several of his ministers were escorted by Bélime through the Nienebale and Kokry (Macina canal) centers of colonization. The delegation also visited the Marakala construction site and the major derivation canals. Office du Niger officials reiterated to the Mossi delegation the principle of maintaining intact in these irrigated lands "a social organization resembling their native villages." Moreover, the delegation was assured that Mossi traditions and established political system would be retained. Under Yatenga Naba's pressure and constant propaganda from recruiters, nine Mossi families consisting of 129 people moved to Office du Niger lands in 1936.[27] A stream of settlers to the Office du Niger lands was maintained, although the numbers disappointed Office and colonial officials. Desperate for increased recruitment of settlers, Bélime proposed to the Administrative Council in Paris in 1937 that immigrants from Algeria be encouraged to settle in the irrigated areas of the Office du Niger. Bélime even dispatched Inspector Martial of the Office du Niger's medical service to Algeria to examine the possibilities on the ground.[28] The council was not enthusiastic, and the governor-general quickly squashed the proposal. African recruits remained the only ones seriously considered for the task.

Despite assurances that indigenous traditions would be maintained in Office du Niger lands, the new settlers soon found themselves intricately involved in Bélime's brave new world. Between October and December 1937 the commandants from the districts of San, Bamako, Koutiala, and Nioro accompanied leading chiefs on tours of Office lands to encourage their participation in recruitment policies. What they found, however, fueled instead the renewed debate about the Office du Niger coincident with the advent of the Popular Front. The Bamako commandant wrote:

The first impressions [of the Office du Niger] are of the prodigious labor which has already been realized. Canals are dug over long distances and rice fields extend as far as one can see. And all this in a land which only recently was unusable due to lack of water. All these admirable works are for the settlers. . . . Nothing is lacking for the agricultural life of the settler and his dependents. Everything possible is done for the success of the crops and for the physical health of the natives. But something was clearly missing: it seems that joy, that pleasure of living, is unknown in these new concessions cultivated by modern procedures. . . .

The native [normally] contents himself with little beyond assuring that his granary is full and sufficient to nourish his family. In addition, he sells different artisanal and consumer goods, which allow him to buy some clothes, a few animals, and to pay off an old bridewealth debt. The native is satisfied to demand no more than to pass long days in visits to villages near and far and to pass interminable hours chatting under the larger trees of the village center.

This idleness is not admitted in any of the irrigated lands. But it is exactly this independence, this nearly perfect freedom after having paid their taxes, made their prestations, and brought their goods to market that had played such an important role in their former lives. Compared to their former lives, the settlers only work, work without stopping, even after the harvest is in.[29]

Toby, commandant of Nioro, filed a similar report:

The first impression which imposes itself on the sensibility of a district commandant used to visiting native villages and living in close contact with Africans is an impression of sadness which one feels in the agricultural colonization villages of the Office du Niger.

Even though the settlers all responded with perfect unanimity that they are very happy to be there, that they earn three times as much money as they did in their native villages, that they are pleased with the modern agricultural procedures supervised by agents of the Office du Niger, the visitor is struck by the absence of gaiety which is so habitual among African communities.

Here there are no tom-toms, no griots, no singing. Upon our arrival all the settlers greeted us in their finest festival attire, but none showed any spontaneity. It was as if they had become mechanical, set in motion by the agent of colonization through the application of new agricultural practices. It seemed that there was something artificial in their attitudes and demeanor.[30]

André Morel, commandant of Koutiala, likened the village of colonization he visited to a "bird in a cage." All the inhabitants, young and old, bore an appearance of sadness and lassitude.[31] Such were the conditions in the Office du Niger when the Popular Front was voted into power.

Debate and Criticism, 1936–1938

The Popular Front government of Léon Blum came to power in 1936 facing significant domestic and international challenges. France's industrial production remained depressed and unemployment high. On the international scene, Blum's government faced the outbreak of the Spanish Civil War and the swelling fascist movements in Germany, Italy, and France itself. Political cohesion in the Popular Front was based on its antifascist platform. Its domestic agenda was considerably more ambiguous. Nor was it surprising that the socialist and antifascist inclinations of the Popular Front should manifest themselves also in colonial issues and, in particular, in a critical stance vis-à-vis Bélime's brave new world in the Soudan.

In June 1936, Blum appointed Marius Moutet as colonial minister, and shortly thereafter Moutet appointed Jules Marcel de Coppet as governor-general of AOF. Both were socialists and both were committed to the extension of maximum social justice to the colonies. Almost immediately, Minister Moutet appointed a parliamentary commission to inquire into the colonial policies throughout the French empire. Between 1936 and 1938, a series of commissions and inquiries examined the labor and colonization policies of the Office du Niger as well as financial and organizational issues.[32] These inquiries into Bélime's irrigation project opened a wedge in the wall of silence surrounding the Office du Niger and inaugurated a heated public controversy.

One of de Coppet's first acts regarding the Office du Niger was to bring greater supervision to the use of second portion labor. Bélime had subordinated recruited labor to the goals of construction, especially in the third arrondissement labor camps. This had led to significant abuses, as officials and workers testified to the Lasalle Séré inspection of 1935, the report of which had been presented to Brévié's administration on the eve of the transition. Based on Lasalle Séré's findings, de Coppet argued that "service of the second portion labor must be organized independently of its direct employers" and placed it under the control of the lieutenant governor of the Soudan. Although further regulations regarding labor, pensions, and disability assistance were to follow shortly, the governor-general expected that this separation of labor use from supervision would result immediately in an amelioration of working conditions. Thereafter, the lieutenant governor was obligated to file an annual report on labor uses in the colony, including a section on the Office du Niger.[33] Whether this separation made much difference on the ground is not clear from the evidence, especially inasmuch as the Popular Front government collapsed less than two years after its formation.

In 1937, de Coppet turned his attention to colonization practices in the Office du Niger by authorizing inquiries into the medical situation in the irrigated lands and the practices of recruitment and colonization. Inspector Sorel of the colonial health service conducted an inspection of the health facilities and public health situation in late 1937 or early 1938. Sorel reported a particularly troubling incident at Nara, where he noticed that the inhabitants of that village were especially reticent in answering his questions. "I had the clear and painful impression," he wrote, "that I was running into commanded silences, into men who were influenced if not terrorized." Sorel's impressions were borne out when, after his tour of Nara, one of his former students from Dakar, Omar Ba, whispered that "you will never know the truth; no one will ever speak. They are frightened." Omar Ba described practices of social control conducted by agents of the Office, including harsh penalties involving withholding food rations, commonly applied to both old and new settlers. In a signed affidavit, Ba recounted an incident in which the inhabitants of Nara had their fishing nets confiscated and their catch thrown back because fishing was prohibited. Even though the Nara settlers were fishing at night, after their agricultural tasks were completed, the Office agent punished them. Fishing even during hours of rest was apparently prohibited because it damaged the embankments of the canals and it "might make the settlers less apt to work the next day."[34] This incident was indicative of the control over daily life that was part of Bélime's model of labor and living in the Office du Niger.

Inspector Henri Carbou's detailed report on colonization arrived on de Coppet's desk around the same time as the reports of the Bamako, Nioro, Koutiala, and San commandants. Included in the commandants' reports was a covering letter from Lieutenant Governor Ferdinand Jacques Louis Rougier. Rougier also visited the colonization sites in the Office du Niger, which by the end of 1937 already had more than a thousand settlers, and reiterated the impressions of his subordinates. Rougier argued in his letter that the Office du Niger should respect native customs concerning labor, days of rest, and festivals. It should, moreover, "reduce the discipline it imposes on the settlers" with a goal of rendering to these new agglomerations something of "their original character, including admitting artisans, griots, and even the village idiot." Rougier suggested that the government-general take a more interventionist role in the enterprise of colonization by appointing a colonial administrator who had long experience with natives as the head of the Service de colonisation. Rougier's recommendation thus challenged Bélime's hold over the organization of colonization by urging that it be returned to the hands of the colonial administration.[35] De Coppet's strategy was now clear. He tried to dismantle Bélime's unchallenged control over the Office du Niger by removing the supervision and organization of both construction labor and colonization.

During the course of 1938, Lieutenant Governor Rougier exerted much more control over the recruitment of settlers. All new recruitment was to be supervised by the district commandants, who were charged with assuring that all inducements were legal and that the decisions made by Africans were completely voluntary. A formal record of the interview with each prospective settler was to be made. Lieutenant Governor Jean Desanti, who replaced Rougier, reported that in 1939 no serious difficulties were recorded between the local administration and agents of the Office du Niger during the course of that year's recruitment.[36]

The Popular Front's attack on the Office du Niger did not confront the project as a whole, but only the stranglehold Bélime exerted over it. Even so, the official challenge to Bélime set the tone for a more general debate. Merchants in French West Africa and the press took up the challenge. In a coordinated series of meetings, the Chambers of Commerce of Dakar, Abidjan, Lomé, and Conakry petitioned the governor-general to halt, at least temporarily, the construction of the Office so as to assess its fiscal impact throughout the federation. As men of affairs, the members of the various Chambers of Commerce worried that the huge construction costs of the Office du Niger were an "excessive drain" on the budget of the federation and resulted in the lack of funds for local development projects. Even if construction could not be completely stopped at this stage, the members of the Abidjan Chamber of Commerce urged that construction should be limited to completing the tasks actually in progress. Moreover, they argued that the present organization of the Office should be suppressed and its functions acquired by the government-general.[37] The Conakry Chamber of Commerce was especially critical of the tension between the promised future rewards and the current fiscal and labor abuses.

The assemblies of merchants, habituated by their trade to judge results, do not take lightly future promises of substantial profits and humanitarian assistance made by the Office du Niger promoters. Because here we enter into a purely speculative domain, where calculations are based on hypotheses which contain abundant contradictions and uncertainties. In addition, no arguments, no promises, and no calculations can justify the abuses and waste, which are revealed all too frequently by the functioning of the Office du Niger. And in the end, it will be the natives of Senegal, Guinée, Dahomey, and the Côte d'Ivoire, who must bear the costs of this prodigality.[38]

Although all these Chambers of Commerce shared a concern with the Office du Niger's drain on federation resources, they did not agree on a solution. Most suggested that because so much capital had already been invested, some of the construction must be completed. But the "effort should be brought into equilibrium with the possibilities, that the project take into account material and human resources available, and that the government-general take charge of the project."[39]

If the leading Chambers of Commerce in French West Africa were more or less agreed on their critique of the Office du Niger, this was not the case in the public press, which, in contrast, was sharply divided by political affiliations. On the left, metropolitan papers, including La Flèche and La Lumière, and colonial ones, including L'AOF and Le Périscope africain, reveled in the attack on Bélime, calling it the "great scandal of French West Africa" and chastising the government-general and the National Assembly for supporting a man they dubbed the "Illusionist." The right-wing press, including L'Action française and Gringoire, defended Bélime and attacked de Coppet as the "builder of ruins."[40]

Bélime and his supporters in Paris were not silent. Senator Jourdain, long one of Bélime's supporters and member of the administrative council, called the governor-general's measures demanding more supervision over labor, colonization, and finances "asphyxiating." He threatened to go directly to the minister of colonies and to appeal to the higher authority of the National Assembly itself. Bélime let his proxies do battle for him as he shrewdly sidestepped criticism by claiming ignorance over specific allegations and by agreeing to some measures of accountability.[41] Bélime and his supporters need not have worried. By 1938 Blum's Popular Front was in trouble and it collapsed shortly thereafter, only to be revived briefly as the wave of war in Europe was building. By 1939 Europe was at war and in June 1940 France fell to the Germans.

From Reprieve to Collapse:
The Office du Niger Under Vichy, 1940–1944

A new France struggled to emerge from military defeat at the hands of the Germans in June 1940. Marshal Henri Pétain established the collaborationist Vichy regime, dedicated to the revival of France through a "national revolution." Pétain's national revolution was designed along corporatist lines, involving the state in a directed economy to minimize the excesses of capitalism and the threats of social upheaval. For the history of French colonial cotton policies, two aspects of Pétain's national revolution deserve attention. First, there was a renewed call for the responsibility of colonies to aid France; and second, there was a renewal of government and private sector consortia, akin to those developed during World War I, to control the supply and allocation of raw materials. The renewal of a managed economy provided Bélime with a new mandate to develop the Office du Niger as he wished.

Under a reorganized colonial ministry, Pierre Boisson, former governor-general of French Equatorial Africa, was appointed as haut commissaire de France pour l'Afrique Noire, essentially the post of governor-general of AOF. Even as French Equatorial Africa slipped from Vichy's hands and sided with the Free French, Boisson saw his task as to assist in reaffirming the federation's supply of raw materials to meet metropolitan needs. Pétain's position on the role of the colonies within the national revolution was affirmed in a major policy statement in December 1941: "France should not lose for a second time her colonial empire. The national revolution must extend, without delay, to the colonies and direct economic mobilization to the fullest potential of France overseas. . . . Veritable riches spring forth from the soil and the metropole will finally find there the material support which is hers by right."[42] Pétain called upon the haut commissaires to develop as quickly as possible detailed plans for the production and supply of colonial goods to the metropole. As part of the national revolution, Pétain also called for unquestioned loyalty from all colonials, Frenchmen and natives. Addressing Africans, Pétain promised them material and moral security in return for their obligation to work. "The native peasant will follow the example of his elder brother, the French peasant, and he will furnish an equal effort." Through a revived politics of production, the Soudan was to provide cotton to the vertically organized metropolitan *comité d'organisation* for textiles, and Bélime was to push more cotton out from the Office du Niger.

Regarding cotton, the comité d'organisation gave rise to the more tightly structured Groupement d'importation et de répartition du coton (GIRC), presided over by M. Senn, a representative of metropolitan textile industries. The purpose of the GIRC was exactly like that of the Consortium of Cotton created during the World War I mobilization of the economy. Senn's task was to develop "programs for the production, the acquisition, and distribution of primary material necessary to this branch of industry."[43] The GIRC was constituted as the sole buyer of cotton.

In legislation developed in 1941, GIRC, representing the state, agreed to buy all the cotton in French West Africa at a price fixed in relationship to the prevailing world price. The haut commissaire in Dakar was to set this price, which also included transportation costs, fees, and profits. Cotton producers were obliged to sell their harvests. Obligatory cotton sales with the state acting as the collector were part of an elaborate "imperial policy" and a "directed economy" decided on by Vichy but having little effect in the Soudan. By 1942, Vichy's colonial cotton policy was clearly a disaster. The Union cotonnière de l'empire français (UCEF), formerly the Association cotonnière coloniale, assessed the situation. "With the coming of the war, the GIRC emerged under the direction of M. Senn. Because of the obvious importance of cotton to a country at war, colonial production was to be encouraged. The contrary occurred."[44] As in the previous 45 years of colonial cotton policy, Vichy foundered on the assumption that the state could control Africans' production decisions. Vichy policy also failed because of the wartime blockade of the Atlantic coast. Whatever cotton the state acquired lay waiting in colonial warehouses.[45]

Despite the meager results measured in cotton imports, Vichy's industrial policy gave Bélime a virtually unrestrained mandate to pursue his irrigated cotton scheme. Vichy's call for colonial cotton and its corporatist social and industrial philosophy liberated Bélime from the constraints and public scrutiny of the Popular Front era. For the first time since he floated his project in 1920 the metropolitan government shared Bélime's vision of society and the place of labor and settlers within it.

In particular, Bélime benefited from a fresh infusion of capital in May 1941, desperately needed to keep construction going. And in December 1941, the Office du Niger was fundamentally reorganized, effectively placing it directly under the authority of the colonial ministry. The Administrative Council was restructured as a smaller consultative unit, staffed by members of the colonial ministry. With the memory of de Coppet's intervention in Office du Niger affairs still very bitter, Bélime managed to write even the pro-Vichy Boisson out of the organization of Office affairs. Further strengthening Bélime's hand over the management of all Office tasks was the legislation in 1942 centralizing responsibility for labor organization (essentially compulsory recruitment through STIN) in the hands of the Office du Niger and responsibility for colonization in the hands of a consortium charged with settlement and irrigation.[46] Under Vichy's commitment to impose an obligation to work in the colonies, Bélime promised to irrigate more than 150,000 hectares of cotton and rice over the next ten years.

Although Bélime shared much in common with Vichy, he was not averse to seeking allies among the Germans, who had been deprived of their colonies at the end of World War I. The goal of acquiring new colonies—or at least tapping into the wealth of occupied Europe's colonies—stimulated a revival of German colonial interests. In 1941, Bélime published a German translation of his self-congratulatory assessment of the Office du Niger, written originally for Vichy. The German version featured a glowing introduction by the leader of the Gruppe Deutscher Kolonialwirtschaftlicher Unternehmung.[47]

The reality was much different. Even armed with a newly formed but complicit oversight council and with Vichy's blessing for Bélime's labor and colonization strategies, Vichy's commitment to fund Bélime's irrigation project confronted increasing demands for cash payments to Germany. Moreover, the continued scarcity of imported cloth in the Soudan led to the sustained disparity between domestic and export cotton prices. Thus GIRC obligatory cotton sales policy confronted Africans unwilling to sell their harvest. The colonial state was still not prepared to pay the going rate for cotton in the domestic market, so whatever it acquired was done only through compulsion. Even the agents of the Office du Niger struggled to retain control over the cotton harvest grown on irrigated lands. Throughout the war years, the Office was increasingly unable to stem the hemorrhage of irrigated cotton to the "clandestine market, which results in considerable reductions in cotton brought to collection centers."[48] By 1946, the Office du Niger abandoned any pretense to controlling the cotton harvest from irrigated lands. Thereafter, all settlers were free to dispose of their cotton as they saw fit.

Bélime could point to accomplishments only regarding compulsory labor and forced settlement. By the end of 1942, he had 11,857 workers recruited from the second portion, nearly double the numbers at the beginning of construction. Bélime had anticipated that the Sansanding dam, the key to his management of the Niger waters, would be finished by 1941. It was not completed until 1949. With Vichy approval and federation complicity, however, the pace of work was increased and more recruits were put to work. More supervisory personnel were sought, but those available or willing to serve in the Office du Niger were drawn increasingly from the flotsam of Europeans in Africa. They were of "deplorable quality" and utterly "contemptuous of the blacks and of the Soudan," complained Lieutenant Governor Ernest Louveau. Not surprisingly, working conditions for the second portion labor deteriorated even further.[49]

Compulsion also produced a significant increase in the number of settlers on Office lands. From 1940 to 1944, between 1,000 and 1,500 new settlers were brought to the Office each year. In 1944, more than 28,000 settlers were actually farming in the irrigated zone. Few, however, were there because they wanted to be. Lieutenant Governor Louveau conceded that most of the settlers considered the Office du Niger "their land of exile." He suggested that the best the Office could hope for was to make their exile as clement and as hospitable as possible.[50]

Bélime's grasp over his newfound mandate was short-lived. Squeezed as it was between an ever more demanding occupation force in the northern part of France and the Allied invasion of North Africa in November 1942, Vichy never managed to put much teeth into its corporatist social and industrial philosophy or into its promised funding for the Office du Niger. The final blow to Bélime came in July 1943, when French West Africa sided with the Free French.

Bélime returned to France. Indeed, in 1944 the local administration took the initiative away from the Office du Niger by working in collaboration with the Macina Société de prévoyance to establish what it called an experiment in "free colonization." Not far from the Macina canal, the local administration constructed a rice zone consisting of "relatively costless" floodwater irrigation of nearly 10,000 hectares in the densely populated Dia-Tenenkou region. The estimated cost of less than 60 francs per irrigated hectare stood in sharp contrast to the millions of francs each hectare cost in the Office du Niger.[51]

The End of Compulsion, 1946

Early in 1944, senior Free French colonial officials met with French political and trade union leaders in Brazzaville to discuss postwar colonial policy. The Brazzaville meetings were advisory, but they nonetheless set an agenda for the inclusion of colonial issues in the future constitutional discussions about remaking France. The delegates urged that both forced labor and the indigénat be abolished and that they be replaced by regulations concerning the rights of free labor and by a unified penal code. Africans, to whom the Free French were indebted for their support, had long campaigned against both forms of compulsion. On 11 April 1946 forced labor was formally abolished.[52]

The end of compulsion had deep ramifications throughout the Soudan, touching all aspects of the colonial order. Lieutenant Governor Louveau described the end of compulsion and the associated reforms of 1946 as a "vertible revolution." "The suppression of requisitioned labor cannot but bring forth serious perturbations. The population, unprepared for such a sudden change in all that they have experienced, confuses free labor with the right not to labor at all, especially for the administration." Louveau complained that even the postal service between Mopti and Timbuktu was halted because it was impossible to hire voluntary sailors.[53] If Africans saw in the 1946 law the freedom to say no to the mail run, the impact on the Office du Niger was much greater.

The end of compulsion, however, did not apply immediately to the second portion labor so that freedom to work was not extended to those recruited under the military draft. Africans continued to protest the maintenance of compulsion, and second portion labor was abolished in 1948 and phased out in 1949. The effect of the 1946 legislation on the settlers in the Office du Niger was much more direct. Between 1946 and 1947, nearly 4,000 settlers and family members, representing 16 percent of the total number, picked up and left. More might have left except that so many settlers were in arrears for advances on fertilizer, food, and water and they were not permitted to leave until they had paid their debts. It was not until 1955 that the number of settlers again reached 1946 levels.

With the end of compulsion, settlement in the Office du Niger became more attractive. Many of the new migrants were former employees of the colonial administration, including mechanics, clerks, guards, laborers, and others who saw new opportunities, especially in irrigated rice cultivation.[54] Migrants willingly came after 1948 because of the changes in the organization of the Office itself. By 1946, Bélime's carefully constructed architecture of undisputed authority and administrative autonomy in the Office du Niger was in shambles. The Office du Niger was restructured to be a service center, without direct authority over settlement or construction. The Office du Niger was to emphasize agricultural modernization, especially mechanization of production, and it benefited directly from the newly created metropolitan development funds. Moreover, the newly structured Administrative Council was to be more sensitive to African interests, and it had a majority representation of federation and Soudanese members.[55]

The end of compulsion did not end the illusion of irrigated cotton. Paradoxically, the reorganization of the Office du Niger under the authority of the Fourth Republic only perpetuated the unsound agronomic practices introduced by Bélime and supporters of the capital-intensive irrigation model of cotton development. By 1946 it was already clear that the Niono region along the Sahel canal was unsuitable for cotton, even though cotton remained a central part of the Office du Niger's ten-year plans launched in 1947.[56] It was not, however, until 1970, fully ten years into the independence of the Republic of Mali, that the Office du Niger publicly ended its commitment to cotton.

If the Office du Niger ultimately failed in its mission to make the Soudan into the cotton center of the French Empire, it did so because of deeply flawed agronomic, hydraulic, economic, and social policies. The Office du Niger represented in the fullest the expression of European efforts to control cotton production directly in French West Africa. It failed not because the Soudan was poorly endowed for cotton but because Europeans could not control Africans or force them to adhere to the production decisions made for them. During this same period, 1932–46, significant advances were made in the production of rain-fed cotton, although it was not until after 1946 that cotton exports from the Soudan became significant. The period 1932–46 also witnessed the continued struggle between the export and the domestic markets for control over the cotton harvest.

The Triumph of Rain-Fed Cotton Production and the Persistence of the Handicraft Textile Industry, 1932-1946

The early 1930s were a difficult time for Soudanese peasants and administrators alike. The Depression, although affecting the Soudan somewhat later than the African coast, settled in with a vengeance in 1932, weakened commercial activity, and made the collection of taxes more difficult. It resulted, wrote the lieutenant governor of the Soudan in his second quarter economic report of 1932, in "an almost complete economic marasmus."[1] Equally disturbing for those promoting peasant cotton, however, was the ascendancy of Bélime's irrigation model of cotton production. The establishment of the Office du Niger seemed to signal a further eroding of the commitment by the colonial state to support peasant cotton, if for no other reason than that the financial and manpower resources of the West Africa Federation and the colony were increasingly drawn into the program of massive construction of irrigation works.

But the Depression did no more than what each previous world economic crisis had done: it reaffirmed the continental basis of the Soudanese economy. The fall in export prices for cotton did not, as Acting Lieutenant Governor Camille Maillet of the Soudan feared, produce a "fatal tendency for the cultivator to produce simply what is necessary for his own needs." On the contrary, wrote the director of economic services for the West Africa Federation in 1932, the peasant "utilizes his cotton to have bands made by local artisans and exported toward Senegal and the Côte d'Ivoire."[2]

Cotton was still being produced during the Depression years, but it was not flowing to the export sector. This was, of course, nothing new. The domestic market had plagued the politique cotonnière since its inception in the late 1890s. What was different, however, was that the pro-peasant advocates were increasingly under pres-

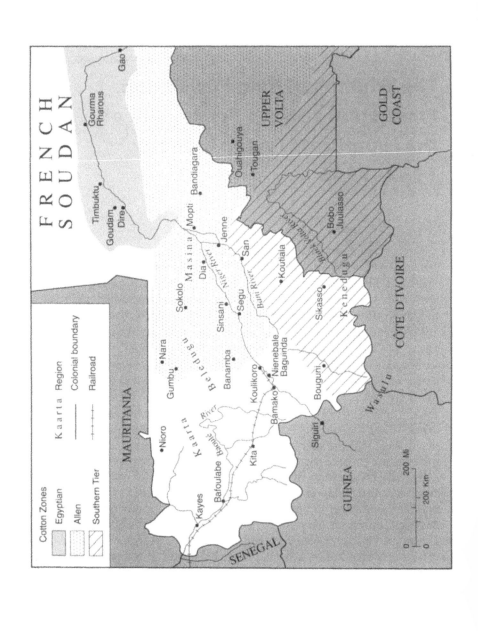

sure by the new commitment to irrigated cotton to ensure that Soudanese peasants did not lose all interest in producing cotton. The redoubling of pro-peasant propaganda after 1932 coincided with the
agronomic advances in acclimating new cotton hybrids to the Soudanese environment. These new varieties promised significant increases in yields. The renewal of the pro-peasant cotton development
model also generated debates about Soudanese peasants as workers
and as members of organic village communities based on the stability of the family. This was part of an ideological effort to differentiate rain-fed cotton programs from those of irrigation, which after
1936 had articulated the ideas of îlots de prospérité and entrepreneurial households.

The politique cotonnière from the onset of the Depression to 1937,
when a significant shift in policy occurred during the Popular Front,
had to confront the long-established relationship between cotton
prices on the export market, cotton prices on the domestic market,
and the volume and prices of imported cloth. There was, nonetheless, a shift in the politique cotonnière after 1932 which reflected
pro-peasant efforts not to cede the colonial economy, which was virtually synonymous with cotton development, to the irrigation camp.
These efforts consisted primarily of the abandonment of the Middle
Niger Valley, the heartland of the first 40 years of colonial cotton
policies, to the Office du Niger and to focus instead on the zone to
the southeast. This shift led to the articulation of a two cotton/two
market/two zone strategy of cotton production and involved a redoubling of efforts to control the production and commercialization
of cotton under the rubric of ensuring stocks of cotton seed. In 1937,
the Popular Front colonial governor reacted against the increasing
incidence of compulsion in cotton production by reaffirming the
freedom of peasants to produce and dispose of their cotton. Peasants
directed their cotton to the domestic market.

For the period from 1940 to late 1943, the politics of cotton production shifted again to conform more closely to Vichy's model of a
corporatist society and a command economy. Vichy cotton programs
were largely stillborn. The colonial state in the 1940s was no more
able to control African peasants' production and marketing decisions
than it had been before. Instead, just as they had done throughout the
previous 45 years, peasant cotton producers directed their cotton harvest to the domestic market and Soudanese spinners and weavers directed their efforts to satisfy local and West African continental demand for handcrafted cloth.

The Politics of Cotton Production, 1932–1936:
Promoting Cotton and Social Stability

If 1932 was bad for peasants producing cotton for export, 1933 was worse. Prices plunged even lower for many colonial commodities and the volume of exports shrank, leaving cotton producers with their harvests and little opportunities to buy imported cloth. The first inkling of increasing world cotton prices occurred late in 1934, when the price of American cotton rose on the Le Havre exchange. World cotton prices firmed on the Le Havre exchange in December 1934, and by 1935 they percolated into the Soudanese market. "The rise in the rate for native products," wrote Lieutenant Governor Alfassa as the volume of the 1935–36 harvest became known, "and the abundant harvest has encouraged the native producer and contributes to a very favorable political situation in the colony."[3] Figure 13 portrays the impact of the Depression and the gradual recovery of exports. The improving climate for commodity production intensified the pro-peasant politique cotonnière in the Soudan.

The most important new weapon in the hands of the pro-peasant

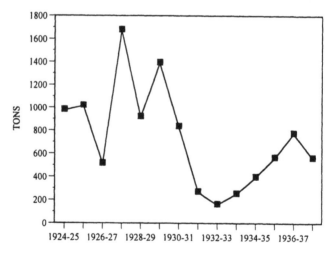

Fig. 13. Exports of Cotton Fiber, 1924–1938. Sources: Charles Godard, Ingénieur en chef des travaux d'agriculture aux colonies, Rapport annuel, campagne 1936–37, Bamako, 24 May 1937, ANS-AOF 2 G 37-53; Service d'agriculture, Soudan, Rapport annuel, campagne 1937–38, ANS-AOF 2 G 38-53; P. Coleno, Ingénieur des travaux agricoles, Rapport sur la culture sèche du cotonnier du Soudan, n.p., 31 Jan. 1935, ANM 1 R 319.

camp in the period after 1932 was new cotton varieties. Soudanese cotton, *koronini* and *koroniba*, consistently sold at a discount at Le Havre. French industrial spinners did not like the short, irregular fibers of indigenous cottons.[4] Allen cotton, originally a Georgia medium staple, remained an important part of the colonial state's efforts to promote colonial cotton to the metropole. But the most significant addition was Karangani–Garrah Hills. Based originally on an Indian variety, this cotton was domesticated to the Soudanese environment by the agronomist Budischowsky at the M'Pesoba experimental farm in 1929–30. By 1932–33, Budi, as the cotton was popularly called, was being distributed in and around M'Pesoba, Baguinda, and Nienebale. Budi promised farmers significant advantages over its two rivals: indigenous cotton on the one hand and Allen on the other. In comparison to indigenous cotton, Budi offered significant improvements in yields. At M'Pesoba, half-hectare plots of Budi yielded the equivalent of between 526 and 632 kilograms per hectare.[5]

Compared to Allen, Budi was far more tolerant of humid conditions and it was highly resistant to cotton diseases and predators. Even under actual farming conditions, peasants could squeeze 250 to 300 kilograms of Budi from each hectare, nearly double the yield for Allen. But most important from the standpoint of the Soudanese farmer, Budi could succeed in a variety of agronomic settings. Whereas Allen did not do well when planted near millet or maize, Budi thrived under these conditions. Allen was also highly susceptible to degradation by cross-fertilization with local cottons, requiring that farmers isolate their Allen fields. Budi was not easily modified by the presence of local varieties and did not require exclusive cotton fields.[6]

Because of its ability to withstand humidity, Budi was targeted to the southeastern tier of the cotton zone, essentially the districts of Koutiala, Sikasso, and San. Koutiala received its first shipment of Budi seeds in time for the 1932–33 season. Koutiala peasants produced only 9,438 kilograms of Budi that year; by 1933–34 they produced 59 tons. Charles Godard, chief agricultural engineer of the colony, noted that Budi had received a "justified popularity" among peasants in the southern part of the colony. Budi seeds were aggressively distributed in Koutiala, Sikasso, and Bouguni districts over the course of the next three cotton campaigns. In Sikasso, the administration sought to work through the *conseil des notables* in its efforts to distribute Budi. "Abderramane Berete, attending the council of notables, thanks the president [of the council] for his efforts to find a variety of cotton which yielded superior harvest than the local cotton, *koroniba*, which the natives cultivate without enthusiasm and which they will abandon without regret."[7] Was it any surprise that the president of the council was also the administrator of the district?

In just four years from its introduction in the 1932–33 cotton season, the Budi harvest was double that of Allen and exceeded even that of the recorded indigenous cotton harvest in several districts (see Table 2).

Budi promised a new future for the pro-peasant defense of its share of the colonial economy. Nearly all of the 1936 harvest was bought by merchants. Metropolitan spinners were not nearly as sanguine, however. Although Budi was selling at a premium of 15 to 25 francs per ton over indigenous cotton, Budi produced short, spindly fibers ill-suited to metropolitan machinery.[8]

Nonetheless, peasant response to Budi signaled a significant change in the priorities among the pro-peasant camp. For the first time, the zone of cotton politics shifted from the precolonial cotton center along the Middle Niger Valley toward the southeastern quadrant. By the 1934–35 harvest, it was becoming increasingly clear that "the Soudan contains two varieties of cotton production on a large scale: Allen in the districts of Kayes, Nara, north Bamako, Segu, Macina,

TABLE 2

1936–37 Harvest of Cotton by Variety and District

Cercle	Allen	Budi	Indigenous	Total
Bamako subdivisions				284.7T
Koulikoro	188.7T	—	—	
Mourdiah	1.8	—	—	
Kolokani	29.1	65.1	—	
Segu	134.2	128.3	—	262.5
Kita	—	87.4	—	87.4
Bafoulabe	—	26.4	—	26.4
San	51.1	114.1	—	165.2
Ouahigouya	144	—	45	189
Sikasso	—	148.6	240.9	389.5
Koutiala	—	354.3	273.5	627.8
Bouguni	—	146.5	—	146.5
Kayes	20	—	300	320
TOTAL	568.9	1,070.7	859.4	2,499 T

SOURCE: Charles Godard, Service de l'Agriculture, Rapport annuel, campagne 1936–37, Bamako, 25 May 1937, ANS-AOF 2 G 37-53.

NOTE: Figures for the harvest of indigenous cotton remained guesswork in large measure because it fed into the domestic market not controlled by the colonial state.

San, Ouahigouya and Tougan; and Karangani–Garrah Hills in the other districts of the colony."[9]

The opening of the southeastern tier of the colony to the pro-peasant politique cotonnière represented a significant shift in strategy. It ceded the old, established cotton zone of the Middle Niger Valley to the Office du Niger, which had already laid claim to the experimental farms and extension services in the region. More important, the promoters of peasant cotton were taking a big gamble. Although the initial data were extremely promising, the cotton potential of the San-Koutiala-Sikasso triangle was untested. It was a zone of greater rainfall, 700 to 850 millimeters annually, and it contained a fairly dense and productive population. The fairly rapid conflation of this new zone with a specific crop, however, was a mistake. The pro-peasant camp quickly realized that despite the rapid acceptance of Budi by the peasants in this zone, the crop itself would not satisfy metropolitan industrial needs. Metropolitan spinners preferred Allen cotton, which was the closest Soudanese cotton to the American medium staple widely used in European industry.

Production of Allen had been making some progress since its introduction in 1927–28. The Depression, however, came at an inauspicious moment for those supporting the expansion of Allen. Figure 14 traces the annual exports of Allen against those of Egyptian long

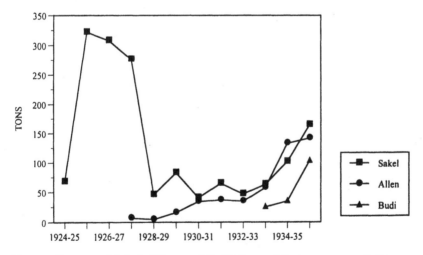

Fig. 14. Exports of Sakel, Allen, and Budi Cotton Fiber, 1924–1936. Source: Charles Godard, Ingénieur en chef des travaux d'agriculture aux colonies, Rapport annuel, campagne 1936–37, Bamako, 24 May 1937, ANS-AOF 2 G 37-53.

staple (Sakel)—grown primarily in CICONNIC Dire plantations and nearby—from 1924 to 1936. Budi exports date from 1933–34 only. Allen production was challenged by falling world cotton prices during the Depression and by peasant preference for Budi.

Already by the beginning of the 1935–36 harvest, the administrator of the Dioila district reported that Allen was increasing by coming into direct competition with Budi and Budi promised even larger harvests.[10] Budi's march northward from Koutiala effectively limited the expansion of Allen into the higher rainfall region of the southeast. The variety of Allen in use in the late 1920s and early 1930s would not have survived well in the more humid conditions of Koutiala and Sikasso anyway. Moreover, the colonial state was having difficulty justifying its continued subsidies of the Allen harvest and the financial losses involved.[11] In 1935, Lieutenant Governor Félix Eboué argued that the administration's price incentives were "artificial and surpass that normally offered by the commercial sector under conditions of free trade." He admitted that the operation consistently ran a deficit, but he justified it as a necessity to encourage "producers to extend a variety of cotton requiring more care and attention than indigenous varieties."[12] In the 1935–36 harvest, the administration turned increasingly to the recently created Sociétés de prévoyance, local provident societies, to act as the regulator of cotton prices to assure producers a fair return. An incident in February 1936, reported by the Koutiala administrator, demonstrates how the provident societies were supposed to function as regulators of the market and of commercial tensions.

M. Fronteau, of Daniel et Fronteau of Segu, arrived in the morning of the Koutiala market and announced a very recent decline in the metropolitan cotton market. He easily persuaded the assembled buyers to reduce their offers from 0.50F/kilogram to 0.45F. The native producers, who brought their cotton to the market expecting the previously fixed price, engaged in lively discussions, but refused to deliver their product. My efforts to have the buyers increase their prices were in vain. . . . That day in Koutiala, there were no transactions in cotton. At M'Pesoba the next day, the same incidents occurred. The stalemate between native producers and buyers threatened to continue.

Commerce, convinced of its omnipotence, waited mockingly. The pressing need for cash, the requirements to satisfy their fiscal obligations to the state, and the general weakness [of the economy] would in the end, it thought, undermine the peasants' resistance. The peasants turned to the administration to assist them.

The administration has an obligation to assist commerce, but does it also have an obligation to protect the native . . . and particularly in the case of cotton, which the administration has everywhere sought to encourage? Hasn't the administration promised that cotton would be a source of wealth for peasants?

The governor intervened by advancing the Société de prévoyance a credit of 300,000 francs and instructed it to buy on the colony's account all the cotton at between 0.50F and 0.55F/kilogram. On the markets held between 5 and 7 February, commerce encountered unexpected competition. Stopped [in its efforts to dictate the market price] and confused, the buyers accepted the new prices for cotton. In conforming to its instructions, the provident society thus managed to create a free market. The conflict thus ended.[13]

In 1936, the provident societies of Kita, Bafoulabe, and Nioro bought all the Allen harvest. In Ouahigouya, the society bought nearly a quarter of the harvest to keep prices from falling below what the administration considered to be a disincentive rate of return.[14] Fadita Tounkara, a former agricultural monitor, described the strategic role of the state in protecting Allen producers. "Prices," he noted, "were fixed at the beginning of each harvest season by the administration. There was no free market."

Question: Why was a price on cotton imposed?
Response: If one allowed the merchants to do what they wanted, they would respond by offering only a derisory price for our products. The fixed price was to defend the peasants.[15]

Despite state intervention, by 1936 the Allen harvest had leveled off and its deficiencies had become clear.[16] The colonial agricultural service was already at work further acclimating Allen to the Soudanese environment. Agronomists were especially interested in maintaining Allen's characteristic fiber while breeding in greater adaptability to humid conditions. N'Kourala cotton, an improved indigenous variety, was first introduced in the Sikasso district during the 1933–34 season. During the 1934–35 season, Sikasso peasants produced 40 tons of N'Kourala cotton, and its future in the more humid southeastern tier seemed promising. By the end of the 1936–37 cotton season, however, agronomists were backpeddling on N'Kourala, calling its role in cotton development "episodic." Agronomists were, however, on the right track and efforts to produce a better Allen eventually succeeded in making the southeastern tier the premier cotton-exporting region in the Soudan.[17]

The colonial state nonetheless persisted in its efforts to supervise and control Allen production. In 1936, the administrator from Kolokani in the Allen zone described the politics of production employed in his district. "In order to effect more efficient control, villages cul-

tivating Allen have been visited and notables have been encouraged
to group together in one field a surface of 20 hectares for this crop.
This accomplished, a master-plower will be sent to these locations,
and after discussion with the heads of the families involved, he will
clear and prepare in each of the villages a surface area proportional to
the population."[18]

Production politics surrounding Allen smacked of a return to the
discredited *champs collectifs*.[19] Lieutenant Governor Rougier argued
strongly that even if these fields of Allen resembled collective fields,
this was certainly not his intention. "The grouped fields for the production of cotton, advised by my predecessor and by me, have the
object to facilitate surveillance and to give superior yields. In no
case, however, were these grouped fields transformed into collective
fields . . . that procedure is eminently condemnable and would go
against the goals we pursue." Rougier tried to draw a fine line between control over production, so necessary for the success of cotton
as an export crop, and individual liberty, so central to the ideology of
the colonial state before the advent of Vichy policies. In trying to find
a middle ground, Rougier's administration privileged the family as
the unit of production. "The grouped fields are located close to the
village and cultivated by the inhabitants of a single village. Clearing
the land would be a collective enterprise, but the plots are divided
among each family, proportional to its size. All the work, from the
seeding to the harvest, is done by the family on the plot designated
to it, and the amount of the sale obtained is given to the head of the
family." The tasks of the politique cotonnière thus had three parts:
first, to assist the native in selecting the best fields with a view toward producing the highest possible return for a similar amount of
labor; second, to ensure that the fields were divided into "family
plots"; and third, to ensure that there would be a free sale of the
harvest and, in all cases, a remuneration payable to each family.[20]

On 4 November 1935, interim lieutenant governor Eboué enacted
a decree profoundly sharpening the colonial state's control over rain-
fed cotton cultivation from preparation of cotton fields to planting
and marketing.[21] It essentially made cotton production in the Soudan compulsory and drew colonial officials ever more fully into its
rhythm and intensity. The decree also recognized the existence of
two parallel models of colonial cotton development in the Soudan.
The revival of the champs collectifs and the subsequent debate focusing on family plots were part of the politics of cotton production
which sought to differentiate the irrigated zones of the Office du Ni-

ger from the long-established "village" of the rain-fed cotton zone. Inspector Bagot defined the two zones of cotton politics as follows:

In contrast to that which occurs in the irrigated lands, where villages of colonization are newly created, the extension of cotton production into the rainfed zone must respect the native administrative unity: the village. The advantage of this latter system is that if it causes any perturbation in ancestral customs, it nonetheless leaves to the native his own land and permits production within the framework of the family. If there is any progress toward individual property, it occurs so slowly that it is virtually unnoticeable.[22]

The revived politique cotonnière targeted the village and through the village the family as the principal unit of cotton production. Neither the village nor the family, however, was an enduring and unproblematical category. The Depression had forced the return of significant numbers of migrant farmers from Senegal, the Côte d'Ivoire, and the Gold Coast, many of whom came back to households and household tensions they had long left behind. They returned, according to a report from Bouguni, "with more deceptions than money."[23] The contraction of the colonial economy and colonial cotton programs seemed to reinforce the authority of the household head and oftentimes village and canton chiefs over young men who had used the boom times of the 1920s to pursue independent opportunities.[24] Elders did not, however, always get their way. In 1934, Lieutenant Governor Eboué wrote that "especially in regions where indigenous authority resides upon less stable bases or is patently deficient, one can discern a certain propensity for the dispersion of constitutive elements of collectivities. Some of the latter suffer from the departures by those who are animated by a spirit of malcontentment or rivalry or who are influenced by unfavorable economic conditions to separate and found independent associations."[25] Governor-General Brévié reiterated Eboué's findings in his annual report of 1934, stating more clearly that the tendency toward change came "principally from young men's efforts to liberate themselves from traditional discipline." Brévié warned, moreover, that in the current state of development of the indigenous society, "all such actions have as a consequence the dissolution of collectivities with fatal repercussions for indigenous authority."[26] The governor of Soudan was even more specific about the motivations of those who chose to leave their villages. In 1936, he wrote that "the young people in particular look for work with the construction gangs, in the towns as porters, or go to the frontiers [of the colony] in order to earn a nest egg. That way they can liberate themselves from the tutelage of their families."[27] Such were

the general conditions in which the revival of the pro-peasant politique cotonnière exacerbated latent or barely concealed tensions and
conflicts at the village and household levels. Far from promoting cotton exports and domestic stability, the politique cotonnière led to
conflict and social change.

Cotton Politics During the Popular Front, 1936–1938

When the Popular Front governor Rougier took office late in 1936,
world commodity prices were firming and the enhanced control over
cotton production was biting deep into rural life. As the 1937 planting season opened, the commandant of Siguiri in neighboring Guinea
wrote to his counterpart across the border in Bouguni that the exodus
of 400 to 500 residents of Ba-Sidibe district seemed over. "When I
asked them why they had come, they responded that they simply
wanted to move to Siguiri because in Bouguni they are obliged to
cultivate cotton." The Bouguni commandant was convinced that the
exodus was prompted because the Ba-Sidibe residents considered the
"cotton campaign a supplementary tax or a corvée. As a consequence
[of this perception], the fields were not well prepared or maintained,
the yields were deficient, and the harvest much smaller than we had
expected."[28]

The 1937 cotton exodus was not, however, limited to Bouguni. In
May, the Bamako commandant counted 664 young men from the
subdivision of Dioila who had departed, adding to the 1,600 young
men who had departed the previous year and not returned. In addition, 700 young men had left Bamako subdivision so far that year and
the numbers were increasing daily. The train to Senegal on the third
of May caught the Bamako commandant's attention because it had
at least ten passenger cars overflowing with *navetanes*, the migrant
farmers who worked the groundnut farms of Senegambia. They were
attracted, he argued, "by the possibility of gain and also to escape the
prestations of forced cotton production." In a separate report written
around the same time, the Bamako commandant reported that "native chiefs have confirmed the declarations of young men for whom
the cultivation of cotton represents a second series of forced labor
surrounding a crop they do not like and the labor on which they consider injurious to their interests."[29]

The exodus of young men from the compulsion of cotton production confronted the Popular Front governors of the Soudan, Ferdinand Jacques Louis Rougier and Jean Desanti, with the deep con-

tradictions of the politique cotonnière. To make Soudanese cotton viable on the export market the colonial state was obliged to intervene in all phases of production and marketing. Yet these policies resulted in an egregious disregard for basic human freedoms, and Popular Front governors could not long support them. Desanti, in particular, elaborated a policy that had in fact been the reality since the inception of the politique cotonnière 40 years before: the tendency for cotton producers to direct their harvests to the domestic market. In late 1938, he wrote to commandants of the major cotton-producing regions that only "when the local needs [of the handicraft industry] are met, then the surplus will be delivered to the export market. Moreover, saturation of the local market will result in a reduction in local prices and thus a reduction in the disequilibrium currently existing [between the export and domestic markets]: at that point, the sale to export markets will resume advantageously."[30] Desanti warned his administrators, however, to "keep an eye toward the provisioning of seeds." Under Desanti's administration, the new twist to the politique cotonnière was what he termed his "absolute principle: the priority is that the needs of the local artisanat must be satisfied first. We cannot oblige the natives to sell for export at a price lower than domestic rates the fibers that they need to clothe themselves."[31] Desanti's new policy was based on one empirical observation and at least one false premise. It was altogether too obvious that the disequilibrium between domestic and export prices for cotton would result in a net flow of the harvest to the sector willing to pay more. The debate about prices during the interwar period (see Chapter 9) was based on this observation. The new policy was designed to operate under the assumption that there was a point of saturation beyond which the domestic market could not absorb additional cotton.

Desanti probably received the idea about saturation from an authoritative 1935 report on rain-fed cotton cultivation written by agricultural engineer P. Coleno. "The local weaving industry is considerably developed. Cotton is exchanged between natives at prices superior to those prevailing on the export market. But the power to absorb cotton by weavers is limited. We estimate that 500T of fiber seems to be the platform."[32] At about 20 percent yield of fiber from capsules, 500 tons of fiber translates roughly to 2,500 tons of raw cotton. In 1937, Charles Godard, the director of agricultural services in the colony, doubled his assessment of the saturation platform to 5,000 tons of raw cotton or about 1,000 tons of fiber. Godard also estimated that the domestic market consumed twice as much cotton as was delivered to the export sector, making the total estimated cotton harvest for 1936–37 about 7,500 tons of raw cotton.[33]

By the 1937–38 harvest, the effects of the Popular Front policy to permit the "free" trade in cotton were beginning to be felt. Administrators expected a significant decline in exports. Instead of the usual 70 to 80 tons exported from Segu, they expected only one-tenth; from Kita, they expected less than one-third of the annual 50 tons exported. Similar reductions were anticipated from all the peasant cotton regions. The annual report stated: "Despite increases in cultivated surfaces this year, the change in the politique coton-nière will have as a consequence the notable and continued reduction in tonnage exported from previous years until saturation of the domestic market is obtained."[34] Cotton producers were obviously pleased with their newfound freedom for they planted even larger fields than the previous year. "Natives in all the regions," noted the annual cotton report that year, "are more and more in favor of this crop since they have been able to conserve their harvest." But because the colonial state could not renounce its control over seeds, the administration increased its pressure on native chiefs to "encourage" cotton producers to bring their harvests to the ginning stations. Cotton producers were promised that they would be able to retain the fiber once the cotton was ginned and a portion kept to cover the costs. Nonetheless, producers also used their new freedom to plant their local varieties of cotton rather than the exotic ones favored by the export market and the colonial state.[35]

Similarly, expatriate and African merchants, who were supposed to ply the cotton export market, sought to maximize their own profits by trading cotton on the domestic market. The "controlled" markets still operated during this period, but increasingly merchants took advantage of the efforts by the colonial state to centralize the trade and to "fix" export prices so as to buy cotton cheaply at the official cotton markets only to sell it again in a different region of the colony for domestic prices often two to three times as high. Administrator Vernay called this "an immoral speculation in buying cotton at export prices and then reselling it at the local rate to natives."[36] Lieutenant Governor Desanti termed these actions "prejudicial to natives who see some intermediaries turn profits without taking on the financial sacrifices in order to develop this crop." Although the governor could not prohibit the commercial sector from making profits, he suggested that the best way to prevent these practices was to have the "provident societies gin all cotton on account of its members and return to them the quantity necessary for their consumption."[37]

These were the imperfections and unforeseen consequences of the Popular Front's policy of saturation. But it was the premise that there actually was a finite "platform" beyond which the domestic industry could no longer consume cotton that was faulty. This premise was flawed in two ways. First, as I discussed in Chapter 9 and as I will discuss more fully later in this chapter, the size of the domestic market for cotton was highly elastic. As the price rose and/or the volume of imported cloth declined, the demand for handicraft textiles increased. Thus the platform was never stationary. Second, because the Soudan was deeply enmeshed in continental circuits of commerce, a purely "domestic" market could never be satisfactorily defined. The 1936 annual report described the special circumstances of the Soudanese economy, which had been observed and repeated many times before. "The Soudan, unlike the other colonies of the federation, does not have to turn all its efforts toward exports to ensure the equilibrium of its economy. The export sector is but a complement to the interior and intercolonial commerce, which escapes all control, and constitutes in reality the principal economic basis of the colony."[38] Although the Popular Front politics of cotton production did seem to reduce the level of compulsion, it did not yield a supply of cotton for the metropole. With the approach of yet another war in Europe, the needs of the metropole for colonial raw materials led to a profound reassessment of the Popular Front policies.

The War, Vichy, and Cotton, 1939–1944

The outbreak of war, the fall of France, and the blockade of Europe profoundly shaped the colonial politique cotonnière. Although Vichy elaborated a colonial policy predicated on the supply of colonial raw materials to the metropole, policy made very little difference on the ground in the Soudan. Colonial cotton policy during the war years operated with virtually the same tool kit used previously. The one innovation was an intriguing barter program introduced in 1942 to stimulate cotton exports. In the end, however, the politique cotonnière under Vichy produced decrees for the colony and not cotton for the metropole.

Three aspects of the political economy of colonial cotton policy formed the core of the history of this period. First, there was a decline in imported cloth. As France under the Third Republic and later under Vichy turned toward wartime production, a significant part of annual textile production in France was directed to military needs. Without cheap and plentiful imports of cloth, the handicraft textile industry in the Soudan remained strong. Second, Vichy attempted to introduce a variant of the "directed economy" in the Soudan which reflected models established in France. The problem was one of implementation because the directed economy assumed that the state could actually control production and marketing. Under the failing Third Republic and under Vichy, the colonial state produced a host of new committees and agencies to control production and marketing. The colonial state reimposed compulsory cotton production in parts of the Soudan. And third, the politics of food production for export to the West Africa Federation increasingly took precedence over the production of cotton for export. This was a concession to the market because the average return on labor for millet, rice, and groundnuts was higher than for cotton. Soudanese peasants continued to grow cotton, but the domestic market was booming and it absorbed most of the cotton produced.

Already in 1939, it was clear that the other colonies of the federation were calling on the food production of the Soudan to satisfy their food deficits at a time when their economies were being called upon to supply raw materials to France. Wartime mobilization of colonial resources privileged food production and requisition over cotton production.[39] The 1939 annual economic report noted that "the production of food was definitely increasing." Nonetheless, the overall plan for the national defense envisioned a sustained supply of Soudanese cotton for export. Peasants were thus confronted with two seemingly contradictory demands. On the one hand, they were responding to the needs of a continental market by producing more food; on the other, they were still being asked to produce cotton for export at significant cost to their income. "There is no question," remarked the lieutenant governor of the Soudan early in 1940, "that while the native accepts without hesitation his military obligations, he seems perplexed by the equally imperious demands made on him in the economic domain."[40] Colonial officials were also perplexed when exports of cotton fell by over 30 percent from 1938 to 1939.

Vichy, however, was not prepared to have the Soudan not play its assigned role in the provision of the metropole. In 1940–41 it tightened its grip through legislation on circulation and consumption of targeted commodities at the expense of "free trade." "More and more, it has become a necessity," stated the annual economic report of 1941, "that tighter control over import and export commerce be exerted. The previous system of economic liberty will little by little yield a directed economy developed by the Service of Commercial Exchanges." The tentacles of the directed economy, however, did not reach too far beyond the government buildings in which it was elaborated. Cotton exports for 1940–41 declined further, and Soudanese cotton remained in the domestic sector, where prices for cotton were buoyant. The annual report conceded that there was a crisis, "but it was not a crisis of production, because there is still cotton in the Soudan." The crisis was the failure to capture the cotton for export.[41]

The failure to capture cotton for export was linked to the failure of imported cloth to capture the domestic market. The outbreak of war in Europe led to a period of "arrest and indecision" on the part of the import-export sector. Because of uncertainty about future deliveries, prices of imported goods rose between 45 and 50 percent in the last months of 1939 alone. As merchants slowed and then stopped buying Soudanese commodities, the administration began to worry again about the deleterious effects this would have on the politics of production. "It is clear that it is the native producer who will bear the costs of this experience, because at best he will receive only a very inferior return for his production. This situation will have serious repercussions on the political and social order: the native knows that huge efforts are demanded of him to produce, but he does not comprehend that he will not be served by his efforts." The administration floated the solution of building massive warehouses capable of stocking the entire export harvest to wait for a return of more normal prices.[42]

Prices did not return to normal nor did the volume of imported cloth increase. Although I shall explore the volume of imported cloth and yarn more fully in the next section, it is clear from the record that imported cloth remained scarce and its price high throughout the war years. Without a significant volume of imported cloth, the domestic market continued to bid up the price of cotton and produce handcrafted cloth to satisfy the needs of the population. Weavers were active throughout the colony, but especially in Bouguni, Sikasso, and San, where the local weaving industry had not been well developed during the interwar period. The price of cotton in local markets went as high as six francs per kilogram in 1941, and the volume of domestic transactions in cotton and cotton fiber "increased without stopping." Pierre Viguier, the director of agricultural services in 1942, admitted that without administrative pressure, deliveries of cotton to the ginneries would fall to zero.[43]

Already with the outbreak of war, Governor-General Boisson suggested that the colonial state intervene to provide price subsidies for cotton exports. He suggested that a tax of 0.50 francs per kilogram on imported foreign cloth be charged on entry into West Africa to provide a fund for cotton exports, to defray the costs of irrigation, and to support centers of cotton research. The war, however, effectively curtailed the international commerce in cloth, especially from Great Britain and the Netherlands, undercutting Boisson's plan.[44] As the war deepened its hold over colonial commerce, the administration saw its control over cotton, so needed by metropolitan industries, slip further through its fingers. The disequilibrium between the domestic and export markets for cotton widened considerably. Both peasants and European merchants abandoned the export market. Deprived of imported goods, European merchants increasingly bought ginned cotton destined for export and sold it back on the domestic market. In 1942 the colonial state reached into its tool kit and returned with a series of prohibitions against this type of "inadmissible speculation."[45]

More intriguing and more representative of Vichy's efforts to give substance to its directed economy was the idea of bartering cotton cloth for raw cotton, floated by M. Mieg, the director of the committee of metropolitan cotton spinners. Such bartering would reconcile the two sides of the cotton supply problem: it would provide Soudanese with cloth they were currently deprived of and it would allow the colonial state to control directly a supply of raw cotton. At administrative council meetings of the Union cotonnière de l'empire français (formerly the ACC) in April and September 1942 Mieg suggested that a Société d'achat des produits contingentés be formed to acquire four million meters of cloth and then distribute it throughout the interior of French West Africa to encourage producers to cultivate cotton and bring it to the market. Mieg anticipated that the exchange would take the form of a barter through which the Soudanese peasant would receive a coupon exchangeable for cloth for a fixed quantity of cotton. The UCEF expected that at the rate of 1.5 meters of cloth for every 10 kilograms of cotton, 4 million meters of cloth would yield 26,400 tons of raw cotton. The concept was intriguing, but the success of the venture rested on the solution of "practical" difficulties, including the creation of an administrative structure able to deliver on both ends of the program. Vichy could generate elaborate organizational models, but its record of delivering the goods was quite different. Mieg's idea was quietly dropped, and the colonial administration retreated to the well-honed tactic of compulsion.[46]

Vichy considered compulsion a natural obligation of individuals to society. Vichy administrators understood that although Soudanese peasants would respond to crops that were in their interest, the "imperious" needs of raw materials for the metropole permitted compulsion. In the cotton regions of Ouahigouya and Tougan, the colonial state continued to impose the compulsory production of Allen and Budi.[47] In other regions, it differentiated "free" production from "controlled" production. "One must distinguish," Viguier wrote in 1942, "two types of cotton cultivation in the Soudan in addition to that of irrigation. The first is controlled cultivation, where seeds are distributed by the administration and production is destined, in principle, to be ginned by the UCEF. The second is free cultivation, where natives spontaneously cultivate cotton, which is destined for the local artisanat." Viguier stressed the term *in principle* because he admitted that without compulsion, even the cotton from the controlled zone would not flow toward the official ginneries.[48]

As increased submarine warfare in the Atlantic cut the supply of cotton from traditional sources, metropolitan officials and industrialists were faced with a critical need for colonial sources of cotton. In the Soudan, the administration proposed a new plan. Named after the chief agricultural engineer of the colony, the Sagot plan anticipated a "return to a system of production analogous to that of obligatory production, which had been used under different circumstances in the past." It focused on "controlled" production exclusively, defining for each region a quota based on the population's agricultural "avocation." Central to the Sagot plan was administrative pressure, which was to operate through the native authority. Subsidies were to be distributed to canton chiefs in direct proportion to the effort they exerted to assist the administration in encouraging cotton production. Control over production was also to be tightened by more frequent visits by agricultural and local administrative agents, who were empowered to encourage careful production through the application of punishments.[49] The deepening of war in Europe in 1942 shattered Sagot's plan. With virtually no imported cloth available, consumers in the Soudan turned exclusively to the domestic sector.

What was necessary, suggested Viguier, was "not the control over cotton production, but its mobilization." Indeed, the figures Viguier reported on cotton production for 1942–43 indicated clearly that the net result of Vichy's insistence on compulsion had the opposite effect. Production and delivery of Allen and Budi to official ginneries in Ouahigouya fell to zero and in Tougan it fell by half of the previous year even though total cotton production for the colony increased.[50] As Figure 15 indicates, a significant amount of cotton was still being ginned, although how much was actually exported to France is not clear from the extant data. Both the politics of saturation, practiced under the Popular Front, and the politics of controlled cotton, applied under Vichy, may well have been concessions to the self-evident failure of the colonial state to capture the cotton harvest. The following sections explore more fully the performance of the handicraft textile industry and the domestic supply of cotton during this period.

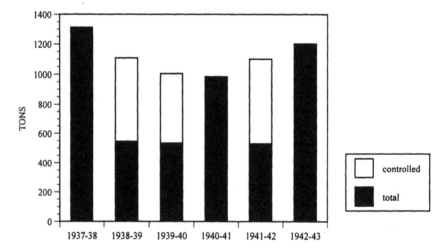

Fig. 15. Estimated Volume of Total Fiber and Volume of Fiber from Controlled Cotton, 1937–1943. Figures for total harvest are based on yields of 20 percent fiber after ginning. Sources: Service de l'Agriculture, Rapport annuel, campagne 1937–38, Soudan, ANS-AOF 2 G 38-53; Service de l'Agriculture, Rapport annuel, campagne 1938–39, Soudan, ANS-AOF 2 G 39-60; Rapport économique pour l'année 1939, Soudan, ANS-AOF 2 G 39-37; Rapport économique, annuel, 1942, Soudan, ANS-AOF 2 G 42-25; Service de l'Agriculture. Rapport annuel, campagne 1939–40, Soudan, ANS-AOF 2 G 40-88; Acting lt.-gov., Plan de Production par Cercles des principaux produits, Kouluba, 21 Apr. 1942, ANS 1 R 56; Service de l'Agriculture, Rapport annuel, campagne 1941–42, ANS-AOF 2 G 42-35; Service de l'Agriculture, Rapport, 14 June 1943, ANS-AOF 2 G 43-47.

The Persistence of the Domestic Market for Cotton and Handcrafted Cotton Textiles, 1932–1946

The period between the Depression and the end of World War II was the single longest stretch since the French conquest of the Soudan in the 1880s in which imports of manufactured cloth did not witness a sustained rebound following shocks to the world economic system. There was a little window between late 1934 and 1938, when industrial productivity returned to the metropole and trade flowed more freely, but it closed abruptly with the German military advance in Europe. The closing window of imported cloth merely reinforced the domestic and continental basis of cotton production, textile manufacturing, and cloth commerce in the Soudan. As the estimates of the total cotton harvest became slightly more reliable during the course of the 1930s and 1940s, it became equally clear that the French had underestimated the size of the domestic market for handcrafted cloth. During this period, the Soudanese—as well as many Senegalese and Ivorians—turned increasingly to the domestic market to supply their needs and desires for cloth.

As the Depression took hold of the import-export sector, the administrator of San in 1933 wrote that "commerce is dead; buyers with money are rare." Responding to the lack of goods in the boutiques of the colony, peasants took their harvests and converged on the major centers such as Bamako. But they did not deal with the export sector. Instead, they turned to these larger, central markets to "exchange [their cotton] directly for products which they do not possess."[51] Nama Jara of Dio in the Bamako district harvested about one ton of cotton from his ten-hectare plot. He took his entire cotton harvest to local markets, where the prevailing prices were higher than those offered by the commercial houses of Bamako.[52] "Cotton culture," the lieutenant governor reassured his superior in Dakar, "is not in regression. Instead, it feeds a very abundant current of exchanges from village to village and from district to district in the form of woven bands."[53] In the first quarter of 1936, nine tons of cotton bands were sold in the markets of Sikasso, roughly equal to 270,000 meters. About half was destined for export to the Côte d'Ivoire.[54] Throughout 1936, cotton bands were selling briskly in Bouguni. There was also a significant trade from Bouguni westward across the border into Guinea and into other Soudanese markets. "Cotton," remarked the administrator there, "is not the object of interest of the export sector. Natives, however, produce much cotton

TABLE 3

Cotton Production and Cotton Consumption in Selected Subdivisions
of Bamako, 1941–1942

Subdivision	Production	Local Use	Export
Bamako	55 T	55 T	none
Koulikoro	55	45	10 T
Kolokani	10	55	−45
Dioila	150	85	65
Kourémalé	none	10	−10
TOTAL	270 T	250 T	20 T

SOURCE: Administrator Bamako, telegram to governor Soudan, Bamako, 26 Jan. 1942,
ANM 1 Q 1909.

and give it to the weavers, who are widespread throughout the villages where their industry is in resurgent prosperity." Juula went to San and other cotton districts to buy and transport cotton to districts where demand from weavers outstripped local production.[55] Table 3 provides data on the production and consumption of cotton in one district.

Dahou Traore of the left bank village of Sibila remembered this interdistrict trade in cotton, particularly from the southern tier regions. Although his village continued to cultivate cotton, it did so in very small quantities and relied on imports of cotton from Koutiala.[56] By 1938, the administrator of Bouguni noted a "very clear increase in the number of native weavers," many of whom were engaged in servicing the demand by gold miners for clothing. In 1943, the administration counted more than two million meters of cotton bands and more than 30,000 kosso blankets exported from the Soudan to markets in Senegal and Mauritania. These figures, admitted the lieutenant governor, were "certainly well below reality."[57]

The basic principles for interpreting the relationships between the output of the handicraft textile industry, imported cloth, and the size of the cotton harvest have been discussed at considerable length in Chapter 9. Precisely because the colonial economic system never fully captured the economy of the Soudan, it was relatively well insulated from rapid shifts in the world economy and thus better able to withstand international economic crises. There was thus no paradox in the capacity of the handicraft textile industry to cater to the needs of both the domestic and neighboring economies. Central to the argument I have been making in this book is that the domestic market for cotton in the Soudan consistently proved resistant to the efforts of the colonial state to shape its production and to capture the cotton harvest. Peasants resisted the intrusion of the state into their decisions about the timing and cycles of production, and Soudanese consumers turned to the domestic market to satisfy their needs for cloth precisely because European imports had never fully captured the domestic economy. Soudanese consumers bought imported cloth when it was available at prices they considered attractive. But they never were attractive long enough to erode the handicraft textile industry. The handicraft textile industry persisted throughout the colonial period because it remained central to the domestic and continental economy of West Africa.

Figures 16 and 17 on the volume of cloth imported into the Soudan illustrate the larger context in which the handicraft textile industry performed from 1931 to 1942. Figure 16 portrays the imports of yarn and two varieties of cloth by value from 1931 to 1935. In 1936, the customs bureau introduced a system of accounting by weight, and Figure 17 traces the imports of the same categories of yarn and cloth from 1936 to 1942.[58] Taken together, these two figures show a fairly strong recovery of cloth imports into the Soudan from 1934 through 1938 and then a dramatic fall in imports of all types of cloth.

Colonial officials had long recognized the persistence of the handicraft textile industry as a primary cause of the meager results of the

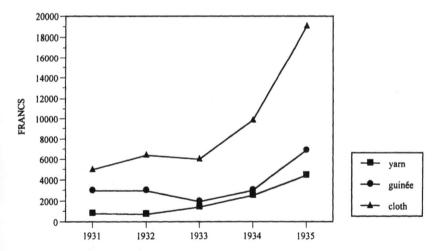

Fig. 16. Imports of Yarn, Cloth, and Guinée, 1931–1935. Sources: Rapport économique annuel, Soudan, 1934, ANS-AOF 2 G 34-34; Rapport économique annuel, Soudan, 1935, ANS-AOF 2 G 35-37.

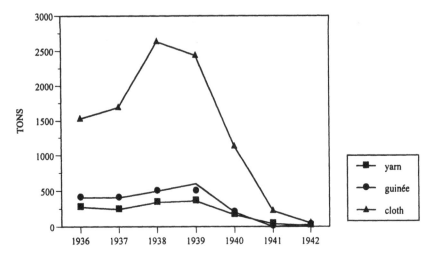

Fig. 17. Imports of Yarn, Cloth, and Guinée, 1936–1942. Sources: Acting lt-gov., Plan de production par cercles des principaux produits, Kouluba, 21 Apr. 1942, ANS 1 R 56; Rapport économique, Soudan, année 1942, ANS-AOF 2 G 42-25.

politique cotonnière. But none had turned to the handicraft textile industry as a source of revenue and of cloth. In the midst of the Depression, as revenue from duties on manufactured imports declined, the administration of the Côte d'Ivoire imposed a tariff of one franc per kilogram on handcrafted cotton bands imported from neighboring colonies. The quarterly economic report from the Soudan noted that the local markets were "brusquely encumbered" by this tariff, although there appears to have been little long-term damage to the intercolonial trade in cotton bands. By 1935, for example, the annual economic report from the Soudan noted that "the large share of the cotton harvest is transformed locally into cotton bands, which feed an abundant exchange between districts and with neighboring colonies, especially the coastal ones."[59] Because borders throughout the interior of West Africa were permeable, it was never easy for colonial administrators to measure the size of the intracontinental trade or to control or tax its movements. Reports from the Depression through the war years make amply clear that the domestic economy remained vibrant and catered to the needs of an intercontinental market as well as to the needs of the colonial administration itself.

When imports of cloth into the Soudan virtually collapsed after 1939, several colonial services turned to the handicraft textile industry for supplies. In 1939, the governor-general wrote to the minister of colonies arguing that in a pinch the Medical Service could use local cloth to satisfy its needs. "The width [of local cloth] is larger than the bands most frequently used by the Medical Service and their texture does not permit them to be cut into smaller strips. But it is not impossible that bands of 5 cm could be furnished by the local artisanat, but it will require a change in customary techniques of production and might involve delays."[60] As the supply of cloth during the war became even more precarious, Lieutenant Governor Louveau wrote that the solution to the "alarming" reports that too many conscripted STIN laborers in the Office du Niger were "very badly clothed" would be found by providing them with complete outfits made from local cloth.[61] Warike Jara of Koulikoro described the decline in imports of cloth during World War II as a leveling experience. "This was when no, absolutely no cloth or imported goods arrived and when everyone, peasants, clerks, and even French officials, wore clothing made of local cloth."[62] These sentiments about wartime scarcity were echoed in the annual economic report of 1942. "Because of the difficulties stemming from the circumstances [of the war], the colony was forced to rely much more on itself, to reap the maximum it could from its soil, and to seek to replace certain imported merchandise with the production of its artisans."[63] The lack of imported cloth for the administration induced some peculiar innovations. Cebarama Dembele of Banankoro described how the Segu administration organized the production of cloth under the auspices of the provident society of Segu, probably to provide cloth to the laborers in the Office du Niger.

Question: During the last war, the administration had weavers established in Segu to work for the "prévoyance." Were you involved in that corvée?
Response: Yes, I participated.
Question: Who spun the cotton? Did the women?
Response: Yes, women were forced to do that work. Some men would sort the cotton, others would weave.
Question: Were the spinners paid for their work?
Response: They received something. The women worked for fifteen days, then they were replaced by other groups of women. They came by groups of ten or fifteen from each village. Some villages provided as many as twenty. They stayed fifteen days and then they were replaced. That which they spun was woven by us in order to make cotton bands.
Question: What was done with those cotton bands?
Response: I don't know, but all profit went to the authorities. Those were difficult times. . . . Shirts and pants were made of cotton bands.[64]

As late as 1945, the director of economic affairs noted that the Soudan was suffering from "extreme penury" of cloth. Imported cloth remained scarce well into the postwar period.[65]

These incidents, reports, and recollections reveal that the handicraft textile industry's share of the cotton market actually increased in response to the decline in cloth imports and to the fall in market price for cotton on the export sector. Measures of the relative importance of market shares held by the export and the domestic sectors are notoriously subject to guesswork and speculation. Nor could anyone agree on the size of the cotton harvest absorbed locally or its capacity. Estimates ranged 2,500 tons of raw cotton, made in 1935, to more than 10,000 tons, made in 1938.[66] The agricultural service's report for the 1937–38 cotton season made clear that the previous estimates of 1,500 tons of fiber for the domestic market were being consistently raised upward "stemming from the considerable increase in the price of imported cloth and yarn."[67] With the virtual collapse of cloth imports in 1939, the size of the handicraft textile industry's share of the cotton harvest increased rapidly to meet the needs of the domestic and regional markets. By 1942, stated the annual economic report, "the entire cotton harvest of the Soudan could easily be absorbed locally."[68]

The Depression and wartime shortages in imported cloth proved yet again that the existence of a robust domestic market for cotton and handcrafted cotton cloth was far stronger than colonial efforts to capture the cotton harvest.

The Handicraft Textile Industry, 1932–1946

Demand for handcrafted textiles during this period seems to have broken the pattern of reversible social change among textile workers. Colonial reports are consonant that during this period weavers were working everywhere. The data only hint at this process, but sustained demand for handcrafted textiles coupled with the apparent diminishing of the household head's authority to organize production and the increasing availability of the factors of production on the market indicate that the household was no longer the primary locus of handicraft production in the Middle Niger Valley. Despite colonial policies designed to support the village and the family, the return of migrant workers from Senegal and the Côte d'Ivoire during the Depression and their general reluctance to fold themselves unquestioningly under the authority of the household head further eroded the household as the locus of all types of production. This pattern may have been different in other regions of the Soudan. Further research is needed to assess these changes.

I interviewed several elderly informants who were active in the handicraft textile sector during this period. Most, however, described changes in production and in the social relations of production in general terms. The tensions between household-based and independent production, so characteristic of the industry's dynamic since the early part of the century, remained part of the gloss on their memories. Only Hadja Toumata Contao, an elderly female entrepreneur of indigo dyeing and of handcrafted cloth, who began her business in the late 1930s, provided the detail on production I sought. Because her memory was so keen, I have included a lengthy segment of this interview, which provides precious detail.

Question: Did you make pagnes especially for sale?
Response: Yes, that was my work.
Question: Did you begin this work by ginning cotton, or did you begin by buying yarn?
Response: I began by ginning and spinning cotton. . . .
Question: Did you buy cotton already ginned?
Response: I bought cotton which I ginned in my home, then I spun it with a bow in order to give the yarn to a weaver. Here is a spinning tool which is not yet broken. . . .
Question: Did you not make white cloth?
Response: Of course, I made white cloth. Some years there was no boloti [imported yarn] available without presenting an identity card, that was 1943, 1944, and 1945. Then I spun cotton. I spun enough yarn for 50 pagnes which I dyed in indigo and enough yarn for 50 white pagnes. I had all of it woven. That was the last time I used [local] indigo. . . .
Question: Was it because of lack of boloti that you did not make more pagnes?
Response: No, it was because of lack of money.[69]

Three aspects of this interview with Hadja Toumata are worth exploring insofar as the data permit. First, she considered the entrepreneurship of textile production her "work." She was prepared to invest time and resources in securing both raw material and labor. Hadja Toumata was also the informant who had three weavers working exclusively for her and five others who wove in exchange for food and lodging (see Chapter 9). Second, the scale of Hadja Toumata's output of white and indigo-dyed cloth was limited by her capital. Because most of her capital was tied up in cloth stocks or in yarn, she could not easily expand production as much as the market could support. In this regard, Hadja Toumata was similar to most small-scale handicraft entrepreneurs who were constrained by limited capital. More directly, the scale of her output was also a function of the availability of yarn. She could spin cotton by hand, but she clearly preferred to buy boloti on the market. During the Depression and during the supply interruptions of World War II, boloti was not abundantly available. As Figure 17 indicates, after 1939 boloti was very scarce. Hadja Toumata stated that industrial yarn was rationed, although I have not seen archival references to support this assertion. And third, Hadja Toumata mentions that it was during the 1940s that she stopped dyeing with local indigo. Imported chemical indigo had made its appearance on a small scale already during the interwar period. I do not have the statistics on chemical indigo imports, but we can assume that because of wartime production needs, little was available for export to the colonies.

Natural indigo had long been a commodity available on the market in the Middle Niger Valley. Most commercially available indigo during the early part of the century probably came from the indigo plantations of Nyamina and Baraweli. Women cultivated small amounts in the kitchen gardens. The arrival of chemical dyes made the work of female dyers much easier, but it tied dyers more fully into the supply of imported commodities. Kissima Makadji noted this pattern. "Women used to gather the indigo leaves and prepare them for use. Then the indigo of the whites arrived and put an end to that. Everyone bought that indigo. But it became too expensive and we stopped using it."[70] According to Mokan Fofana, "imported indigo replaced the indigo plant. It [originally] cost less and it was easier to use. . . . It was rare to find even an isolated field of indigo."[71] Indigo-dyed pagnes and blankets remained a staple in the regional and intracontinental trade, so my informants' assessment that natural indigo virtually disappeared needs to be taken with some skepticism. Nonetheless, the trajectory of change was clear. Even though natural indigo dye produced a more esteemed color, chemical inputs dominated the production of dyed cloth from the interwar period onward.[72]

The periodic interruptions in imported cloth supply from 1932 to 1946 certainly added to demand for handcrafted textiles because they were the only reliable source of cloth available. Older weaving centers along the Middle Niger boomed. Demand also spurred additional production from regions where commercial weaving was not as well established. In 1941, two years after the dramatic decline in cloth imports, Godard, the director of the Service d'agriculture, pointed to Koutiala, which he argued "possessed the largest proportion of weavers to total population."[73] Weavers in Koutiala could also draw on the increasing supplies of Budi and N'Kourala cotton. How were all these weavers organized? Were they independent contractors, weaving in exchange for a fixed sum? Entrepreneurs like Hadja Toumata Contao in Segu established patron-client relations with weavers, whom she housed and fed in her own concession and whose labor she more or less controlled. Weavers could earn considerable sums, equivalent to the best paying agricultural labor. According to Toumata Contao, in the 1930s and 1940s she paid 2 francs to have a pagne woven. The most efficient weavers could weave one pagne per day and thus earn 60 francs per month. If we subtract the costs of lodging and food (labor equivalent to 5 pagnes), then the net earned could be as high as 50 francs per month, with the average running 20 percent less at about 40 francs per month.[74] Other weavers probably plied their trade openly, inviting those with yarn to engage them. As a dry-season activity, many weavers would migrate to the major commercial centers, where weavers from the same village often stayed in the same quarters and wove side by side.[75] In the previous section, I cited the organization of weaving under the direction of the Société de prévoyance. A similar atelier was established just outside the administrative center in Koutiala, which employed 40 weavers producing extra-wide cloth (0.60m) for use as household linen.[76] Most weavers, however, wove as an off-farm, dry-season activity, which contributed to keeping handicraft textiles accessible to a large part of the domestic market.

Weavers' productivity depended upon yarn. Increasingly, weavers used boloti and produced cloth using both imported and handspun yarn. Between 1931 and 1934 (just before and just after the worst of the Depression), imports of industrial yarn increased by 300 percent while cloth imports barely doubled. This pattern persisted during the period when imports flowed more generously into the Soudan. By 1939, the annual economic report for the Soudan noted that "a very strong increase in imported cotton yarn confirms the activities of weavers, who confect more and more cloth using cotton supplied from the harvest and imported cotton yarn." Indeed, the only activity reported from the boutiques of the colony was the purchase of white and colored yarn.[77] The increased reliance on the market for the supply of raw materials and labor indicates that by the beginning of World War II the household was no longer the primary locus of handicraft textile production.

Because cloth was such a significant part of colonial commerce and because the Soudan produced vast amounts of cotton, it had been the seductive dream of some European entrepreneurs and colonial officials to bring European capital and technology to African raw materials and labor. In 1941, Louis Laprade and Louis Colombier approached the administration with a proposal to erect a spinning mill on a 30-hectare site along the Niger River with an initial capacity of 3,000 spindles to be expanded in two stages to 10,000 spindles. Laprade and Colombier also promised to erect an adjoining factory of 300 to 400 automatic looms, which would use 250 tons of ginned cotton annually. Where Colombier expected to get the capital and the equipment under wartime conditions was not mentioned. The administration, however, balked at his request for a concession and the plan folded.[78] Over at Kayes, the Compagnie soudanaise could point to the first industrial success story of the politique cotonnière. The Compagnie soudanaise was already active in cotton ginning. It sought to use its source of cotton to feed a spinning mill. The company acquired and actually installed mechanized spindles in the early 1930s. But the most the company could point to was an average production of 150 kilograms of yarn per year.[79] This was a tiny fraction of the 300 tons of cotton yarn imported annually in the late 1930s.

The New Politics of Cotton Production, 1944–1946

By 1944, Lieutenant Governor Louveau could unambiguously declare that "the principal effort asked of the Soudan concerns food products, especially rice." Certainly the politique cotonnière was not dead; it was, instead, relegated to the second tier level of production targets.[80] In 1944 France was liberated and the politique cotonnière was subjected to the sweeping changes promised during the Brazzaville Conference.

The end of the war in Europe brought renewed vigor to colonial development issues. France followed through on its promises made at Brazzaville and ended compulsory labor. The end of compulsion profoundly changed the politique cotonnière, as I indicated in the previous chapter. The provisional postwar government in France also committed itself to significant investment in colonial development projects through the linked programs of the Fonds d'investissement et de développement économique et social des territoires d'outre-mer (FIDES) and the Fonds d'équipement rural de développement économique et social (FERDES). Neither the metropole, Dakar, nor

Kouluba renounced Soudanese cotton, however. But the postwar politics of cotton production focused on the southern tier and introduced different production and marketing incentives.

Ever since the introduction of Budi and N'Kourala cotton varieties in the more humid southeastern tier in the 1930s, administrators and agronomists expected great things. The old cotton centers of the Middle Niger Valley seemed unable to push beyond a low yield per hectare threshold forced on them by irregular rainfall, lack of fertilizer, and peasant disdain for state intervention in cotton production. By the 1944–45 planting season, the colonial state announced that it was devoting fully 70 percent of its resources toward encouraging cotton production in the districts of Sikasso and Koutiala. In Sikasso alone, cotton was being planted on 15,000 hectares, and its harvest that season exceeded the expected 800 tons by 10 percent.[81]

But even in Sikasso, cotton producers remained financially disadvantaged in relationship to other crops, including millet and rice. A detailed comparison of labor output to return for nine different crops was collected in Sikasso during the 1944–45 agricultural season. Unfortunately, the report does not make clear the exact size of the sample used to assemble the data, but the comparisons of labor days expended and returns per hectare are worth recounting in some detail.

Table 4 is somewhat misleading because it suggests that no crop— neither food, groundnuts, nor cotton—returned a significant income in relationship to the effort expended. Within the scope of the data presented, it is nonetheless clear that cotton returned even less than food crops such as millet and rice and other export crops such as groundnuts. The director of agricultural services stated bluntly in that report that "at current world prices, remuneration in cotton does not justify the labor expended." The director went on to argue that high domestic cotton prices, lower export prices, and the high costs of transport conspired to limit export production. "The situation of our colony, in the heart of French Africa, handicaps all commodities of interest to the metropole or other foreign countries. Its 1,200 kilometers of narrow rail and its trains capable of transporting only small quantities at prohibitive rates have for a long time hindered the development of this vast but poor land."[82] Nonetheless, a postwar pattern of increasing commodity prices was set in motion, which saw prices rise from 3 francs per kilogram in 1946 to 18 francs per kilogram in 1949.[83]

Despite the postwar tendency for prices of Soudanese cotton to

TABLE 4

Sikasso Agricultural Study, 1944–1945

Expenses/Income	Millet	Sorghum	Corn	Rice	Ground-nuts	Cotton inter-cropped	Cotton separate
Expenses							
Preparation of fields	17	17	21	24	18	—	20
Seeding	5	5	5	4	4	5	5
Weeding	24	24	24	30	35	15	30
Harvesting	8	8	8	15	8	25	25
Transport	4	4	4	5	4	3	3
Threshing, clean-ing, preparation	10	12	15	6	17	8	8
Unforeseen	4	4	4	4	4	4	4
Total days	72	74	82	89	91	60	95
Value	504F	518F	574F	623F	637F	420F	665F
Cost of seeds	15F	15F	15F	80F	70F	—	—
TOTAL	519F	533F	589F	703F	707F	420F	665F
Income							
yields/hectare	800k	559k	700k	1000k	600k	250k	250k
gross return	525F	535F	600F	705F	710F	420F	665F
less total expenses	519F	533F	589F	703F	707F	420F	665F
NET INCOME	6F	3F	11F	2F	3F	0F	0F

SOURCE: Chef du Service de l'agriculture, Rapport annuel du Service de l'agriculture, année 1945, Soudan, 11 May 1946, Bamako, ANS-AOF 2 G 45-33. Assumption, 1 day = 7F.

rise, Lieutenant Governor Louveau worried that "the production of cotton in the Soudan continues to be unprofitable. The harvest will be consumed locally because world price bars the export route."[84] Louveau added that if "the metropole wants to buy significant stocks of Soudanese cotton, it must resolve to pay prices superior to those on the world market. Without doing that, despite all the efforts of the Office du Niger and the agricultural technical services, production of cotton will continue to stagnate for years." Although it is beyond the scope of this chapter, economic development resources under FIDES and FERDES were mobilized by the Compagnie française du développement textile beginning in 1950 to target the southeastern tier for cotton production using price subventions, intensive agricultural outreach, introduction of new seed varieties, and provision of hefty support for investment in fertilizer and agricultural machinery. CFDT also pursued the policy of "saturating" the handicraft textile industry to minimize the disparities between the domestic and export prices. Eventually, this combination was to break the "barrier of world prices" and make the Sikasso-Koutiala-San triangle the leading cotton-exporting region in the Soudan.[85]

In the years through 1946, the period under examination here, the attractiveness of domestic cotton prices meant that "the native does not bring his cotton harvest to the market voluntarily. He prefers, instead, to conserve it and sell it locally at prevailing market rates."[86] Despite higher world prices percolating into the export sector, as late as 1948, Lieutenant Governor Louveau reported that almost the entire cotton harvest was being consumed locally.[87] The introduction of free labor and free markets in 1946 combined with continuing high prices for imported cloth further solidified the power of the domestic market to draw virtually the entire Soudanese cotton harvest. Nearly 140 years of the politique cotonnière in Senegal and the Soudan had proven only the remarkable vitality of the domestic market for cotton and for handcrafted cotton textiles.

CHAPTER TWELVE

Conclusion

In 1949, Governor Ernest Louveau of the Soudan surveyed the economic condition of his colony in a section of his annual report titled "a chapter of difficulties." Despite his expectations that the rise in postwar commodity prices would translate into active commercial transactions, Louveau could not point to any appreciable change in exports. Cotton export prices, in particular, rose threefold between 1946 and 1947 and by another 65 percent between 1947 and 1948. By 1949 the price of cotton on the export markets was 17.40 francs, a monumental leap of nearly 600 percent from the 1946 price of 2.90 francs. Nonetheless, almost all of the 1,800 tons of cotton produced in the 1948–49 campaign was consumed locally. Louveau lamented that "cotton just does not seem sufficiently profitable." Louveau went through the by then common rhetorical practice of comparing cotton with other crops, in this case millet. A hectare of cotton yielded, Louveau estimated, no more than 80 to 100 kilograms, whereas a hectare of millet yielded 600 kilograms. In pursuing his calculations, Louveau assumed that freight charges were the same for millet and cotton. Cotton fetched 16.939 francs per kilo and millet 10 francs.

cotton	80 × 16.939 francs	=	1,355.12 francs
millet	600 × 10 francs	=	6,000 francs

According to Louveau's calculations, a Soudanese farmer would therefore lose 4,645 francs in cultivating cotton for export instead of millet. Unfortunately for the colonial economy, as Louveau noted, Soudanese farmers sold neither millet nor cotton to the export sector.[1]

In contrast, Louveau described the vibrant interior commerce of the Soudan. "Many [economic] zones are superimposed on the geographical regions of the Soudan: the districts of the north bring to those of the south their livestock and their salt; there, they find cereal, karité, etc. . . . In contrast, the transverse zones are smaller. Kayes barely attracts commerce from Kita, which focuses more on Bamako. Bamako, as the capital, barely attracts commerce upstream from San and Mopti, which in their turn, supply those chronically cereal deficient districts further downstream."[2] This was a sobering note, describing how little economically the French had accomplished in their nearly 70 years of colonization in the French Soudan.

No part of France's economic agenda for the Soudan was more ambitious and less successful than her cotton development program. Louveau clung tenaciously to the dominant ideological assumption that the Soudanese were rational economic actors and that adequate price incentives would yield cotton for export. Despite the increase in cotton prices in the export sector, "the parity between what exporters are prepared to pay and what natives receive when they sell to their countrymen to be made into cotton bands is still far from being realized." According to figures Louveau provided, export prices would have to double if not triple again to be competitive with the domestic market for cotton. "Boubous, pagnes, and scarves of bold colors are not found except in the cities, where money flows more readily. In contrast, the cotton band reigns uncontested in the bush, except perhaps on festival days."[3]

The failure of the French to capture the cotton of the Soudan for export to metropolitan mills has to be measured against the stated goals of French policy. From the moment when France reestablished colonization in Senegal in 1817, the French wanted tropical produce for metropolitan consumption. Their interest in cotton was prominent, although it faded in the face of the difficulties of actually acquiring sufficient cotton to interest metropolitan weavers. As the French metropolitan cotton spinning and weaving industry expanded during the first half of the nineteenth century, its reliance on the world supply of cotton became much more pronounced. French industrialists and government officials worried about the drain of French gold reserves to pay for imported cotton and about the industry's reliance on one major producer, the United States. The American Civil War proved their worries founded; the world supply of cotton declined, although its impact was exacerbated by hording and speculation. More than any other event, the cotton supply crisis during the Civil War forced colonial officials to elaborate programs of colonial cotton development. Policies to promote production and commerce of Senegalese cotton were implemented, but the results were far from encouraging. Within a decade after the cessation of hostilities in the American South, a seemingly inexhaustible supply of cotton was flowing onto the world market. Cotton prices plummeted. Declining world prices and ample supplies made colonial cotton schemes less imperative.

Increasing industrialization of the world cotton textile industry in the last quarter of the nineteenth century contributed to renewed worries about world cotton supplies and to debates about tariffs and economic protectionism. These worries coincided with the realization that European nations had laid claim to most of tropical Africa and that these colonies were awaiting their missions. Cotton and colonialism were therefore inextricably linked in Africa.[4]

La politique cotonnière—France's colonial cotton policy—in the French Soudan began with Lieutenant Governor Trentinian's efforts to promote cotton for export in 1896. Trentinian, together with the semiofficial Association cotonnière coloniale, which commenced its operations in the Soudan in 1904–5, defined the tool kit for cotton development. The concept of a colonial cotton development tool kit, as I argued in the introduction and in Chapter 4, reflected the assumption that the problems of promoting cotton for export were amenable to technical solutions. Officials could thus draw out of the tool kit ideologies and conceptual blueprints as well as practical policies and technologies to fix the imperfections in colonial cotton development: quality control, marketing, and labor (or production). Although the solutions to cotton development were most often presented as "technical" ones, they had their own politics. Proponents of different models of colonial cotton development promoted different mixes of these "tools."

I described colonial cotton development as la politique cotonnière, which was the widely used contemporary term. The term was not merely a slogan; it carried with it two linked meanings. On the one hand, the term politique meant policy. As policy, colonial cotton development was based on certain assumptions about the outcomes or goals of colonialism. All partisans of colonial cotton development expected that the Soudan would become the premier source of cotton for metropolitan mills. There was, however, little agreement on how the Soudan should become la France cotonnière. Thus the policy component of la politique cotonnière confronted the politics of colonial cotton development. This was the second meaning of the term. Politics, as the practice of political power, makes sense only if we understand it to operate within an environment of contending social, economic, and cultural forces. Various groups of French administrators, entrepreneurs, agronomists, and merchants and African peasants, workers, consumers, and chiefs all aligned themselves differently. Their alliances were prompted not merely by the actors' interests in cotton. The stakes were much bigger, particularly as cotton came to represent colonialism in the French Soudan. The struggle over colonial cotton policy was simultaneously a struggle to control the colonial state and its fiscal and ideological resources. In analyzing the failure of French colonial economic policy, I have drawn upon three sets of interpretations: those dealing with the colonial state; those examining the connections between culture and colonialism; and those relating to the encounter between local processes and the world system.

In applying several of Lonsdale and Berman's conceptualizations of the colonial state to this study, I have suggested that their approach, although presented as a general paradigm for the study of the colonial state in Africa, may not be fully applicable to the West African context. In particular, the absence of a strong and politically focused settler component in West Africa and the more developed precolonial webs of production and exchange thwarted the development of the "strong" East African interventionist state in the West African context. In contrast, the colonial state in the French Soudan revealed itself woefully unable to become a "factor in the cohesion of a heterogeneous social formation."[5] Rather than promote either consolidation of state power or economic development, the struggles over colonial economic policy fragmented colonial power. The terms *strong* and *weak* for colonial states must be understood to be descriptive and relative. They must be measured against the stated goals of colonial policy. It was in the articulation of goals that the Soudanese colonial state appeared irrational by establishing unrealistic outcomes and by failing to implement policies congruent with those outcomes.

The fracturing of power in the colonial state was caused by the struggles between two camps in the colonial administration for control over colonial cotton development. A group of senior administrators favored a pro-peasant orientation, which saw price incentives, long-term hybridization schemes, and distribution of new varieties of seed as the key to making cotton the king of the Soudan. Opposed to them was a group consisting of entrepreneurs, public works officials, and some agronomists who saw massive investment in irrigation as the pivotal solution to the problem of cotton supply to the metropole. To most of them, irrigation was linked to European-managed cotton plantations because they considered Africans unable or unwilling to produce sufficient cotton on their own terms. Colonial officials, entrepreneurs, public works officials, agronomists, and European merchants all participated in these struggles over cotton development policy, and each had a role to play. Indeed, each set of actors fiercely guarded its sphere of activities and distrusted any encroachment upon what its members considered their privileged space for economic action. The colonial state was to enact broad policy regarding the colonial economy; agronomists, public works officials, and the Association cotonnière coloniale were to provide technical services to promote broad policy; expatriate French merchants and their African agents regarded the commercial sphere of market incentives and transactions as their domain. Africans were to be the producers of cotton either as peasant growers, tenant farmers, or laborers. Tensions arose when the actors did not play—or were presumed not to play—their assigned roles.

In drawing on the connections between culture and colonialism, I have argued that cotton colonialism was not only about economic development policies. It was about efforts to impose order on African societies and to render intelligible Africans' economic and social behavior. The debates among the contending groups of colonial officials, entrepreneurs, and Africans were not merely about the most efficacious means of encouraging cotton production and controlling the cotton harvest of the Soudan. These debates must be seen as part of a colonial development discourse. As such, cotton colonialism also produced cultural representations of Africans, of their societies and economies, of their capacities to conform to prevailing European cognitive categories of laborers and peasants, and of the roles and functions of colonialism.

A study of the cultural side of French cotton colonialism reveals at least two different models of Africans. These models helped to narrow the field of intervention because they imposed recognizable interpretations on unfamiliar—or nonconforming—economic behavior. There was, first, a group of senior colonial officials who promoted the idea that the Soudanese peasant was a rational economic actor who would respond positively to market incentives. Therefore, they pursued a model of colonialism which sought market incentives to improve the quality and quantity of cotton brought to the export markets. In applying this model of colonialism, these officials sought to impose economic and social behavior based on the universalizing market concepts of self-interest, maximization, and profits. Because of the privileged place of commerce within the colonial political economy, these officials were obliged to rely on the private sector to provide many of the market incentives they assumed motivated the Soudanese cotton producers. This obligation to respect the privileges of "free enterprise" even against irrefutable evidence that it did not deliver the goods led to efforts to "manage" the economy in spite of the efforts of the private sector. Such policies resulted, for example, in the bizarre compulsion of free trade in the official cotton market.

The other prevailing model of Africans was elaborated by those who saw cotton development in terms of massive investment in irrigation, which would yield vast plantations managed by Europeans. According to this model, Africans were inherently unsuited to producing high-quality cotton on their own terms. They needed to be disciplined into productive workers for their own good and for the good of the metropole. In promoting cotton development through irrigation, the proponents of this model drew on analogies to the Nile River in lower Egypt and to the history of European and Egyptian efforts to promote cotton development there. The examples of CICONNIC and the Office du Niger testify to the power of this language of discourse to create illusion rather than cotton and prosperity. Both models rested on the assumption that Europeans could control the economic decisions of West Africans. Thus the debates about cotton development were simultaneously debates about colonialism, about the Europeans' mission in Africa, and about Africans. Precisely because cotton was so deeply conjoined with colonialism, these struggles over cotton development provide a privileged discourse about colonialism and about various roles assigned to the metropolitan and colonial states, to local administrators, to agricultural and technical experts, to expatriate and local merchants, and to Africans.

The failure of both models of colonial cotton development rested upon the actions of the Soudanese themselves. And this brings us to the third interpretive field through which this study passes. This book is about the encounter between the world economy and dynamic local processes. It is about the resiliency of the regional economy of the Soudan to withstand colonial efforts to bend its deeper structures of production and exchange to satisfy metropolitan needs. The explanation for the failure of colonial cotton development presented here rests on the sustained capacity of the domestic and regional markets for cotton and handcrafted cotton cloth to satisfy the demands of West African consumers. It also rests on the fact that cotton producers were enmeshed in complex social and cultural processes of change. French colonial assumptions of African peasants' economic rationality confronted Africans engaged in local processes of change and conflict. These processes can be interpreted only through local histories sensitive to the encounter between world transformative events and the "interior architecture" of local groups.

The French gravitated to cotton in the French Soudan because they saw cotton being widely produced throughout the savanna and because they believed that they could fairly easily tap into the existing supply of cotton for export to the metropole. Precisely because the handicraft textile industry fed a dynamic domestic and intracontinental market in West Africa, which persisted despite huge imports of European manufactured cloth, Soudanese cotton producers were able to withstand pressure from the colonial state to sell their cotton harvest to the export markets. The failure of the colonial state to capture the supply of cotton in the Soudan also rests with the failure of the world economy and the imperial economy to subsume the domestic handicraft textile industry in its orbit. Soudanese (and West African) consumers' demand for textiles was highly elastic. Textiles were a relatively inexpensive "luxury." Consumers were willing to buy vast amounts of cloth when they had the means, and they were prepared to do with much less when they did not. French efforts to promote cotton production for export and to encourage the imports of manufactured cloth were two sides of the same encounter.[6] This encounter provided cotton producers, spinners, and weavers in the Soudan with opportunities and challenges to reconsider their economic strategies. The cultivators of cotton and the workers of the handicraft textile industry applied a complex production calculus to their decisions about how and where to unload their social product. In the end, the workers in the handicraft textile industry persisted because West African consumers continued to demand handcrafted cloth and because they were prepared to pay significantly more than the export market could bear.

The price differences between the domestic and export markets for cotton in the Soudan were the principal obstacle to the goals of cotton colonialism. These price differences were the result of the peculiar outcome of the encounter between the world economy and local processes in the Soudan. Because French metropolitan spinners and weavers were part of a highly competitive world market for cotton and for textiles, they were not prepared to pay more for colonial cotton than prevailing world prices for the medium-staple industry standard. Despite neomercantilist protectionism prevailing at various times during this period, the metropolitan industry consistently refused to pay a premium for secure colonial cotton. This unwillingness profoundly hobbled colonial efforts to promote cotton for export. Thus colonial assumptions about African economic behavior—especially those held by senior colonial administrators regarding peasants' inherent economic rationality—combined with the persistence of a dynamic regional market for handcrafted cloth led to policies that ultimately fostered the development of a colonial economy over which officials had little control. More research needs to be conducted into the social and economic history of what I have called "reversible social processes" to gain a better understanding of the meanings of this encounter.

Students of the development of development will also find here a cautionary tale. Recent studies of economic development have revealed most to have an arrogant disregard for local realities of social and economic life. Most development programs founder on fundamentally faulty assumptions about the world economy and regional economic processes and because they often fail to involve targeted populations in planning and implementing programs.[7] This history of French colonial cotton development should make development experts aware of the long tradition of arrogance and failure to which they belong.

Governor Louveau's sober assessment of colonial cotton policy in the Soudan as late as 1949 clearly shows that French policy did not yield a steady supply of cotton to metropolitan mills. But this assessment does not capture the complexities of the problem of colonial cotton development in the Soudan. Louveau's concluding comment on cotton in his 1949 chapter on "difficulties" distilled the larger problem simply: "The cultivation of cotton in the Soudan seems compromised precisely because it is not profitable. The harvest is consumed locally because the world price bars the route to exports."[8]

Three issues emerge from Louveau's assessment. These were virtually the same issues that dogged colonial cotton development from its outset. First, producing cotton for export was not profitable enough compared to alternative crops. Cotton was a demanding crop; it required significant rainfall and high average temperatures. It also required intense labor at irregular intervals. And because cotton yields were low, only high commodity prices could compensate for the labor expended. Second, the prices French metropolitan mill owners were prepared to pay were determined by the world market supply. Because the French textile industry was part of a highly competitive world market, industrialists in France were not going to pay more for colonial cotton than they paid for cotton available on the world cotton market. Thus fluctuations in world cotton supply and price sent confusing signals to African cotton producers and to colonial officials charged with encouraging cotton exports. The propeasant policies held the price to be the key incentive to promoting cotton production, and widely changing prices were seen as disincentives to cotton growers. Much of the discussions about cotton marketing and how to fix its imperfections revolved around the role of expatriate commercial houses. Colonial administrators and cotton "experts" assigned to the private sector the tasks of commercialization of cotton, which included providing adequate incentives through the marketplace. Because merchants also operated in a highly competitive world market for cotton, they too were constrained by the prevailing world price of cotton. Administrators were quick to condemn merchants for their failure to uphold their side of the politique cotonnière, and in the process, administrators often revealed their deep-seated disdain for merchants, even though they relied on them to promote cotton through price incentives.

Third, Louveau argued, as did his many predecessors, that the domestic economy serving local and regional demand was a major cause of the failure of France to capture the cotton supply of the Soudan. French failure to capture the cotton of the Soudan for export has allowed me to examine the nature of the encounter between the world capitalist system emanating from France and dynamic local processes. I have argued that an examination of the power of capitalist industry's demand for raw materials to organize a world cotton supply cannot adequately explain the complex interactions between the world economy and local systems of production and exchange. This book has examined the persistence of the handicraft textile industry in the French Soudan and has advanced a set of assumptions concerning its history, which I elaborate as a multilayered "production calculus." Central to the outer layer was the availability of imported cloth and the elasticity of African demand. Prices for imported cloth were determined not just by supply and demand but by political and world economic factors. Similarly, African consumers' ability to buy imported cloth depended on their incomes, and their incomes in turn depended on the prevailing prices for their agricultural goods.

The inner set of the production calculus was made by cotton producers and handicraft weavers, and they made their decisions based on world, regional, and local economic conditions. The story presented here demonstrates that Africans did indeed make their own history, even under conditions of European colonialism.

Reference Matter

Notes

Complete authors' names and publication data for sources cited in short form are given in the Bibliography under "Published Sources, Theses, and Manuscripts," pp. 352–68.

Chapter 1

1. The history of the technological changes in the spinning and weaving industries is well known. For a sampling, see Cameron, *Concise Economic History*; Landes, *Unbound Prometheus*; Chapman, *Cotton Industry*; Dodge, *Cotton*. For a detailed discussion of Kay's flying shuttle, see Wadsworth and Mann, *Cotton Trade*, chap. 22.

2. Wright, *Political Economy*, p. 13; Bruchey, ed., *Cotton*, Table 2A.

3. Sugar was perhaps the first commodity of the newly emerging world economy of the seventeenth century because it linked Europe to the New World and Africa to both. Sugar, however, gave way to cotton as the premier commodity of the world economy in 1831. That year, cotton supplanted sugar as Britain's leading import.

4. For background, see Pollard, *Peaceful Conquest*, chaps. 3–4; Brauland, *British Technology*.

5. Wadsworth and Mann, *Cotton Trade*; Schmidt, "Les Débuts de l'industrie cotonnière en France, 1ère Partie" and Schmidt, "Les Débuts de l'industrie cotonnière en France, 2ième Partie."

6. See esp. Cohen, *French Encounter with Africans*, which builds on Curtin, *Image of Africa*. On the managerial tendencies in the French state, see esp. Kuisel, *Capitalism*, and Chapman, *State Capitalism*. On French ideas of modernism, specifically as they relate to urban design and colonialism, see Rabinow, *French Modern*, and Wright, *Politics of Design*.

7. Marseille, *Empire colonial*, pp. 31–32, 187–97, 371–73; Marseille, "Industrie cotonnière."

8. For a Portuguese counterpart to Marseille's project, which is much more sensitive to the interplay of metropolitan and colonial forces, see Pitcher, *Politics in the Portuguese Empire*.

9. Said, *Culture and Imperialism*, refers to his method as "contrapuntal analysis," pp. 18, 66–67, 279.

10. Wallerstein, *Modern World System*, pp. 347–48.

11. Stern, "Feudalism," p. 862. See also Wallerstein, "Comment," and Stern, "Reply," pp. 873–97.

12. Tomich, *Slavery*, p. 4; Cooper, "Africa and the World Economy," pp. 96–97.

13. See esp. Isaacman, *Cotton*.

14. See esp. Kanya-Forstner, *Conquest*.

15. Weber, *Peasants into Frenchmen*; Cooper, *On the African Waterfront*.

16. Mitchell, *Colonising Egypt*, pp. 161, 33. See also Mitchell, "The World as Exhibition." For a more detailed study of French urban planning in Morocco and Madagascar, see Wright, *Politics of Design*.

17. Said, *Culture*, pp. 11, 99.

18. Dirks, "Introduction," pp. 7–8, 14. See also Prakash, "Writing Post-Orientalist Histories." For a useful critique, see O'Hanlan and Washbrook, "After Orientalism."

19. Fog usually lifts to reveal a wider landscape. In a similar manner, I can only hope that the turn to interpretation will also seek a wider landscape for its inquiries.

20. Ludden, "India's Development Regime," pp. 251, 257. For a fuller assessment of Western attitudes about non-Western development in the age of imperialism, see Adas, *Machines*, esp. chap. 4. For an important discussion of the role of knowledge and policy making in colonial Kenya, see Berman, *Control*, pp. 88–97.

21. For a preliminary account of the uses of "human" sciences in French colonial conquest, see Nordman and Raison, eds., *Sciences*.

22. Labouret, *Recommendations*; *Ethnologie coloniale*; *Main d'oeuvre*; *Tribus du Rameau Lobi*; *Manding*; "Géographie alimentaire." These studies led to *Paysans d'Afrique occidentale*.

23. On the transformation of African workers, see Cooper, *On the African Waterfront*, and *Decolonization*.

24. Berman, "Structure," pp. 142–43.

25. Berman and Lonsdale, "Coping with the Contradictions," pp. 490–91; reprinted as chapter 4 in Berman and Lonsdale, *Unhappy Valley*.

26. Berman, *Control*, pp. 424–25.

27. I have described this process as "linked sets of transformations set in motion by colonialism." For preliminary statements, see Roberts, "End of Slavery," and most recently in "Divorce."

28. For Young, civil society and international relations appear to be the main challenges to the autonomy of the colonial state (*African Colonial State*, pp. 95–133).

29. Ibid., pp. 124–33, 182–213; Scott, *Weapons*, and Scott, *Domination*.

30. Hopkins, *Economic History*, p. 237.

31. For example, see Austen, *African Economic History;* Munro, *Africa;* Wickins, *Africa.*

32. For example, the monthly and quarterly economic reports from colonial districts in the French Soudan, beginning with the earliest French foothold in 1882–83, were obliged to report on the volume of goods moving through their districts and on the prices of goods brought to market. The use of these data, however, is not unproblematic.

33. Rimmer, *Economies,* p. 18.

34. MacGaffey, "Issues and Methods," pp. 7, 10. See also her earlier study, *Entrepreneurs and Parasites,* where many of these ideas were originally broached.

35. For further discussion, see Roberts, "Linkages"; Roberts, *Warriors.*

36. Cohen, "Doing Social History," p. 195; Berry, *No Condition Is Permanent,* p. 8.

37. For example, Rodney, *How Europe Underdeveloped Africa;* Palmer and Parsons, eds., *Roots of Rural Poverty;* Sheriff, *Slaves.*

38. Tilly, "Retrieving European Lives," p. 11.

39. Even if historians are now much more conscious about how the past is invented, they are less certain about how the meanings of the past are generated. For suggestive leads, see Hobsbawm and Ranger, eds., *Invention of Tradition;* Chanock, *Law, Custom and Social Order;* Scott, *Weapons;* and Berry, *No Condition Is Permanent.*

40. Scott, *Weapons,* p. 178.

41. Of course, there were enough variations among what my informants recounted to identify points of conflict and to develop a historical account of changes within the handicraft textile industry.

42. Escott, *Slavery Remembered,* pp. 7–8. See also Blassingame, *Slave Testimony.*

43. Irwin, *Liptako Speaks,* p. 20; Cohen, "Reconstructing a Conflict in Bunafu." See also Cohen, "Doing Social History," and Cohen and Odhiambo, *Siaya.*

44. For the oral history I collected on Faama Mademba Sy in 1992 I tried a different approach. I opened each interview with a simple request, "Please tell me about Faama Mademba," and let the informant range in whatever direction she or he chose. Only after the informant had finished would I ask for more detail or pursue specific lines of questioning I knew from previous oral and archival research would probably be important to my project.

45. Gov. Schmaltz, letter to Cunca, Roi de Galam et Sombra Congol Batcheri et autres principaux du Royaume de Galam, Saint Louis, 10 Feb. 1817, ANF-DOM Sénégal et Dépendences XIII 34a.

46. Gov-gen. Clozel, circulaire to lt govs., Dakar, 12 Dec. 1912, AMN 1 R 118.

47. Le Gouverneur-général de l'Afrique occidentale française aux Messieurs les Lieutenant-gouverneurs des Colonies du groupe, Circulaire relative à l'application de l'arrêté du 6 Mars 1924, organisant la production des

textiles en Afrique occidentale française, 15 Mar. 1924, *Journal officiel de l'Afrique occidentale française*, 15 Mar. 1924, p. 173.

48. For an important challenge to ethnic categorizations, see Amselle, *Logiques métisses*, pp. 71–88, 209–28. For challenges to our thinking about peasants, resistance, and culture, see Feierman, *Peasant Intellectuals*.

49. Young, *Politics in the Congo*. Administrator De Loppinot was the one exception in this study; see Chapter 7.

50. Londres, *A Very Naked People*, pp. 173–74.

51. A more detailed study of the economic and social history of the production, circulation, and use of textiles in the Soudan is needed to develop more fully the complexities of the domestic handicraft textile industry.

52. They did, of course, have significant experience in metropolitan public works. See, for example, French efforts to control the Rhône and Saône rivers under the Second Empire, in Leonard, *Lyon Transformed*, and Third Republic debates about massive public works, in Saly, *Politique des grands travaux*. The one major exception, which stood outside of the public sphere, was French participation in the Suez Canal, see Marlowe, *Making of the Suez Canal*, and Duff, *100 Years of the Suez Canal*.

53. Bélime appears as an actor in several accounts of the Office du Niger, but he has not been subject to a more thorough study. In many ways, Bélime was the quintessential petty colonial official who became *le roi de la brousse*. I discuss Bélime in Chapters 6, 8, and 10.

Chapter 2

1. Brown and Ware, *Cotton*, pp. 529–30. A host of man-made or synthetic fibers, especially rayon and nylon, entered the textile market in the interwar period. They competed with cotton but more so with wool and silk.

2. Braudel, *Structures*, 1: 325–27.

3. Braudel, *The Mediterranean*, 1: 84, 155, 2: 725, 762. See also International Institute of Agriculture (Rome), *Cotton Growing Countries*.

4. Spinning under mechanized conditions favored cotton fiber of regular length and tensile strength. For a general overview, see Brown and Ware, *Cotton*, pp. 464–504. See also Henri Bondoit, "Le problème du coton colonial au point de vue du textile français," Rapport présenté au nom de l'Association des Anciens Elèves de Filature et de Tissage de Mulhouse, Congrès d'Agriculture coloniale, May 1918, ANF-DOM Comité Française pour l'Outre-mer 344.

5. Brown and Ware, *Cotton*, pp. 1–2, 20–36; Todd, *Cotton World*, pp. 5–7; Owen, *Cotton*, pp. 28–36.

6. See Porter, "Note." On the colonial science and international exchange, see Headrick, *Tentacles of Progress*, pp. 209–50, and for the French case during the Second Empire, see Osborne, *Nature*.

7. Brown and Ware, *Cotton*, pp. 264–312; Todd, *Cotton World*, pp. 7–9; Cox, *Cotton*, pp. 103–28; International Institute of Agriculture (Rome), *Cotton Growing Countries*, pp. xiv–xvii.

8. See esp. Chaudhuri, *Trading World*, chap. 12; Chaudhuri, *Asia Before Europe*, pp. 306–22.

9. Chapman and Chassagne, *European Textile Printers*.

10. Smelser, *Social Change*.

11. At the same time, linen imported from Ireland rose from 1,538,000 pounds in 1731 to over 2,490,000 pounds in 1751. Cotton had not yet achieved its dominance over linen or woolen textile production. See Ellison, *Handbook*, pp. 127–28.

12. Ellison, *Cotton Trade*, pp. 15–16, 81; Wadsworth and Mann, *Cotton Trade*, pp. 183–87.

13. Wadsworth and Mann, *Cotton Trade*, pp. 185–87. Despite the low priority West Indian planters gave cotton, they guarded their prerogatives to exclusive production jealously. Wadsworth and Mann cite the planters' successful efforts in 1751 to squash the Africa Company's plans to cultivate cotton near its Gold Coast Castle (p. 187).

14. Ellison, *Cotton Trade*, pp. 81–82.

15. This was actually the second capitalist reorganization. The first capitalist transition occurred in response to the destruction of the guild control over weaving and the institution of the putting-out system. The transition from artisanal hand-loom production to industrial production was the second capitalist transformation in the textile industry, and it resulted in a significant increase in spinning and weaving productivity and gave rise to the first identifiable industrial proletariat. In the process, the hand-loom weaving industry was destroyed. Friedrich Engels privileged the cotton textile industry in his *Condition of the Working Class*. See also Bythell, *Handloom Weavers*.

16. Ellison, *Handbook*, pp. 128–30; Ellison, *Cotton Trade*, pp. 81–86; Bruchey, *Cotton*, Table 2-A.

17. Ellison, *Handbook*, pp. 128–30; Ellison, *Cotton Trade*, pp. 83–85; Brown and Bates, *Cotton*, pp. 369–71; Wright, *Political Economy*, pp. 13–14; Bruchey, *Cotton*, pp. 43–47.

18. Wadsworth and Mann, *Cotton Trade*, pp. 192–99, 503–4, 517; Carponnier, *Crise*, p. 31. On technology flows in the cotton textile industry see Brauland, *British Technology*.

19. Schmidt, "Débuts de l'industrie cotonnière en France, 1ère Partie," pp. 261–95; Schmidt, "Débuts de l'industrie cotonnière en France, 2ième partie," pp. 26–55; Wadsworth and Mann, *Cotton Trade*, pp. 204–8.

20. See, for example, Kindleberger, *Economic Growth*; Clapham, *Economic Development*; Cameron, *France*; Gerschenkron, *Backwardness in Historical Perspective*; Landes, *Prometheus Unbound*; Kemp, *Economic Forces*; Wadsworth and Mann, *Cotton Trade*, pp. 204–8.

21. Fohlen, "Industrial Revolution," pp. 217–20; Caron, *Histoire économique*, pp. 128–29; Caron, "Croissance industrielle," p. 290.

22. Fohlen, *Industrie textile*, pp. 205–314; Carponnier, *Crise*, pp. 37–40; Farnie, *English Cotton Industry*, pp. 141–45.

23. El Bekri, *Description de l'Afrique septentrinonale*, pp. 325–26, 329, 339, quoted in Mauny, *Tableau géographique*, p. 699; Monteil, *Coton*, pp. 3, 10, 12. Boser-Sarivaxévanis, *Tissus*, p. 141, dates the cloth industry in the Upper Senegal the same way.

24. For an overview of weaving more generally, see Barber, *Prehistorical Textiles*. For a discussion of plant genetics, see Hutchinson, Silow, and Stephens, *Evolution of Gossypium*, and Hutchinson, "New Evidence," pp. 225–41.

25. McIntosh and McIntosh, *Prehistoric Investigations*, pp. 159–60, 415; McIntosh and McIntosh, "Inland Niger Delta," p. 17.

26. See Schaedler, *Weaving*, pp. 10–31, 447–51; Thornton, "Precolonial African Industry."

27. Mauny, *Tableau géographique*, p. 231; Mauny, "Notes historiques," pp. 698–99. Mauny cited al Hamdani, Macoudi, al Moullahabi, el Bekri, and Idrisi, among other travelers' accounts.

28. Tellier, *Autour Kita*, p. 238.

29. Braudel, *Structures*, 1: 333.

30. See, for example, Hay, "Constructing a Modern Identity." See also Gilfoy, *Patterns of Life*; Eicher, *African Dress*; and *African Dress II*. For some intriguing leads on clothing, adornment, and aesthetics see Roach and Eicher, "Language of Personal Adornment"; Brincard, ed., *Beauty by Design*; Martin, "Contesting Clothes."

31. See Weiner and Schneider, eds., *Cloth*. For an introduction to the relationship between political economy and social identity in the Western Sudan, see Roberts, *Warriors*, pp. 7–16, 201–7.

32. Ibn Battuta, *Voyage*, pp. 36, 30; see Mauny, *Tableau géographique*, for an assessment of luxury cloth in the trans-Saharan trade (pp. 344, 369–70).

33. Mollien, *Travels*, p. 256.

34. Mage, *Voyage*, p. 150.

35. Ibn Battuta, *Voyage*, p. 47.

36. See Mauny, "Notes historiques"; Dalziel, *Useful Plants*.

37. Mage, *Voyage*, p. 89.

38. Note sur le coton, Segu, 28 Apr. 1897, ANM 1 R 116.

39. Raffenel, *Nouveau Voyage*, 1: 407. For the 1897 description see Note sur le coton, Segu, 28 Apr. 1897, ANM R 116.

40. Raffenel, *Nouveau Voyage*, 1: 385. Among the Fulbe, weaving was a major activity of a caste called *mabo* (Monographie du cercle de Jenne, 20 Nov. 1909, ANM 1 D 38#3). On castes, see Tamari, "Development of Caste Systems" and Conrad and Hoffman, eds., *Nyamakalaw*.

41. Captain Kibes, letter [to lt gov.], Bamako, 19 Apr. 1897, ANM 1 R 81.

42. Roberts, "Linkages"; Roberts, "Long Distance Trade." See also Roberts, *Warriors*, pp. 3–20.

43. Baillaud, *Sur les routes du Soudan*, p. 67.

44. Women's preference for the *tambe sembe* during the agricultural season raises important issues about the structure and organization of the

household and about the relationships between men and women more generally. For a preliminary statement, see Roberts, "Women's Work."

45. Dubois, *Tombouctou*, pp. 80–81.

46. On *bokolanfini* see Imperato and Shamin, "Bokolanfini" and Bayol, *Voyage*, p. 132. On the red pagnes of Kong, see Binger, letter, Kong, 10 Mar. 1888, ANS-AOF 1 G 199.

47. Indigo production was linked to this expanded sphere of cloth production, but it was socially much more complex. See Roberts, "Women's Work," and Roberts, "Reversible Social Processes."

48. See esp. Shea, "Development of an Export Oriented Dyed Cloth Industry"; Shea, "Approaching the Study of Production in Rural Kano"; Kriger, "Textile Production." This shift from female to male tasks may reflect the social changes associated with the expansion of the scale of production.

49. Roberts, *Warriors*.

Chapter 3

1. Faillot, *Histoire*, pp. 31–34; Barry, *Sénégambie*, pp. 187–90; Klein, *Islam*; Miers, *Britain*; Saint-Martin, *Sénégal*.

2. Hardy, *Mise en valeur*, pp. 9–11; Faillot, *Histoire*, p. 35; Webb, "Trade," pp. 155–63; McLane, "Commercial Rivalries," pp. 44–57.

3. Gov. Schmaltz, letter to Cunca, Roi de Galam et Sombra Congol Batcheri et autres principaux du Royaume de Galam, Saint Louis, 10 Feb. 1817, ANF-DOM Sénégal et Dépendances XIII 34a.

4. Gov. Schmaltz, letter to Baron Portal, Minister of Colonies, [Saint Louis], 1 May 1817, ANF-DOM Sénégal et Dépendances XIII 34a.

5. For more detail on guinée and the commerce in guinée, see Roberts, "Guinée Cloth."

6. [Cotton courtier], letter to Baron Portal, Rouen, 28 Aug. 1817, ANF-DOM Sénégal et Dépendances XIII 34a. See the very similar statement by Thomas Valentin, Capitaine de navire commandant le Brig-goelette La Petite Famille du Havre, Declaration, Le Havre, 6 Aug. 1818, ibid.

7. Hardy, *Mise en valeur*, pp. 36–39; Schmaltz, Développement sur le projet de colonisation dans les Etablissements français d'Afrique, Paris, 19 Mar. 1818, ANF-DOM Sénégal et Dépendances XIII 18.

8. Commissaire de la Marine, letter to Ministre Secrétaire d'Etat de la Marine et des Colonies, Nantes, 24 Aug. 1819, ANF-DOM Sénégal et Dépendances XIII 34a; Commissaire de la Marine, letter to Ministre Secrétaire d'Etat de la Marine et des Colonies, Nantes, 19 Dec. 1820, ANF-DOM Sénégal et Dépendances XIII 34b. See also Hardy, *Mise en valeur*, p. 65.

9. Faure, *Histoire*, p. 53; Hardy, *Mise en valeur*, pp. 67–105. See also Robinson, *Chiefs*, and Barry, *Le Royaume de Waalo*.

10. For more detail on the science and politics of the acclimation movement in mid-nineteenth-century France, see Osborne, *Nature*.

11. See, for example, Chef de Bataillon du Génie, Rapport sur deux modèles de machines à égrener le coton, Saint Louis, 8 Aug. 1822, ANF-DOM

Sénégal et Dépendances XIII 35a; letter to Ministre Secrétaire d'Etat de la Maison du Roi, Paris, 11 June 1822, ANF-DOM Sénégal et Dépendances XIII 35; Ministre de la Marine et des Colonies, letter to M. de Villaret Joyeuse, Capitaine de Vaisseu, Paris, Apr. 1823, ANF-DOM Sénégal et Dépendances XIII 35a; Vice Consul de France, letter to Ministre de Marine et des colonies, Savannah, 10 Sept. 1823, ANF-DOM Sénégal et Dépendances XIII 35; Le Commissaire général de la Marine, letter, Bordeaux, 31 July 1824, ANF-DOM Sénégal et Dépendances XIII 39a; Le Commissaire général, ordonnateur de la Marine, letter to Ministre de la Marine et des Colonies, Rochfort, 12 Jan. 1826, ANF-DOM Sénégal et Dépendances XIII 35b. See also Hardy, *Mise en valeur*, pp. 117, 128–43, 158–64.

12. L'état Major Hesse, Rapport sur les cultures du Sénégal, Paris, 15 Jan. 1824, ANF-DOM Sénégal et Dépendances XIII 19c.

13. No author, Du commerce et de la culture du coton au Sénégal et dans ses Dépendances, n.p., n.d. [probably 1863], ANF-DOM Sénégal et Dépendances XIII 37a.

14. For example, Klein, "Slavery"; Searing, *West African Slavery*; and Renault, *Liberation d'esclaves*.

15. No author, Du commerce et de la culture du coton au Sénégal et dans ses Dépendances, n.p., n.d. [probably 1863], ANF-DOM Sénégal et Dépendances XIII 34a; Hardy, *Mise en valeur*, pp. 143–51, 194–202, 232–40; Barry, *Sénégambie*, pp. 196–99.

16. Berton, letter to Gov. Senegal, Richard-Toll, 13 Jan. 1829, ANF-DOM Sénégal et Dépendances XIII 22.

17. Fohlen, *Industrie textile*.

18. Hose, "Britain and the Development of West African Cotton"; Ratcliffe, "Cotton Imperialism."

19. No author, Du commerce et de la culture du coton au Sénégal et dans ses Dépendances, n.p., n.d. [probably 1863], ANF-DOM Sénégal et Dépendances XIII 37a; Pasquier, "En marge de la guerre de secession." A parallel effort to encourage cotton took place in Algeria; see Reybaud, "Culture du coton," pp. 692–717.

20. Reybaud, *Coton*, pp. 5, 24–25.

21. The best source for the French cotton crisis of 1861–65 is Fohlen, *Industrie textile*, pp. 128, 255–57, 284–314.

22. Gov. Faidherbe, letter to Ministre de la Marine et des Colonies, Saint Louis, 14 June 1860, ANF-DOM Sénégal et Dépendances XIII 36a. For more detail on French policies during this period, see Saint-Martin, *Sénégal*, pp. 446–596.

23. Certificate de reception, envoi du Consul de France de Nouvelle Orleans, Port du Havre, Jan. 1861, ANF-DOM Sénégal et Dépendances XIII 36a; Le Gérant du Consulat, letter to Ministre de la Marine et des Colonies, Edinburgh, 18 Oct. 1861, ANF-DOM Sénégal et Dépendances XIII 36b. The figure of threefold increase appears in Gustave Begouen, Charles Gallois, S. Meunier, courtiers à le Havre, Renseignements ont été fournis à la Cham-

bre de Commerce, Le Havre, 15 Jan. 1861, ANF-DOM Sénégal et Dépendances XIII 36a. See also Pasquier, "En marge de la guerre de secession," pp. 1–22.

24. Gov. Pinet-Laparde, letter to Minister de la Marine et des Colonies, Gorée, 21 Oct. 1860, ANF-DOM Sénégal et Dépendances XIII 36a.

25. Commandant Pinet-Laparde, Note sur le Dionden et le Pays des Sérés Nones annexes à nos possessions de la Presqu'île du Cap Vert, Gorée, 8 May 1861, ANF-DOM Sénégal et Dépendances XIII 36a. I develop this argument in Chapters 4, 8, 9, and 11.

26. Directeur des Colonies, 2ième Bureau, Rapport au Ministre de la Marine et des Colonies, Paris, [?] Aug. 1861, ANF-DOM Sénégal et Dépendances XIII 36b.

27. Barrows, "General Faidherbe"; Barrows, "The Merchants and General Faidherbe"; McLane, "Commercial Rivalries," pp. 44–57.

28. M. Prefect de la Seine-Inférieure, Note, n.p., 25 Nov. 1861, ANF-DOM Sénégal et Dépendances XIII 36b. A longer version appears in a letter to Ministre de l'Agriculture, Commerce, et Travaux publics, Paris, 2 Dec. 1861, ANF-DOM Sénégal et Dépendances XIII 38 and Drouet, Des moyens de doter les possession françaises en Afrique.

29. Le Moniteur de la Flotte, 15 Sept. 1863. Clippings found in ANF-DOM Sénégal et Dépendances XIII 37a. Louis Drouet fils, letter to Fritz Koechlin, Gorée, 29 Mar. 1863; Fritz Koechlin, letter to Louis Drouet, Mulhouse, 23 Apr. 1863, ANF-DOM Sénégal et Dépendances XIII 37a.

30. Pinet-Laparde, Exposé général sur la situation de la colonie, des causes qui ont influé sur cette situation et des améliorations qu'elle reclame, Saint Louis, 1 Sept. 1865, ANF-DOM Senegal I 51c; H. V. Dupuis, Rapport fait le 21 Jan. 1866 par le Président de la Compagnie Agricole de la Presqu'île du Cap Vert à l'Assemblée générale des actionnaires, Gorée, 21 Jan. 1866, ANF-DOM Sénégal et Dépendances XV 14; Dossier Herzog, ANF-DOM Sénégal et Dépendances XV 14.

31. Monsignor Kobès, letter to Minister of Colonies, Paris, 27 Oct. 1862, ANF-DOM Sénégal et Dépendances XV 13.

32. Fritz Koechlin, letter to Minister of Marine and Colonies, Mulhouse, 30 Nov. 1867, ANF-DOM Sénégal et Dépendances XV 14; Dossier Herzog, ANF-DOM Sénégal et Dépendances XV 14.

33. Notes de M. Brunil, n.p., Aug. 1864, ANS R 1.

34. Msg Kobès, Aperçu des faits observés relatifs à la culture du coton dans la colonie agricole de Saint Joseph pendant les années 1863–64, Saint Joseph, 4 Apr. 1864, ANS R 1.

35. H. V. Dupois, Rapport faît le 21 Jan. 1866 par le Président de la Compagnie Agricole de la Presqu'île du Cap Vert à l'Assemblée générale des actionnaires, Gorée, 21 Jan. 1866, ANF-DOM Sénégal et Dépendances XV 14.

36. Ibid.; Fritz Koechlin, letter to Minister of Marine and Colonies, Mulhouse, 30 Nov. 1867, ANF-DOM Sénégal et Dépendances XV 14.

37. Notes de M. Brunil, n.p., Aug. 1864, ANS R 1.

38. Gov. Pinet-Laparde, Exposé général de la situation de la colonie, des causes qui ont influé sur cette situation et des améliorations qu'elle reclame, Saint Louis, 25 Sept. 1866, ANF-DOM Sénégal I 51a.

39. Gov. Jauréguibéry, letter to Minister of Marine and Colonies, Saint Louis, 22 Aug. 1862, ANF-DOM Sénégal I 48b.

40. Minister of Colonies, Instructions générales to Gov. Jauréguibéry, Paris, 17 Dec. 1861, ANF-DOM Sénégal I 48a; No author, Du commerce et de la culture du coton au Sénégal et dans ses Dépendances, n.p., n.d. [probably 1863], ANF-DOM Sénégal et Dépendances XIII 37a; Gov. Jauréguibéry, letter to Minister of Marine and Colonies, Saint Louis, 22 Aug. 1862, ANF-DOM Sénégal I 48b.

41. Agence et Consulat Général de France en Egypte, letter to Minister of Marine and Colonies, Alexandria, 18 Nov. 1862, ANF-DOM Sénégal et Dépendances XIII 37a; Vice Consul, letter to Minister of Marine and Colonies, Liverpool, 14 May 1863, ANF-DOM Sénégal et Dépendances XIII 37a; Pasquier, "En marge de la guerre de secession," pp. 1–22.

42. Brooks, "Peanuts." See also Hogendorn, Nigerian Groundnut Exports; and Hogendorn, "Cotton Campaign."

Chapter 4

1. Rapport commercial, agricole et industriel sur le Soudan français, 1898, ANF-DOM Soudan XIII 13; P. Georges Mias, letter to Colonel [Commandant Supérieur], Kayes, 6 Apr. 1893, ANF-DOM Soudan XIII 1 a.

2. Lt gov. Trentinian, letter to commandants des cercles de Kayes, Kati, Bamako, Segu, Sumpi, Goundam, Jenne, San, Bandiagara, and the Faama de Sansanding, Kayes, 21 Dec. 1898, ANM B 77; Lecomte, Coton, pp. 424–25.

3. Ratcliffe, "Cotton Imperialism"; Farnie, English Cotton Industry.

4. Lt gov. Trentinian, letter to Commandant Cercle of Bamako, Kouluba, 11 Aug. 1899, ANM B 77.

5. In 1903 the ACC estimated that the freight rates, which did not favor cotton, would be 112 francs per ton from the field to France (22 francs per ton for movement along river to Koulikoro; 45 francs per ton rail freight from Koulikoro to Kayes; 45 francs per ton freight from Kayes to France). This rate was still higher than transport costs from the American South: cotton shipped from Galveston to France was 105 francs per ton; from New Orleans, 88.3 francs per ton; and from Savannah, 72.25 francs per ton (Nautilus, "Le Soudan et la question cotonnière," Bull ACC, annex 1, 1903, p. 44; Rapport de M. Maigret, Secrétaire-général de ACC, in Bull ACC, 3, 1904, p. 56).

6. Captain Charnet, Rapport commercial et agricole, Bamako, 2d Quarter 1899, ANM 1 R 31.

7. Indeed, the first tentative request to establish a textile factory in Bamako, made by Louis Colombier and Company in 1941, was rejected by the administration, ANM 1 Q 1909. See Chapter 11 for more detail.

8. Rapport commercial et agricole, n.p., 1891, AM 1 R 31. In June of that

year 54,000 meters of cloth were imported. By 1916, imports of cloth were worth 49 percent of the value of total imports reported for Bamako, which was both the capital city and the effective terminus of the railway (Rapport commercial, Bamako, 4th Quarter 1916, AMN 1 Q 44).

9. "La culture du coton," *Dépêche Coloniale*, 7 Jan. 1903. See also Andrews, Grupp, and Kanya-Forstner, "Mouvement colonial français."

10. Lenfant, letter to Charles Marande, Paris, 5 Feb. 1903, quoted in J. Brenier, "La culture du coton dans les colonies françaises," *Bull ACC*, 2, 1903, annex.

11. Note sur l'Association cotonnière, n.d., [file 1901–6] ANM 1 R 118; "Introduction," *Bull ACC*, 1, 1903, pp. 27–28.

12. William Ponty, Note sur la Colonie du Haut-Sénégal-Niger, Paris, 25 June 1905, ANF-DOM Soudan I ii bis.

13. Vuillet, Régions cotonnières du Soudan, 18 Aug. 1904, AMN 1 R 79.

14. Captain Charnet, Rapport commercial et agricole, Bamako, 2d Quarter 1899, ANM 1 R 31.

15. Rapport sur le coton americain, Bamako, 1899, ANM 1 R 301.

16. Lt gov., letter to commandant de Région Niger (Bamako), 18 Nov. 1899, ANM B 74.

17. Captain Charnet, Rapport commercial et agricole, Bamako, 2d Quarter 1899, ANM 1 R 31.

18. Captain Charnet, letter to lt gov., Haut-Sénégal-Niger, Bamako, 18 Aug. 1899, ANM 1 R 81.

19. Captain Didio, letter to lt gov., Haut-Sénégal-Niger, Bamako, 20 Jan. 1899, ANM 1 R 31.

20. Lt gov., letter to Commandant Bamako, Kayes, 19 Sept. 1899, ANM B 74.

21. Bulletin politique, Bamako, Mar. 1899, ANM 1 E 18.

22. Commandant adjoint, Notice accompagnie 400kg coton destiné à un essai d'égrenage, Segu, 20 Dec. 1903, ANM 1 R 95.

23. Roume, "Discourse de M. Roume," 12 Oct. 1903, *Bull ACC*, 2, 1903.

24. For background, see Mbodj, "Un example d'économie coloniale"; Pelissier, *Paysans du Sénégal*; Brooks, "Peanuts."

25. Gov. William Ponty, letter to ACC, Kayes, 22 Jan. 1906, *Bull ACC*, 8, Mar. 1906.

26. ACC representative, letter to lt gov., Haut-Sénégal-Niger, Bamako, 17 May 1905, ANM 1 R 81.

27. Esnault-Pelterie, Président de l'ACC, letter to Gov-gen. Roume, Paris, 2 Apr. 1904, ANM 1 R 79.

28. Maigret, secrétaire-général, "Rapport de l'ACC," *Bull ACC*, 3, 1903, p. 51. "Much of the cotton of the Soudan has been able to replace advantageously the cotton from the U.S., especially the Mississippi product" (Rapport sur la campagne 1906, ACC, ANM 1 R 118).

29. "Revue des colonies," *Bull ACC*, 7 June 1905, p. 8.

30. Ibid., pp. 5–6.

31. Esnault-Pelterie, "L'oeuvre de l'ACC française," presented at the Congrès International de l'Association des filateurs and manufacteurs de coton, Bremen, 25–27 June 1906, cited in *Bull ACC*, 1907, p. 181. This notion of a grand collaboration between the colonial administration and private enterprise overcoming previous distrust was reiterated by Paul Doumergue, Minister of Colonies, in a speech cited in Bourdette, *Etude sur la culture du coton*, p. 117.

32. Vuillet, Rapport, Koulikoro, 13 Oct. 1904, ANM 1 R 81; Rapport sur l'emploie des subventions accordées par le Département à l'ACC, n.d., [1909 file], ANM 1 R 118; Allocution de M. Esnault-Pelterie, 21 Mar. 1906, *Bull ACC*, Mar. 1906, p. 15.

33. Rapport sur l'emploie des subventions accordées par le Département à l'ACC, n.d., [1909 file], ANM 1 R 118; Jacquey, agent de l'ACC, Notice sur le cercle de Segu, 1904, ANS-AOF 1 G 320.

34. Esnault-Pelterie, President de l'ACC, letter to Gov-gen. Roume, Paris, 2 Apr. 1904, ANM 1 R 79.

35. "Revue des colonies," *Bull ACC*, June 1905, pp. 5–6; "Allocution de M. Esnault-Pelterie," 21 Mar. 1906, *Bull ACC*, Mar. 1906, p. 13.

36. "We estimate that colonial production can be profitable in sending to Havre 5,000 kg lots of the same cotton already ginned" (C-A. Marande, "Rapport commercial sur les qualités et les défauts des cotons coloniaux et sur les moyens paraissant indiqués pour éviter les défauts," *Bull ACC*, 8 Feb. 1906). On the homogeneity of cotton fibers see Henri Bondoit, "Le problème du coton colonial au point de vue textile français," Rapport presenté au nom de l'Association des anciens élèves de filature et de tissage de Mulhouse, Congrès d'Agriculture coloniale, May 1918, ANF-DOM CFOM 344. Efforts to achieve greater homogeneity in cotton were also central to the renewed politique cotonnière following World War I.

37. Gov-gen., letter to lt gov., Dakar, 28 Dec. 1909, ANM 1 R 118; Rapport sur l'emploie des subventions accordées par le Département à l'ACC, n.d., [1909 file], ANM 1 R 118; Rapport agricole, Haut-Sénégal-Niger, 2d Quarter 1911, ANS-AOF 2G 11-30.

38. Esnault-Pelterie, Président ACC, letter to Gov-gen. Roume, Paris, 2 Apr. 1904, ANM 1 R 79; Guérin, *Colonies cotonnières*.

39. Jacquey, agent de l'ACC, Notice sur le cercle de Segu, 1904, ANS-AOF 1 G 320; Level, "Note au sujet des essais de coton entrepris par l'ACC," 30 June 1912, *Bull ACC*, 1912, p. 368.

40. Rapport commercial, 3d Quarter 1911, Segu, ANM 1 Q 83; Rapport sur l'emploie des subventions accordées à l'ACC, [n.d., probably 1912], ANM 1 R 118; Level, agent de l'ACC, Avant projet des travaux à 1912, n.d., ANM 1 R 118; Rocaché, administrator Segu, letter to lt. gov., Haut-Sénégal-Niger, Segu, 30 May 1913, ANM 1 R 118.

41. Esnault-Pelterie, letter to gov. [H-S-N], Paris, 23 Nov. 1907, ANM 1 R 118.

42. President, ACC letter to William Ponty, gov-gen. AOF, Paris, 17 Feb.

1910, ANM 1 R 118; Rapport agricole, Haut-Sénégal-Niger, 2d Quarter 1911, ANS-AOF 2 G 11-30; Spitz, *Sansanding*, p. 44.

43. Rapport politique, San, Jan. 1910, ANM 1 E 67.

44. Rapport sur la situation économique pendant l'année 1913, Haut-Sénégal-Niger, ANS-AOF 2 G 13-11.

45. Carrié and Dabrigeon, letter to gov-gen., Bamako, 4 Dec. 1912, ANM 1 R 118. For a critique of the relationship between the ACC and CCC see also Yves Henry, "Comment la France peut se procurer le coton dont elle a besoin," Rapport presenté au Congrès d'Agriculture colonial, May 1918, ANF-DOM CFOM 41.

46. Gov-gen. Ponty, letter to Ministre des Colonies, Dakar, 27 Feb. 1913, ANM 1 R 118; Gov-gen. Ponty, letter to Ministre des Colonies, Dakar, 14 May 1914, ANS 1 R 18.

47. Gov-gen. Ponty, telegram to [gov.] French Soudan, 15 Dec. 1912, ANM 1 R 118.

48. Colliaux, Rapport sur le coton, Koutiala, 25 Mar. 1910, ANS 1 R 35.

49. Gov-gen. Clozel, circulaire to lt gov in AOF, Dakar, 12 Dec. 1912, ANM 1 R 118.

50. Rapport politique, circonspection de San, Jan. 1910, ANM 1 E 67.

51. Rapport sur l'Association cotonnière coloniale 1912–13, file 1913, ANM 1 R 118.

52. Barth, *Ethnic Groups*; Roberts, *Warriors*, pp. 16–17; Amselle, *Logiques métisses*.

53. Rapport général sur la politique du cercle pendant l'année 1905, ANM 1 E 77. See also Roberts, *Warriors*, pp. 203–7, and Roberts, "Emergence of a Grain Market."

54. Interviews with Cebarama Dembele, Banankoro, 22 Jan. 1984; Bamoussa Keita, Sinsani, 21 Jan. 1984; Rapport commercial, 1st Quarter 1903, Bouguni; Rapport commercial, 3d Quarter 1906, Bouguni, ANM 1 Q 47; Roberts, "End of Slavery."

55. Vuillet, Rapport agricole, Haut-Sénégal-Niger, 1st Quarter 1908, ANS-AOF 2 G 8-2; Rapport annuel sur la politique, Segu, 1909, ANM 1 E 72.

56. Marcel Quesnel, "Rapport," *Bull ACC*, 4, 1904, pp. 10–11.

57. "Discourse d'Esnault-Pelterie," Nov. 1907, *Bull ACC*, 1906–7.

58. ACC representative, letter to lt. gov. du H-S-N, Bamako, 17 May 1905, ANM 1 R 81; Rapport sur l'égrenage du coton recolté, Segu, 1906, ANM 1 R 116.

59. Interview with Tijani Sylla, Baraweli, 20 Jan. 1984. See also the interview with Ko Togola, M'Peba, 23 Jan. 1984.

60. Colliaux, Rapport sur le coton, Koutiala, 25 Mar. 1910, ANM 1 R 113.

61. Rapport commercial, Segu, 1st Quarter 1908, ANM 1 Q 83.

62. Interview with Bamoussa Keita, Sinsani, 21 Jan. 1984. See also interview with Hadja Toumata Contao, Segu, 23 Jan. 1984.

63. I have developed this theme more fully in Roberts, "End of Slavery."

64. Rapport commercial, Bamako, 19 Mar. 1917, ANM 1 Q 44.

65. Rapport commercial, Segu, 1st Quarter 1907, ANM 1 Q 83.

66. Rapport politique, circonscription du San, Jan. 1910, ANM 1 E 67.

67. Rapport commercial, Segu, 4th Quarter 1908, ANM 1 Q 83.

68. Colliaux, "Rapport sur la culture du coton dans le cercle de Koutiala, 1910," Bull ACC, 1910–11, p. 746.

69. See Goody, ed., Development Cycle, and Lewis, "Descendants and Crops."

70. Rapport sur l'ACC campagne 1912–13, file 1913, ANM 1 R 118.

71. Roberts, "End of Slavery," pp. 300–302.

72. Rapport sur l'ACC, campagne 1912–13, Koutiala, 12 May 1913, ANM 1 Q 113.

73. Gov. Soudan, telegram to Union coloniale française, Kouluba, 20 Jan. 1915, ANF-DOM CFOM 514.

74. Rapport d'ensemble sur la situation économique de la colonie du Haut-Sénégal-Niger, 1915, ANM 1 Q 40.

75. Rapport commercial, Bamako, 4th Quarter 1916, ANM 1 Q 44. Prices for 1918 are in Rapport commercial, Bamako, 3d Quarter 1918, ANM 1 Q 44. See also Note sur la situation économique de l'AOF en 1915 comparée à celle de l'année précédente, ANS-AOF 2 G 15-19.

76. Rapports commerciaux, Bamako, 2d, 3d, and 4th Quarters 1916, ANM 1 Q 44; Chef de Service d'agriculture, letter, Kouluba, 16 Apr. 1918, ANM 1 R 118.

77. Chef de Service d'agriculture, letter, Kouluba, 16 Apr. 1918, ANM 1 R 118.

78. Gov-gen., letter to lt gov., Haut-Sénégal-Niger, Dakar, 6 Sept. 1918, ANM 1 R 118.

79. Marseille, Empire colonial.

80. President, Ligue coloniale française, letter to Gov.-gen. Van Vollenhoven, Le Havre, 4 July 1917, ANS 1 R 65.

81. Comments sur l'avant-projet d'un rapport sur "Les questions coloniales d'après-guerre en Afrique occidentale française," 1916, drafted by Pierre Pégard, President, Union coloniale française, Section de l'Afrique occidentale, ANF-DOM CFOM 31. See also Marseille, Empire Colonial.

82. Sarraut, Mise en valeur, p. 48.

83. Gov-gen., letter to Minister of Colonies, Paris, 24 May 1917, ANF-DOM Défense Nationale, Utilisation des produits coloniaux 10; Procès-verbal, Comité commercial de l'AOF, séance du 12 Juin 1917, ANF-DOM Défense Nationale, Utilisation des produits coloniaux 10.

84. Maginot, Minister of Colonies, letter to Gov.-gen. AOF, Paris, 23 July 1917, ANF-DOM Défense Nationale, Service d'Utilisation des produits coloniaux, 10. The minister's concern for African merchants was piqued by a letter strongly critical of Van Vollenhoven's "commercial consortium" written by the Blaise Diagne, the African deputy in the National Assembly representing Senegal.

85. Gov. du Haut-Sénégal-Niger, letter to Gov-gen., Bamako, 12 Aug. 1918, ANF-DOM Union coloniale française 467.

Chapter 5

1. Marseille, *Empire colonial*; see also Michel, *Appel à l'Afrique*.

2. This argument pushes backward Low and Lonsdale's assumptions that the 1940s constituted the "second colonial occupation." There were likely three phases of colonial occupation in Africa: the conquest phase lasting up to World War I, the second interwar phase of intensification of colonial development issues, and the third phase following World War II, when significant new political and economic forces were at work. See Low and Lonsdale, "Introduction," p. 12.

3. Renouvin, *Forms of War Government*, pp. 5–51; Delemer, *Bilan de l'étatisme*, pp. 21–35; Kemp, *French Economy*, pp. 30–45. For a general introduction to the impact of the war on French colonial policies, see Heisser, "Impact of the Great War."

4. Renouvin, *Forms of War Government*, pp. 54–55.

5. Kuisel, *Capitalism*, p. 86, see chap. 3.

6. Convention du Consortium cotonnier français avec le Ministère du Commerce, n.d., ANF-DOM Aff écon 888. See also Delemer, *Bilan de l'étatisme*, pp. 42–43; Renouvin, *Forms of War Government*, pp. 62–63; Aftalion, *Industrie textile*, p. 103; Aftalion, "Effect of the War," pp. 115–19.

7. Aftalion, *Industrie textile*, pp. 30–31; Mazel, "Effect of the War," pp. 20–27.

8. As in the case of the ACC, enterprises with direct or indirect state participation were barred from earning profits on their own.

9. Delemer, *Bilan de l'étatisme*, pp. 42–43.

10. In 1925, many of the functions of the Consortium of Cotton were taken over by Office National français du coton, projet de création d'un Office national du coton, Paris, n.d. [1925], ANF-DOM Aff écon 889-5.

11. Fontaine, *French Industry*, p. 203; Aftalion, "Effect of the War," pp. 63–66; Caron and Bouvier, "Guerre, crise, guerre," p. 636. For background to the place of the textile industry within the debates about a national economy see Ready, *Rise of Market Culture*.

12. General A. Messimy, Rapport fait, au nom de la Commission des colonies, après l'examen, auquel a procédé la Commission des conditions dans lesquelles la France peut se ravitailler en coton dans ses colonies, n.d. [1924], ANS 1 R 102. A version of this report was published as Messimy, "Ravitaillement," pp. 161–98.

13. Ogburn and Jaffe, *Economic Development*, p. 342; General Messimy, Rapport, [1924], ANS 1 R 102.

14. Delemer, *Bilan de l'étatisme*, pp. 53–54; Kemp, *French Economy*, pp. 66–68; Ogburn and Jaffe, *Economic Development*, pp. 37, 358–59.

15. For the textile industry as a whole, including wool, linen, silk, jute,

and hemp, the imports for 1923 were 7.186 billion francs (Messimy, "Ravitaillement," pp. 162–64).

16. The prewar base includes postwar acquisition of Alsace-Lorraine industrial capacity. Fontaine, *French Industry*, pp. 440–41; Ogburn and Jaffe, *Economic Development*, pp. 52–53, 343.

17. Ministers Daladier (Colonies), Clementel (Finance), and Raynaldy (Commerce and Industry) used the term "to liberate" in discussing colonial cotton policy (Projet de loi, portant de création des taxes spéciales destinées à subventionner l'ACC, n.d. [1926], ANF-DOM Aff écon 889-5). See also Robert, *Culture du coton*, p. iii.

Chapter 6

1. Henry was the leading cotton "expert" in French West Africa. Henry, *Culture pratique du cotonnier; Détermination de la valuer commercial des fibres de coton; Eléments d'agriculture coloniale; Irrigations et cultures irriguées; Coton aus Etats-Unis; Coton dans l'Afrique occidentale française.*

2. Yves Henry, "Comment la France peut se procurer le coton dont elle a besoin," draft of a paper presented to the Congrès d'agriculture coloniale, May 1918, ANF-DOM CFOM 41.

3. Henry, *Irrigations et cultures irriguées*, pp. 257–59, quote on p. 150.

4. Ibid., p. 2. In 1913 Henry had voiced his support for irrigation, although he did not elaborate an argument (*Culture pratique du cotonnier*, p. 120).

5. Henry, *Irrigations et cultures irriguées*, pp. 4–5, 148.

6. Gov.-gen. Angoulvant, letter to Hirsch, Dakar, 4 Mar. 1918, ANS-AOF 1 R 73. The best study of CICONNIC, indeed the only study, is Saint-André, "Compagnie de culture cotonnière," pp. 299–316. Saint-André's thesis is based on a very close reading of the Malian archives, but not those of the AOF or the Ministry of Colonies. He also ends his study in 1927, just when CICONNIC's troubles became evident. In many ways, the subsequent period raised even more significant policy considerations for the future of irrigated cotton. A cursory discussion of CICONNIC appears in Schreyger, *Office du Niger*, pp. 32–35. See also Suret-Canale, *French Colonialism*, p. 181.

7. Bélime, *Irrigations du Niger*; Bélime, *Production du coton*.

8. Bélime, *Production du coton*, pp. 112–15, 141.

9. Bélime, *Irrigations du Niger*, p. 41; Bélime, *Production du coton*, pp. 161–62. Henry borrowed the graphic representation of this convergence in Henry, Vuillet, and Lavergne, *Irrigations au Niger*, p. 41.

10. Bélime, *Production du coton*, p. 178.

11. Bélime, *Irrigations du Niger*, pp. 101–44.

12. Bélime, *Production du coton*, pp. 116–17.

13. Sarraut, *Mise en valeur*, p. 54.

14. Ibid., pp. 168, 88–89. For more discussion on the Sarraut ministry, see Heisser, "Impact of the Great War," chaps. 5–6.

15. Sarraut, *Mise en valeur*, pp. 171, 182.

16. Gov-gen. Angoulvant, letter to Minister of Colonies, Dakar, 13 June 1918, ANS-AOF 1 R 18.

17. Angoulvant, Gouverneur-général honoraire des colonies, "Nos colonies de l'Afrique occidentale française peuvent ravitailler largement en coton notre industrie textile, mais il faut une politique d'action," n.d. [1924], ANF-DOM CFOM 344. Angoulvant's arguments also appeared in *La journée industrielle*, 2 Feb. 1924.

18. Gov-gen. Angoulvant, letter to President ACC, Dakar, 4 Sept. 1918, ANF-DOM Aff écon 889-1.

19. M. Nougès, "Compte rendu des travaux de l'année 1922," *Bull ACC*, May 1923, pp. 34–35. On the redefinition of tasks, Culture du coton, Programme pour les campagnes 1918–19 et suivant, ANS-AOF 1 R 48. On the declining budgetary allocations, see M. Landry, Rapporteur du Budget des colonies, Projet du Budget, 1919, ANF-DOM Aff écon 889-1.

20. Gustave Roy, "Rapport," May 1920, *Bull ACC*, 1920.

21. Gov-gen. Merlin, Rapport au Comité interministériel des consortiums sur l'attribution à l'Afrique occidentale française d'une somme de 26 million francs, n.d. [ca. Nov. 1920], ANF-DOM Aff écon 888.

22. Inspecteur général Y. Henry, Essais cotonniers en 1905, n.p., 26 May 1905, ANM R 79; J. Vuillet, letter, Koulikoro, 18 Dec. 1904, ANM R 79.

23. Barois argued that plans to manage rivers were necessarily different from plans to build railways. For a railway, a study once undertaken can be considered definitive. To understand the life of a river, however, studies have to be undertaken over many years (Procès-verbal, Comité d'action agricole, Union coloniale française, n.p. [Paris], 4 July 1919, ANF-DOM CFOM 529).

24. In 1913, Governor-general Ponty commissioned Inspector Younès to evaluate the Senegal and Niger River valleys for irrigation (Gov.-gen. Ponty, letter to lt gov. Haut-Sénégal-Niger, Dakar, 11 Oct. 1913, ANM R 79). The results of the Younès mission, which was concluded in 1919, were seriously flawed and of little value. See Inspecteur-général Demaret, Rapport concernant la vérification de M. Younès, chef de la mission d'études d'irrigation dans les vallées du Sénégal et du Niger, 9 Apr. 1919, ANM 2 D 14, cited in Saint-André, "Compagnie de culture cotonnière," pp. 285–86. See also J. Barois, Inspecteur-général des Ponts et Chaussées, en retraite, L'irrigation de la vallée du Niger, n.d., n.p. [1922–23], ANF-DOM CFOM 519; Directeur des Services économiques, Notice sur la Compagnie de cultures cotonnières du Niger, Dakar, 3 Aug. 1937, ANS-AOF 1 R 73; Bélime, *Production du coton*, pp. 58–62; Henry, Vuillet, and Lavergne, *Irrigations au Niger*, pp. 27–30.

25. Rapport de M. Aron, l'Ingénieur des Ponts et Chaussées, Sur l'Irrigation dans le bassin du Niger, Dakar, 15 Dec. 1910, ANS-AOF P 401.

26. Hardel, Etude sur l'irrigation dans la vallée du Niger, n.d. [1911], ANS-AOF P 402.

27. Bélime, *Production du coton*, pp. 62–63; Saint-André, "Compagnie de

culture cotonnière," pp. 261–62; Lemmet and Vitalis, "Note sur la mise en valeur des terres de la vallée du Moyen Niger," p. 122. Younès filed several reports from 1914 to 1918, see his reports, ANS-AOF P 405 and P 406.

28. Etesse, Rapport au sujet de la convention Hirsch, irrigation de la vallée du Sénégal, Saint Louis, 13 Dec. 1918, ANF-DOM CFOM 467. See also anon., Compagnie de culture cotonnière du Niger: historique et résultats obtenus, n.p., 20 July 1932, ANF-DOM Aff écon 72-2.

29. Saint-André, "Compagnie de culture cotonnière," pp. 316–22.

30. Ibid., p. 347.

31. Arrêté promulguant en Afrique occidentale française le décret du 27 Novembre 1919, approuvant une convention conclue en vue de l'exécution de travaux d'irrigation et du développement de la culture du cotonnier en Afrique occidentale française, Journal officiel de l'Afrique occidentale française, 3 Jan. 1920, pp. 6–11, particularly title II and articles 3, 7, and 8.

32. "Rapport," Bull ACC, May 1920, p. 25; Inspecteur de 3ième classe de colonies, Bargues, Rapport sur les conditions d'exploitation, par la Compagnie de culture cotonnière du Niger, du Domaine de Dire, Dire, 22 Apr. 1935, ANF-DOM Aff écon 107 bis-3.

33. Hirsch, letter to gov-gen. AOF, Paris, 2 Apr. 1921, ANF-DOM Aff écon 73-11.

34. De Loppinot, director of CICONNIC, letter to lt gov. of Soudan, Hirschville, 10 May 1920, ANS-AOF 1 R 18.

35. Arrêté 25 Nov. 1919.

36. De Loppinot, letter to lt gov., Hirschville, 10 May 1920, ANS-AOF 1 R 18.

37. Acting lt gov. Terrasson, letter to de Loppinot, Kouluba, 16 June 1920, ANM 1 R 305. A copy of this letter is in ANS-AOF 1 R 18.

38. De Loppinot, letter to acting lt gov., Hirschville, 28 Mar. 1920, cited in Saint-André, "Compagnie de culture cotonnière," p. 386.

39. Acting lt gov. Terrasson, letter to de Loppinot, Kouluba, 19 Apr. 1920, cited ibid.

40. Gov-gen. Merlin, letter to lt gov. Soudan, 25 Oct. 1920, cited ibid., p. 388.

41. Ibid., pp. 390–95.

42. The establishment of the company had nonetheless stimulated some economic growth in the region. By the beginning of 1923, a village had sprung up just outside Hirschville and Syrian merchants had established themselves there. By the beginning of 1927, the company boasted of 327 permanent and 275 "specialized" workers, presumably paid at a higher rate, in addition to the gang of contractual labor. Given its precarious hold over labor, CICONNIC management pursued three additional strategies of labor recruitment, retention, and control. See Chapter 7 for further discussion. R. Forbes and E. Barthaburu, Rapport sur la situation en Février 1927 des travaux de mise en valeur entreprise par la Compagnie de culture cotonnière

du Niger sur la concession de Dire, les concessions de Saga, Dioro, et Sene-kou, Segu, 19 Feb. 1927, ANS-AOF 1 R 73.

43. Inspecteur-général des colonies, Kair, Rapport sur la Concession cotonnière de Dire, Kouluba, 15 Jan. 1923, ANF-DOM Aff écon 72-4.

44. Saint-André, "Compagnie de culture cotonnière," p. 392.

45. Kair, Rapport, 15 Jan. 1923, ANF-DOM Aff écon 72-4.

46. Forbes and Barthaburu, Rapport, 19 Feb. 1927, ANS-AOF 1 R 73; Schlumberger, La production du coton en AOF, n.p., 1927, ANS-AOF 1 R 102; Saint-André, "Compagnie de culture cotonnière," pp. 485–90.

47. Directeur des Services économiques (AOF), Note au sujet de la Compagnie de culture cotonnière du Niger, Dakar, 18 Aug. 1932, ANS 1 R 73; Bélime, Production du coton, p. 64; Saint-André, "Compagnie de culture cotonnière," pp. 457–63.

48. Inspecteur-général des colonies Coste, Au sujet de la CICONNIC, Dakar, 7 May 1938, ANF-DOM AFF écon 97-6.

49. Société civile d'études et de colonisation, Rapport sur l'étude du cotonnier égyptien et de la colonisation dans la zone lacustre de la Vallée Moyenne du Niger, exécution du contrat d'études du 4 février 1932, ANS 1 R 73; Inspecteur de 3ième classe des colonies, Bargues, Rapport sur les conditions d'exploitation, par la Compagnie de culture cotonnière du Niger, du Domaine de Dire, Dire, 22 Apr. 1935, ANF-DOM Aff écon 107 bis-3. Yield discrepancies cited in Bargues report and in Vuillet report cited in Saint-André, "Compagnie de culture cotonnière," pp. 464–67. On degeneration, see Henry, Culture pratique du cotonnier, pp. 188–89.

50. A. de Monzie, senator and former under secretary of state for merchant marine, G. Angoulvant, former governor-general of French West Africa, L. Archinard, the conqueror of the Soudan and former governor of Madagascar, and General Hélo, former officer in the colonial army, were among the officers of the administrative council.

51. J. Barois, Inspecteur-général des Ponts et Chaussées en retraite, L'irrigation de la vallée du Niger, n.p., n.d. [1922–23], ANF-DOM CFOM 519; E. Bélime, "Où est le problème," n.p., 1921, ANS 1 R 35.

52. Chevalier, "Etudes," pp. 113–17. A version of this article appears in Bélime et al., Discussions et controverses, pp. 3–10. Hardel, "Irrigation en Afrique occidentale française," pp. 494–509. A synopsis of Hardel's study appears in Chevalier, "Etudes," pp. 118–20, but no mention of Hardel appears in the version published in Bélime et al., Discussions et controverses. Bélime was present at the 1918 Congress, where he presented a study of irrigation in France's Indian colonies. Bélime must, therefore, have been aware of Hardel's arguments.

53. Chevalier, "Etudes," p. 117.

54. Bernard, "Mise en valeur," pp. 368, 389. The article appears in a truncated form in Irrigations du Niger, pp. 81–89.

55. Bernard, "Mise en valeur," pp. 371–74.

56. Ibid., pp. 389–90.

57. Colonel F. Bernard, untitled report, n.p., 10 Apr. 1922, ANF-DOM CFOM (Agence des colonies) 13.

58. Henry, Vuillet, and Lavergne, *Irrigations au Niger*, pp. 11, 9, 16–22.

59. Ibid., pp. 21–30, 48.

60. By 1927 Bélime was prepared to abandon the Nyamina canal, which was the least well conceived in his 1921 study. See Bélime, "Grands travaux coloniaux," p. 246.

61. Bélime et al., *Discussions et controverses*, pp. 42–43.

62. Ibid., pp. 45–46.

63. Bélime, *Production du coton*, p. 229.

64. Gov-gen. Carde, "Circulaire relative à l'application de l'arrêté du 6 mars 1924, organisant la production des textiles en Afrique occidentale française," *Journal officiel de l'Afrique occidentale française*, 15 Mar. 1924, pp. 175–76. See Chapter 8 for more detail on Carde's program.

65. Bélime, *Production du coton*, pp. 245, 249.

66. Ibid., pp. 254–56.

67. Ibid., pp. 96, 254, 262.

Chapter 7

1. Schreyger, *Office du Niger*, pp. 35–37.

2. Forbes, *Coton*, pp. 116–17, 128–30; Bélime, *Production du coton*, pp. 66–69.

3. Le Gouverneur-général de l'Afrique occidentale française à Messieurs les Lieutenant-gouverneurs des Colonies du groupe, Circulaire relative à l'application de l'arrêté du 6 mars 1924, organisant la production des textiles en Afrique occidentale française, 15 Mar. 1924, *Journal officiel de l'Afrique occidentale française*, 15 Mar. 1924, p. 170.

4. Ibid., pp. 172–73.

5. Ibid., pp. 174–75.

6. Ibid., pp. 175–76.

7. Ibid., p. 179.

8. By 1927, nine European-managed cotton plantations had been established in the Soudan: Société anonyme des plantations de Diakandape (capitalized largely by the commercial house of Dèves and Chaumat), Kayes district; Etablissements Delage, Kayes district; Leger, Kayes district; Colombani, Kayes district; Delbos (Mission catholique de Kakoulu), Kayes district; Labe, Kayes district; Sociéte du Niger, Bamako district; Société du Coton et des Textiles Africaines, Bamako and Segu districts; CICONNIC, Dire and Segu districts. Gov-gen. Carde, letter to Direction des Affaires économiques, 15 Apr. 1927, ANS 1 R 102; Waddington, Notes de voyage de M. Waddington au cours de sa mission en AOF, Dec. 1923 au fin de Fév. 1924, Paris, n.d., ANF-DOM Aff écon 889-1.

9. J. Rocache, Inspecteur des affaires administratives, Rapport au lieuten-

ant-gouverneur du Soudan, Kouluba, 10 Nov. 1922, ANS 1 R 18. A copy of the report can be found in ANF-DOM Aff écon 888. In 1924, the Société auxiliare africaine became the Société du coton et des textiles africaines, in part because it began to diversify into sisal and other textile products. I refer to the company throughout this chapter by its acronym, SAA.

10. Representative SAA, letter to lt gov. Soudan, [Kenenkou], 2 Feb. 1924; Terrasson, telegram to commandant Segu, Kouluba, 13 Feb. 1924, ANM 2 Q 6.

11. Terrasson, letter to representative of SAA at Kenenkou, Kouluba, 8 Apr. 1924, ANM 2 Q 6.

12. Primel, letter to gov-gen., Kenenkou, 19 May 1924; Battesti, telegram to lt gov. Soudan, Segu, 7 Aug. 1924, ANM 2 Q 6.

13. Primel, letter to lt gov. Soudan, Kenenkou, 4 Nov. 1924; Terrasson, note attached to Primel, letter to lt gov. Soudan, Kenenkou, 11 Feb. 1925; Terrasson, letter to Director, SAA, Kouluba, 3 June 1925, ANM 2 Q 6.

14. Battesti, telegram to lt gov. Soudan, Segu, 2 Jan. 1926; Dr. Galland, Rapport medico-legal, n.p., 6 Jan. 1926; Battesti, letter to lt gov., Segu, 7 Jan. 1926, ANM 2 Q 6.

15. Interview with Cebarama Dembele, Banankoro, 22 Jan. 1984.

16. Primel, letter to administrator Segu, Kenenkou, 27 Jan. 1926; Terrasson, letter to director SAA, Kouluba, 30 Jan. 1926, ANM 2 Q 6.

17. Administrator Koutiala, letter to lt gov. Soudan, Koutiala, 20 Apr. 1926, ANM 2 Q 6.

18. Terrasson, letters to directors of SAA, Kouluba, 18 Nov. 1927 and 16 Apr. 1928; Agent SAA, letter to lt gov. Soudan, Kenenkou, 20 Apr. 1928, ANM 2 Q 6.

19. Terrasson, Rapport à Direction des affaires économiques, Kouluba, 13 Apr. 1928, ANM 1 R 305.

20. Schlumberger, La production du coton en AOF, 1927, ANS 1 R 102; Terrasson, letter to gov-gen., Bamako, 25 Mar. 1927, ANF-DOM Aff écon 73-13.

21. Terrasson, letter to gov-gen., Bamako, 25 Mar. 1927, ANF-DOM Aff écon 73-13; Inspecteur de 3ième classe des colonies, Bargues, Rapport sur les conditions d'exploitation, par la Compagnie de culture cotonnière du Niger, du domaine de Dire, Dire, 22 Apr. 1935, ANF-DOM Aff écon 107 bis 3.

22. Avenant no. 2 du 26 Mars 1926, cited in Bargues, Rapport, 22 Apr. 1935, ANF-DOM Aff écon 107 bis-3; Inspecteur-général de 1ère Classe des colonies Coste, au sujet de la CICONNIC, Dakar, 7 May 1938, ANF-DOM Aff écon 97-6. By the end of 1927, the three delta concessions totally abandoned cotton (Rapport agricole d'ensemble pour l'année 1927, Soudan, ANS-AOF 2 G 27-41).

23. R. Forbes and E. Barthaburu, Rapport sur la situation en Fev 1927 des travaux de mise en valeur entreprise par la Compagnie de culture cotonnière du Niger sur les concessions de Dire, de Sama, Dioro, et Senenkou, Segu, 19 Feb. 1927, ANS 1 R 73.

24. Administrateur des Colonies, Controleur de la Société civile d'études et de colonisation Dongier, Rapport sur l'expérience de colonisation mixte à Dire, campagne 1930–31, n.d., n.p., ANS 1 R 73; Inspecteur de 3ième Classe des colonies Bargues, Rapport sur les conditions d'exploitation, par la Compagnie de culture cotonnière du Niger, du Domaine du Dire, Dire, 22 Apr. 1935, ANF-DOM Aff écon 107 bis-3.

25. Bargues, Rapport sur les conditions d'exploitation, 22 Apr. 1935, ANF-DOM Aff écon 107 bis 3.

26. Henry, Vuillet, and Lavergne, *Irrigations au Niger*, pp. 6–7. On Nienebale, see Becker, "Experiment."

27. Inspecteur de 2ième classe, Chastenet de Gery, Rapport concernant la ferme de Nienebale et les essais de colonisation au Soudan, Kouluba, 15 Mar. 1930, ANF-DOM Aff écon 107 bis-2. By 1938 Nienebale had 1,500 inhabitants in three villages. See Spitz, *Sansanding*, pp. 48–49, 111–13.

28. Gov-gen. Carde, Note, attached to Chastenet de Gery, Rapport, 25 May 1930, ANF-DOM Aff écon 107 bis-2.

29. Ibid.; Duthoit, Chef du Bureau des affaires économiques du Soudan, Kouluba, 8 Apr. 1930, attached to Chastenet de Gery, Rapport, 15 Mar. 1930, ANF-DOM Aff écon 107 bis-2. Chanock, "Paradigms," and Berry, *No Condition Is Permanent*, examine the unintended consequences of policy on local processes surrounding access to land and other resources.

30. Dongier, Rapport sur l'expérience de colonisation mixte à Dire, campagne 1930–31, ANS 1 R 73; Bargues, Rapport sur les conditions d'exploitation, 22 Apr. 1935, ANF-DOM Aff écon 107 bis-3.

31. Gov-gen. De Coppet, letter to Minister of Colonies, Dakar, 22 Apr. 1938, ANS 1 R 73; Direction générale des services économiques (AOF), Note sur la Compagnie de culture cotonnière du Niger et sur la question de Dire, n.p., Aug. 1939, ANS 1 R 73.

Chapter 8

1. Carde, Circulaire, 15 Mar. 1924, pp. 171, 179.

2. Hesling, gouverneur honoraire, directeur de l'ACC, to Ministre des Colonies, Développement des méthodes et des services de technique agricole aux colonies en vue de l'intensification de la production, n.p., 15 Apr. 1928, ANS 1 R 102.

3. Roume, "Discourse de M. Roume," 12 Oct. 1903, *Bull ACC*, 2, 1903; Carde, Circulaire, 15 Mar. 1924. See also Bélime, Rapport annuel sur la culture du cotonnier en AOF, Kouluba, 15 Apr. 1928, ANS-AOF 2 G 27-99.

4. Inspecteur du Service général des textiles, Bélime, La campagne cotonnière 1924–25 en Afrique occidentale, Compte-rendu de tournée, Kouluba, 10 May 1925, ANS 1 R 102. See also Notice mensuelle pour l'Agence économique de l'AOF, Soudan, June 1925, ANS-AOF 2 G 25-4.

5. Dulles, *French Franc*; Neurisse, *Histoire du franc*; Fohlen, *France de l'entre-deux-guerres*; Ogburn and Jaffe, *Economic Development*.

6. For example, Commandant Bamako, Rapport de tournée administrative, [Bamako], n.d. [July 1927], ANM 1 Q 330.

7. Affaires économiques [AOF], Compte rendu de la situation agricole pour 1926, Dakar, ANS 1 R 56.

8. Lt gov. Terrasson, circulaire aux M. les commerçants, Kouluba, n.d. [around 28 Feb. 1927], ANM 1 Q 18.

9. Bélime, Note relative à l'établissement d'une taxe d'exportation sur les cotons ouest-africains, n.p., Mar. 1924, ANS 1 R 102.

10. Inspecteur-général de 1ère classe des colonies Mérat, Affaires économiques, l'Association cotonnière coloniale, Dakar, 22 Feb. 1931, ANF-DOM Aff écon 97-3.

11. Carde, Circulaire, 15 Mar. 1924, p. 171. In 1931, Governor-General Brevié held to these same pro-peasant positions: "The native has the right to all our solicitude, because he is the source, the only one, of the commercial movement which enriches our colony. In addition, he is the buyer of the large majority of all imported goods. . . . As is well known, the native can buy only to the extent which he produces and in proportion to the prices offered to him" (Discours prononcé par M. J. Brevié, gouverneur-général de l'AOF à l'ouverture de la session du Conseil de Gouvernement, Dec. 1931, ANF-DOM CFOM 206).

12. Already in 1902, the agronomist Vuillet had argued that "the lack of homogeneity in cotton is not due to the climate in our colony, but to the mode of cultivation practiced by the natives" (Vuillet, letter to gov-gen., Koulikoro, 10 Mar. 1902, ANM 1 R 81).

13. Carde, Circulaire, 15 Mar. 1924, pp. 171–72. Lieutenant governor Ponty had made this point in 1904 when he wrote that far from adapting to the new environment, "American and Egyptian cottons produce hybrids, which degenerate to the point where the varieties introduced have disappeared" (Ponty, Rapport).

14. Barthaburu, Chef du Service agronomique des régions tropicales, Notice sur la culture du coton Allen, Segu, 22 June 1931, ANS 1 R 100. For more detail on Allen cotton see Chapter 9 below.

15. Carde, Circulaire, 15 Mar. 1924, p. 172.

16. Etesse, Grands produits africains, p. 146; Commissariat de l'Afrique occidental française, Grands produits de l'Afrique occidentale française, p. 2. See also Henry, Coton dans l'Afrique occidentale française, pp. 50, 148–49, 154–55; Bélime, Rapport sur la production cotonnière en Afrique occidentale française, Kouluba, 15 May 1926, ANF-DOM Aff écon 72-4.

17. Procès-verbal, Chambre de Commerce, Kayes, 22 Dec. 1923, ANS 1 R 18; Waddington, Notes de voyage de M. Waddington au cours de sa mission en AOF, Déc. 1923 à fin de Fev. 1924, [Paris], ANF-DOM Aff écon 889-1; Inspecteur-général des 1ère Classe des colonies Mérat, Affaires économiques: l'Association cotonnière coloniale, Dakar, 22 Feb. 1931, ANF-DOM Aff écon 97-3; La Dépêche coloniale, 27–28 Jan. 1924, cited in Bull ACC, 1924.

18. Minister of Colonies, circular 18 Mar. 1923 to gov-gen., cited in Lt gov. Fousset, Rapport sur le coton et l'Association cotonnière coloniale, Kouluba, 5 Jan. 1932, ANM 1 R 305; Minister of Colonies, letter to gov-gen., Paris, 24 Mar. 1924, ANF-DOM Aff écon 889-1, which supported both the monopoly of classification and the notion of a consortium of buyers.

19. Arrêté promulguant en Afrique occidentale française du 11 Jan. 1924, règlement les conditions de circulation, de mise en vente et d'exportation de produits naturels de l'AOF, 11 Jan. 1924 *Journal Officiel de l'AOF*, 9 Feb. 1924, p. 112; Carde, Circulaire, 15 Mar. 1924, p. 171.

20. Administrator Koutiala, letter to lt gov. Soudan, Koutiala, 18 Oct. 1923, ANM 1 R 305. The ACC was not yet prepared to abandon its claim to experimental farms, and it received a five-year grant to a 200-hectare concession in Koutiala (Receiver of Registers, letter to lt gov. Soudan, [Kouluba], 27 Jan. 1931, ANM 1 R 305).

21. The private ginneries were in Kayes district: Diakandape, Delage-Diamou, and Entreprises Africaines; in Bamako: Macina-Niger and Entreprises Africaines; in Koutiala: Entreprises Africaines; and in Goundam: CICONNIC. The M'Pesoba ginnery was sold to the Entreprises Africaines. See Lt gov. Soudan, to gov-gen., Production du coton en 1925–26, Kouluba, 24 Sept. 1926, ANS 1 R 102; Lt gov. Fousset, Rapport sur le coton et l'Association cotonnière coloniale, [Kouluba], 5 Jan. 1932, ANM 1 R 305.

22. Terrasson, note to directeur des Affaires économiques, Kouluba, 13 Nov. 1925, ANM 1 R 305; Terrasson, telegrams 3976 and 3978 to administrator Bouke and agent ACC at Segu, Kouluba, 4 July 1925, ANM 2 Q 4; Terrasson, letter to agent ACC at Segu, Kouluba, 24 Feb. 1925, ANM 1 R 305; Mérat, Affaires économiques: l'Association cotonnière coloniale, Dakar, 22 Feb. 1931, ANF-DOM Aff écon 97-3.

23. Direction des Affaires économiques, Rapport, May 1926, cited in Mérat, Affaires économiques: l'Association cotonnière coloniale, 22 Feb. 1931, ANF-DOM Aff écon 97-3. For a 1926 critique of the ACC, see Terrasson, letter to Directeur des Affaires économiques, Kouluba, 13 Apr. 1926, ANM 1 R 305.

24. Projet de loi, portant la création des taxes spéciales destinées à subventionner l'Association cotonnière coloniale, présenté au nom de M. Gaston Doumergue, Président de la République française, par Edouard Daladier, Ministre des Colonies, par M. Clementel, Ministre des Finances, et par M. Raynaldy, Ministre du Commerce et de l'Industrie, n.d. [1926], ANF-DOM Aff écon 889-5; *La Dépêche coloniale*, 1 Apr. 1927, cited in *Bull ACC*, June 1927; Mérat, Affaires économiques: l'Association cotonnière coloniale, 22 Feb. 1931, ANF-DOM Aff écon 97-3.

25. Rapport présenté au nom du Comité de Direction de l'ACC, Assemblée générale, 15 June 1927, *Bull ACC*, June 1927, pp. 14–15.

26. Mérat, Affaires économiques: l'Association cotonnière coloniale, 22 Feb. 1931, ANF-DOM Aff écon 97-3; Gov-gen. Brévié, Note (attached to

Mérat, Affaires économiques, 22 Feb. 1931), 28 Apr. 1932, ANF-DOM Aff écon 97-3; Fousset, Rapport sur le coton et l'Association cotonnière coloniale [Kouluba], 5 Jan. 1932, ANM 1 R 305; Bélime, Rapport annuel sur la culture du cotonnier en AOF, Kouluba, 15 Apr. 1928, ANS-AOF 2 G 27-99.

27. Bulletin économique pour l'Agence économique de l'AOF, Soudan, 2d Quarter 1929, ANS-AOF 2 G 29-4; Fousset, Rapport sur le coton et l'Association cotonnière coloniale, Kouluba, 5 Jan. 1932, ANM 1 R 305.

28. Angoulvant, Gouverneur-général honoraire des colonies, "Nos colonies de l'Afrique occidentale française peuvent ravitailler largement en coton notre industrie textile, mais il faut une politique d'action," n.d. [1924], ANF-DOM CFOM 344. Angoulvant's arguments also appeared in La Journée industrielle, 2 Feb. 1924.

29. Carde, Circulaire, 15 Mar. 1924, p. 173.

30. Ibid.

31. Procès-verbal, Comité d'action agricole coloniale, Paris, 5 Mar. 1924, ANF-DOM CFOM 309. See also Suret-Canale, French Colonialism, pp. 229–30.

32. Despite his general concordance with big business, as in Hirsch's CICONNIC, Bélime shared with many other colonial administrators a deep disdain for the pettiness of small French merchants, who seemed interested only in maximizing their immediate gain.

33. Bélime, Rapport annuel sur la culture du cotonnier en AOF, Kouluba, 15 Apr. 1928, ANS-AOF 2 G 27-99. French merchants requested that the Upper Volta model be applied to the Soudan (Robert Boussac, agent général de Comptoirs de l'industrie cotonnière, letter to lt gov. Soudan, Bouguni, 9 Jan. 1926, ANM 1 Q 18).

34. Commandant Bouguni, letter to lt gov. Soudan, Bouguni, 27 May 1926, ANM 2 Q 4.

35. Robert Boussac, agent général de Comptoirs de l'industrie cotonnière, letter to lt gov. Bouguni, 9 Jan. 1926, ANM 1 Q 18.

36. Interview with Cebarama Dembele, Banankoro, 22 Jan. 1984.

37. Interview with Ko Togola, M'Peba, 23 Jan. 1984.

38. Administrator Sikasso, letter to lt gov. Soudan, Sikasso, 28 Mar. 1927, ANM 1 Q 18.

39. Commandant Bamako, Rapport de tournée administrative du chef de la subdivision, [Bamako], n.d. [July 1927], ANM 1 Q 330. Emphasis in the original.

40. Spitz, Sansanding, p. 155.

41. Rapport sur la situation générale du Soudan français, situation économique, June 1923, ANS-AOF 2 G 23-5; Bulletin de renseignements pour l'Agence économique de l'AOF, Soudan, 3d and 4th Quarters 1927, ANS-AOF 2 G 27-6; Bulletin économique pour l'Agence économique de l'AOF, Soudan, 1st Quarter 1929; Rapport économique, Soudan, 4th Quarter 1930, ANS-AOF 2 G 30-31.

42. Administrator Bamako, telegram to lt gov. Soudan, Bamako, 5 May 1937, ANM 1 Q 705; Rapport sur la culture du coton dans le cercle de Bamako, Bamako, n.d. [probably May 1937], ANM 1 Q 705; Rapport économique, Bouguni, 1st Quarter 1937, ANM 1 Q 705. For more detail see Chapter 11.

43. Procès-verbal, Chambre de Commerce, Kayes, 22 Dec. 1923, ANS 1 R 18.

44. Notice mensuelle pour l'Agence économique de l'AOF, Soudan, May 1925, ANS-AOF 2 G 25-4.

45. Procès-verbal, Assemblée générale de l'ACC, Paris, 18 June 1924, Bull ACC, June 1924.

46. For notions of moral economy in historical perspective, see Thompson, "Moral Economy," and Scott, Moral Economy.

47. Bélime, Note relative à l'établissement d'une taxe d'exportation sur les cotons ouest-africains, n.p., Mar. 1924, ANS 1 R 102.

48. Bulletin économique pour l'Agence économique de l'AOF, Soudan, Jan.–Feb. 1927, ANS-AOF 2 G 27-6.

49. "Le Tariff d'égrenage dans les usines de l'ACC," Bull ACC, Apr. 1927, pp. 13–15.

50. Bulletin économique pour l'Agence économique de l'AOF, Soudan, Mar.–Apr. 1927, ANS-AOF 2 G 27-6.

51. Terrasson, letter to M. Président, Chambre de Commerce de Bamako, Kouluba, 29 Dec. 1927, ANM 1 R 306; Bulletin économique pour l'Agence économique de l'AOF, Soudan, Jan.–Feb. 1927, ANS-AOF 2 G 27-6.

52. Colomb, commandant Bouguni, telegram to Terrasson, Bouguni, 31 Mar. 1928, and annotation by Terrasson, n.d., ANM 1 R 306.

53. Robert Boussac, agent général de Comptoirs de l'industrie cotonnière, letter to Lt gov. Soudan, Bouguni, 9 Jan., 1926, ANM 1 Q 18.

54. Bélime, Rapport annuel sur la culture du cotonnier en AOF, Kouluba, 15 Apr. 1928, ANS-AOF 2 G 27-99.

55. Terrasson, Rapport à Direction des affaires économiques, Kouluba, 13 Apr. 1928, ANM 1 R 305.

56. For more detail, see "The Cotton Fair" section. These prohibitions refer to Arrêté 1477, règlement le conditionnement du coton au Soudan français, Kouluba, 9 Oct. 1925, ANS 1 R 102.

57. Bulletin économique pour l'Agence économique de l'AOF, Soudan, 1st Quarter 1930, ANS-AOF 2 G 30-31; Conseil du Gouvernement, Office de la production et du credit, Soudan, Dec. 1930, ANM 1 R 300.

58. Mérat, Affaires économiques; ACC, Dakar, 22 Feb. 1931, ANF-DOM Aff écon 97-3.

59. Ibid.; Fousset, Rapport sur le coton et l'ACC, Kouluba, 5 Jan. 1932, ANM 1 R 305. The following table depicts the official fixed prices by district.

TABLE FOR NOTE 59
Fixed Cotton Prices, 1927–32

District	1927	1929	1930	1932
Bamako	1.10	1.50	1.25	
Bafoulabe	1.00	1.25	1.25	
Bouguni	.80	1.00	1.15	
Kayes	1.30	1.55	1.40	.30–.40
Kita	1.00	—	1.20	
Koutiala	.80	1.25	1.20	
San	.80	1.50	1.20	
Segu	.90	.85–1.00	1.10–1.25	
Sikasso	.90	1.15	1.15	

SOURCES: Bulletin de renseignements pour l'Agence économique de l'AOF, Soudan, Mar. 1927, ANS-AOF 2 G 27-6; Direction des Affaires économiques, Renseignements sur la culture du coton en AOF pendant l'année 1929, n.d., n.p., ANS 1 R 100; Bulletin économique pour l'Agence économique de l'AOF, Soudan, 1st Quarter 1930, ANS-AOF 2 G 30-31; Bulletin économique, Soudan, 1st Quarter 1932, ANS-AOF 2 G 32-9; Governor de Fousset, Le coton et l'ACC, Kouluba, 5 Jan. 1932, ANM 1 R 305.
NOTE: I have not been able to locate 1928 or 1931 prices.

60. Carde, Circulaire, 15 Mar. 1924, p. 171.

61. Gov-gen. Carde, Notice des instructions aux lt govs. Soudan, Haute Volta, Côte d'Ivoire, Dakar, n.d. [1924], ANS 1 R 102.

62. Notice mensuelle pour l'Agence économique de l'AOF, Soudan, Feb. 1925; Notice mensuelle pour l'Agence économique de l'AOF, Soudan, Mar. 1925, ANS-AOF 2 G 25-4.

63. Terrasson, télégramme aux cercles Bamako, Kayes, Bouguni, Mopti, San, Koutiala, Sikasso, Bafoulabe, Kita, Nioro, Segu, Kouluba, 7 May 1925, ANM 1 R 303. See also Notice mensuelle pour l'Agence économique de l'AOF, Apr. 1925, Soudan, ANS-AOF 2 G 25-4.

64. Arrêté 1477, règlement le conditionnement du coton au Soudan français, Kouluba, 9 Oct. 1925, ANS 1 R 102.

65. Terrasson, Rapport à Direction des affaires économiques, Kouluba, 13 Apr. 1928, ANM 1 R 305. In his report, Terrasson was alluding to a particular incident in Koutiala earlier that month. The inspecteur des affaires administratives wrote that "before the opening of the cotton fair the merchants resident in the district and in neighboring ones agreed on a price. They also agreed on how to share the harvest: one part for all merchants not resident and one and a half parts for those resident [in Koutiala]." The administrator of Koutiala agreed to this arrangement as long as the producers remained free to sell or not. African traders and intermediaries based in Segu were excluded from this cartel. They complained to the administrator, and their grievance moved up the chain of command to Terrasson. Terrasson telegraphed Koutiala and Sikasso that any threats or intimidations against any traders, which had the consequence of diminishing the freedom of trade, would not be tol-

erated and would be punished by the courts (Inspecteur des affaires administratives, letter to lt gov. Soudan, Kouluba, 1 May 1928; Acheteurs de Segou,
telegram to lt-gov. Soudan, [Segu], 3 Mar. 1928; Terrasson, telegram to administrator Sikasso, Kouluba, 5 Apr. 1928, ANM 1 R 306).

66. Notice mensuelle pour l'Agence économique de l'AOF, Soudan, Mar.
1925, ANS-AOF 2 G 25-4; Rapport agricole, Soudan, 1926, ANS-AOF 2 G 26-
33; Gov-gen. Carde, letter to Minister of Colonies, 3 May 1927, Paris, ANF-
DOM Agence des colonies 13; Rapport agricole d'ensemble pour l'année
1928, Soudan, ANS-AOF 2 G 28-41. The cotton markets for 1927 were sched-
uled as follows: Bamako, 3; Bouguni, 1; Kayes, 2; Koutiala, 3; San, 1; Segu, 3;
Sikasso, 5.

67. Bélime, Rapport sur la production cotonnière de l'AOF en 1925–26,
Kouluba, 15 May 1926, ANF-DOM Aff écon 72-4; Bélime, Rapport annuel
sur la culture cotonnière en AOF, Kouluba, 15 Apr. 1928, ANS-AOF 2 G 27-
99; Duranthon, administrator Sikasso, letter to lt gov. Soudan, Sikasso, 28
Mar. 1927, ANM 1 Q 18; President, Chambre de Commerce de Bamako, letter to lt gov. Soudan, Bamako, 20 May 1925, ANM 1 R 303; Robert Boussac,
letter to lt gov. Soudan, Bouguni, 9 Jan. 1926, ANM 1 Q 18.

68. Bélime, Rapport sur la production cotonnière de l'AOF en 1925–26,
Kouluba, 15 May 1926, ANF-DOM Aff écon 72-4; Bélime, Rapport annuel
sur la culture cotonnière en AOF, Kouluba, 15 Apr. 1928, ANS-AOF 2 G 27-
99; Duranthon, administrator Sikasso, letter to lt gov. Soudan, Sikasso, 28
Mar. 1927, ANM 1 Q 18.

69. Bulletin de renseignements pour l'Agence économique de l'AOF, Soudan, Mar.–Apr. 1927, ANS-AOF 2 G 27-6.

70. Hesling (former gov. and director of the ACC), Rapport de mission en
AOF, Dec. 1928–Mar. 1929, Paris, 15 Apr. 1929, ANS 1 R 102. For a similar
description, see Lalande, "L'achat du coton aux indigènes," p. 260.

71. Bulletin économique, Soudan, 2d Quarter 1931, ANS-AOF 2 G 31-37.
The official cotton fairs persisted through the end of the decade, after which
they withered away. In 1935, with the resurgence of world commodity
prices, efforts were made to revive them (Rapport économique annuel, Soudan, 1935, ANS-AOF 2 G 35-37).

72. Mérat, Affaires économiques, ACC, Dakar, 22 Feb. 1931, ANF-DOM
Aff écon 97-3; Lt gov. Fousset, Rapport sur le cotton et l'ACC, Kouluba, 5
Jan. 1932, ANM 1 R 305.

73. Cultivated originally in Georgia, Allen was introduced in Africa first
in Zeidad, Anglo-Egyptian Sudan, just after the turn of the century. It was
first introduced to the Soudan in the early 1920s via Dahomey. Indeed,
Forbes was intrigued by this variety and traveled to Nigeria to secure a
"purer" seed source (P. Coleno, Ingénieur des travaux agricoles, Rapport sur
la Culture sèche du cotonnière au Soudan, n.p., 31 Jan. 1935, ANM 1 R 319).

74. Lt. gov. Fousset, Rapport sur le coton et l'ACC, Kouluba, 5 Jan. 1932,
ANM 1 R 305; R. H. Forbes, Situation de la culture cotonnier en AOF, n.d.
[probably 1931], ANS 1 R 100.

75. Bureau des affaires économiques et commerciales, Rapport annuel, Soudan, 1929, ANS-AOF 2 G 29-4; Rapport économique, Soudan, 4th Quarter 1930, ANS 2 G 30-31; Bulletin économique, Soudan, 4th Quarter 1931, ANS-AOF 2 G 31-37; E. Barthaburu, Note sur l'organisation de l'egrenage du coton Allen dans le region de Segou, Segu, 14 Apr. 1931, ANM 1 R 304.

76. Lt Gov. Fousset, Rapport sur le coton et l'ACC, Kouluba, 5 Jan. 1932, ANM 1 R 305.

77. Similar concerns were voiced in France concerning the metropolitan state's managerial and commercial competence. See Kuisel, *Capitalism,* pp. 2–3, 36–37, 64.

Chapter 9

1. In a slightly modified form, these assumptions were revived as "vent for surplus" theories. For example, Myint, "Classical Theory of International Trade"; for African applications, see Gemery and Hogendorn, "Atlantic Slave Trade"; and Hogendorn, *Nigerian Groundnut Exports.*

2. M. Etesse, "Le coton des terres sèches en Afrique occidentale," paper presented to the Secrétaire-général, Union coloniale française, Paris, 28 Dec. 1923, ANF-DOM CFOM 344.

3. Johnson, "Technology," p. 267. See also Johnson, "Cotton Imperialism."

4. Raúl Prebisch developed these arguments in reports of the Economic Commission for Latin America. See also Prebisch, *Change and Development;* Frank, "Development of Underdevelopment," pp. 10–11. The fullest expression of Frank's thesis is in *Capitalism.* See also Cooper, "Africa and the World Economy," pp. 93–94.

5. See, for example, Boser-Sarivaxévanis, *Tissus de l'Afrique occidentale,* and *Recherche;* Idiens and Ponting, eds., *Textiles of Africa;* Menzel, *Textilen aus Westafrika;* Weiner and Schneider, eds., *Cloth;* and the papers presented at "The Artisan, Cloth, and the World Economy" Conference, Dartmouth College, Apr. 1993.

6. Commandant Aubin, letter to lt gov., Segu, 18 Feb. 1927, ANM 1 Q 18.

7. The concept of "normal surplus" is derived from Allan, *African Husbandman.* On the Maraka slave plantations, see Roberts, "Long Distance Trade," and Roberts, *Warriors,* pp. 46–50, 112–28.

8. M. Costes, Ingénieur des Services agricoles, Rapport annuel du Service des l'agriculture du Soudan français, Koulikoro, 2 Mar. 1922, ANS-AOF 2 G 21-22.

9. Notice mensuelle pour l'Agence économique, Soudan, July 1926, ANS-AOF 2 G 26-5.

10. Rapport sur la situation générale du Soudan français, situation économique, Jan. 1922; Rapport sur la situation générale du Soudan français, situation économique, Mar. 1922, ANS-AOF 2 G 22-3. For more detail on the concept of cotton imperialism, see Johnson, "Technology," and "Cotton Imperialism."

11. Bélime, Inspecteur de la Service générale des textiles, La campagne cotonnière (1924–25) en Afrique occidentale, 19 May 1925, ANF-DOM Aff écon 889.

12. Rapports sur la situation générale du Soudan français, situation économique, Jan. 1923, Apr. 1923; Notice mensuelle sur l'état des cultures et des récoltes, l'élevage et les épizooties Soudan, Dec. 1923, ANS-AOF 2 G 23-5.

13. Notice mensuelle pour l'Agence économique de l'AOF, Soudan, Apr. 1925, ANS-AOF 2 G 25-4.

14. Rapport sur la situation générale du Soudan français, situation économique, Apr. 1923, ANS-AOF 2 G 23-5.

15. La Dépêche coloniale, 23 Feb. 1924, quoted in Bull ACC, Feb. 1924. See also Président-directeur de Pozzo di Borgo, letter to Président UCF, Marseille, 2 Apr. 1924; Président de l'Industrie cotonnière française, letter to Président UCF, Paris, 24 Mar. 1924; Président UCF, letter to M. Vézia, Président du Syndicat de défense des intérêts sénégalaises, Paris, 28 Jan. 1928, ANF-DOM UCF 514.

16. Bulletin économique, Soudan, 2d Quarter 1931, ANS 2 G 31-37.

17. Lt. Gov. Louis de Fousset, Rapport sur le coton et l'ACC, Kouluba, 5 Jan. 1931, ANM 1 R 305.

18. Bulletin économique pour l'Agence économique de l'AOF, Soudan, 1st Quarter 1929, ANS-AOF 2 G 29-4. See also Rapport de fin d'année sur le commerce, Segu, 4th Quarter 1929, ANM 1 Q 358.

19. Rapport politique d'ensemble (AOF) pour 1928, ANS-AOF 2 G 28-6.

20. Bulletin économique, Soudan, 2d Quarter 1931, ANS-AOF 2 G 31-37.

21. Bulletin économique, Soudan, 1st Quarter 1932, ANS-AOF 2 G 32-9. See also Rapport d'ensemble d'AOF, Agriculture, forêts, élevage, n.d., n.p. [1932], ANS 1 R 56.

22. Governor Fousset understood this point. "If cotton does not offer [the producer sufficient] returns, the effort we will ask of him must take the form of a supplementary tax or a corvée" (Lt. Gov. Fousset, Rapport sur le coton et l'ACC, Kouluba, 5 Jan. 1932, ANM 1 R 305).

23. Notice mensuelle sur l'état des cultures et des récoltes, l'élevage et épizooties, Soudan, Dec. 1924, ANS-AOF 2 G 23-5.

24. Notice mensuelle pour l'Agence économique de l'AOF, Soudan, Aug. 1924, ANS-AOF 2 G 24-6; Notice mensuelle pour l'Agence économique de l'AOF, Soudan, Mar. 1925, ANS-AOF 2 G 25-4.

25. Dulles, French Franc; Neurisse, Histoire du franc; Fohlen, France de l'entre-deux-guerres; Ogburn and Jaffe, Economic Development.

26. Notice mensuelle pour l'Agence économique de l'AOF, Soudan, Apr. 1924, ANS-AOF 2 G 24-6.

27. Notice mensuelle pour l'Agence économique de l'AOF, Soudan, Apr. 1925, ANS-AOF 2 G 25-4.

28. Bulletin économique, Soudan, July 1926, ANS-AOF 2 G 26-5; on cloth prices, Bulletin mensuelle pour l'Agence économique de l'AOF, Soudan, Dec. 1926, ANS-AOF 2 G 26-5.

29. Bulletins de renseignements pour l'Agence économique de l'AOF, Soudan, Mar.–Apr. 1927; Bulletin de renseignements pour l'Agence économique de l'AOF, Soudan, 4th Quarter 1927, ANS-AOF 2 G 27-6.

30. Notice mensuelle pour l'Agence économique de l'AOF, Soudan, Mar. 1925, ANS-AOF 2 G 25-4.

31. Bulletin économique, Soudan, Dec. 1926, ANS-AOF 2 G 26-5.

32. Inspecteur-général de 1ère classe des colonies, Mérat, Affaires économiques: l'Association cotonnière coloniale, Dakar, 22 Feb. 1931, ANF-DOM Aff écon 97-3.

33. Descemet, le Secrétaire-général chargé de l'expédition des affaires, Rapport d'agricole d'ensemble pour l'année 1926, Soudan, ANS-AOF 2 G 26-33.

34. Bulletin mensuelle pour l'Agence économique de l'AOF, Soudan, Dec. 1926, ANS-AOF 2 G 26-5.

35. "The figures furnished by the ginning factories represent only a very small part of the harvest" (ibid.).

36. Acting lt gov. [Descemet], Soudan, Production du coton en 1925–26, Kouluba, 24 Sept. 1926, ANS 1 R 102.

37. Descemet, le Secrétaire-général chargé de l'expédition des affaires, Rapport d'agricole d'ensemble pour l'année 1926, Soudan, ANS-AOF 26-33; Bulletin de renseignements pour l'Agence économique de l'AOF, Soudan, Mar. 1927, ANS-AOF 2 G 27-41. See also "Rapport sur l'AOF," *Bull ACC,* June 1924.

38. Of this total, 4,300 tons were ginned by ginning factories and 5,525 tons were consumed locally. How these figures were arrived at remains questionable; taken together, cotton ginned and cotton consumed locally account for only 9,825 tons, leaving unaccounted 4,575 tons (Bulletin économique pour l'Agence économique de l'AOF, Soudan, 3d Quarter 1930, ANS-AOF 2 G 30-31).

39. Rapport économique, 1st Quarter 1931, San, ANM 1 Q 359.

40. Commandant Aubin, letter to lt gov., Segu, 28 Feb. 1927, ANM 1 Q 18.

41. Bulletin de renseignements pour l'Agence économique de l'AOF, Soudan, Nov. 1925, ANS-AOF 2 G 25-4. Bélime was much taken by the economic potentialities of establishing mechanized spinning and weaving industries in French West Africa. Such an industry would provide two very important functions: first, it could produce wide cloth to compete better with the narrow strips of local handicraft textile producers; and second, it could absorb the vast quantities of low-grade cotton, which was not of export quality but yielded short, strong fibers. Bélime cited with enthusiasm the success of the Gonfreville mill in Bouake (Bélime, Rapport sur la production cotonnière de l'Afrique occidentale française en 1925–26, Kouluba, 15 May 1926, ANF-DOM Aff écon 72-4). In 1931, La Compagnie soudanaise in Kayes began tests of a mechanized weaving factory it erected, using 18 tons of

local cotton (Bulletin économique, Soudan 2d Quarter· 1931, ANS-AOF 2 G 31-37).

42. Terrasson, letter to gov-gen., Bamako, 19 May 1930, ANM 1 Q 115. Terrasson, however, was not describing anything new. In 1921, Costes had already described how in Bamako European and Syrian merchants were dealing in the local cotton trade. Some even bought raw cotton, had it ginned, and sold ginned cotton locally at 6 francs per kilogram (Costes, Rapport annuel du Service de l'agriculture du Soudan français, Koulikoro, 2 Mar. 1922, ANS-AOF 2 G 21-3).

43. Acting lt gov. Soudan, to gov-gen., Production du coton en 1925–26, Kouluba, 24 Sept. 1926, ANS 1 R 102.

44. Bélime, Inspecteur du Service général des textiles, Compte-rendu de tournée, Kouluba, 10 May 1925, ANF-DOM Aff écon 889-1.

45. Interview with Bamoussa Keita, Sinsani, 21 Jan. 1984.

46. Gaffiot, Coton, pp. 14–15.

47. "The hand carders will permit producers and intermediaries to transport the same volume of cotton, but a load of ginned cotton is valued at 150–200 francs in Bamako compared to 30–40 francs for the same load of raw cotton. This profit should be an encouragement for cotton production" (Notice mensuelle sur l état des cultures et des récoltes, l'élevage et les épizooties, Soudan, Mar. 1924, ANS-AOF 2 G 24-6).

48. Meillassoux, "Etat et condition des esclaves à Goumbou (Mali)," pp. 249–50; Meillassoux, "Female Slavery," p. 58.

49. Interview with Hadja Toumata Contao, Segu, 23 Jan. 1984.

50. Bélime, Rapport sur la production cotonnière de l'Afrique occidentale française en 1925–26, Kouluba, 15 May 1926, ANF-DOM Aff écon 72-4.

51. Interview with Dahou Traore, Sibila, 21 Jan. 1984.

52. Interview with Tijani Sylla, Baraweli, 20 Jan. 1984; interview with Cebarama Dembele, Banakoro, 22 Jan. 1984, reiterated Sylla's point that husbands were not informed about what women entrepreneurs did. "Women bought yarn at the market and they made it into cloth. Husbands knew nothing of this."

53. Interview with Bamoussa Keita, Sinsani, 21 Jan. 1984.

54. Interview with Hadja Toumata Contao, Segu, 23 Jan. 1984.

55. Interview with Cebarama Dembele, Banakoro, 22 Jan. 1984. Dembele's allusion to "salary" here is symbolic of the changes in household reciprocity. Salary is a modern misnomer for the shares involved in household ginning, but it reflects the negotiated nature of household social relations in the colonial and postcolonial periods.

56. Interview with Cebarama Dembele, Banakoro, 22 Jan. 1984.

57. Interview with Hadja Toumata Contao, Segu, 23 Jan. 1984.

58. Interview with Cebarama Dembele, Banakoro, 22 Jan. 1984. See also interviews with Ko Togola, M'Peba, 23 Jan. 1984.

59. Interview with Dramane Kone, Nyamina, 23 July 1981. For a similar account, see the interview with Diasse Diabite, collection Aliou Kone, 1984.

60. Kemp, *French Economy*, pp. 100–114; Kuisel, *Capitalism*; Sauvy, "Economic Crisis."

61. *Bull ACC*, Apr. 1932, p. 58.

62. Bulletin économique, Soudan, 2d Quarter 1932, ANS-AOF 2 G 32-9.

63. Gaffoit, *Coton*, pp. 50–51.

64. Notes by Colonel Vallée, Chef du secrétariat permanent de la Défense Nationale; Inspecteur Mérat; Bélime, Directeur de la Service des textiles; and Mondor, Directeur des Affaires économiques in Mérat, Des affaires économiques; l'Association cotonnière coloniale, Dakar, 22 Feb. 1931, ANF-DOM Aff écon 97-3.

65. Mérat, Des affaires économiques: Association cotonnière coloniale, Dakar, 22 Feb. 1931, ANF-DOM Aff écon 97-3.

66. Bulletin économique, Soudan, 4th Quarter 1931, ANF-AOF 2 G 31-37.

Chapter 10

1. Compare Coquery-Vidrovitch, "L'Afrique coloniale française," pp. 386–424, and Martin, "Long Depression," pp. 74–95.

2. The notion of a personal fief is expressed in Manue's obituary, "Emile Bélime," p. 5.

3. Schreyger, *Office du Niger*, pp. 35–37; see also Jean Filipovitch, "Office du Niger," pp. 90–97; van Beusekom, "Colonial Rural Development"; and Aw, "Historique de l'Office du Niger."

4. Schreyger, *Office du Niger*, p. 45. Filipovitch argues that the preliminary report issued by La Compagnie générale in November 1923 advised strongly against irrigation without first undertaking further studies. When the final report was submitted, it contained a grudging approval of a dam and canal near Bamako, but the objectives were no longer primarily to irrigate cotton but to provide a means of navigating the rapids and a means of generating electricity. The report indicated that some thousands of hectares could also be irrigated but that these were to be experimental in nature ("Office du Niger," pp. 95–96, 123–25). On the role of rice and irrigation along the Niger, see van Beusekom, "Colonial Rural Development," chap. 1.

5. Filipovitch, "Office du Niger," pp. 123–30; Becker, "Experiment."

6. Echenberg, "Migrations militaires"; Echenberg, "Paying the Blood Tax"; Echenberg, *Colonial Conscripts*.

7. Echenberg and Filipovitch, "African Military Labour," pp. 537–39; Mercier, *Travail obligatoire*, pp. 35–36, 45. For more general information on prestation and corvée labor, see Fall, "Travail forcé"; Buell, *Native Problem*.

8. Interview with Cebarama Dembele, Banankoro, 22 Jan. 1984.

9. Mercier, *Travail obligatoire*, pp. 13–15, 17–18. To counter charges that compulsory labor contradicted basic metropolitan principles of free labor, Mercier argued on pages 17–18 that even in France, where the notion of "individual liberty forms the base of all European institutions, it too is be-

coming more and more relative: it is sufficient to consider the numerous and imperative regulations, made necessary by the complexity of contemporary social life, which intrude into the very tissue of our lives more and more fully." For more detail on neo-Malthusian aspects of French colonial thinking, see van Beusekom, "Colonial Rural Development," chap. 2.

10. Echenberg and Filipovitch, "African Military Labour," pp. 541–45; Schreyger, *Office du Niger*, p. 46; Mercier, *Travail obligatoire*, p. 66.

11. Spitz, *Sansanding*, pp. 51–52; Filipovitch, "Office du Niger," pp. 131–35; Schreyger, *Office du Niger*, pp. 47–49.

12. Kuisel, *Capitalism*, pp. 66–67. For a wider background on French *travaux publics* during this crucial period, see Saly, *Politique des grands travaux*, and Kuisel, "Technocrats," pp. 228–53. It was fitting that when Bélime left the Soudan in 1944, he bought an old castle in Haute-Savoie, overlooking the Rhône, swollen and tamed by a hydroelectric and irrigation dam. See Manue, "Emile Bélime," p. 5.

13. See Schreyger, *Office du Niger*, pp. 58–69, and Filipovitch, "Office du Niger," pp. 170–73, n. 97, p. 200. Filipovitch establishes a more exact chronology for the subsumption of the second portion recruits under Bélime. In 1929, according to her account, authority for the STIN was taken out of the hands of the lieutenant governor of the Soudan and placed under the authority of the governor-general. By 1933, Bélime created a special division of STIN labor for the irrigation works, which virtually made him king over this coerced labor pool.

14. Filipovitch, "Office du Niger," pp. 162–64.

15. For background, see Paxton, *Vichy France*.

16. Bélime, *L'Heure de la France*; Bélime, *L'Ordre réel*. His political philosophy, according to Filipovitch, reflected "nearly every strain of French right-wing thinking" and had much in common with Charles Maurras and Italian corporatist thinking. See Filipovitch, "Office du Niger," pp. 164–66, and Manue, "Emile Bélime," p. 5.

17. Paradoxically, for someone as prolific as Bélime was in the period before the establishment of the Office du Niger, he left surprisingly few detailed records of the orders and instructions he obviously gave to his subordinates at the Office. Perhaps a trove of Bélime memoranda may yet be found to provide a clearer picture of the evolution of Bélime's vision of a new society both in Africa and in France.

18. Filipovitch, "Office du Niger," pp. 139–40, 153–89.

19. Quoted ibid., p. 173; see also Magassa, *Papa Commandant*, pp. 50–52.

20. Filipovitch, "Office du Niger," pp. 181–89.

21. In 1933, Arthur Waddington reported that the success of the irrigation project was assured because "labor costs, compared to the black worker in Texas, are also less expensive" ("Mission du M. Waddington au Soudan," *Bull ACC*, Apr. 1933, pp. 39–40). Waddington was referring to labor costs in cotton production, but his remark also applied to construction.

22. Bélime, "L'Afrique s'éveille," p. 7.

23. Filipovitch, "Office du Niger," pp. 256–59; Magassa, *Papa Commandant.*

24. The term was used officially in the National Assembly debate of 27 March 1933 by Deputy Nouvelle, *Journal officiel de la république française,* no. 43, p. 1574, quoted in Schreyger, *Office du Niger,* p. 77, n. 1. See also Marchal "Office du Niger," pp. 73–90, and Marchal, Kohler, and Remy, *Colons Mossi.*

25. Bauzil, *Note,* pp. 2, 4.

26. Van Beusekom, "Colonial Rural Development," pp. 106–8.

27. Lt gov. Alfassa, Rapport politique annuel, Soudan, 1935, ANS-AOF 2 G 35-9. See also van Beusekom, "Colonial Rural Development," pp. 112–18; Filipovitch, "Office du Niger," pp. 333–37; Schreyger, *Office du Niger,* pp. 76–82. For a discussion of Mossi recruitment, see Marchal, Kohler, and Remy, *Colons Mossi.*

28. Bélime, letter to gov-gen. AOF, Paris, 9 July 1937, ANF-DOM Aff pol 2808.

29. Czenave, Commandant, Rapport sur le voyage effectué en Octobre 1937 sur les terres irriguées de l'Office du Niger, Bamako, 6 Nov. 1937, ANF-DOM Aff pol 620-9.

30. Toby, Commandant Nioro, Au sujet peuplement des terres irriguées, Nioro, 18 Dec. 1937, ANF-DOM Aff pol 620-9.

31. André Morel, Commandant Koutiala, Rapport, Koutiala, 27 Dec. 1937, ANF-DOM Aff pol 620-9.

32. Bernard-Duquenet, "Front populaire," pp. 159–60; Filipovitch, "Office du Niger," pp. 204–5.

33. Gov-gen. de Coppet, Rapport politique du gouvernement général de l'AOF, année 1936, ANS-AOF 2 G 36-25.

34. Sorel, Inspecteur Général du Service de santé des colonies, letter to gov-gen., Dakar, 30 Mar. 1938, ANF-DOM Aff pol 620-3.

35. Lt gov. Rougier, letter to gov-gen., Kouluba, 10 Jan. 1938, ANF-DOM Aff pol 620-9; Rapport de mission de M. Henri Carbou, Administrateur en Chef des Colonies, Annexes 1-20, n.d. [1938], ANF-DOM Aff écon 167; Gov-gen. de Coppet, confidential letter to Minister of Colonies, n.d. [but arrived in Paris 9 June 1938] ANF-DOM Aff écon 167. See also Rapport politique de gouvernement-général de l'AOF, année 1937, ANS-AOF 2 G 37-1.

36. Lt gov. Desanti, Rapport politique annuel, année 1939, Kouluba, 19 Apr. 1940, ANS-AOF 2 G 39-8.

37. Petition, Lasserre, Président de la Chambre de Commerce à M. le Gouverneur de la Côte d'Ivoire, 14 June 1938, ANF-DOM Aff pol 620-6.

38. Copy of a telegram, Chambre de Commerce de la Guinée, to gov-gen., included in a letter, gov-gen. to Minister of Colonies, Dakar, 18 July 1938, ANF-DOM Aff écon 167.

39. Ibid. See also Voeu concernant l'Office du Niger, Chambre de Commerce, Dakar, 21 Mar. 1938, ANF-DOM Aff pol 620-3; Voeu émis par la

Chambre de Commerce du Dahomey dans sa séance du 19 Mai 1938 and petition, Lasserre, Président de la Chambre de Commerce à M. le Gouverneur de la Côte d'Ivoire, 14 June 1938, ANF-DOM Aff pol 620-6.

40. Collections of 1938–39 press clippings are located in ANF-DOM Aff pol 620-3 and ANF-DOM Aff écon 167. See also Filipovitch, "Office du Niger," pp. 210–11.

41. For a discussion of this period, see Filipovitch, "Office du Niger," pp. 209–16.

42. Marshal Pétain, Fondements d'une économie impériale, Vichy, 13 Dec. 1941, ANF-DOM Aff écon 64 bis.

43. Organismes administratifs de nouvelle création intéressant la production cotonnière coloniale française, Vichy, 16 Jan. 1941, ANF-DOM Aff écon 223. For more detailed discussion of Vichy's organization of production, see Kuisel, *Capitalism*, pp. 128–44.

44. UCEF, Rapport, Paris, 17 Feb. 1942, ANF-DOM Aff écon 223. On the GIRC, see Projet de contrat du coton, n.d. [but 1941]; Senn, letter to Direction des textiles et cuirs, Ministère de production industrielle et du travail, n.p., 27 Mar. 1941; Gov-gen. Boisson letter to General Weygand, Dakar, 28 Apr. 1941, ANF-DOM Aff écon 223.

45. Sec. d'Etat à la production industrielle, letter to Sec. d'Etat aux colonies, Paris, 7 July 1942, ANF-DOM Aff écon 64 bis; Rapport économique annuel, Soudan, 1941, ANS-AOF 2 G 41-28.

46. Inspecteur des affaires administratives Marchand, Rapport politique [du Soudan] annuel, 1942, ANS-AOF 2 G 42-3; gov-gen., letter, to governors des colonies du groupe, Dakar, 1942, ANS 1 R 56. See also Filipovitch, "Office du Niger," pp. 219–24.

47. Bélime, *Das innere Nigerdelta*.

48. Soudan, Rapport économique annuel, 1941, ANS-AOF 2 G 41-28; Service de l'exploitation, Office du Niger, Rapport annuel sur l'activité du Service, Campagne agricole, 1943–44, ANS-AOF 2 G 44-84. The organization of settler life surrounded their obligatory participation in Association agricole indigène, formed in 1931 as a formally constituted agricultural cooperative. All settlers were to be represented by their AAI council, but in reality, the AAI became an institution of Office intervention in the daily lives of the settlers. Compare Schreyger, *Office du Niger*, pp. 88–93, and van Beusekom, "Colonial Rural Development," pp. 182–83. For more on settler resistance to Office marketing and supervision, see van Beusekom, "Colonial Rural Development," chap. 6.

49. Lt gov. Louveau, Rapport annuel sur le travail, année 1943, Kouluba, ANS-AOF 2 G 43-24; Lt gov. Louveau, Annexe au rapport annuel sur l'emploie de la main d'oeuvre au Soudan pendant l'année 1942, ANS-AOF 2 G 42-23. See also Filipovitch, "Office du Niger," chap. 8.

50. Lt gov. Louveau, Rapport politique annuel, 1944, Kouluba, ANS-AOF 2 G 44-22.

51. Ibid.

52. Decree, 11 Apr. 1946, cited in *Journal officiel de l'Afrique occidentale française*, 4 May 1946, p. 547. See also Morgenthau, *Political Parties*, pp. 37–48. The end of coercion was also enshrined in the October constitution of the Fourth Republic.

53. Lt gov. Louveau, Rapport politique annuel, Soudan, 1946, ANS-AOF 2 G 46-21. Louveau reiterated the same point in Rapport économique, année 1947, Soudan, ANS-AOF 2 G 47-27.

54. Van Beusekom, "Colonial Rural Development," pp. 123, 201; Filipovitch, "Office du Niger," pp. 361–66, also 429–41.

55. Schreyger, *Office du Niger*, pp. 130–69. The various metropolitan funds were Fonds d'investissement pour le développement économique et social des territoires d'Outre-Mer and from the spin-off Fonds d'équipement rural et de développement économique et social.

56. Schreyger, *Office du Niger*, pp. 159–63.

Chapter 11

1. Bulletin économique, Soudan, 2d Quarter 1932, ANS-AOF 2 G 32-9.

2. Acting lt gov. Maillet, Soudan: Rapport économique annuel, 1932, ANS-AOF 2 G 32-9; Direction générale des services économiques, AOF: Rapport d'ensemble, année 1932, ANS-AOF 2 G 32-3.

3. Rapport économique annuel, Soudan, 1933, ANS-AOF 2 G 33-5; Rapport économique annuel, Soudan, 1934, ANS-AOF 2 G 34-34; Lt gov. Alfassa, Rapport politique, Soudan, année 1935, ANS-AOF 2 G 35-9.

4. Les Etablissements Koeklin, under the technical direction of M. Soering, is "one of the rare, I dare not say the only, cotton spinner that I know, who is not an enemy of African cotton" (De Coninck, Considérations générales sur les cotons coloniaux, n.p., n.d. [probably 1938], ANS 1 R 131).

5. Président de la Chambre d'agriculture de Pondichéry, letter to gov. des Etablissements français dans l'Inde, Pondichéry, 29 Apr. 1929, ANS 1 R 48; Rapport économique annuel, Soudan, 1934, ANS-AOF 2 G 34-34; Rapport annuel du Service de l'agriculture, campagne 1933–34, ANS-AOF 2 G 34-45; P. Coleno, Ingénieur des travaux agricoles, Rapport sur la culture sèche du cotonnier du Soudan, n.p., 31 Jan. 1935, ANM 1 R 319. Karangani-Garrah also appears as Karangani-garo in the records.

6. Inspecteur de 1ère classe des colonies Bagot, Rapport sur le Service agronomique de l'Office du Niger, Paris, 4 July 1935, ANF-DOM Aff écon 107 bis 3; Le Chef du Service de l'agriculture et des forêts, Rapport annuel, campagne 1934–35, Kouluba, 12 May 1935, ANS-AOF 2 G 35-51; Ingénieur en chef des travaux d'agriculture aux colonies Charles Godard, Service d'agriculture, Rapport annuel, campagne 1936–37, Bamako, 25 May 1937, ANS-AOF 2 G 37-53.

7. Conseil des Notables de Sikasso, procès verbal de la réunion du 16 Mai 1936, [Sikasso], ANM 1 R 321.

8. Le Chef du Service de l'agriculture et des forêts, Rapport annuel, cam-

pagne 1934–35, Kouluba, 12 May 1935, ANS-AOF 2 G 35-51; Bulletin économique, Soudan, 1st Quarter 1936, ANS-AOF 2 G 36-6; Ingénieur en chef
des travaux d'agriculture aux colonies Charles Godard, Service de l'agriculture, Rapport annuel, campagne 1936–37, Bamako, 25 May 1937, ANS-AOF
2 G 37-53.

    9. Le Chef du Service de l'agriculture et des forêts, Rapport annuel du
Service de l'agriculture et des forêts, campagne 1934–35, Kouluba, 12 May
1935, ANS-AOF 2 G 35-51; Rapport d'ensemble AOF, agriculture, forêts
élevage 1933, ANS 1 R 56.

    10. Lt gov. de Fousset, letter to Director, ACC, Kouluba, 1 June 1934,
ANM 1 R 309; Administrator Dioila, telegram to gov., Oct. 1935, ANM 1 Q
330.

    11. When costs of ginning, packaging, and transportation were added, the
administration estimated that it lost 300 francs per ton exported during the
1934–35 harvest. See Rapport économique annual, Soudan, 1933, ANS-AOF
2 G 33-5; Rapport économique annuel, Soudan, 1934, ANS-AOF 2 G 34-34;
Chef du Service de l'agriculture et des forêts, Rapport annuel du Service de
l'agriculture et des forêts, Kouluba, 12 May 1935, ANS-AOF 2 G 35-21; Rapport économique annuel, Soudan, 1935, ANS-AOF 2 G 35-37. See also
Charles Godard, Chef du Service de l'Agriculture, Rapport annuel du Service
de l'agriculture, campagne 1936–37, Soudan, n.d., ANF-DOM Agence FOM
149-133.

    12. Lt gov. Eboué, note 30 Apr. 1935, appended to Inspecteur de 3ième
classe des colonies Bargues, Rapport concernant la verification de M. Pinchon, Conducteur principal des Travaux agricoles à Baraweli, 12 Feb. 1935,
ANF-DOM Aff écon 107 bis 3.

    13. Administrator Leccia, Rapport sur la traite du coton, campagne 1935–
36, Koutiala, 16 Apr. 1936, ANM 1 R 315.

    14. Rapport économique annuel, Soudan, 1935, ANS-AOF 2 G 35-37; Bul-
letin économique, Soudan, 1st Quarter 1936, ANS-AOF 2 G 36-6.

    15. Interview with Fadita Tounkara, Segu, 22 Jan. 1984.

    16. Bulletin économique, Soudan, 1st Quarter 1936, ANS-AOF 2 G 36-6;
Gov-gen. Boisson, letter to Direction des affaires économiques, Ministry of
Colonies, Paris, 19 Nov. 1938, ANF-DOM Aff écon 1223.

    17. Rapport annuel du Service de l'agriculture, campagne 1933–34, ANS-
AOF 2 G 34-45; Le Chef du Service de l'agriculture et des forêts; Rapport
annuel du Service de l'agriculture et des forêts, campagne 1934–35, ANS-
AOF 2 G 35-51; Ingénieur en chef des travaux d'agriculture aux colonies
Charles Godard; Service de l'agriculture, Rapport annuel, campagne 1936–
37, ANS-AOF 2 G 37-53.

    18. Rapport économique, Subdivision of Kolokani, 2d Quarter 1936,
ANM 1 Q 330.

    19. Rapport économique, Bamako subdivision, Bamako, 2d Quarter 1936,
ANM 1 Q 330.

20. Lt gov. Rougier, letter to Commandant of Bouguni, Kouluba, 13 May 1937, ANM 1 Q 704; Lt gov. Rougier, Note, n.d., appended to Charles Godard, Chef du Service de l'agriculture, Rapport annuel du Service de l'agriculture, campagne 1936–37, Soudan, ANF-DOM Agence FOM 149-133. Consistent with this strategy, the administrator from San reported that "family fields grouped together give the best results" (Rapport économique annuel, San, [1938], 5 Apr. 1939, ANM 1 R 359).

21. Arrêté du Lieutenant-gouverneur p.i. au sujet de l'amélioration de la culture cotonnière au Soudan français, 5 Nov. 1935, Journal officiel du Soudan français, 1 Jan. 1936, pp. 19–21. See also Bull ACC, Apr. 1936. Article I prohibited the introduction without prior permission of the lieutenant governor into the Soudan of any cotton seeds not approved by the administration. Under Article 2, peasants were obliged to sow their fields exclusively with seeds provided by the administration. The 1935 decree went further than any previous legislation on cotton and empowered the local administration to intervene in all phases of cotton production and marketing. To enforce these first two articles, the legislation further required that all cotton transactions between producers and buyers take place in officially designated cotton fairs. Requiring cotton sales to take place in fairs, which were geographically linked to ginneries, was critical to the administration's ability to control the supply of cotton seeds, so necessary to renew the cotton cycle in the following season. The politics of recovering seeds was critical to the reproduction of the politique cotonnière; for example, see Inspecteur de 3ième classe des colonies Bargues, Rapport concernant la verification de M. Pinchon, Conducteur principal des travaux agricoles à Baraweli, Segu, 12 Feb. 1935, ANF-DOM Aff écon 107 bis-3; Lt gov. Descanti, circulaire to commandants Bouguni, Koutiala, Mopti, Nema, Ouahigouya, Sikasso, San, Segu, Tougan, Bamako, Kita, Kayes, and Nioro, 1939, ANM 1 Q 684. To control production more fully, Article 6 obliged cotton producers, upon questioning by any colonial official, to identify the source of the cotton seeds they planted. Article 7 required peasants to burn and destroy all cotton plants and capsules from the previous year and plant only cotton designated for that region and provided by the administration. Article 10 enshrined into law the division of the colony into distinct zones, each of which was identified with a particular cotton variety: Egyptian long-staple cotton was to be cultivated exclusively in the districts of Goundam, Timbuktu, Gao, Niafunke, and Gourma-Rharous; Allen and other upland medium-staple varieties were to be planted exclusively in Kayes, Nara, Segu, Bamako, subdivision of Koulikoro North, Kolokani, subdivision of Bamako North, subdivision of Dioila North, San, Tougan (except for Nouna district), Mopti, Bandiagara, and Ouahigouya; Karangani–Garrah Hills was the exclusive cotton of Koutiala, Sikasso, Bouguni subdivision of Bamako South, subdivision of Dioila South, Kita, Bafoulabe, and Nouna subdivision of Tougan; the N'Kourala hybrid was targeted to the thin zone between Budi and Allen. Article 10 made some

provision for the continued cultivation of indigenous cotton, essentially permitting its cultivation throughout the Soudan "except in regions defined each year by the lieutenant governor."

22. Inspecteur de 1ère classe des colonies Bagot, Rapport sur les essais de vulgarisation agricole en "terre sèche," Paris, 31 July 1935, ANF-DOM Aff écon 107 bis 3.

23. Rapport économique et commercial, Bouguni, 1st Quarter 1931, ANM 1 Q 332.

24. For an example, see Klein and Roberts, "Resurgence of Pawning," pp. 23–38.

25. Lt gov. Eboué, Rapport politique annuel, Soudan, 1934, ANS-AOF 2 G 34-6.

26. Gov-gen. Brévié, Rapport politique annuel du gouvernement-général de AOF, 1934, ANS-AOF 2 G 34-12.

27. Bulletin économique, Soudan, 1st Quarter 1936, ANS-AOF 2 G 36-6.

28. Rapport économique, Bouguni, 1st Quarter 1937, ANM 1 Q 705.

29. Commandant Bamako, telegram to lt gov. Soudan, Bamako, 5 May 1937; Rapport sur la culture du coton dans le cercle de Bamako, n.d. [probably May 1937], ANM 1 Q 705.

30. Lt gov. Desanti, telegram to commandants Bouguni, Sikasso, Koutiala, Segu, San, Tougan, Ouahigouya, 24 Dec. 1938, ANM 1 R 709.

31. Lt gov. Desanti, telegram to commandants Bamako, Koutiala, Tougan, Ouahigouya, San, Bouguni, Sikasso, Kita, Kayes, Nioro, 13 Dec. 1940, ANM 1 Q 684.

32. P. Coleno, Ingénieur des travaux agricoles, Rapport sur la culture sèche du cotonnière du Soudan, n.p., 31 Jan. 1935, ANM 1 R 319.

33. Ingénieur en chef des travaux d'agriculture aux colonies Charles Godard, Service de l'agriculture, Rapport annuel, campagne 1936–37, 25 May 1937, ANS-AOF 2 G 37-53. A duplicate of the report appears in ANF-DOM Agence FOM 149-133.

34. Service de l'agriculture, Rapport annuel, campagne 1937–38, Soudan, ANS-AOF 2 G 38-53.

35. Service de l'agriculture, Rapport annuel de l'agriculture, [campagne 1938–39], Bamako, 10 June 1939, ANS-AOF 2 G 39-60.

36. Vernay, Le problème de l'exportation du coton du Soudan français, 1938–40 [dated 1939], ANM 1 Q 684.

37. Lt gov. Desanti, telegram to all cercles, 9 Nov. 1938, ANM 1 R 709.

38. Rapport économique annuel, Soudan, 1936, ANS-AOF 2 G 36-6.

39. See van Beusekom, "Colonial Economic Development," pp. 54–60.

40. Rapport économique pour l'année 1939, Soudan, ANS-AOF 2 G 39-37.

41. Other committees established during this period included the Comité colonial de la production agricole, see Rapport économique annuel, Soudan, 1941, ANS-AOF 2 G 41-28.

42. Rapport économique pour l'année 1939, Soudan, ANS-AOF 2 G 39-37.

43. Le chef du Service de l'agriculture, Rapport annuel, campagne 1940–41, Bamako 3 June 1940, ANS-AOF 2 G 41-39; Rapport économique annuel, Soudan, 1941, ANS-AOF 2 G 41-28; Pierre Viguier, Chef p.i. du Service de l'agriculture, Rapport annuel du Service de l'agriculture, campagne 1941–42, Kouluba, 14 June 1943, ANS-AOF 2 G 42-35.

44. Gov-gen. Boisson, letter to Ministry of Colonies, Direction des affaires économiques, Dakar, 24 Nov. 1939, ANF-DOM Aff écon 223.

45. Gov-gen. Boisson, letter to Secrétaire d'Etat aux colonies, Dakar, 13 Feb. 1942, ANF-DOM Aff écon 224; Rapport économique annuel, Soudan, 1941, ANS-AOF 2 G 41-28.

46. Union cotonnière de l'empire française, Conseil de l'administration, Paris, 18 Apr. 1942 and 25 Sept. 1942, ANF-DOM Aff écon 224.

47. Lt gov. p.i., Rapport politique annuel, Soudan, 1940, Kouluba, 19 Apr. 1941, ANS-AOF 2 G 40-10.

48. Pierre Viguier, Chef p.i. du Service de l'agriculture, Rapport annuel du Service de l'agriculture, campagne 1941–42, Kouluba, 14 June 1943, ANS-AOF 2 G 42-35.

49. Inspecteur des Affaires administratives Marchand, Rapport politique annuel, Soudan, 1942, Kouluba, 19 July 1943, ANS-AOF 2 G 42-3.

50. Pierre Viguier, Chef p.i. du Service de l'agriculture, Rapport, Bamako, 14 June 1943, ANS-AOF 2 G 43-47.

51. Rapport économique, 3d Quarter 1933, San, ANM 1 Q 359; Rapport économique, 3d Quarter 1933, Bamako, ANM 1 Q 330.

52. Rapport économique, 1st Quarter 1933, Bamako, ANM 1 Q 330.

53. Rapport économique annuel, 1934, Soudan, ANM 1 Q 1075.

54. Rapport économique, 1st Quarter 1936, Sikasso, ANM 1 Q 360.

55. Rapport économique, 1st Quarter 1936, San, ANM 1 Q 359.

56. Interview with Dahou Traore, Sibila, 21 Jan. 1984.

57. Commandant Bouguni, telegram to governor Soudan, Dionsi, 15 Feb. 1934, ANM 1 R 312; Rapport économique, 4th Quarter 1936, Bouguni, and Rapport économique annuel, 1938, Bouguni, ANM 1 Q 332; Lt gov. Louveau, Rapport économique annuel, 1943, Soudan, Kouluba, 30 Sept. 1944, ANS-AOF 2 G 43-30. Not all of this commerce was conducted by African traders. European merchant houses were also actively involved. In 1945, for example, La Coste et compagnie of Saint Louis bought 2,000 woolen blankets in the Soudan for export to Senegal. European commerce continued to look toward the African continental market for at least a part of its profits (Lt gov., letter and authorization to La Coste, n.p., 11 May and 12 May 1945, ANM 1 Q 241).

58. By 1936, the customs bureau had begun to specify more precisely the varieties of cloth imported. Instead of the three categories used before 1935, eight categories were used after 1936. Yarn and guinée remained separate categories, but cloth now consisted of *tissus coton écrus, tissus coton blan-*

chis, *tissus teintes autres de guinée, tissus imprimés et fabriqués, tissus fa-çonnés, autres.* For the purposes of equivalences, I have lumped these European cloth varieties together.

59. Bulletin économique, 1st Quarter 1932, Soudan, ANS-AOF 2 G 33-140; Rapport économique annuel, 1935, Soudan, ANS-AOF 2 G 35-37.

60. Gov-gen., letter to Minister of Colonies, Dakar, 13 Nov. 1939, ANF-DOM Aff écon 223.

61. Lt gov. Louveau, Annex au rapport annuel sur l'emploi de la main d'oeuvre au Soudan pendant l'année 1942, Kouluba, 16 July 1943, ANS-AOF 2 G 42-23.

62. Interview with Warike Jara, Koulikoro, 29 Jan. 1984.

63. Rapport économique, année 1942, Soudan, ANS-AOF 2 G 42-25.

64. Interview with Cebarama Dembele, Banankoro, 22 Jan. 1984.

65. Chef du Bureau des affaires économiques, note to lt gov., Kouluba, 6 Apr. 1945, ANM 1 Q 241. On postwar scarcity, see Direction des services économiques, Rapport économique pour l'année 1948, Soudan, ANF-DOM Agence FOM 150.

66. P. Coleno, Ingénieur des travaux agricoles, Rapport sur la culture sèche du cotonnier du Soudan, n.p., 31 Jan. 1935, ANM 1 R 319; Service de l'agriculture, Rapport annuel, campagne 1937–38, Soudan, ANS-AOF 2 G 38-53.

67. Service de l'agriculture, Rapport annuel, campagne 1937–38, Soudan, ANS-AOF 2 G 38-53.

68. Rapport économique, année 1942, Soudan, ANS-AOF 2 G 42-25. For a similar assessment, see lt gov. p.i., Plan de production par cercles des principaux produits, Kouluba, 21 Apr. 1942, ANS 1 R 56.

69. Interview with Hadja Toumata Contao, Segu, 23 Jan. 1984.

70. Interview with Kissima Makadji, Tenimbala, 19 July 1981.

71. Interview with Mokan Fofana, Banamba, 20 July 1981. See also the interview with Batene Kale, an elderly dyer from Segu, 31 July 1981.

72. See, for example, the interview I conducted with a female entrepreneur of dyed cloth, Fanta Ballo, Segu, 23 Jan. 1984. See also Polakoff, *Into Indigo*; Byfield, "Women, Economy, and the State."

73. Le Chef du Service de l'agriculture, Rapport annuel, campagne 1940–41, Bamako, ANS-AOF 2 G 41-39.

74. Interview with Hadja Toumata Contao, Segu, 23 Jan. 1984.

75. See esp. Grosz-Ngate, "Bambara Men and Women."

76. Rapport économique annuel, Koutiala, 1942, ANM 1 Q 346.

77. Rapport économique pour l'année 1939, Soudan, ANS-AOF 2 G 39-37; Vernay, Le problème de l'exportation du coton au Soudan français, 1938–40 [dated 1939], ANM 1 Q 684.

78. Louis Laprade, letter to Gov. Soudan, Marseille, 14 June 1941; Louis Colombier et Comp, letter to Gov. Soudan, Periguiaux, 18 July 1941; Lt. gov. Soudan, letter to Colombier, Kouluba, 6 Aug. 1941, ANM 1 Q 1909.

79. Rapport économique annuel, 1943, Soudan, ANS-AOF 2 G 43-30.

80. Lt gov. Louveau, Rapport économique annuel, Soudan, Kouluba, 1943, 30 Sept. 1944, ANS-AOF 2 G 43-30.

81. Rapport agricole de la campagne 1944–45, Soudan français, ANS-AOF 2 G 44-57.

82. Chef, Service de l'agriculture, Rapport annuel du Service de l'agriculture, année 1945, Bamako, 11 May 1946, ANS-AOF 2 G 45-33.

83. Lt gov. Louveau, Direction locale des services économiques, Rapport annuel, Soudan, 1949, ANS-AOF 2 G 49-26.

84. Ibid.

85. For an early discussion of CFDT, see A. Renard, Ingénieur principal de 1ière classe, Chef du Service de l'agriculture, Rapport annuel, Soudan, 1950, Bamako, 20 Aug. 1950, ANS-AOF 2 G 50-28. On CFDT's strategy to saturate the domestic industry see Torre, Direction générale des services economiques et du plan, letter to Ministry of France for Overseas, n.p., 14 Nov. 1955, ANM 1 R 1573. On the introduction of new seed varieties, especially Allen no. 49, derived from experiments in Chad, see Rapport économique, Soudan, année 1953, ANS-AOF 2 G 53-10. For more general discussion of CFDT, see Bassett, "Development of Cotton," and de Wilde, with the assistance of McLoughlin et al., *Experiences with Agricultural Development*, 2: 301–36.

86. Chef, Service de l'agriculture, Rapport annuel du Service de l'agriculture, année 1945, Soudan, ANS-AOF 2 G 45-33.

87. Lt gov. Louveau, Rapport annuel, Direction des services économiques, Soudan, 1948, ANS-AOF 2 G 48-54.

Conclusion

1. Lt gov. Louveau, Direction locale des services economiques, Rapport annuel, 1949, Soudan, ANS-AOF 2 G 49-26.

2. Ibid.

3. Lt gov. Louveau, Direction locale des services économiques, Rapport annuel, 1950, Soudan, ANS-AOF 2 G 50-37; see also Rapport économique, 1950, Services des affaires économiques, Soudan, ANF-DOM Aff écon 916. Louveau calculated on the following formula: five kilograms of seed cotton yielded one kilogram of cotton woven into bands. One kilogram of cotton bands equaled 18 meters. At 25 francs for each meter, cotton fetched 90 francs per kilogram. Of course, it is necessary to subtract what women received for carding and spinning and what weavers received for their work, thus reducing the market prices for cotton considerably. Nonetheless, the export price of even 25 francs per kilo would not be sufficiently attractive.

4. For comparative studies of cotton and colonialism in Africa, see Isaacman and Roberts, eds., *Cotton*.

5. Lansdale and Berman, "Coping with the Contradictions," pp. 470–91.

6. This encounter is examined from the perspective of metropolitan industry in Marseille, *l'Empire colonial*.

7. For example, Ferguson, *Anti-Politics Machine;* Klitgaard, *Tropical Gangsters*. For an example of how development refracts local struggles, see Moore, "Contesting Terrain."

8. Lt gov. Louveau, Direction locale des Services économiques, Rapport annuel, Soudan, 1949, ANS-AOF 2 G 49-26.

Bibliography

Archival Sources

Archives Nationales de France–Dépôt d'Outre-Mer Series

ANF-DOM Aff écon 64 bis. Marshal Pétain, Fondements d'une économie impériale, Vichy, 13 Dec. 1941; Sec. d'Etat à la Production industrielle, letter to Sec. d'Etat aux colonies, Paris, 7 July 1942.

ANF-DOM Aff écon 72-2. anon., Compagnie de culture cotonnière du Niger: historique et résultats obtenus, n.p., 20 July 1932.

ANF-DOM Aff écon 72-4. Inspecteur-général des colonies, Kair, Rapport sur la Concession cotonnière de Dire, Kouluba, 15 Jan. 1923; Bélime, Rapport sur la production cotonnière en Afrique occidentale française en 1925–26, Kouluba, 15 May 1926.

ANF-DOM Aff écon 73-11. Hirsch, letter to gov-gen. AOF, Paris, 2 Apr. 1921.

ANF-DOM Aff écon 73-13. Terrasson, letter to gov-gen., Bamako, 25 Mar. 1927.

ANF-DOM Aff écon 97-3. Inspecteur-général de 1ère classe des colonies Mérat, Affaires économiques: l'Association cotonnière coloniale, Dakar, 22 Feb. 1931; Direction des affaires économiques, Rapport, May 1926, cited in Mérat, Affaires économiques: l'Association cotonnière coloniale, 22 Feb. 1931; Gov-gen. Brévié, Note (attached to Mérat, Affaires économiques, 22 Feb. 1931), 28 Apr. 1932; notes by Colonel Vallée, Chef du secrétariat permanent de la Defense Nationale; Inspecteur Mérat; Bélime, directeur du Service des textiles; and Mondor, Directeur des Affaires économiques in Mérat, Des Affaires économiques: ACC, Dakar, 22 Feb. 1931.

ANF-DOM Aff écon 97-6. Inspecteur-général de 1ère classe des colonies Coste, Au sujet de la CICONNIC, Dakar, 7 May 1938.

ANF-DOM Aff écon 107 bis-2. Inspecteur de 2ième classe, Chastenet de Gery, Rapport concernant la ferme de Nienebale et les essais de colonisation au Soudan, Kouluba, 15 Mar. 1930; Duthoit, Chef du Bureau des affaires économiques du Soudan, 8 Apr. 1930, Kouluba, attached to Chastenet de Gery, Rapport, 15 Mar. 1930; Gov-gen. Carde, Note, attached to Chastenet de Gery, Rapport, 25 May 1930.

ANF-DOM Aff écon 107 bis-3. Inspecteur de 3ième classe des colonies Bargues, Rapport concernant la verification de M. Pinchon, Conducteur principal des travaux agricoles à Baraweli, Segu, 12 Feb. 1935; Inspecteur de 3ième classe des colonies, Bargues, Rapport sur les conditions d'exploitation, par la Compagnie de culture cotonnière du Niger, du Domaine de Dire, Dire, 22 Apr. 1935; Lt-gov. Eboué, note, 30 Apr. 1935, appended to Inspecteur de 3ième classe des colonies Bargues, Rapport concernant la verification de M. Pinchon, Conducteur principal des travaux agricoles à Baraweli, 12 Feb. 1935; Inspecteur de 1ère classe des colonies Bagot, Rapport sur le Service agronomique de l'Office du Niger, Paris, 4 July 1935; Inspecteur de 1ère classe des colonies Bagot, Rapport sur les essais de vulgarisation agricole en "terre sèche," Paris, 31 July 1935; Avenant no. 2 du 26 Mars 1926, cited in Bargues, Rapport, 22 Apr. 1935.

ANF-DOM Aff écon 167. Rapport de mission de M. Henri Carbou, Administrateur en Chef des colonies, Annexes 1-20, n.d. [1938]; Gov-gen. de Coppet, confidential letter to Minister of Colonies, n.d. [but arrived in Paris 9 June 1938]; Copy of a telegram, Chambre de Commerce de la Guinée, to gov-gen. included in a letter, gov-gen. to Minister of Colonies, Dakar, 18 July 1938; Collections of 1938–39 press clippings.

ANF-DOM Aff écon 223. Gov-gen., letter to Minister of Colonies, Dakar, 13 Nov. 1939; Gov-gen. Boisson, letter to Ministry of Colonies, Direction des affaires économiques, Dakar, 24 Nov. 1939; Organismes administratifs de nouvelle création intéressant la production cotonnière coloniale française, Vichy, 16 Jan. 1941; UCEF, Rapport, Paris, 17 Feb. 1942; Projet de contrat du coton, n.d. [but 1941]; Senn, letter to Direction des textiles et cuirs, Ministère de production industrielle et du travail, n.p., 27 Mar. 1941; Gov-gen. Boisson, letter to General Weygand, Dakar, 28 Apr. 1941.

ANF-DOM Aff écon 224. Gov-gen. Boisson, letter to Secrétaire d'Etat aux colonies, Dakar, 13 Feb. 1942; Union cotonnière de l'empire français, Conseil d'administration, Paris, 18 Apr. 1942 and 25 Sept. 1942.

ANF-DOM Aff écon 888. Gov-gen. Merlin, Rapport au Comité interministeriel des consortiums sur l'attribution à l'Afrique occidentale française d'une somme de 26 million francs, n.d. [ca. Nov. 1920]; Convention du Consortium cotonnier français avec le Ministère du Commerce, n.d.

ANF-DOM Aff écon 889. Bélime, Inspecteur du Service général des textiles, La campagne cotonnière (1924–25) en Afrique occidentale, 19 May 1925.

ANF-DOM Aff écon 889-1. Gov-gen. Angoulvant, letter to President ACC, Dakar, 4 Sept. 1918; M. Landry, Rapporteur du Budget des colonies, Projet du Budget, 1919; Waddington, Notes de voyage de M. Waddington au cours de sa mission en AOF, Déc. 1923 à fin de Fev. 1924, [Paris] n.d.; Minister of Colonies, letter to gov-gen., Paris, 24 Mar. 1924; Bélime, Inspecteur du

Service général des textiles, Compte-rendu de tournée, Kouluba, 10 May 1925.

ANF-DOM Aff écon 889-5. Office national français du coton, Projet de création d'un Office national du coton, Paris, [1925]; Ministers Daladier (Colonies), Clementel (Finance), and Raynaldy (Commerce and Industry) Projet de loi, portant de création des taxes spéciales destinées à subventionner l'ACC, n.d. [1926]; Projet de loi, portant la création des taxes spéciales destinées à subventionner l'Association cotonnière coloniale, présenté au nom de M. Gaston Doumergue, Président de la République Française, par Edouard Daladier, Ministre des Colonies, par M. Clementel, Ministre des Finances, et par M. Raynaldy, Ministre du Commerce et de l'Industrie, n.d. [1926].

ANF-DOM Aff écon 916. Rapport économique, 1950, Services des affaires économiques, Soudan.

ANF-DOM Aff écon 1223. Gov-gen. Boisson, letter to Direction des affaires économiques, Ministry of Colonies, Paris, 19 Nov. 1938.

ANF-DOM Aff pol 620-3. Voeu concernant l'Office du Niger, Chambre de Commerce, Dakar, 21 Mar. 1938; Sorel, Inspecteur Général du Service de santé des colonies, letter to gov-gen., Dakar, 30 Mar. 1938; Collections of 1938–39 press clippings.

ANF-DOM Aff pol 620-6. Voeu émis par la Chambre de Commerce du Dahomey dans sa séance du 19 Mai 1938; petition, Lasserre, Président de la Chambre de Commerce à M. le Gouverneur de la Côte d'Ivoire, n.p., 14 June 1938.

ANF-DOM Aff pol 620-9. Czenave, Commandant, Rapport sur le voyage effectué en Octobre 1937 sur les terres irriguées de l'Office du Niger, Bamako, 6 Nov. 1937; Toby, Commandant Nioro, Au sujet peuplement des terres irriguées, Nioro, 18 Dec. 1937; André Morel, Commandant Koutiala, Rapport, Koutiala, 27 Dec. 1937; Lt gov. Rougier, letter to gov-gen., Kouluba, 10 Jan. 1938.

ANF-DOM Aff pol 2808. Bélime, letter to gov-gen. AOF, Paris, 9 July 1937.

ANF-DOM Agence FOM (Agence des colonies) 13. Colonel F. Bernard, untitled report, n.p., 10 Apr. 1922; Gov-gen. Carde, letter to Minister of Colonies, Paris, 3 May 1927.

ANF-DOM Agence FOM 149-133. Lt gov. Rougier, Note, appended to Charles Godard, Chef du Service de l'agriculture, Rapport annuel du Service de l'agriculture, campagne 1936–37, Soudan, n.d.; Charles Godard, Service de l'agriculture, Rapport annuel, campagne, 1936–37, 25 May 1937.

ANF-DOM Agence FOM 150. Direction des services économiques, Rapport économique pour l'année 1948, Soudan.

ANF-DOM Comité français pour l'Outre-mer 31. Comments sur l'avant-projet d'un rapport sur "Les questions coloniales d'après-guerre en Afrique occidentale française," drafted by Pierre Pégard, President, Union coloniale française, Section de l'Afrique occidentale, 1916.

ANF-DOM CFOM 41. Yves Henry, "Comment la France peut se procurer le coton dont elle a besoin," Rapport présenté au Congrès d'agriculture coloniale, May 1918.

ANF-DOM CFOM 206. Discours prononcé par M. J. Brevié, gouverneur-général de l'AOF à l'ouverture de la session du Conseil de gouvernement, Dec. 1931.

ANF-DOM CFOM 309. Procès-verbal, Comité d'action agricole coloniale, Paris, 5 Mar. 1924.

ANF-DOM CFOM 344. Henri Bondoit, "Le problème du coton colonial au point de vue textile français," Rapport présenté au nom de l'Association des anciens élèves de filature et de tissage de Mulhouse, Congrès d'Agriculture coloniale, May 1918; M. Etesse, "Le coton des terres sèches en Afrique occidentale," paper presented to the Secrétaire-général, Union coloniale française, Paris, 28 Dec. 1923; Angoulvant, Gouverneur-général honoraire des colonies, "Nos colonies de l'Afrique occidentale française peuvent ravitailler largement en coton notre industrie textile, mais il faut une politique d'action," n.d. [1924].

ANF-DOM CFOM 467. Etesse, Rapport au sujet de la convention Hirsch, irrigation de la vallée du Sénégal, Saint Louis, 13 Dec. 1918.

ANF-DOM CFOM 514. Lt. gov. Soudan, telegram to Union coloniale française, Kouluba, 20 Jan. 1915.

ANF-DOM CFOM 519. J. Barois, Inspecteur-général des ponts et chaussées, en retraite, L'irrigation de la vallée du Niger, n.d., n.p. [1922–23].

ANF-DOM CFOM 529. Procès-verbal, Comité d'action agricole, Union coloniale française, n.p. [Paris], 4 July 1919.

ANF-DOM Défense Nationale, Utilisation des produits coloniaux 10. Gov-gen., letter to Minister of Colonies, Paris, 24 May 1917; Procès-verbal, Comité commercial de l'AOF, séance du 12 Juin 1917; Maginot, Minister of Colonies, letter to gov-gen. AOF, Paris, 23 July 1917.

ANF-DOM Sénégal I 48a. Minister of Colonies, Instructions générales to Gov. Jauréguibéry, Paris, 17 Dec. 1861.

ANF-DOM Sénégal I 48b. Gov. Jauréguibéry, letter to Minister of Marine and Colonies, Saint Louis, 22 Aug. 1862.

ANF-DOM Sénégal I 51a. Gov. Pinet-Laparde, Exposé général de la situation de la colonie, des causes qui ont influé sur cette situation et des améliorations qu'elle reclame, Saint Louis, 25 Sept. 1866.

ANF-DOM Sénégal et Dépendances XIII 18. Schmaltz, Développement sur le projet de colonisation dans les Etablissements français d'Afrique, Paris, 19 Mar. 1818.

ANF-DOM Sénégal et Dépendances XIII 19c. L'état Major Hesse, Rapport sur les cultures du Sénégal, Paris, 15 Jan. 1824.

ANF-DOM Sénégal et Dépendances XIII 22. Berton, letter to Gov. Senegal, Richard-Toll, 13 Jan. 1829.

ANF-DOM Sénégal et Dépendances XIII 34a. Gov. Schmaltz, letter to Cunca, Roi de Galam et Sombra Congol Batcheri et autres principaux du Royaume de Galam, Saint Louis, 10 Feb. 1817; Gov. Schmaltz, letter to Baron Portal, Minister of Colonies, [Saint Louis], 1 May 1817; [Cotton courtier], letter to Baron Portal, Rouen, 28 Aug. 1817; Thomas Valentin, Capitaine de navire commandant le Brig-goelette La Petite Famille du Havre, Declaration, Le Havre, 6 Aug. 1818; Commissaire de la Marine, letter to Ministre Secrétaire d'Etat de la marine et des colonies, Nantes, 24 Aug. 1819.

ANF-DOM Sénégal et Dépendances XIII 34b. Commissaire de la Marine, letter to Ministre Secrétaire d'Etat de la marine et des colonies, Nantes, 19 Dec. 1820.

ANF-DOM Sénégal et Dépendances XIII 35. Letter to Ministre Secrétaire d'Etat de la Maison du Roi, Paris, 11 June 1822; Vice Consul de France, letter to Ministre de marine et des colonies, Savannah, 10 Sept. 1823.

ANF-DOM Sénégal et Dépendances XIII 35a. Chef de Bataillon du Génie, Rapport sur deux modèles de machines à égrener le coton, Saint Louis, 8 Aug. 1822; Ministre de la marine et des colonies, letter to M. de Villaret Joyeuse, Capitaine de Vaisseau, Paris, Apr. 1823.

ANF-DOM Sénégal et Dépendances XIII 35b. Le Commissaire général, ordonnateur de la marine, letter to Ministre de la marine et des colonies, Rochfort, 12 Jan. 1826.

ANF-DOM Sénégal et Dépendances XIII 36a. Gov. Faidherbe, letter to Ministre de la marine et des colonies, Saint Louis, 14 June 1860; Gov. Pinet-Laparde, letter to Ministre de la marine et des colonies, Gorée, 21 Oct. 1860; Certificat de reception, envoi du Consul de France de Nouvelle Orleans, Port du Havre, Jan. 1861; Gustave Begouen, Charles Gallois, S. Meunier, courtiers à Le Havre, Renseignements ont été fournis à la Chambre de Commerce, Le Havre, 15 Jan. 1861; Commandant Pinet-Laparde, Note sur le Dionden et le Pays de Sérés Nones annexes à nos possessions de la Presqu'île du Cap Vert, Gorée, 8 May 1861.

ANF-DOM Sénégal et Dépendances XIII 36b. Directeur des Colonies, 2ième Bureau, Rapport au Ministre de la marine et des colonies, Paris, Aug. 1861; Le Gérant du Consulat, letter to Ministre de la marine et des colonies, Edinburgh, 18 Oct. 1861; M. Préfet de la Seine-Intérieure, Note, n.p., 25 Nov. 1861 [A longer version appears in letter to Ministre de l'agriculture, commerce, et travaux publics, Paris, 2 Dec. 1861, ANF-DOM Sénégal et Dépendances XIII 38].

ANF-DOM Sénégal et Dépendances XIII 37a. Agence et Consulat Général de France en Egypte, letter to Minister of Marine and Colonies, Alexandria, 18 Nov. 1862; Anon., Du commerce et de la culture du coton au Sénégal et dans ses Dépendances, n.p., n.d. [probably 1863]; Clippings file; Louis Drouet fils, letter to Fritz Koechlin, Gorée, 29 Mar. 1863; Fritz Koechlin, letter to Louis Drouet, Mulhouse, 23 Apr. 1863; Vice Consul, letter to Minister of Marine and Colonies, Liverpool, 14 May 1863.

ANF-DOM Sénégal et Dépendances XIII 39a. Le Commissaire général de la marine, letter, Bordeaux, 31 July 1824.

344   Bibliography

ANF-DOM Senegal I 51c. Pinet-Laparde, Exposé général sur la situation de la colonie, des causes qui ont influé sur cette situation et des améliorations qu'elle reclame, Saint Louis, 1 Sept. 1865.

ANF-DOM Sénégal et Dépendances XV 13. Monsignor Kobès, letter to Minister of Colonies, Paris, 27 Oct. 1862.

ANF-DOM Sénégal et Dépendances XV 14. H. V. Dupuis, Rapport fait le 21 Jan. 1866 par le President de la Compagnie Agricole de la Presqu'île du Cap Vert à l'Assemble générale des actionnaires, Gorée, 21 Jan. 1866; Dossier Herzog; Fritz Koechlin, letter to Minister of Marine and Colonies, Mulhouse, 30 Nov. 1867.

ANF-DOM Soudan I ii bis. William Ponty, Note sur la Colonie du Haut-Sénégal-Niger, Paris, 25 June 1905.

ANF-DOM Soudan XIII 1 a. P. Georges Mias, letter to Colonel [Commandant Supérieur], Kayes, 6 Apr. 1893.

ANF-DOM Soudan XIII 13. Rapport commercial, agricole et industriel sur le Soudan français, 1898.

ANF-DOM Union coloniale française 467. Governor du Haut-Sénégal-Niger, letter to Gov-gen., Bamako, 12 Aug. 1918; Etesse, Rapport au sujet de la convention Hirsch, irrigation de la vallée du Sénégal, Saint Louis, 13 Dec. 1918.

ANF-DOM UCF 514. Président-directeur de Pozzo di Borgo, letter to Président UCF, Marseille, 2 Apr. 1924; Président de l'Industrie cotonnière française, letter to Président UCF, Paris, 24 Mar. 1924; Président UCF, letter to M. Vézia, Président du Syndicat de Défense des intérêts sénégalais, Paris, 28 Jan. 1928.

Archives Nationales, République du Mali (ANM Series)

ANM B 74. Lt gov. to Commandant Bamako, Kayes, 19 Sept. 1899; Lt gov., letter to Commandant du Région Niger (Bamako), 18 Nov. 1899.

ANM B 77. Lt gov. Trentinian to commandants des cercles de Kayes, Kati, Bamako, Segu, Sumpi, Goundam, Jenne, San, Bandiagara, and the Faama de Sansanding, Kayes, 21 Dec. 1898; Lt gov. Trentinian to Commandant, Cercle of Bamako, Kouluba, 11 Aug. 1899.

ANM 1 D 38#3. Monographie du cercle de Jenne, 20 Nov. 1909.

ANM 1 E 18. Bulletin politique, Bamako, Mar. 1899.

ANM 1 E 67. Rapports politiques, San.

ANM 1 E 72. Rapport annuel sur la politique, Segu, 1909.

ANM 1 E 77. Rapport général sur la politique du cercle pendant l'année 1905.

ANM 1 Q 18. Robert Boussac, agent général de Comptoirs de l'industrie cotonnière, letter to lt gov. Soudan, 9 Jan. 1926, Bouguni; Commandant Aubin, letter to lt gov., Segu, 28 Feb. 1927; Lt gov. Terrasson, circulaire aux M. les commerçants, Kouluba, n.d. [around 28 Feb. 1927]; Administrator Sikasso, letter to lt gov. Soudan, Sikasso, 28 Mar. 1927; Duranthon, administrator Sikasso, letter to lt gov. Soudan, Sikasso, 28 Mar. 1927.

ANM 1 Q 40. Rapport d'ensemble sur la situation économique de la colonie du Haut-Sénégal-Niger, 1915.

ANM 1 Q 44. Rapports commerciaux, Bamako.

ANM 1 Q 47. Rapports commerciaux, Bouguni.

ANM 1 Q 83. Rapports commerciaux, Segu.

ANM 1 Q 113. Rapport sur l'ACC, campagne 1912–13, Koutiala, 12 May 1913.

ANM 1 Q 115. Terrasson, letter to gov-gen., Bamako, 29 May 1930.

ANM 1 Q 241. Chef du Bureau des affaires économiques, note to lt gov., Kouluba, 6 Apr. 1945; Lt gov., letter and authorization to La Coste, n.p., 11 May and 12 May 1945.

ANM 1 Q 330. Rapports économiques, Bamako and Kolokani subdivisions; Commandant Bamako, Rapport de tournée administrative du chef de la subdivision, [Bamako], n.d. [July 1927]; Administrator Dioila, telegram to lt gov., Oct. 1935.

ANM 1 Q 332. Rapports économiques, Bouguni.

ANM 1 Q 346. Rapport économique annuel, Koutiala, 1942.

ANM 1 Q 358. Rapport de fin d'année sur le commerce, Segu, 4th Quarter 1929.

ANM 1 Q 359. Rapports économiques, San.

ANM 1 Q 360. Rapport économique, Sikasso, 1st Quarter 1936.

ANM 1 Q 684. Lt gov. Desanti, circulaire to commandants Bouguni, Koutiala, Mopti, Nema, Ouahigouya, Sikasso, San, Segu, Tougan, Bamako, Kita, Kayes, and Nioro, 1939; Vernay, Le problème de l'exportation du coton du Soudan Français, 1938–40, [dated 1939]; Lt gov. Desanti, telegram to commandants Bamako, Koutiala, Tougan, Ouahigouya, San, Bouguni, Sikasso, Kita, Kayes, Nioro, 13 Dec. 1940.

ANM 1 Q 704. Lt gov. Rougier, letter to Commandant of Bouguni, Kouluba, 13 May 1937.

ANM 1 Q 705. Rapport économique, Bouguni, 1st Quarter 1937. Commandant Bamako, telegram to lt gov. Soudan, Bamako, 5 May 1937; Rapport sur la culture du coton dans le cercle de Bamako, n.d. [probably May 1937].

ANM 1 Q 1075. Rapport économique annuel, 1934, Soudan.

ANM 1 Q 1909. Louis Laprade, letter to lt gov. Soudan, Marseille, 14 June 1941; Louis Colombier et Comp, letter to lt gov. Soudan, Periguiaux, 18 July 1941; Lt gov. Soudan, letter to Colombier, Kouluba, 6 Aug. 1941.

ANM 2 Q 4. Terrasson, telegrams 3976 and 3978 to administrator Bouke and agent ACC at Segu, Kouluba, 4 July 1925; Commandant Bouguni, letter to lt gov. Soudan, Bouguni, 27 May 1926.

ANM 2 Q 6. Representative SAA, letter to lt gov. Soudan, [Kenenkou], 2 Feb. 1924; Terrasson, telegram to commandant Segu, Kouluba, 13 Feb. 1924; Terrasson, letter to representative of SAA at Kenenkou, Kouluba, 8 Apr. 1924; Primel, letter to gov-gen., Kenenkou, 19 May 1924; Battesti, telegram to lt gov. Soudan, Segu, 7 Aug. 1924; Primel, letter to lt gov. Soudan,

Kenenkou, 4 Nov. 1924; Terrasson, note attached to Primel, letter to lt gov. Soudan, Kenenkou, 11 Feb. 1927; Terrasson, letter to Director, SAA, Kouluba, 3 June 1925; Battesti, telegram to lt gov. Soudan, Segu, 2 Jan. 1926; Dr. Galland, Rapport médico-légal, n.p., 6 Jan. 1926; Battesti, letter to lt gov., Segu, 7 Jan. 1926; Primel, letter to administrator Segu, Kenenkou, 27 Jan. 1926; Terrasson, letter to director SAA, Kouluba, 30 Jan. 1926; Administrator Koutiala, letter to lt gov. Soudan, Koutiala, 20 Apr. 1926; Terrasson, letters to directors of SAA, Kouluba, 18 Nov. 1927 and 16 Apr. 1928; Agent SAA, letter to lt gov. Soudan, Kenenkou, 20 Apr. 1928.

ANM R 79. J. Vuillet, letter, Koulikoro, 18 Dec. 1904; Inspecteur-général Y. Henry, Essais cotonniers en 1905, n.p., 26 May 1905; Gov-gen. Ponty, letter to lt gov. Haut-Sénégal-Niger, Dakar, 11 Oct. 1913.

ANM 1 R 31. Rapport commercial et agricole, n.p., 1891; Captain Didio, letter to lt gov., Haut-Sénégal-Niger, Bamako, 20 Jan. 1899; Captain Charnet, Rapport commercial et agricole, Bamako, 2d Quarter 1899.

ANM 1 R 79. Esnault-Pelterie, President de l'ACC, letter to Gov-gen. Roume, Paris, 2 Apr. 1904; Vuillet, Régions cotonnières du Soudan, 18 Aug. 1904.

ANM 1 R 81. Captain Charnet, letter to lt gov., Haut-Sénégal-Niger, Bamako, 18 Aug. 1899; Captain Kibes, letter [to lt gov.], Bamako, 19 Apr. 1897; Vuillet, letter to gov-gen., Koulikoro, 10 Mar. 1902; Vuillet, Rapport, Koulikoro, 13 Oct. 1904; ACC representative, letter to lt gov., Haut-Sénégal-Niger, Bamako, 17 May 1905.

ANM 1 R 95. Commandant adjoint, Segu, Notice accompagnie 400kg coton destiné à un essai d'égrenage, Segu, 20 Dec. 1903.

ANM 1 R 113. Colliaux, Rapport sur le coton, Koutiala, 25 Mar. 1910.

ANM 1 R 116. Note sur le coton, Segu, 28 Apr. 1897, Segu; Rapport sur l'égrenage du coton recolté, Segu, 1906.

ANM 1 R 118. Note sur l'Association cotonnière, n.d., [file 1901–6]; ACC, Rapport sur la campagne 1906; Esnault-Pelterie, letter to lt gov. [H-S-N], Paris, 23 Nov. 1907; Rapport sur l'emploie des subventions accordées par le Département à l'ACC, n.d., [1909 file]; Gov-gen., letter to lt gov., Dakar, 28 Dec. 1909; President, ACC letter to William Ponty, gov-gen. AOF, Paris, 17 Feb. 1910; Gov-gen. Clozel, circulaire to lt govs., Dakar, 12 Dec. 1912; Carrié and Dabrigeon, letter to gov-gen. Bamako, 4 Dec. 1912; Rapport sur l'emploie des subventions accordées à l'ACC, [n.d., probably 1912]; Level, agent de l'ACC, Avant projet des travaux à 1912, n.d.; Gov-gen. Ponty, letter to Ministre des colonies, Dakar, 27 Feb. 1913; Rocaché, administrator Segu, letter to lt gov., Haut-Sénégal-Niger, Segu, 30 May 1913; Gov-gen. Ponty, telegram to [lt gov.] French Soudan, n.p., 15 Dec. 1913; Rapport sur l'Association cotonnière coloniale campagne 1912–13, file 1913; Rapport sur l'ACC campagne 1912–13, file 1913; Chef du Service d'agriculture, letter, Kouluba, 16 Apr. 1918; Gov-gen., letter to lt gov., Haut-Sénégal-Niger, Dakar, 6 Sept. 1918.

ANM 1 R 300. Conseil du Gouvernement, Office de la production et du credit, Soudan, Dec. 1930.

ANM 1 R 301. Rapport sur le coton americain, Bamako, 1899.

ANM 1 R 303. Terrasson, télégramme aux cercles Bamako, Kayes, Bouguni, Mopti, San, Koutiala, Sikasso, Bafoulabe, Kita, Nioro, Segu, Kouluba, 7 May 1925; President, Chambre de Commerce de Bamako, letter to lt gov., Soudan, Bamako, 20 May 1925.

ANM 1 R 304. Commandant Aubin, letter to lt gov., Segu, 18 Feb. 1927; E. Barthaburu, Note sur l'organisation de l'egrenage du coton Allen dans le région de Segou, Segu, 14 Apr. 1931.

ANM 1 R 305. Acting lt gov. Terrasson, letter to de Loppinot, Kouluba, 16 June 1920. A copy of this letter also appears in ANS-AOF 1 R 18; Ministre des colonies, circular 18 Mar. 1923 to gov-gen., cited in Lt gov. Fousset, Rapport sur le coton et l'Association cotonnière coloniale, 5 Jan. 1932, Kouluba; Administrator Koutiala, letter to lt gov. Soudan, Koutiala, 18 Oct. 1923; Terrasson, letter to agent ACC at Segu, Kouluba, 24 Feb. 1925; Terrasson, note to Directeur des affaires économiques, Kouluba, 13 Nov. 1925; Terrasson, letter to Directeur des affaires économiques, Kouluba, 13 Apr. 1926; Terrasson, Rapport à Direction des affaires économiques, Kouluba, 13 Apr. 1928; Receiver of Registers, letter to lt gov. Soudan, [Kouluba], 27 Jan. 1931; Lt gov. de Fousset, Rapport sur le coton et l'ACC, Kouluba, 5 Jan. 1932.

ANM 1 R 306. Terrasson, letter to M. Président, Chambre de Commerce de Bamako, Kouluba, 29 Dec. 1927; Acheteurs de Segou, telegram to lt gov. Soudan, [Segu], 3 Mar. 1928; Colomb, commandant Bouguni, telegram to Terrasson, Bouguni, 31 Mar. 1928, and annotation by Terrasson, n.d.; Terrasson, telegram to administrator Sikasso, Kouluba, 5 Apr. 1928; Inspecteur des Affaires administratives, letter to lt gov. Soudan, Kouluba, 1 May 1928.

ANM 1 R 309. Lt gov. de Fousset, letter to Director, ACC, Kouluba, 1 June 1934.

ANM 1 R 312. Commandant Bouguni, telegram to governor Soudan, Dionsi, 15 Feb. 1934.

ANM 1 R 315. Administrator Leccia, Rapport sur la traite du coton, campagne 1935–36, Koutiala, 16 Apr. 1936.

ANM 1 R 319. P. Coleno, Ingénieur des travaux agricoles, Rapport sur la culture sèche du cotonnier au Soudan, n.p., 31 Jan. 1935.

ANM 1 R 321. Conseil des Notables de Sikasso, procès verbal de la réunion du 16 Mai 1936, [Sikasso].

ANM 1 R 359. Rapport économique annuel, San, [1938], 5 Apr. 1939.

ANM 1 R 709. Lt gov. Desanti, telegram to commandants Bouguni, Sikasso, Koutiala, Segu, San, Tougan, Ouahigouya, 24 Dec. 1938; lt gov. Desanti, telegram to all cercles, 9 Nov. 1938.

ANM 1 R 1573. Torre, Direction générale des services économiques et du plan, letter to Ministry of France for Overseas, n.p., 14 Nov. 1955.

Archives Nationales, République du Sénégal (ANS) Series

ANS R 1. Msg Kobès, Aperçu des faits observés relatifs à la culture du coton dans la colonie agricole de Saint Joseph pendant les années 1863–64, Saint Joseph, 4 Apr. 1864; Notes de M. Brunil, n.p., Aug. 1864.

ANS 1 R 18. Gov-gen. Ponty, letter to Ministre des Colonies, Dakar, 14 May 1914; J. Rocache, Inspecteur des affaires administratives, Rapport au lieutenant-gouverneur du Soudan, Kouluba, 10 Nov. 1922 (a copy of the report can be found in ANF-DOM Aff écon 888); Procès-verbal, Chambre de Commerce, Kayes, 22 Dec. 1923.

ANS 1 R 35. Colliaux, Rapport sur le coton, Koutiala, 25 Mar. 1910; E. Bélime, "Où est le problème," n.p., 1921.

ANS 1 R 48. Président de la Chambre d'agriculture de Pondichéry, letter to gov. des Etablissements français dans l'Inde, Pondichéry, 29 Apr. 1929.

ANS 1 R 56. Affaires économiques [AOF], Compte rendu de la situation agricole pour 1926, Dakar [1927]; Rapport d'ensemble d'AOF, Agriculture, forêts, élevage, 1933; Gov-gen. letter to lt gov des colonies du groupe, Dakar, 1942; Acting lt gov., Plan de production par cercles des principaux produits, Kouluba, 21 Apr. 1942.

ANS 1 R 65. Président, Ligue coloniale française, letter to Gov-gen. Van Vollenhoven, Le Havre, 4 July 1917.

ANS 1 R 73. Administrateur des Colonies, Contrôleur de la Société civile d'études et de colonisation Dongier, Rapport sur l'expérience de colonisation mixte de Dire, campagne 1930–31, n.p., n.d.; Société civile d'études et de colonisation, Rapport sur l'étude du cotonnier égyptien et de la colonisation dans la zone lacustre de la Vallée Moyenne du Niger, exécution du contrat d'études du 4 Février 1932; Directeur des Services économiques (AOF), Note au sujet de la Compagnie de culture cotonnière du Niger, Dakar, 18 Aug. 1932; Gov-gen. De Coppet, letter to Minister of Colonies, Dakar, 22 Apr. 1938; Direction générale des services économiques (AOF), Note sur la Compagnie de culture cotonnière du Niger et sur la question de Dire, n.p., Aug. 1939.

ANS 1 R 100. Direction des affaires économiques, Renseignements sur la culture du coton en AOF pendant l'année 1929, n.d., n.p.; R. H. Forbes, Situation de la culture cotonnière en AOF, n.d. [probably 1931]; Barthaburu, Chef du Service agronomique des régions tropicales, Notice sur la culture du coton Allen, Segu, 22 June 1931.

ANS 1 R 102. Gov-gen. Carde, Notice des instructions aux lt govs. Soudan, Haute Volta, Côte d'Ivoire, Dakar, n.d. [1924]; General A. Messimy, Rapport fait, au nom de la Commission des colonies, après l'examen, auquel a procédé la Commission des conditions dans lesquelles la France peut se ravitailler en coton dans ses colonies, n.d. [1924]; Bélime, Note relative à l'établissement d'une taxe d'exportation sur les cotons ouest-africains, n.p., Mar. 1924; Inspecteur du Service général des textiles, Bélime, La campagne cotonnière 1924–25 en Afrique occidentale, Compte rendu de tournée, Kouluba, 10 May 1925; Arrêté 1477, règlement le conditionnement du coton au Soudan français, Kouluba, 9 Oct. 1925; lt gov. Soudan, to gov-gen., Production du coton en 1925–26, Kouluba, 24 Sept. 1926; Acting lt gov. [Descemet], Soudan, Production du coton en 1925–26, Kouluba, 24 Sept. 1926; Gov-gen. Carde, letter to Direction des affaires économiques, n.p., 15 Apr. 1927; Schlumberger, La production du coton en AOF, n.p., 1927; Hesling, gouverneur honoraire, directeur de l'ACC, Ministre des Colonies, Développement des méthodes et des services de technique agri-cole aux colonies en vue de l'intensification la production, n.p., 15 Apr. 1928; Hesling (former gov. and director of the ACC), Rapport de mission en AOF, Dec. 1928–Mar. 1929, Paris, 15 Apr. 1929.

ANS 1 R 131. De Coninck, Considérations générales sur les cotons colon-iaux, n.p., n.d. [probably 1938].

Archives Nationales, République du Sénégal, Government-General AOF Series

ANS-AOF 1 G 199. Binger, letter, Kong, 10 Mar. 1888.

ANS-AOF 1 G 320. Jacquey, agent de l'ACC, Notice sur le cercle de Segu, 1904.

ANS-AOF 2 G 8-2. Vuillet, Rapport agricole, Haut-Sénégal-Niger, 1st Quar-ter 1908.

ANS-AOF 2G 11-30. Rapport agricole, Haut-Sénégal-Niger, 2d Quarter 1911.

ANS-AOF 2 G 13-11. Rapport sur la situation économique pendant l'année 1913, Haut Sénégal-Niger.

ANS-AOF 2 G 15-19. Note sur la situation économique de l'AOF en 1915 comparée à celle de l'année précédente.

ANS-AOF 2 G 21-3. Costes, Rapport annuel du Service de l'agriculture du Soudan français, Koulikoro, 2 Mar. 1922.

ANS-AOF 2 G 21-22. E. Barthaburu, Note sur l'organisation de l'égrenage du coton; M. Costes, Ingénieur des Services agricoles, Rapport annuel du Ser-vice de l'agriculture du Soudan français, Koulikoro, 2 Mar. 1922.

ANS-AOF 2 G 22-3. Rapport sur la situation général du Soudan français, situ-ation économique, Jan. 1922; Rapport sur la situation général du Soudan français, situation économique, Mar. 1922.

ANS-AOF 2 G 23-5. Rapport sur la situation générale du Soudan français, situation économique, Apr. 1923; Rapport sur la situation générale du Soudan français, situation économique, June 1923; Notice mensuelle sur l'état des cultures et des récoltes, de l'élevage et des épizooties, Soudan, Dec. 1924.

ANS-AOF 2 G 24-6. Notice mensuelle pour l'Agence économique de l'AOF, Soudan, Apr. 1924.

ANS-AOF 2 G 25-4. Notice mensuelle pour l'Agence économique de l'AOF, Soudan, Feb. 1925; Notice mensuelle pour l'Agence économique de l'AOF, Soudan, Mar. 1925; Notice mensuelle pour l'Agence économique de l'AOF, Soudan, Apr. 1925; Notice mensuelle pour l'Agence économique

de l'AOF, Soudan, May 1925; Notice mensuelle pour l'Agence économique de l'AOF, Soudan, June 1925; Bulletin de Renseignement pour
l'Agence économique de l'AOF, Soudan, Nov. 1925.

ANS-AOF 2 G 26-5. Notice mensuelle pour l'Agence économique, Soudan,
July 1926; Bulletin économique, Soudan, Dec. 1926.

ANS-AOF 26-33. Descemet, le Secrétaire-général chargé de l'expédition des
Affaires, Rapport d'agricole d'ensemble pour l'année 1926, Soudan; Rapport agricole, Soudan, 1926.

ANS-AOF 2 G 27-6. Bulletin économique pour l'Agence économique de
l'AOF, Soudan, Jan.–Feb. 1927; Bulletin des renseignements pour l'Agence
économique de l'AOF, Soudan, Mar.–Apr. 1927; Bulletin des renseignements pour l'Agence économique de l'AOF, Soudan, 3d and 4th Quarters 1927.

ANS-AOF 2 G 27-41. Bulletin des renseignements pour l'Agence économique de l'AOF, Soudan, Mar. 1927; Rapport agricole d'ensemble pour
l'année 1927, Soudan.

ANS-AOF 2 G 27-99. Bélime, Rapport annuel sur la culture cotonnière en
AOF, Kouluba, 15 Apr. 1928.

ANS-AOF 2 G 28-6. Rapport politique d'ensemble (AOF) pour 1928.

ANS-AOF 2 G 28-41. Rapport agricole d'ensemble pour l'année 1928,
Soudan.

ANS-AOF 2 G 29-4. Bulletin économique pour l'Agence économique de
l'AOF, Soudan, 1st Quarter 1929; Bulletin économique pour l'Agence
économique de l'AOF, Soudan, 1st Quarter 1929; Bulletin économique
pour l'Agence économique de l'AOF, Soudan, 2d Quarter 1929; Bureau des
affaires économiques et commerciales, Rapport annuel, Soudan, 1929.

ANS-AOF 2 G 30-31. Bulletin économique pour l'Agence économique de
l'AOF, Soudan, 1st Quarter 1930; Bulletin économique pour l'Agence
économique de l'AOF, Soudan, 3d Quarter 1930; Rapport économique,
Soudan, 4th Quarter 1930.

ANS-AOF 2 G 31-37. Bulletin économique, Soudan, 2d Quarter 1931; Bulletin économique, Soudan, 4th Quarter 1931.

ANS-AOF 2 G 32-3. Direction générale des services économiques, AOF:
Rapport d'ensemble, année 1932.

ANS-AOF 2 G 32-9. Bulletin économique, Soudan, 1st Quarter 1932; Bulletin économique, Soudan, 2d Quarter 1932; Acting lt gov. Maillet, Soudan:
Rapport économique annuel, 1932.

ANS-AOF 2 G 33-5. Rapport économique annuel, Soudan, 1933.

ANS-AOF 2 G 33-140. Bulletin économique, Soudan, 1st Quarter.

ANS-AOF 2 G 34-6. Lt gov. Eboué, Rapport politique annuel, Soudan, 1934.

ANS-AOF 2 G 34-12. Gov-gen. Brevié, Rapport politique annuel du gouvernement-général de AOF, 1934.

ANS-AOF 2 G 34-34. Rapport économique annuel, Soudan, 1934.

ANS-AOF 2 G 34-45. Rapport annuel du Service de l'agriculture, campagne
1933–34.

ANS-AOF 2 G 35-9. Lt gov. Alfassa, Rapport politique annuel, Soudan, 1935.

ANS-AOF 2 G 35-21. Chef du Service de l'agriculture et des forêts, Rapport annuel du Service de l'agriculture et des forêts, Kouluba, 12 May 1935.

ANS-AOF 2 G 35-37. Rapport économique annuel, Soudan, 1935

ANS-AOF 2 G 35-51. Le Chef du Service de l'agriculture et des forêts, Rapport annuel du Service de l'agriculture et des forêts, campagne 1934–35, Kouluba, 12 May 1935.

ANS-AOF 2 G 36-6. Rapport économique annuel, Soudan, 1936; Bulletin économique, Soudan, 1st Quarter 1936.

ANS-AOF 2 G 36-25. Gov-gen. de Coppet, Rapport politique du gouvernement-général de l'AOF, année 1936.

ANS-AOF 2 G 37-1. Rapport politique du gouvernement-général de l'AOF, année 1937.

ANS-AOF 2 G 37-53. Ingénieur en chef des travaux d'agriculture aux colonies Charles Godard, Service d'agriculture, Rapport annuel, campagne 1936–37, Bamako, 25 May 1937.

ANS-AOF 2 G 38-53. Service d'agriculture, Rapport annuel, campagne 1937–38, Soudan.

ANS-AOF 2 G 39-8. Lt gov. Desanti, Rapport politique annuel, année 1939, Kouluba, 19 Apr. 1940.

ANS-AOF 2 G 39-37. Rapport économique pour l'année 1939, Soudan.

ANS-AOF 2 G 39-60. Service d'agriculture, Rapport annuel de l'agriculture, [campagne 1938–39], Bamako, 10 June 1939.

ANS-AOF 2 G 40-10. Lt gov. p.i., Rapport politique annuel, Soudan, 1940, Kouluba, 19 Apr. 1941.

ANS-AOF 2 G 41-28. Rapport économique annuel, Soudan, 1941.

ANS-AOF 2 G 41-39. Le Chef du Service de l'agriculture, Rapport annuel, campagne 1940–41, Bamako.

ANS-AOF 2 G 42-3. Inspecteur des affaires administratives Marchand, Rapport politique annuel, Soudan, 1942, Kouluba, 19 July 1943.

ANS-AOF 2 G 44-22. Lt gov. Louveau, Rapport politique annuel, 1944, Kouluba.

ANS-AOF 2 G 42-23. Lt gov. Louveau, Annexe au rapport annuel sur l'emploi de la main d'oeuvre au Soudan pendant l'année 1942, Kouluba, 16 July 1943.

ANS-AOF 2 G 42-25. Rapport économique, année 1942, Soudan.

ANS-AOF 2 G 42-35. Pierre Viguier, Chef p.i. du Service de l'agriculture, Rapport annuel du Service de l'agriculture, campagne 1941–42, Kouluba, 14 June 1943.

ANS-AOF 2 G 43-24. Lt gov. Louveau, Rapport annuel sur le travail, année 1943, Kouluba.

ANS-AOF 2 G 43-30. Lt gov. Louveau, Rapport économique annuel, 1943, Soudan, Kouluba, 30 Sept. 1944.

ANS-AOF 2 G 43-47. Pierre Viguier, Chef p.i. du Service de l'agriculture, Rapport, Bamako, 14 June 1943.

ANS-AOF 2 G 44-57. Rapport agricole de la campagne 1944–45, Soudan français.

ANS-AOF 2 G 44-84. Service de l'exploitation, Office du Niger, Rapport annuel sur l'activité du service, campagne agricole, 1943–44.

ANS-AOF 2 G 45-33. Chef, Service de l'agriculture, Rapport annuel du Service de l'agriculture, année 1945, Bamako, 11 May 1946.

ANS-AOF 2 G 46-21. Lt gov. Louveau, Rapport politique annuel, Soudan, 1946.

ANS-AOF 2 G 47-27. Lt gov. Louveau, Rapport économique, année 1947, Soudan.

ANS-AOF 2 G 48-54. Lt gov. Louveau, Rapport annuel, Direction des services économiques, Soudan, 1948.

ANS-AOF 2 G 49-26. Lt gov. Louveau, Direction locale des services économiques, Rapport annuel, Soudan, 1949.

ANS-AOF 2 G 50-28. A. Renard, Ingénieur principal de 1ière classe, Chef du Service de l'agriculture, Rapport annuel, Soudan, 1950, Bamako, 20 Aug. 1950.

ANS-AOF 2 G 50-37. Lt gov. Louveau, Rapport annuel, 1950, Soudan, Direction locale des services économiques.

ANS-AOF 2 G 53-10. Rapport économique, Soudan, année 1953.

ANS-AOF P 401. Rapport de M. Aron, l'Ingénieur des ponts et chaussées, sur l'irrigation dans le bassin du Niger, Dakar, 15 Dec. 1910.

ANS-AOF P 402. Hardel, Etude sur l'irrigation dans la vallée du Niger, n.d. [1911].

ANS-AOF P 405 and P 406. Younès reports.

ANS-AOF 1 R 18. Gov-gen. Angoulvant, letter to Minister of Colonies, Dakar, 13 June 1918; De Loppinot, director of CICONNIC, letter to lt gov. of Soudan, Hirschville, 10 May 1920.

ANS-AOF 1 R 48. Culture du coton, Programme pour les campagnes 1918–19 et suivant.

ANS-AOF 1 R 73. Gov-gen. Angoulvant, letter to Hirsch, Dakar, 4 Mar. 1918; R. Forbes and E. Barthaburu, Rapport sur la situation en Février 1927 des travaux de mise en valeur entreprise par la Compagnie de culture cotonnière du Niger sur la concession de Dire, les concessions de Saga, Dioro, et Senekou, Segu, 19 Feb. 1927; Directeur des Services économiques, Notice sur la Compagnie de culture cotonnière du Niger, Dakar, 3 Aug. 1937.

Published Sources, Theses, and Manuscripts

Adas, Michael. *Machines as the Measure of Men: Science, Technology, and Ideologies*. Ithaca: Cornell University Press, 1989.

Aftalion, Albert. "The Effect of the War upon French Commercial Policy." In Charles Gide, ed., *Effect of the War upon French Economic Life: A Collection of Five Monographs*. Oxford: Clarendon Press, 1923.

————. L'Industrie textile en France pendant la guerre. Paris: Les Presses Universitaires de France, n.d. [1926–27].

Allan, William. The African Husbandman. New York: Barnes and Noble, 1965.

Amselle, Jean-Loup. Logiques métisses: Anthropologie de l'identité en Afrique et ailleurs. Paris: Payot, 1990.

Andrews, C. M., P. Grupp, and A. S. Kanya-Forstner. "Le Mouvement colonial français et ses principales personalités. Revue française d'histoire d'Outre-Mer 42, no. 4 (1975): 640–73.

Austen, Ralph. African Economic History: Internal Development and External Dependency. London and Portsmouth, N.H.: James Currey and Heinemann, 1987.

Aw, Djibril. "Historique de l'Office du Niger." Unpublished manuscript [no place], 1963.

Baillaud, Sur les routes du Soudan. Toulouse: Imprimerie et Librairie Edouard Privat, 1902.

Barber, E. J. W. Prehistorical Textiles: The Development of Cloth in the Neolithic and Bronze Ages with Special Reference to the Aegean. Princeton: Princeton University Press, 1991.

Barrows, Leland. "General Faidherbe, the Maurel and Prom Company, and French Expansion in Senegal." Ph.D. diss., University of California at Los Angeles, 1975.

————. "The Merchants and General Faidherbe." Revue française de l'histoire d'Outre-Mer 61, no. 2 (1974): 236–83.

Barry, Boubacar. Le Royaume Waalo: Le Sénégal avant la conquête. Paris: Maspero, 1972.

————. La Sénégambie du XVᵉ au XIXᵉ siècle: Traite négrière, Islam, et conquête coloniale. Paris: Editions l'Harmattan, 1988.

Barth, Frederick. Ethnic Groups and Boundaries: The Social Organization of Cultural Difference. Boston: Little, Brown, 1969.

Bassett, Thomas. "The Development of Cotton in Northern Ivory Coast, 1910–1965." Journal of African History 19, no. 2 (1988): 267–84.

Bauzil, V. Note sur les méthodes de colonisation indigène de l'Office du Niger. Paris: Imprimerie Nationale, 1938.

Bayol, Jean. Voyage en Sénégambie, Haut Niger, Bambouck, Fouta Djallon et Bélédugu, 1880–1885. Paris: L. Baudin, 1888.

Becker, Laurence C. "An Experiment in the Reorganisation of Agricultural Production in the French Soudan (Mali), 1920–40." Africa 64, no. 3 (1994).

Bélime, Emile. Das innere Nigerdelta: Ein Baumwollgebiet der Zukunft. Berlin: Verlag Walter de Gruyter, 1941.

————. "L'Afrique s'éveille." Hommes et mondes, no. 50 (Sept. 1950): 1–18.

————. "Les Grands Travaux coloniaux: Que fait-on sur le Niger?" Revue politique et parlementaire 132 (1927): 233–63.

————. Les Irrigations du Niger: Études et projets. Paris: E. Larose, 1921.

——. *L'Heure de la France: Réflexions sur la crise.* Paris: Librairie Felix Alcan, 1933.

——. *L'Ordre réel: Ni capitalisme ni communisme.* Paris: Les Oeuvres Françaises, 1935.

——. *La production du coton en Afrique occidentale française: Le programme Carde.* Paris: Publications du Comité du Niger, 1925.

Bélime, Emile, and Auguste Chevalier, Yves Henry, and Fernand Bernard, *Les Irrigations du Niger: Discussions et Controverses.* Paris: Comité du Niger, n.d. [1923].

Berman, Bruce. *Control and Crisis in Colonial Kenya: The Dialectic of Domination.* London: James Currey, 1990.

——. "Structure and Process in the Bureaucratic States of Colonial Africa." In Bruce Berman and John Lonsdale, eds., *Unhappy Valley: Conflict in Kenya and Africa.* London: James Currey, 1992.

Berman, Bruce, and John Lonsdale. "Coping with the Contradictions: The Development of the Colonial State, 1895–1914." *Journal of African History* 20, no. 4 (1979): 487–505.

Bernard, Colonel F. "La Mise en valeur des colonies et le programme de M. Sarraut." *La revue de Paris,* 15 Sept. and 1 Oct. 1922, pp. 365–94, 543–60.

Bernard-Duquenet, Nicole. "Le Front populaire et le problème des prestations en AOF." *Cahiers des Etudes africaines* 61–62 (1976): 159–72.

Berry, Sara. *No Condition Is Permanent: The Social Dynamics of Agrarian Change in Sub-Saharan Africa.* Madison: University of Wisconsin Press, 1993.

Blassingame, John W. *Slave Testimony: Two Centuries of Letters, Speeches, Interviews, and Autobiographies.* Baton Rouge: Louisiana State University Press, 1972.

Boser-Sarivaxévanis, Renée. *Recherche sur l'histoire des textiles traditionnels tissés et teints de l'Afrique occidentale.* Basel: Naturforschende Gesellschaft, 1975.

——. *Les tissus de l'Afrique occidentale: Méthode de classification et catalogue raisonné des étoffes, tissus de l'Afrique de l'Ouest établis à partir de données techniques et historiques.* Bâle: Pharos-Verlag, H. Schwabe, 1972.

Bourdette, Victor. *Etude sur la culture du coton dans les colonies françaises: Thèse pour le doctorat.* Paris: Henri Jouve, 1909.

Braudel, Fernand. *The Mediterranean and the Mediterranean World in the Age of Philip II.* Translated by Sian Reynolds, vols. 1 and 2. New York: Harper Colophon, 1972–73.

——. *The Structures of Everyday Life: Civilization and Capitalism, 15th–19th Century.* Translated by Sian Reynolds, vol. 1. New York: Harper & Row, 1981.

Brauland, Kristine. *British Technology and European Industrialization: The Norwegian Textile Industry in the Mid-Nineteenth Century.* Cambridge: Cambridge University Press, 1989.

Brincard, Marie Thérèse, ed. *Beauty by Design: The Aesthetics of African Adornment.* New York: African-American Institute, 1984.

Brooks, George. "Peanuts and Colonialism: Consequences of Peanuts in West Africa, 1830–70." *Journal of African History* 16, no. 1 (1975): 29–54.

Brown, Harry Bates, and Jacob Osborn Ware. *Cotton.* 3d ed. New York: McGraw Hill, 1958.

Bruchey, Stuart, ed. *Cotton and the Growth of the American Economy, 1790–1860: Sources and Readings.* New York: Harcourt, Brace and World, 1967.

Buell, Raymond Leslie. *The Native Problem in Africa.* 2 vols. New York: Macmillan, 1928.

Byfield, Judith. "Women, Economy, and the State: A Study of the Adire Industry in Abeokuta (Western Nigeria), 1890–1939." Ph.D. diss., Columbia University, 1993.

Bythell, Duncan. *The Handloom Weavers: A Study in the English Cotton Industry During the Industrial Revolution.* Cambridge: Cambridge University Press, 1969.

Cameron, Rondo. *A Concise Economic History of the World: From Paleolithic Times to the Present.* New York: Oxford University Press, 1993.

———. *France and the Economic Development of Europe.* Princeton: Princeton University Press, 1961.

Caron, François. "La Croissance industrielle: Secteurs et branches." In Jean Bouvier et al., eds., *Histoire économique et sociale de la France,* vol. 4, part 1. Paris: Presses Universitaires de France, 1979.

———. *Histoire économique de la France, XIXe–XXe siècles.* Paris: Armand Colin, 1981.

Caron, François, and Jean Bouvier. "Guerre, crise, guerre: 1914–1949." In Fernand Braudel and Ernest Labrousse, eds., *Histoire économique et sociale de France,* vol. 4. Paris: Presses Universitaires de France, 1980.

Carponnier, François. *La Crise de l'industrie cotonnière française.* Paris: Editions Génin, 1959.

Chanock, Martin. *Law, Custom and Social Order: The Colonial Experience in Malawi and Zambia.* Cambridge: Cambridge University Press, 1985.

———. "Paradigms, Policies, and Property: A Review of the Customary Law of Land Tenure." In Kristin Mann and Richard Roberts, eds., *Law in Colonial Africa.* Portsmouth, N.H.: Heinemann, 1991.

Chapman, Herrick. *State Capitalism and Working Class Radicalism in the French Aircraft Industry.* Berkeley: University of California Press, 1990.

Chapman, S. D. *The Cotton Industry in the Industrial Revolution.* London: Macmillan, 1972.

Chapman, S. D., and S. Chassagne. *European Textile Printers in the Eighteenth Century: A Study of Peel and Oberkampf.* London: Heinemann, 1981.

Chaudhuri, C. N. *Asia Before Europe: Economy and Civilisation of the In-*

dian Ocean from the Rise of Islam to 1750. Cambridge: Cambridge University Press, 1990.

———. *The Trading World of Asia and the British East India Company.* Cambridge: Cambridge University Press, 1978.

Chevalier, Auguste. "Etudes sur l'irrigation en Afrique occidentale." *Revue de botanique appliquée et d'agriculture coloniale* 1 (1921): 113–17.

Clapham, John Harold. *The Economic Development of France and Germany, 1815–1914.* 3d ed. Cambridge: Cambridge University Press, 1928.

Cohen, David William. *Combing of History.* Chicago: University of Chicago Press, 1994.

———. "Doing Social History from Pim's Doorway." In Olivier Zunz, ed., *Reliving the Past: The Worlds of Social History.* Chapel Hill: University of North Carolina Press, 1985.

———. "Reconstructing a Conflict in Bunafu: Seeking Evidence Outside the Narrative Tradition." In Joseph Miller, ed., *African Past Speaks: Essays in Oral Tradition and History.* Folkestone, Eng.: Dawson, 1980.

Cohen, David William, and E. S. Atieno Odhiambo. *Siaya: The Historical Anthropology of an African Landscape.* London: James Currey, 1989.

Cohen, William B. *The French Encounter with Africans: White Response to Blacks, 1530–1880.* Bloomington: Indiana University Press, 1980.

Commissariat de l'Afrique occidentale française. *Les Grands Produits de l'Afrique occidentale française: Exposition coloniale internationale de Paris.* Rochfort-sur-mer: A. Thoyon-Thèze, 1931.

Conrad, David C., and Barbara E. Frank, eds. *Status and Identity in West Africa: Nyamakalaw of Mande.* Bloomington: University of Indiana Press, 1995.

Cooper, Frederick. "Africa and the World Economy." *African Studies Review* 24, nos. 2–3 (1981), reprinted in Frederick Cooper et al., *Confronting Historical Paradigms: Peasants, Labor, and the Capitalist World System in Africa and Latin America.* Madison: University of Wisconsin Press, 1993.

———. *Decolonization and African Society: The Labor Question in British and French Africa.* Cambridge: Cambridge University Press, 1996.

———. *On the African Waterfront: Urban Disorder and the Transformation of Work in Colonial Mombassa.* New Haven: Yale University Press, 1987.

Coquery-Vidrovitch, Catherine. "L'Afrique coloniale française et la crise de 1930: Crise structurelle et genèse du sous-développement." *Revue française d'Outre-Mer,* 63 (1976): 386–424.

Cox, Alonzo Bettis. *Cotton: Demand, Supply, Merchandising.* Austin, Tex.: Hemphill's, 1953.

Curtin, Philip. *The Image of Africa: British Ideas and Action, 1780–1850.* Madison: University of Wisconsin Press, 1964.

Dalziel, J. M. *The Useful Plants of Tropical West Africa.* London: Crown Agents for the Colonies, 1937.

de Wilde, John, with the assistance of Peter F. M. McLoughlin et al. *Experiences with Agricultural Development in Tropical Africa.* 2 vols. Baltimore: Johns Hopkins Press, 1967.

Delemer, Adolphe. *Le Bilan de l'étatisme.* Paris: Payot, 1922.

Dodge, Bertha. *Cotton: The Plant That Would Be King.* Austin: University of Texas Press, 1984.

Dirks, Nicholas B. "Introduction: Colonialism and Culture." In Nicholas B. Dirks, ed., *Colonialism and Culture.* Ann Arbor: University of Michigan Press, 1992.

Drouet, Louis. *Des moyens de doter les possessions françaises en Afrique de la culture du coton.* Rouen: Imprimerie St-Evron, 1862.

Dubois, Félix. *Tombouctou, la mystérieuse.* Paris: Flammarion, 1897.

Duff, R. E. B. *100 Years of the Suez Canal.* London: Clifton House, 1969.

Dulles, Eleanor L. *The French Franc, 1914–28: The Facts and Their Interpretation.* New York: Macmillan, 1929.

Echenberg, Myron. *Colonial Conscripts: The Tirailleurs Sénégalais in French West Africa, 1857–1960.* Portsmouth, N.H.: Heinemann, 1991.

———. "Les Migrations militaires en Afrique occidentale française, 1900–1945." *Canadian Journal of African Studies* 14, no. 3 (1980): 429–50.

———. "Paying the Blood Tax: Military Conscription in French West Africa, 1914–29." *Canadian Journal of African Studies* 9, no. 2 (1975): 171–92.

Echenberg, Myron, and Jean Filipovitch. "African Military Labour and the Building of the Office du Niger Installations, 1925–50." *Journal of African History* 27, no. 3 (1986): 533–51.

Eicher, Joanne Bubolz. *African Dress: A Select and Annotated Bibliography of Subsaharan Countries.* East Lansing: Michigan State University Press, 1973.

———. *African Dress II: A Selection and Annotated Bibliography.* East Lansing: Michigan State University Press, 1985.

El Bekri, Abou Obed. *Description de l'Afrique septentrionale.* Translated by MacGuckin de Slane. Algiers: Jourdan, 1913.

Ellison, Thomas. *The Cotton Trade of Great Britain: Including a History of the Liverpool Cotton Market and of the Liverpool Cotton Brokers' Association.* London: Effingham-Wilson, 1886.

———. *Handbook of the Cotton Trade: Or, A Glance at the Past History, Present Condition, and Future Prospects of the Cotton Commerce of the World.* London: Longman, Brown, Green, Longmans, and Roberts, 1858.

Engels, Friedrich. *The Condition of the Working Class in England.* Translated by W. O. Henderson and W. H. Chaloner. Stanford: Stanford University Press, 1958.

Escott, Paul D. *Slavery Remembered: A Record of Twentieth-Century Slave Narratives.* Chapel Hill: University of North Carolina Press, 1979.

Etesse, Marius. *Les Grands Produits africains.* Paris: Editions du Comité de l'Afrique française, 1930.

Faillot, Ernest. *Histoire de la colonie française du Sénégal.* Paris: Challamel Ainé, 1884.

Fall, Bouboucar. "Le Travail forcé en Afrique occidentale française, 1900–1946: Cas du Sénégal, de la Guinée et du Soudan." Thèse de 3ᵉ cycle, Université de Dakar, 1984.

Farnie, D. A. *The English Cotton Industry and the World Market, 1815–1896.* Oxford: Clarendon Press, 1979.

Faure, Claude. *Histoire de la Presque'île du Cap Vert et des origines de Dakar.* Paris: Emile Larose, 1914.

Feierman, Steven. *Peasant Intellectuals: Anthropology and History in Tanzania.* Madison: University of Wisconsin Press, 1990.

Ferguson, James. *The Anti-Politics Machine: "Development," Depoliticization, and Bureaucratic Power in Lesotho.* Cambridge: Cambridge University Press, 1990.

Filipovitch, Jean. "L'Office du Niger Under Colonial Rule: Its Origins, Evolution, and Character (1920–60)." Ph.D. diss., McGill University, 1985.

Fohlen, Claude. *La France de l'entre-deux-guerres, 1917–39.* Paris: Casterman, 1966.

———. *L'Industrie textile au temps du Second Empire.* Paris: Librairie Plon, 1956.

———. "The Industrial Revolution in France." In Rondo Cameron, ed., *Essays in French Economic History.* Homewood, Ill.: Richard Irwin, 1970.

Fontaine, Arthur. *French Industry During the War.* New Haven: Yale University Press, 1926.

Forbes, Docteur R. H. *Le Coton dans la Vallée Moyenne du Niger: Essais de culture, 1923–24, rapport.* Paris: E. Larose, 1926.

Frank, Andre Gunder. *Capitalism and Underdevelopment in Latin America.* New York: Monthly Review Press, 1967.

———. "The Development of Underdevelopment." In Robert Rhodes, ed., *Imperialism and Underdevelopment: A Reader.* New York: Monthly Review Press, 1970.

Gaffiot, Robert. *Le Coton en AOF.* Arc-et-Senans: Editions de l'Aile, 1932.

Gemery, Henry, and Jan Hogendorn, "The Atlantic Slave Trade: A Tentative Economic Model," *Journal of African History* 15, no. 2 (1974): 223–46.

Gerschenkron, Alexander. *Backwardness in Historical Perspective.* Cambridge, Mass.: Harvard University Press, 1966.

Gilfoy, Peggy Stoltz. *Patterns of Life: West African Strip-Weaving Traditions.* Washington, D.C.: Smithsonian Institution Press, 1989.

Goody, Jack, ed. *The Development Cycle of Domestic Groups.* Cambridge: Cambridge University Press, 1958.

Grosz-Ngate, Maria. "Bambara Men and Women and the Reproduction of Social Life in Sana Province, Mali." Ph.D. diss., University of Michigan, 1986.

Guérin, Jacques. *Les Colonies cotonnières: Thèse pour le doctorat.* Paris: André Rousseau, 1907.

Hardel. "L'Irrigation en Afrique occidentale française (vallée du Niger)." In J. Chailley and D. Zolla for the Union coloniale française, eds., *Congrès d'agriculture coloniale.* Vol. 1. Paris: A. Challamel, 1920.

Hardy, Georges. *La Mise en valeur du Sénégal de 1817 à 1854.* Paris: Emile Larose, 1921.

Hay, Jean. "Constructing a Modern Identity: Christian Missions, the Labor Market, and Clothing in Colonial Western Kenya." Unpublished paper presented at the "Cloth, the World Economy, and the Artisan: Textile Manufacturing and Marketing in South Asia and Africa, 1780–1950" conference, Dartmouth College, Apr. 1993.

Headrick, Daniel R. *The Tentacles of Progress: Technology Transfer in the Age of Imperialism, 1850–1940.* New York: Oxford University Press, 1988.

Heisser, David Calvin Reynolds. "The Impact of the Great War on French Imperialism, 1914–24." Ph.D. diss., University of North Carolina, Chapel Hill, 1972.

Henry, Yves M. *Le Coton aux Etats-Unis.* Paris: A. Challamel, 1902.

———. *Le Coton dans l'Afrique occidentale française.* Paris: A. Challamel, 1905.

———. *Culture pratique du cotonnier.* Paris: A. Challamel, 1913.

———. *Détermination de la valeur commerciale des fibres de coton.* Paris: A. Challamel, 1902.

———. *Eléments d'agriculture coloniale: Plantes à fibres.* Paris: A. Colin, 1924.

———. *Irrigations et cultures irriguées en Afrique tropicale.* Paris: Emile Larose, 1918.

Henry, Yves, F. Vuillet, and H. Lavergne, *Les Irrigations au Niger et la culture du cotonnier: Etudes et travaux d'agriculture.* Paris: Larose, 1922.

Hobsbawm, Eric, and Terence Ranger, eds. *The Invention of Tradition.* Cambridge: Cambridge University Press, 1983.

Hogendorn, Jan. "The Cotton Campaign in Northern Nigeria, 1902–1914: An Example of a Public-Private Planning Failure in Agriculture." In Allen Isaacman and Richard Roberts, eds., *Cotton, Colonialism, and Social History in Sub-Saharan Africa.* Portsmouth, N.H.: Heinemann, 1995.

———. *Nigerian Groundnut Exports: Origins and Early Developments.* Zaria: Ahmadu Bello University Press, 1978.

Hopkins, A. G. *An Economic History of West Africa.* London: Longman, 1973.

Hose, John Robert. "Britain and the Development of West African Cotton, 1845–1960." Ph.D. diss., Columbia University, 1970.

Hutchinson, J. B. "New Evidence on the Origin of the Old World Cottons." *Heredity* 8 (1954): 225–41.

Hutchinson, J. B., R. A. Silow, and S. G. Stephens. *The Evolution of Gossypium.* London: Oxford University Press, 1947.

Ibn Battuta. *Voyage dans le Soudan.* Translated by MacGuckin de Slane. Paris: Imprimerie Royale, 1843.

Idiens, Dale, and K. G. Ponting, eds. *Textiles of Africa.* Bath: Pasold Research Fund, 1980.

Imperato, Pascal James, and Marli Shamin. "Bokolanfini: Mud Cloth of the Bamana of Mali." *African Arts* 3, no. 4, (Summer 1970): 32–41.

International Institute of Agriculture (Rome). *The Cotton Growing Countries Present and Potential: Production, Trade, and Consumption.* London: P. S. King & Son, 1926.

Irwin, Paul. *Liptako Speaks: History from Oral Tradition in Africa.* Princeton: Princeton University Press, 1981.

Isaacman, Allen. *Cotton Is the Mother of Poverty: Peasants, Agrarian Change and Rural Protest in Colonial Mozambique, 1938–1961.* Portsmouth, N.H.: Heinemann, 1996.

Isaacman, Allen, and Richard Roberts, eds. *Cotton, Colonialism, and Social History in Sub-Saharan Africa.* Portsmouth, N.H.: Heinemann, 1995.

Johnson, Marion. "Cotton Imperialism in West Africa." *African Affairs* 73, no. 291 (Apr. 1974): 178–87.

———. "Technology, Competition, and African Crafts." In Clive Dewey and A. G. Hopkins, eds., *The Imperial Impact: Studies in the Economic History of Africa and India.* London: Athlone Press, 1978.

Kanya-Forstner, A. S. *Conquest of the Western Sudan: A Study in French Military Imperialism.* Cambridge: Cambridge University Press, 1969.

Kemp, Tom. *Economic Forces in French History.* London: Dobson, 1971.

———. *The French Economy, 1913–39.* London: Longman, 1972.

Kindleberger, Charles P. *Economic Growth in France and Britain, 1850–1950.* Cambridge, Mass.: Harvard University Press, 1964.

Klein, Martin. *Islam and Imperialism in Sine-Saloum, 1847–1914.* Stanford: Stanford University Press, 1968.

———. "Slavery and Emancipation in French West Africa." In Martin Klein, ed., *Breaking the Chains: Slavery, Bondage, and Emancipation in Modern Africa and Asia.* Madison: University of Wisconsin Press, 1993.

———. "Studying the History of Those Who Would Rather Forget: Oral History and the Experience of Slavery." *History in Africa* 16 (1989): 209–17.

Klein, Martin, and Richard Roberts. "The Resurgence of Pawning in French West Africa During the Depression of the 1930s." *African Economic History* 16 (1987): 23–37.

Klitgaard, Robert E. *Tropical Gangsters.* New York: Basic Books, 1990.

Kriger, Colleen. "Textile Production and Gender in the Sokoto Caliphate." *Journal of African History* 34, no. 3 (1993): 361–401.

Kuisel, Richard. *Capitalism and the State in Modern France: Renovation and Economic Management in the Twentieth Century.* Cambridge: Cambridge University Press, 1981.

———. "Technocrats and Public Economic Policy: From the Third to Fourth

Republic." In John C. Cairns, ed., *Contemporary France: Illusion, Conflict, and Regeneration*. New York: New Viewpoints, 1978.

Labouret, Henri. *A la recherche d'une politique indigène dans l'Ouest Africain*. Paris: Comité de l'Afrique française, 1931.

———. *Ethnologie coloniale: Un programme de recherches*. Paris: Larose, 1932.

———. "Géographie alimentaire en Afrique occidentale." *Annales géographiques* (1937).

———. *La Main d'oeuvre dans l'ouest africain*. Paris, 1930.

———. *Les Manding et leur langue*. Paris: Larose, 1934.

———. *Paysans d'Afrique occidentale*. Paris: Gallimard, 1941.

———. *Rapport sur le travail et la main d'oeuvre autochtone en Afrique occidentale française*. Paris: Institut International de Cooperation, 1937.

———. *Recommandations pour l'étude de la famille et des chefferies*. Paris, 1929.

———. *Les Tribus du Rameau Lobi*. Paris: Institut d'Ethnologie, 1931.

Landes, David S. *The Unbound Prometheus: Technological Change and Industrial Development in Western Europe from 1750 to the Present*. London: Cambridge University Press, 1969.

Lalande, W. "L'Achat du coton aux indigènes." *Coton et culture cotonnière* 3, no. 3 (1928).

Lecomte, Henri. *Le Coton: Monographie culture, histoire économique*. Paris: G. Carré and C. Naud, 1900.

———. *Le Coton en Egypte: Culture, préparation, exportation. Rapport adressé a M. Le Gouverneur du Sénégal*. Paris: A. Challamel, 1905.

Lemmet, J., and Vitalis. "Note sur la mise en valeur des terres de la vallée du Moyen Niger." *Comité d'Etudes historiques et scientifiques de l'Afrique occidentale française, annuaire et mémoire* (1917).

Leonard, Charlene Marie. *Lyon Transformed: Public Works of the Second Empire, 1855–1864*. Berkeley: University of California Press, 1961.

Lewis, John V. D. "Descendants and Crops: Two Poles of Production in a Malian Peasant Village." Ph.D. diss., Yale University, 1979.

Londres, Albert. *A Very Naked People*. Translated by Sylvia Stuart. New York: Horace Liveright, 1929.

Low, D. A., and John Lonsdale. "Introduction." In D. A. Low and John Lonsdale, *Oxford History of East Africa*, vol. 3. Oxford: Oxford University Press, 1976.

Ludden, David. "India's Development Regime." In Nicholas B. Dirks, ed., *Colonialism and Culture*. Ann Arbor: University of Michigan Press, 1992.

MacGaffey, Janet. *Entrepreneurs and Parasites: The Struggle for Indigenous Capitalism in Zaire*. Cambridge: Cambridge University Press, 1987.

———. "Issues and Methods in the Study of African Economies." In Janet MacGaffey et al., *The Real Economy of Zaire: The Contribution of Smuggling and Other Unofficial Activities to National Wealth*. Philadelphia: University of Pennsylvania Press, 1991.

Magassa, Amidu. *Papa Commandant a jeté un grand filet devant nous: Les Exploités des rives du Niger, 1960–1962.* Paris: François Maspero, 1978.

Mage, M. Eugene. *Voyage dans le Soudan occidental.* Paris: Hachette, 1868.

Manue, Georges R. "Emile Bélime: Le maître de l'eau." *Le Monde,* 31 July 1969.

Marchal, Jean-Yves. "L'Office du Niger: Îlot de prospérité paysanne ou pôle de production agricole." *Canadian Journal of African Studies* 8, no. 1 (1974): 73–90.

Marchal, Jean Yves, J. M. Kohler, and G. Remy. *Les Colons Mossi de l'Office du Niger: L'Expérience de trente années de colonisation agricole dirigée.* Ougadougou: ORSTOM, 1971.

Marlowe, John. *The Making of the Suez Canal.* London: Cresset Press, 1964.

Marseille, Jacques. *Empire colonial et capitalisme français: Histoire d'un divorce.* Paris: Albin Michel, 1984.

———. "L'Industrie cotonnière française et l'impérialisme colonial." *Revue d'histoire économique et sociale* 53, nos. 2–3 (1975): 386–412.

Martin, Phyllis M. "Contesting Clothes in Colonial Brazzaville." *Journal of African History* 35, no. 3 (1994): 401–26.

Martin, Susan M. "The Long Depression: West African Export Producers and the World Economy, 1915–45." In Ian Brown, ed., *The Economies of Africa and Asia in the Inter-War Depression.* London: Routledge, 1989.

Mauny, Raymond. "Notes historiques autour des principales plantes cultivées d'Afrique occidentale." *Bulletin d'IFAN* 15 (1953): 684–730.

———. *Tableau géographique de l'Ouest Africain au Moyen Age d'après les sources écrites, la tradition et l'archéologie.* Mémoires de l'Institut Français d'Afrique Noire, no. 61. Dakar: IFAN, 1961.

Mazel, Henri. "The Effect of the War upon the French Merchant Marine." In Charles Gide, ed., *Effect of the War upon French Economic Life: A Collection of Five Monographs.* Oxford: Clarendon Press, 1923.

McIntosh, Susan Keech, and Roderick J. McIntosh. "The Inland Niger Delta Before the Empire of Mali: Evidence from Jenne-Jeno." *Journal of African History* 22, no. 1 (1981): 1–22.

———. *Prehistoric Investigations in the Region of Jenne, Mali: A Study in the Development of Urbanism in the Sahel.* Cambridge: B.A.R. (Cambridge Monographs in African Archeology, no. 2), 1980.

McLane, Margaret O. "Commercial Rivalries and French Policy on the Senegal River, 1831–58." *African Economic History* 15 (1986): 39–67.

Mbodj, Mohammed. "The Abolition of Slavery in Senegal." In Martin Klein, ed., *Breaking the Chains: Slavery, Bondage, and Emancipation in Modern Africa and Asia.* Madison: University of Wisconsin Press, 1993.

———. "Un exemple d'économie coloniale, Le Sine-Saloum (Sénégal) de 1887 à 1940: Cultures arachidières et mutations sociales." Thèse 3ᵉ cycle, Université Paris VII, 1978.

Meillassoux, Claude. "Etat et condition des esclaves à Goumbou (Mali) au

XIXe siècle." In Claude Meillassoux, ed., *L'esclavage en Afrique précoloniale*. Paris: Maspero, 1975.

———. "Female Slavery." In Claire Robertson and Martin Klein, eds., *Women and Slavery in Africa*. Madison: University of Wisconsin Press, 1983.

Menzel, Brigitte. *Textilen aus Westafrika*. Berlin: Staatliches Museum für Völkerkunde, 1979.

Mercier, Réné. *Le Travail obligatoire dans les colonies africaines*. Paris: Larose, 1933.

Messimy, General A. "Le Ravitaillement de la France en coton par ses colonies." *Revue politique et parlementaire* 120 (1924): 161–98.

Michel, Marc. *L'Appel à l'Afrique: Contributions et réactions à l'effort de guerre en A.O.F. (1914–1919)*. Paris: Publications de la Sorbonne, 1982.

Miers, Suzanne. *Britain and the Ending of the Slave Trade*. New York: Africana Publishing Company, 1975.

Mitchell, Brian R. *European Historical Statistics, 1750–1975*. New York: Facts on File, 1980.

Mitchell, Timothy. *Colonising Egypt*. Cambridge: Cambridge University Press, 1988.

———. "The World as Exhibition." *Comparative Studies in Society and History* 31, no. 2 (1989): 217–36.

Mollien, Gaspar Theodore. *Travels in the Interior of Africa to the Sources of the Senegal and Gambia Performed by the Command of the French Government in the Year 1818*. Reprint. London: Frank Cass, 1967.

Monteil, Charles. *Le Coton chez les noirs: Etat actuel de nos connaissances sur l'Afrique occidentale française*. Paris: Publications du Comité d'etudes historiques et scientifiques de l'AOF, 1932.

Moore, Donald S. "Contesting Terrain in Zimbabwe's Eastern Highlands: Political Ecology, Ethnography, and Peasant Resource Struggles." *Economic Geography* 69, no. 4 (1993): 380–401.

Morgenthau, Ruth Schachter. *Political Parties in French-Speaking West Africa*. Oxford: Clarendon Press, 1964.

Munro, J. Forbes. *Africa and the International Economy, 1800–1960*. London: J. M. Dent, 1976.

Myint, Hla. "The 'Classical Theory' of International Trade and Underdeveloped Countries." *Economic Journal* 68 (1958): 317–37.

Neurisse, A. *Histoire du franc*. Paris: Presses Universitaires de France, 1963.

Nordman, Daniel, and Jean-Pierre Raison, eds. *Sciences de l'homme et conquête coloniale: Constitution et usages des sciences humaines en Afrique (XIXe–XXe siècles)*. Paris: Presse de l'Ecole Normale Supérieure, 1980.

Ogburn, William F., and William Jaffe. *The Economic Development of Post-War France: A Survey of Production*. New York: Columbia University Press, 1929.

O'Hanlan, Rosalind, and David Washbrook. "After Orientalism: Culture,

Criticism, and Politics in the Third World." *Comparative Studies in Society and History* 34, no. 1 (1992): 141–67.

Osborne, Michael A. *Nature, the Exotic, and the Science of French Colonialism.* Bloomington: Indiana University Press, 1994.

Owen, E. R. J. *Cotton and the Egyptian Economy, 1820–1914; A Study in Trade and Development.* Oxford: Clarendon Press, 1969.

Palmer, Robin, and Neil Parsons, eds. *The Roots of Rural Poverty in Central and Southern Africa.* Berkeley: University of California Press, 1977.

Pasquier, Roger. "En marge de la guerre de sécession: Les Essais de culture du coton du Sénégal." *Annales Africaines* 1 (1955): 1–22.

Paxton, Robert O. *Vichy France: Old Guard and New Order, 1940–44.* New York: Random House, 1972.

Pelissier, Paul. *Les Paysans du Sénégal: Les Civilisations agraires du Cayor à la Casamance.* Saint-Yrieix: Imprimerie Fabrègue, 1966.

Pitcher, M. Anne. *Politics in the Portuguese Empire: Industry, State, and Cotton, 1929–1974.* Oxford: Clarendon Press, 1993.

Polakoff, Claire. *Into Indigo.* New York: Anchor Books, 1980.

Pollard, Sidney. *Peaceful Conquest: The Industrialization of Europe, 1760–1970.* Oxford: Oxford University Press, 1981.

Ponty, William. *Rapport sur la situation générale de la colonie du Haut-Sénégal-Niger en 1904.* Paris: Imprimerie Nationale, 1906.

Porter, Philip. "A Note on Cotton and Climate: A Colonial Conundrum." In Allen Isaacman and Richard Roberts, eds., *Cotton, Colonialism, and Social History in Sub-Saharan Africa.* Portsmouth, N.H.: Heinemann, 1995.

Prakash, Gyan. "Can the 'Subaltern' Ride? A Reply to O'Hanlan and Washbrook." *Comparative Studies in Society and History* 34, no. 1 (1992): 168–84.

———. "Writing Post-Orientalist Histories of the Third World: Perspectives from Indian Historiography." *Comparative Studies in Society and History* 32, no. 2 (1990): 383–408.

Prebisch, Raúl. *Change and Development in Latin America: The Great Task.* New York: Praeger, 1971.

Rabinow, Paul. *French Modern: Norms and Forms of the Social Environment.* Cambridge, Mass.: MIT Press, 1989.

Raffenel, Anne. *Nouveau Voyage au pays des Nègres.* 2 vols. Paris: N. Chaix, 1856.

Ratcliffe, Barrie M. "Cotton Imperialism: Manchester Merchants and Cotton Cultivation in West Africa in the Mid-Nineteenth Century." In Catherine Coquery-Vidrovitch and Alain Forest, eds., *Enterprises et Entrepreneurs en Afrique XIXe et XXe siècle*, vol. 2. Paris: Editions l'Harmattan, 1983.

———. "Cotton Imperialism: Manchester Merchants and Cotton Cultivation in West Africa in the Mid-Nineteenth Century." *African Economic History* 11 (1982): 87–113.

Ready, William. *The Rise of Market Culture: The Textile Trade and French Society.* New York: Cambridge University Press, 1984.

Renault, François. *Libération d'esclaves et nouvelle servitude: Les Rachats de captifs africains pour le compte des colonies françaises après l'abolition de l'esclavage.* Dakar: Nouvelles Editions Africaines, 1975.

Renouvin, Pierre. *The Forms of War Government in France.* New Haven: Yale University Press, 1927.

Reybaud, Louis. *Le Coton: Son régime, ses problèmes, son influence en Europe.* 1863; reprint, Geneva: Slatkine, 1982.

———. "La culture du coton en Algérie." *Revue des Deux Mondes* 34, no. 2 (1864): 692–717.

Rimmer, Douglas. *The Economies of West Africa.* London: Weidenfeld and Nicolson, 1984.

Roach, Mary Ellen, and Joanne Bubolz Eicher. "The Language of Personal Adornment." In Justine M. Cordwell and Ronald A. Schwartz, eds., *The Fabrics of Culture: The Anthropology of Clothing and Adornment.* The Hague: Mouton, 1979.

Robert, Louis. *La Culture du coton en Afrique occidentale française.* Paris: Les Editions Domat-Montchristien, 1931.

Roberts, Richard. "Divorce, Social Change, and the 1903 Native Legal Code in the French Soudan." Paper presented at the "Law, Colonialism, and Control over Bodies" symposium, Stanford Humanities Center, May 1993.

———. "The Emergence of a Grain Market in Bamako, 1883–1908." *Canadian Journal of African Studies* 14, no. 1 (1980): 37–54.

———. "The End of Slavery in the French Soudan, 1905–1914." In Suzanne Miers and Richard Roberts, eds., *The End of Slavery in Africa.* Madison: University of Wisconsin Press, 1988.

———. "Guinée Cloth: Linked Transformations of Production Within the French Colonial Empire." *Cahiers d'Etudes Africaines* 32, no. 4 (1992): 597–627.

———. "Linkages and Multiplier Effects in the Ecologically Specialized Trade of Precolonial West Africa." *Cahiers d'Etudes Africaines* 20, nos. 1–2 (1980–81): 135–48.

———. "Long Distance Trade and Production: Sinsani in the Nineteenth Century." *Journal of African History* 21, no. 2 (1980): 169–88.

———. "Reversible Social Processes, Historical Memory, and the Production of History." *History in Africa* 17 (1990): 341–49.

———. *Warriors, Merchants, and Slaves: The State and the Economy in the Middle Niger Valley, 1700–1914.* Stanford: Stanford University Press, 1987.

———. "Women's Work and Women's Wealth: Household Social Relations in the Maraka Textile Industry in the Nineteenth Century." *Comparative Studies in Society and History* 26, no. 2 (1984): 229–50.

Robinson, David. *Chiefs and Clerics: Adbul Bokar Kan and Futa Toro, 1853–1891.* Oxford: Clarendon Press, 1975.

Rodney, Walter. *How Europe Underdeveloped Africa.* Washington, D.C.: Howard University Press, 1981.

Said, Edward W. *Culture and Imperialism.* New York: Knopf, 1993.

Saint-André, Christian. "La Compagnie de culture cotonnière du Niger, 1919–27: Intérêts nationaux ou intérêts privés." Thèse, 3ᵉ cycle, Université Paul Valéry, Montpellier III, 1976.

Saint-Martin, Yves-Jean. *Le Sénégal sous le second empire: Naissance d'un empire colonial.* Paris: Karthala, 1989.

Saly, Pierre. *La Politique des grands travaux en France, 1929–39.* New York: Arno Press, 1977.

Sarraut, Albert. *La Mise en valeur des colonies françaises.* Paris: Payot, 1923.

Sauvy, A. "The Economic Crisis of the 1930s in France." *Journal of Contemporary History* 4, no. 4 (1969): 21–35.

Schaedler, Karl-Ferdinand. *Weaving in Africa South of the Sahara.* Munich: Panterra Verlag, 1987.

Schmidt, Charles. "Les Débuts de l'industrie cotonnière en France, 1760–1806, 1ère Partie: Jusqu'au Traité de 1786." *Revue d'histoire économique et sociale* 6 (1913): 261–95.

———. "Les Débuts de l'industrie cotonnière en France, 1760–1806, 2ième Partie: De 1786 à 1806." *Revue d'histoire économique et sociale* 7 (1914): 26–55.

Schreyger, Emil. *L'Office du Niger au Mali, 1932 à 1982: La Problèmatique d'une grande entreprise agricole dans la zone du Sahel.* Wiesbaden: Steiner, 1984.

Scott, James. *Domination and the Arts of Resistance: Hidden Transcripts.* New Haven: Yale University Press, 1990.

———. *The Moral Economy of the Peasantry.* New Haven: Yale University Press, 1976.

———. *Weapons of the Weak: Everyday Forms of Peasant Resistance.* New Haven: Yale University Press, 1985.

Searing, James. *West African Slavery and the Atlantic Commerce: The Senegal River Valley, 1700–1860.* Cambridge: Cambridge University Press, 1993.

Shea, Philip. "Approaching the Study of Production in Rural Kano." In Bawuro Bakundo, ed., *Studies in the History of Kano.* Ibadan: Heinemann, 1983.

———. "The Development of an Export Oriented Dyed Cloth Industry in the Kano Emirate." Ph.D. diss., University of Wisconsin, 1975.

Sheriff, Abdul. *Slaves, Spices, and Ivory in Zanzibar: Integration of an East-African Commercial Empire into the World Economy, 1770–1873.* London: James Currey, 1987.

Smelser, Neil J. *Social Change in the Industrial Revolution: An Application of Theory to the Lancashire Cotton Industry, 1770–1840*. London: Routledge & Kegan Paul, 1959.

Spitz, Georges. *Sansanding: Les Irrigations du Niger*. Paris: Société géographique, maritime et coloniale, 1949.

Stern, Steve J. "Feudalism, Capitalism, and the World-System in the Perspective of Latin America and the Caribbean." *American Historical Review* 93, no. 4, (1988): 829–72.

———. "Reply: 'Ever More Solitary.'" *American Historical Review* 93, no. 4, (1988): 886–97.

Suret-Canale, Jean. *French Colonialism in Tropical Africa, 1900–1945*. Translated by Till Gottheiner. New York: Pica Press, 1971.

Tamari, Tal. "The Development of Caste Systems in West Africa." *Journal of African History* 32, no. 2 (1991): 221–50.

Tellier, Louis-Henri-Ernest-Edmond-Gaston. *Autour Kita: Etude soudanaise*. Paris: H. Lavauzelle, 1902.

Thompson, E. P. "The Moral Economy of the English Crowd in the Eighteenth Century." *Past and Present* 50 (1971): 76–136.

Thornton, John. "Precolonial African Industry and the Atlantic Trade, 1500–1800." *African Economic History* 19 (1990–91): 1–19.

Tilly, Charles. "Retrieving European Lives." In Olivier Zunz, ed., *Reliving the Past: The Worlds of Social History*. Chapel Hill: University of North Carolina Press, 1985.

Todd, John A. *The Cotton World: A Survey of the World's Cotton Supplies and Consumption*. London: Sir Isaac Pitman & Sons, 1927.

Tomich, Dale. *Slavery in the Circuit of Sugar: Martinique and the World Economy, 1830–1848*. Baltimore: Johns Hopkins University Press, 1990.

van Beusekom, Monica M. "Colonial Rural Development: French Policy and African Response at the Office du Niger, Soudan Français (Mali), 1920–60." Ph.D. diss., Johns Hopkins University, 1989.

Wadsworth, Alfred P., and Julia De Lacy Mann. *The Cotton Trade and Industrial Lancashire, 1600–1780*. Manchester: Manchester University Press, 1931.

Wallerstein, Immanuel M. "Comment on Stern's Critical Tests." *American Historical Review* 93, no. 4, (1988): 873–85.

———. *The Modern World System*. New York: Academic Press, 1974.

———. *The Modern World System II*. New York: Academic Press, 1980.

Webb, James, Jr. "The Trade in Gum Arabic: Prelude to French Conquest in Senegal." *Journal of African History* 26, nos. 2–3 (1985): 149–68.

Weber, Eugen. *Peasants into Frenchmen: The Modernization of Rural France, 1870–1914*. Stanford: Stanford University Press, 1976.

Weiner, Annette B., and Jane Schneider, eds. *Cloth and Human Experience*. Washington, D.C.: Smithsonian Institution Press, 1989.

Wickins, Peter Lionel. *Africa, 1880–1980: An Economic History*. Cape Town: Oxford University Press, 1986.

Wright, Gavin. *The Political Economy of the Cotton South: Households, Markets, and Wealth in the Nineteenth Century.* New York: Norton, 1978.

Wright, Gwendolyn. *The Politics of Design in French Colonial Urbanism.* Chicago: University of Chicago Press, 1991.

Young, Crawford. *The African Colonial State in Comparative Perspective.* New Haven: Yale University Press, 1994.

———. *Politics in the Congo.* Princeton: Princeton University Press, 1965.

Interviews

Fanta Ballo, Segu, 23 Jan. 1984.

Hadja Toumata Contao, Segu, 23 Jan. 1984.

Cebarama Dembele, Banankoro, 22 Jan. 1984.

Diasse Diabite, collection Aliou Kone, 1984.

Mokan Fofana, Banamba, 20 July 1981.

Warike Jara, Koulikoro, 29 Jan. 1984.

Batene Kale, Segu, 31 July 1981.

Bamoussa Keita, Sinsani, 21 Jan. 1984.

Dramane Kone, Nyamina, 23 July 1981.

Kissima Makadji, Tenimbala, 19 July 1981.

Tijani Sylla, Baraweli, 20 Jan. 1984.

Ko Togola, M'Peba, 23 Jan. 1984.

Dahou Traore, Sibila, 21 Jan. 1984.

Fadita Tounkara, Segu, 22 Jan. 1984.

Additional interviews not cited in this book on cotton and on the economy and society of the Middle Niger Valley are located in "Maraka Historical Texts, I," "Maraka Historical Texts, II," and "Maraka Historical Texts, III." Volumes I and II are available at the Institut de Sciences Humaines, Bamako, and at Green Library, Stanford University. Volume III is in preparation.

Index

tion, 37–38, 84–85, 110, 127, 145, 148, 164, 178, 193, 206ff, 224. *See also* agricultural extension; colonial cotton policy; market incentives; price fixing; quality
public works experts, 7, 110, 116, 121. *See also* Bélime, Emile, controversy; compulsory labor; Office du Niger
pumping machines for irrigation, 134

quality: efforts to enhance, 29–37 *passim*, 111, 145, 163, 172, 177, 182, 184; seed and technologies, 81, 110, 150, 165, 168. *See also* Association Cotonnière Coloniale; agricultural extension; cotton varieties; gins
Quesnel, Marcel, off. of ACC, 94

Rabaud, 126
Raffenel, Anne, 55–56
raw materials: length of fiber, 43; supply for France, 1, 3–6, 10, 48, 60, 103, 109–10, 121, 125, 166, 253; policies, 60, 112, 115; imbalance of payments for cotton, 115, 123. *See also* colonial cotton policy, autarky; World War I
reversible social processes, 11, 26, 93, 192, 218, 274
Reybaud, Louis, 67
Rhône Valley, 42
Richard, agronomist, 64
Richard-Toll (Senegal), 65, 71f, 90, 126, 133; agricultural station, 64
Rimmer, Douglas, 22
Roger, Jacques-François, gov., 41, 64–65
Rouen, 49, 63, 71, 125
Rougier, lt.-gov., 240, 258, 260
Roume, Ernest, gov.-gen., 84–88, 116, 164, 182
Roy, Gustave, dir. of ACC, 125
Russia, 5, 42, 81

Saga (Soudan), 134
Sagot, col. official, 267
Sahel canal, 236, 247
Said, Edward, 14–15
Saint Domingue, 46, 48
Saint Joseph concession, 71–73
Saint Louis, 1, 41, 61–70 *passim*, 126

Sama, 155
Samanko, 151
Samory, 76
San (district), 92, 98, 132, 149, 206, 237, 240, 253, 255, 265, 269, 281, 284
Sansanding (Soudan), 57, 137
Sansanding dam, 3, 6, 141, 228, 232–34, 245
Sarraut, Albert, Min. of Colonies, 122–23, 139, 146, 149, 226–28, 231
Sassila (Soudan), 151, 153
Schmaltz, Colonel Julien, gov., 29, 41, 63–65
Scott, James, 20, 27
second European colonial occupation of Africa, 110
Segu, 55, 84–98 *passim*, 146–47, 151, 155, 170, 173, 177, 181, 189, 196, 206–9, 212, 254, 262, 277
Segu canal, 122, 138, 141, 143, 150, 159, 225–28
Seine-Inférieure, 50, 70f
Senegal River, 61, 71, 80, 126, 133
Senegal River valley, 63f, 119, 122, 126f, 140
Senenkou (Soudan), 134, 155
Senn, M., Vichy official, 243
Séré, Lasalle, col. official, 239
Service Temporaire des Irrigations du Niger (STIN), 226–34 *passim*, 244, 273. *See also* compulsion; irrigation; Office du Niger; public works
sharecropping, 89, 145, 157f, 161
Shire and Zambezi river valleys, 43
Sibila (Soudan), 270
Sicily, 42
Siguiri (Guinea), 209, 260
Sikasso (Soudan), 76, 132, 170, 175–77, 183, 185, 206, 208, 210, 253, 255–57, 265, 269, 279
Simon, Henry, min. of colonies, 121, 128
Sinsani (Soudan), 3, 134. *See also* Sansanding
slavery, end of, 217; impact on handicraft textile industry, 93, 96; eroded patriarchal authority, 99. *See also* handicraft textile industry; slaves; weavers
slaves, 27, 56, 59, 94, 197, 212, 216; freed

Library of Congress Cataloging-in-Publication Data

Roberts, Richard L., 1949–
  Two worlds of cotton : colonialism and the regional economy in the
French Soudan, 1800–1946 / Richard L. Roberts.
    p. cm.
  Includes bibliographical references and index.
  ISBN 0-8047-2652-3 (alk. paper)
    1. Cotton textile industry—Mali—History.   2. Cotton trade—Mali—
History.   3. Mali—Colonigal influence.   I. Title.
HD9887.M422R63   1996
338.1′7721′096623—dc20   95-26213
                                                                CIP

Original printing 1996
Last figure below indicates year of this printing:
05 04 03 02 01 00 99 98 97 96